AI IN TEAMS

RESEARCH ON MANAGING GROUPS AND TEAMS

Edited by Marshall Scott Poole

Previous Volumes:

Series Editor: Eduardo Salas

Volume 6:	*Time in Groups*, edited by Sally Blount
Volume 7:	*Status and Groups*, edited by Melissa C. Thomas-Hunt
Volume 8:	*Groups and Ethics*, edited by Ann E. Tenbrunsel
Volume 9:	*National Culture and Groups*, edited by Ya-Ru Chen
Volume 10:	*Affect and Groups*, edited by Elizabeth A. Mannix, Margaret A. Neale and Cameron P. Anderson
Volume 11:	*Diversity in Groups*, edited by Katherine W. Phillips
Volume 12:	*Creativity in Groups*, edited by Elizabeth A. Mannix, Jack A. Goncalo and Margaret A. Neale
Volume 13:	*Fairness and Groups*, edited by Elizabeth A. Mannix, Margaret A. Neale and Elizabeth Mullen
Volume 14:	*Negotiation and Groups*, edited by Elizabeth A. Mannix, Margaret A. Neale and Jennifer R. Overbeck
Volume 15:	*Looking Back, Moving Forward: A Review of Group and Team-based Research*, edited by Margaret A. Neale and Elizabeth A. Mannix
Volume 16:	*Pushing the Boundaries: Multiteam Systems in Research and Practice*, edited by Marissa L. Shuffler, Ramón Rico and Eduardo Salas
Volume 17:	*Team Cohesion: Advances in Psychological Theory, Methods and Practice*, edited by Eduardo Salas, Armando X. Estrada and William B. Vessey
Volume 18:	*Team Dynamics Over Time*, edited by Eduardo Salas, William B. Vessey and Lauren B. Landon
Volume 19:	*Building Intelligent Tutoring Systems for Teams: What Matters*, edited by Joan Johnston, Robert Sottilare, Anne M. Sinatra and C. Shawn Burke

Series Editor: Marshall Scott Poole

Volume 20:	*Managing Meetings in Organizations*, edited by Annika L. Meinecke, Joseph A. Allen, Nale Lehmann-Willenbrock
Volume 21:	AI in Teams, edited by Susannah B. F. Paletz and Samantha R. Dubrow

RESEARCH ON MANAGING GROUPS AND TEAMS VOLUME 21

AI IN TEAMS

EDITED BY

SUSANNAH B. F. PALETZ
University of Maryland, USA

AND

SAMANTHA R. DUBROW
The MITRE Corporation, USA

United Kingdom – North America – Japan
India – Malaysia – China

Emerald Publishing Limited
Emerald Publishing, Floor 5, Northspring, 21-23 Wellington Street, Leeds LS1 4DL.

First edition 2026

British Library Cataloguing in Publication Data
A catalog record for this book is available from the British Library

ISBN: 978-1-83662-357-1 (Print)
ISBN: 978-1-83662-356-4 (Online)
ISBN: 978-1-83662-358-8 (Epub)

ISSN: 1534-0856 (Series)

Printed and bound by CPI Group (UK) Ltd, Croydon, CR0 4YY

For Dalia, who knows what AI should and should not be and deserves a good, not dystopian, AI future; for Chris, without whose support this book would never have been developed; and for David, who always wants his children to generate books and whose support was also invaluable. S.B.F.P.

To my growing family. Thank you for being the light of my world. S.R.D.

CONTENTS

PART 3
AI AND TEAM COGNITION

PART 4
AI IN CONTEXT

PART 5
REFLECTIONS ON AI IN TEAMS

ABOUT THE EDITORS

Susannah B. F. Paletz is an Associate Professor at the UMD College of Information and affiliate Faculty at the Applied Research Laboratory for Intelligence and Security (ARLIS), among other UMD centers. A social/personality psychologist (MA 2000, PhD 2003, UC Berkeley), her research focuses on teams and collaboration (e.g., team cognition, team diversity, processes, and measurement), creativity, culture, and technology, and applied psychology topics such as AI in teams. Her research has been funded by the Minerva Research Initiative, NSF, the Army Research Office, and more. She is also the founding Director of the Organizational Teams and Technology Research Society (ottrs.info.umd.edu). She is on the editorial board of *Small Group Research* and *Group Dynamics: Theory, Research, and Practice*. She was an elected board Member for the Interdisciplinary Network for Group Research (INGroup, 2022–2025), and she chaired the McGrath Lifetime Achievement Award committee for that society.

Samantha R. Dubrow is the SIMEX (Simulation Experiment) Program Manager at The MITRE Corporation. She holds a PhD in Industrial-Organizational Psychology from George Mason University. Her research has focused on team dynamics, multiteam systems, human–machine teaming, and leadership. She has served in multiple leadership roles across MITRE for DoD and DHS sponsors, including as Acting SIMEX Program Manager, SIMEX Director, SIMEX Data Collection and Analysis Lead, and Tabletop Exercise (TTX) Lead. She has been working to enhance SIMEX capabilities and team development by fostering strategic partnerships with other MITRE capabilities such as the Immersion Lab, IDEA Lab, IDEAS TTXs, Wargaming, and Serious Games. She has served as Deputy Chair of the I/ITSEC (Interservice/Industry Training, Simulation, and Education Conference) Human Performance Analysis and Engineering Subcommittee, as an Elected Board Member for INGRoup, and as a scientific advisor for multiple organizations.

ABOUT THE CONTRIBUTORS

Arianna Addis, MS, holds a BS in Psychology from the University of Washington and a MS in Industrial/Organizational Psychology from the Florida Institute of Technology. Her research interests span the intersection of teams, technology, well-being, and humanitarian work psychology. Currently, she applies these interests to consumer research and product development at Brooks Running in Seattle. She has previously worked with the Air Force Office of Scientific Research, Army Research Institute, International Association of Applied Psychology, OpenStreetMap, and the Girl Scout Research Institute.

Mohammed Akib, MS, is an Industrial/Organizational (I/O) Psychology PhD student at the Florida Institute of Technology. He earned his BS in Psychology from the University of Central Florida in 2020 and his MS in I/O Psychology from the Florida Institute of Technology in 2023. His research focuses on trust dynamics in human–agent teaming (HATs), culture, and DEI in organizational systems.

Joseph A. Allen, PhD, is a Professor of Industrial and Organizational (I/O) Psychology at the University of Utah. His research focuses on three major areas of inquiry including the study of workplace meetings, occupational safety and health, and organizational community engagement and outreach. He has more than 300 publications in academic and trade outlets, another 20 under review, and many works in progress for a number of journals. He has published several books including *Suddenly Virtual: Making Remote Meetings Work*, *Suddenly Hybrid: Managing the Modern Meeting*, *Running Effective Meetings for Dummies*, and *The Burned Out Physician*. He has presented over 300 papers/posters at regional and national conferences, given more than 100 invited presentations on his research, and participated in more than 150 interviews, podcasts, and press-related tasks associated with his research.

Elana Blinder is a Child–Computer Interaction Researcher and PhD Candidate at the University of Maryland (UMD)'s College of Information, as well as a former public elementary school teacher, learning designer, and education technology researcher. Her work is centered around understanding how children perceive, interact with, and co-design new technologies, with a focus on directly involving children in the design of their own learning tools and processes and how this can support their developing identities and dispositions as young designers.

Elizabeth ("beth") Bonsignore is an Associate Research Professor at the University of Maryland's (UMD's) College of Information and Human-Computer Interaction Lab (HCIL). Her research explores the design of interactive play and social experiences that promote new media literacies, AI literacy, and arts-integrated STEM learning. She co-designs with youth, families, and local communities with the goal of empowering youth who have been historically underrepresented in STEM to advance in these fields.

Sylvain Bruni, Principal Research Engineer and Division Director for Performance Augmentation Systems, Aptima, Inc., supervises a portfolio of defense and civilian cognitive assistants called Sidekick. His technical work focuses on developing and deploying human–AI collaborative systems and technologies in the defense and healthcare domains. He provides expertise and leadership in human factors and cognitive systems engineering, design thinking, rapid prototyping, and agile methodologies. He holds an SM in aeronautics and astronautics from Massachusetts Institute of Technology (MIT) and a Diplôme d'Ingénieur from CentraleSupélec (France).

Samuel Canter holds a PhD in Politics and International Relations from the University of Leicester (UK) and an MA in Military History from Norwich University. His research focuses primarily on national security organization, bureaucracy, and culture. A former Infantry and Military Intelligence officer in the U.S. Army, he has occupied both civil service and consultant positions for the Pentagon, the White House, and the Intelligence Community, and as an Adjunct Professor in International Security at George Mason University. His views are his own and do not reflect any institution, organization, or entity with which he is affiliated.

Kendall Carmody, MS, graduated with a master's in Aviation Human Factors from the College of Aeronautics at Florida Institute of Technology and is a Project-lead of ATLAS lab, a human factors research lab. She holds a BS in Aeronautical Science and a Minor in Aviation Environmental Science. She currently works collaboratively as a Research Fellow for the Air Force Research Lab and co-leads two projects at the ATLAS LAB on the topics of Human Agent Teaming (HAT) and Urban Air Mobility (UAM). She is pursuing a PhD in Aviation Sciences, with a focus on human factors, virtual environments, and virtual/augmented reality.

Meredith Carroll, PhD, is a Professor of Aviation Human Factors and Director of the Advancing Technology-interaction and Learning in Aviation Systems (ATLAS) Lab at Florida Tech. She has over 20 years of experience studying human/team performance and training, related to decision making in complex systems, cognition and learning, human–autonomy teaming, performance and expertise assessment, and adaptive training. She has been funded by organizations, such as NASA, the Federal Aviation Administration, the Air Force Office of Scientific Research, and the Office of Naval Research (ONR) to study different facets of these areas. She teaches a range of human factors courses aimed at giving students practical, hands-on experience in applying theories of cognition and learning to optimize performance. She holds a BS in Aerospace Engineering from the University of Virginia, an MS in Aviation Science from Florida Tech, and a PhD in Applied Experimental Psychology/Human Factors from the University of Central Florida.

Mark A. Clark, PhD (www.american.edu/kogod/faculty/maclark.cfm), is Professor and Management Department Chair at the Kogod School of Business, American University in Washington DC. His teaching and research focus on leadership and high-performance collaborations across a variety of contexts. His work is published in top academic outlets such as *Academy of Management Journal*, *Group Dynamics*, *Human Resource Management*, *Human Factors*, and *Design Studies*, and he has consulted with some of the largest – and some of the smallest – companies in the world. His book, *Six Paths to Leadership* (2021), outlines lessons learned from working with leaders in a variety of contexts, including politics, corporations, start-ups, and family businesses. He is also a Co-author of a forthcoming book, *Design Thinking with Artificial Intelligence: A Practical Guide for Business Innovation.*

Madeline M. Diep is a Senior Research Scientist at Fraunhofer USA. She received her PhD in Computer Science (University of Nebraska – Lincoln, 2009). She has over 10 years of experience in computer science and software engineering research and application, including project management, AI-based software development, quality assurance, testing, and validation. Her expertise has supported multi-disciplinary research projects in life-science and social-sciences, funded by National Institutes of Health, Intelligence Advanced Research Projects Activity, Army Research Office, Office of the Director of National Intelligence, and NAVAIR. In the Army Research Office-funded Human–Agent Teaming on Intelligence Tasks (HATIT) project, she led and was the primary contributor to the development of the HATIT experimental platform.

Utkarsh Dwivedi is a Designer and Software Engineer whose research focuses on human-centered artificial intelligence and participatory machine learning. He holds a PhD in Information Studies from the University of Maryland (UMD). His dissertation research explored inclusive ways for exposing youth to AI black boxes and earned won best paper honorable mention awards at IEEE VL/HCC and ACM CHI. Prior to conducting research at UMD, he was a Game Designer and Software Engineer, developing games for learning math.

Emilee Eden, MPH, is a Project Manager at the University of Utah's Data Coordinating Center where she oversees multi-site clinical trial research focused on pediatric populations. She brings a strong academic and professional background in epidemiology, biostatistics, and public health. She has led and supported a variety of occupational and environmental health studies throughout her career. She also worked in the Center for Meeting Effectiveness where she managed a research team dedicated to advancing the field of meeting science. Her work in this area has been presented at numerous industrial–organizational psychology and team research conferences. Presentation topics include evidence-based meeting practices, meeting conflict and equity, meeting dynamics and physiological measures, and the influence of technology on team interactions. Her current research includes diverse clinical interventions aimed at improving health outcomes in pediatric populations. Her work involves coordinating complex research initiatives and fostering collaboration across multidisciplinary teams.

Selena Evans is a PhD student in Human Systems Engineering at Arizona State University. Her research interests include human–AI collaboration, AI ethics and fairness, AI for social good, trustworthy AI, and educational technology. Her primary focus is on how AI is transforming education and learning, both in the classroom and in the workplace, and how these changes are shaping the future of learning.

Cherrise Ficke, MS, is a Scientist at Aptima, Inc. working in the Training, Learning, and Readiness, Division. There, she uses her research expertise in aviation human factors, adaptive training, unmanned aerial systems (UAS) operations, and human–agent teaming (HAT). She holds a private pilot's license and has research experience from Florida Institute of Technology's ATLAS Lab, the Naval Air Warfare Center Training Systems Division (NAWCTSD), and the Naval Surface Warfare Center (NSWC). She has an MS in human factors in aeronautics and a BS in aviation management from the Florida Institute of Technology.

Adam Fouse, Principal Research Engineer and Vice President of Technical Operations, Aptima, Inc., leads interdisciplinary research in creating tools to increase performance of individuals and teams in areas such as information analysis, industrial safety, and health. He has served as a principal investigator on numerous research projects with a focus on creating tools that combine human and artificial intelligence to improve performance of sociotechnical systems. He holds a PhD and MS in cognitive science from the University of California, San Diego, and a BA in cognitive science and computer science from Brown University.

Gabriel Ganberg, Principal Software Architect, Aptima, Inc., has more than 20 years of experience leading and architecting software projects in the R&D space. Serving as the Chief Architect for Aptima's Technical Operations Group, his focus is on applying the latest advancements in AI to solve real-world problems and on leading the development of common platforms that support Aptima's cutting-edge R&D programs. He received a BA in Computer Science and Economics from Vassar College.

Marvin Grabowski is a PhD Candidate in Industrial/Organizational Psychology at the University of Hamburg, Germany. His research focuses on the future of workplace meetings, with an emphasis on interactions in the metaverse, hybrid meetings, and their underlying psychological mechanisms. At the interface between

Industrial/Organizational Psychology and Human–Computer Interaction, he investigates, for example, how avatar-mediated interaction influences group dynamics. He also conducts research at the intersection of Virtual Reality and AI to better understand how new technologies can support group interactions.

Daniel Graff, DSc (https://tjdi.tongji.edu.cn/TeacherDetail.do?id=5184&lang=_en), is Distinguished Research Fellow (Professor) and Director of the Strategic Design Lab at the College of Design & Innovation, Tongji University in Shanghai, China. His research explores designing in different contexts, such as how designing is influenced by culture and how designers and design teams collaborate with AI. His work has been published in top academic outlets, including *Design Studies* and *Journal of Engineering Design*. He teaches topics including design thinking, AI design methods, business model innovation, and new product development at multiple universities and has worked with nearly 100 organizations (e.g., KESKO in Finland, VW in Germany, Panasonic in China) helping to develop new products. He is Lead Author of a forthcoming book, *Design Thinking with Artificial Intelligence: A Practical Guide for Business Innovation* (Palgrave MacMillan/SpringerNature).

Mona Leigh Guha is a Researcher, Designer, and Educator focused on early childhood and children's technology and media. She holds a PhD in Human Development from the University of Maryland, where her work focused on human–computer interaction, specifically co-design of technology with children. She is currently a Senior Fellow with the Joan Ganz Cooney Center.

Edmund R. Hunt is a Senior Lecturer (US Associate Professor) in Robotics at the University of Bristol and Co-investigator on the UK EPSRC grant "Satisficing Trust in Human-Robot Teams" (2023–26, reference EP/X028569/1). He holds a research fellowship with the Royal Academy of Engineering (2021–26) focused on multi-robot systems for infrastructure security. His research interests include behavioral bio-inspiration, human–robot interaction, and field robotics. His "field swarm robotics" lab has various research projects investigating the use of robot swarms for environmental monitoring. He received his PhD in complexity sciences from the University of Bristol in 2016.

Laura H. Inderberg is a PhD student in the Human Systems Engineering Department at Arizona State University. Her research interests include human factors in aviation, especially in relation to VTOLs, and the effects of technologies such as LLMs and AI on the human brain and mind.

Rabeya Jamshad is PhD student in the Healthcare Robotics Lab at UC San Diego and is advised by Dr. Laurel Riek. Her work has looked into developing robots that can support human teams in dynamic, fast-paced, and uncertain environments. It lies at the intersection of artificial intelligence, robotics, and team research. In her work, she has also designed experiments in collaboration with cognitive science researchers to support the understanding and design of human–robot teams. She has also worked with stakeholders such as clinicians to design robots that support their tasks in the emergency department. Before joining UC San Diego, she completed her MSc degree in Electrical and Computer Engineering from Georgia Institute of Technology as a Fulbright Scholar. She earned her BS degree in Electrical Engineering from LUMS, Pakistan. She is also a Recipient of the Powell Fellowship at UC San Diego 2021.

Rajeswari Jayakumar (she/her) is a graduate student in the MS User Experience program at Arizona State University. Her work bridges UX design, generative AI, and human-centered design, with a focus on building intuitive, ethical, and inclusive systems. She is especially interested in how AI can support decision-making, foster trust, and enhance collaboration in human–agent teams. At ASU, she contributes to digital accessibility and design system development, while exploring ways to make emerging technologies more human-aware and socially responsible.

Hernisa Kacorri is an Associate Professor at the College of Information and the University of Maryland Institute for Advanced Computer Studies. She holds affiliate appointments in Computer Science and Electrical and Computer Engineering. She is a Member of interdisciplinary research labs, initiatives, and institutes at UMD such as HCIL, MIDA, VCAI, TRAILS, and AIM. Her research explores accessibility and human-centered artificial intelligence, designing technologies that invite people with disabilities, older adults, and youth to shape AI as active creators rather than passive consumers.

Aimée A. Kane is the Donahue Chair in Management and an Associate Professor at Duquesne University's Palumbo-Donahue School of Business. An organizational behavior researcher by training (PhD 2004, Carnegie Mellon University), her research examines team newcomers, knowledge transfer, language and group processes, and most recently human–agent teaming. She is published in diverse outlets including the *Academy of Management Annals*, *CHI Conference on Human Factors in Computing*, *Computers in Human Behavior*, *Group Dynamics: Theory, Research and Practice*, *Group and Organization Management*, *Organization Science*, *Organization Studies*, *Proceedings of the Human Factors and Ergonomics Society*, and *Small Group Research*. She was a co-PI of the Army Research Office-funded Human-Agent Teaming on Intelligence Tasks (HATIT) project and has received other external funding. She served as an Associate Editor at *Group Dynamics: Theory, Research and Practice* and currently serves on the editorial review boards of *Academy of Management Discoveries* and *Small Group Research*.

Zachary Klinefelter, Lead for Collaborative AI Science Innovation, and Scientist, Aptima, Inc., has a background in multi-level and team dynamics research covering the areas of team resilience, fatigue, stress, burnout, team performance, high-stress occupational contexts like military and emergency response, and human–agent teams (HATs). His research has been published at leading conferences and in scholarly journals. He received his PhD in industrial–organizational psychology from Clemson University.

Yi-Hsieh Lin is a UX Designer and Researcher with a master's degree in human–computer interaction from the University of Maryland (UMD) College of Information. She has over five years of experience designing user-centered digital products across diverse domains, including government services, accessibility, and IoT-enabled smart factory systems. From 2023 to 2025, she collaborated with KidsTeam (UMD), contributing to child interaction research with children to co-design tools to support sustainability education and promote environmentally friendly practices in everyday life.

Heather C. Lum (she/her) is an Assistant Professor and Director of the Virtual Environments & Cognitive Training Research (VECToR) laboratory at Arizona State University. She earned her PhD in applied experimental and human factors psychology from the University of Central Florida in 2011. Her research interests focus on perceptions of technology, specifically the ways in which technology impacts the way we interact with each other as humans. She conducted research on human–non-human teaming as part of the U.S. Air Force Research Lab Summer Faculty Fellowship Program (2023). Additionally, she is a K9 handler and training coordinator for the Yavapai County Search and Rescue Team-Search Dog Unit and a trainer/evaluator for the National Association for Search and Rescue.

Rebecca L. Marrone is a Lecturer in Learning Sciences and Development at the University of South Australia, Australia, specializing in Educational Psychology. Her research focuses on creativity, well-being, and the interaction between human and artificial cognition. In particular, she examines the effects of technology on well-being, with an emphasis on how AI influences both teacher and student well-being. She has secured over $2 million in grant and contract funding for projects related to AI in education, creativity, and well-being. She has also received early career researcher awards from both the South Australian State Government and the University of South Australia.

Kelsey E. Medeiros is an Associate Professor of Management at the University of Nebraska at Omaha (UNO). Her research focuses on creativity, leadership, and gender with a specific focus on building more inclusive and creative workplaces. She has published over 50 articles and book chapters on these topics and currently serves as an Associate Editor with the *Creativity Research Journal*. She is also Author of the book, *Painted Wolves: A New Model of Leadership from Powerful Women*. Her work earned her the 2024 UNO Chancellor's Commission on the Status of Women Outstanding Achievement Award.

Dinesh Kumar Nanduri is a UX Designer and Researcher with a master's degree in human–computer interaction from the University of Maryland (UMD) College of Information. He is an Assistant Vice President of UX Design at Swiss Re, where he builds high-impact, user-centered products in the global risk and insurance space. From 2022 to 2025, he worked with KidsTeam (UMD), contributing to child–computer interaction research that engaged children and families in co-design activities to explore and reimagine how generative AI might help develop language learning and culturally responsive systems. During this time, he also conducted exploratory research with the Maryland Initiative for Digital Accessibility (MIDA) on how parents and children use learning management systems and assistive technologies in Maryland public schools.

Daniel Nguyen, PhD, is an Associate Scientist at Aptima, Inc. He received his BA in Psychology at Texas A&M University in 2017 and then went on to receive his MS and PhD in I/O Psychology at Florida Tech in 2020 and 2023. His research interests and experiences are focused on work teams, with a special focus on human–agent teaming which has led him to a broader interest in related human-factors topics such as human performance and trust in automation.

Kara L. Orvis, Executive Vice President, Science and Technology, and Principal Scientist, Aptima, Inc., has more than 25 years of experience in government research and development across the military services. Her expertise is in the areas of training, leadership, teams, culture, distributed work, and unobtrusive measurement, for which she has more than 80 publications/presentations, including one edited book. At Aptima, she leads projects related to military assessment, formation, training, and development. She holds an MA and a PhD in industrial–organizational psychology from George Mason University and a BA in psychology from Ohio Wesleyan University.

Adam A. Porter is a Professor of Computer Science at the University of Maryland and holds appointments in the Institute for Advanced Studies (UMIACS), Institute for Systems Engineering (ISR), and Applied Research Laboratory for Intelligence and Security (ARLIS). He is the Co-executive Director of the University of Maryland Institute for Health Computing. He is also the Executive Director of the Fraunhofer USA Center Mid-Atlantic, a US 501(c) 3 not-for-profit corporation, conducting applied research and technology transfer center. He received his PhD in Computer Science (UC Irvine, 1991), and his research focuses on tools, methods, and processes for cost-effectively designing, developing, testing, and deploying cutting-edge software-intensive systems.

Roni Reiter-Palmon is a Distinguished Professor of Industrial/Organizational (I/O) Psychology and the Director of the I/O Psychology Graduate Program at the University of Nebraska at Omaha (UNO). Her research focuses on creativity and innovation in the workplace, specifically cognitive processes, team creativity, development of teamwork and creative problem-solving skills, and leading creative individuals and teams. She is an Associate Editor for the *European Journal of Work and Organizational Psychology*. She has published four edited books on the topic of creativity and is the Co-editor of the 2nd edition of the *Handbook of Organizational Creativity*. She has obtained over 8 million dollars in grant and contract funding from government and businesses focusing on creativity, leadership, and teams. She has received the University of Nebraska systems award for her research and scholarship, the Arnheim lifetime achievement award from Division 10 of APA, and been recognized by the American Psychological Association APA fellow (Divisions 10 and 14).

Laurel D. Riek, PhD, is Professor and David R. Miller Endowed Chair of Computer Science and Engineering at UC San Diego and also has appointments in the Contextual Robotics Institute, Design Lab and Department of Emergency Medicine. Riek directs the Healthcare Robotics Lab and leads research in human–robot interaction, assistive robotics, and health informatics. Riek's current research projects have applications in acute care, neurorehabilitation, and dementia caregiving, conducted in close collaboration with community organizations, disabled people, and healthcare workers. Riek has received the NSF CAREER Award, AFOSR Young Investigator Award, Qualcomm Research Award, and multiple best paper awards, and leads the ONR MURI HUDDLE project.

Valerie Tuccillo Robbins-Roth, MS, is an Industrial Organizational (I/O) Psychology PhD candidate at the Florida Institute of Technology. She earned her BS in Psychology with minors in Business Administration and Applied Behavior Analysis from Nova Southeastern University and her MS in I/O Psychology with a culture concentration from the Florida Institute of Technology. She is a Recipient of the Boren Fellowship, supporting her language study and international research on leadership and collaboration in Japan. Her research and consulting experience includes leadership, culture, group and team dynamics (including human–agent teaming), and organizational change and development.

Reva Schwartz is a Linguist and Measurement Scientist and the Co-founder of Civitaas Insights, a company driving AI's market readiness by pioneering real-world evaluation methods. With a 20+ year career in federal service, her background blends scientific, technical, and operational expertise. She was a Forensic Scientist at the United States Secret Service, advised the U.S. intelligence community on how to implement advanced technologies for subject matter experts working in high-risk and high-consequence settings, and created and led the U.S. National Institute of Standards and Technology (NIST)'s Assessing Risks and Impacts of AI (ARIA) Evaluation Program. Her research lies at the intersection of measurement science, social science, and machine learning.

Susan Simkins (formerly Mohammed) is Professor of Industrial-Organizational Psychology at Pennsylvania State University, where she leads the Teams, Cognition, and Time (TCaT) lab. For the past three decades, she has investigated the drivers of effective teamwork and performance. Her research focuses on team cognition, team composition/diversity, and the role of time in team and leadership research. Her most recent work is applying these research topics to human–robot teaming. The National Science Foundation, the National Institutes of Health, and the Office for Naval Research fund her research. She is a Fellow of the Association of Psychological Science and the Society for Industrial and Organizational Psychology. As the Director of Team Science for the Penn State Clinical and Translational Science Institute, she merges science and practice by educating and consulting with team leaders and members on improving their team processes. She received her PhD from Ohio State University.

Sreya Suresh is an Architect turned UX Designer. She is currently pursuing her MS in User Experience. She uses her background in spatial design to explore how form and function translate to digital design while creating human-centered experiences for the trends of current technology. At ASU, she researches ways that AI can enhance usability and create digital products that are intuitive, inclusive, and socially responsible.

Medha Tare is the Senior Director of Research at the Joan Ganz Cooney Center at Sesame Workshop. She earned her PhD in Developmental Psychology from the University of Michigan. Her work addresses the needs of the whole child, including considering individual differences among learners, their environments, and the media through which they learn. She currently leads the Cooney Center Sandbox, an initiative to center children's voices in the design of technology and media.

Amanda L. Thayer, PhD, is an Associate Professor of Industrial/Organizational Psychology at Florida Tech. Her research on teams and collaboration has produced more than 100 publications, invited talks, and national and international conference presentations, including outlets such as *American Psychologist*, *Organizational Psychology Review*, and *Human Resource Management Review*, among others. Her current research is focused on team selection, staffing, and composition; trust violation and repair; team cohesion, adaptation, and resilience; neurodiversity in teams; and measurement and methodologies for studying interpersonal relationships and team- and system-level dynamics. Her research spans a variety of contexts, including military units, NASA crews, volunteer nonprofit teams, human–agent teams, and virtual teams. To date, she has secured over $7 million in external funding from clients such as the U.S. Army Research Institute (ARI), NASA, and the Air Force Office of Scientific Research (AFOSR).

Matthew S. Thiese, PhD, MSPH, is a Professor and Epidemiologist at the University of Utah. He directs the Occupational Injury Prevention masters and PhD programs in the Division of Occupational and Environmental Health. His research focuses on the overlap between a person's job and their health and safety, with peer-reviewed 145 articles on the topic.

Svitlana Volkova, Chief Computational Scientist, Aptima, Inc., is a recognized Leader in the field of human-centered artificial intelligence (AI). She leads the development of AI-powered descriptive, predictive, and prescriptive decision intelligence and analytics to model and explain complex systems and behaviors to address national security challenges in the human domain and beyond. She has authored 80+ peer-reviewed conference and journal publications. She received her PhD in Computer Science from the Johns Hopkins University, where she was affiliated with the Center for Language and Speech Processing and the Human Language Technology Center of Excellence.

Nicola Webb is a Postdoctoral Research Associate at the University of Bristol, supported by the UK EPSRC grant "Satisficing Trust in Human-Robot Teams" (2023–26, reference EP/X028569/1). She previously worked as a Research Fellow on the "RoboTIPS: Responsible Robots for the Digital Economy" project. Her PhD research at the University of the West of England focused on measuring group social engagement and improving robots' social situation awareness. During her PhD, she was a Member of the ECHOS research group at the Bristol Robotics Laboratory (Embodied Cognition for Human-RObot Interactions).

Jessica L. Wildman, PhD, is a tenured Professor and Chair of the Industrial Organizational (I/O) Psychology masters and doctoral programs at the Florida Institute of Technology. She also serves as the Research Director for the affiliated Institute for Culture, Collaboration, and Management (ICCM). To date, she has co-authored 52 journal articles and book chapters, and over 100 national and international conference presentations, on topics including human–agent teams, global virtual teams, trust development and repair, and culture in the workplace. She has been associated with over $2.5 million in funded research for clients including the U.S. Office of Naval Research, U.S. Army Research Institute, NASA, the Air Force Office of Scientific Research, and large multinational companies. She is the Co-editor of the 2014 book *Leading Global Teams: Translating Multidisciplinary Science to Practice* and the 2016 book *Critical Issues in Cross Cultural Management*.

FOREWORD

When Susannah and Samantha asked me to write the foreword for this book, I was both honored and excited. The topic of technology and teams is one I've engaged with for many years. As a linguist and research scientist, I've spent over two decades using, overseeing, and evaluating advanced technology like artificial intelligence (AI) in various government contexts. My initial focus was the field of human language technology, specifically in the speech domain (machine translation, speech recognition, and speaker recognition) before expanding to AI evaluation, and then trustworthy and responsible AI.

I started my civil service career as a forensic scientist where I used several specialized tools developed for the laboratory. This led to advising U.S. government agencies about how to develop and implement AI technology that supports practitioners in high-risk operational settings. These experiences were instrumental in my final position in the government, at the U.S. National Institute of Standards and Technology (NIST), where I led the agency's initiatives on AI bias, created the Assessing Risks and Impacts of AI (ARIA) Evaluation Program, and was a member of the core writing team for NIST's AI Risk Management Framework (AI RMF) and the chief architect of the AI RMF Playbook. The consistent thread across my work has been translating between expert end-users and technology development teams. My goal has been to not just improve the performance of technology but to build understanding between different fields to solve hard problems.

I first met Susannah through a mutual friend when I was working on a DARPA program helping government analysts leverage data-driven approaches in their workflows. Since then, I've teamed up with Susannah to help researchers understand the operational challenges that expert teams encounter in their various contexts. This has been invaluable in revealing the evolving needs and demands that affect how teams adapt to and integrate technology in their own settings.

Many teams looking to integrate AI struggle with communicating their needs and expectations during the system design or procurement process. While describing workflows and tasks is relatively straightforward, articulating implicit factors like organizational demands, procedural requirements, internal communication, and inter-team coordination can be more demanding. The tendency in technology development to rely on readily available data, familiar models, and established algorithms can also inadvertently narrow problem definitions. This narrowing effect can limit exploration of more adaptable or creative solutions, restrict the options available to teams and, ultimately, constrain the path for AI integration.

Technologists often mistakenly believe that a team's lack of understanding the technical aspects of AI prevents them from fully embracing it. However, my experience shows that trust is the key element and building it takes time. Like other subject matter experts who use AI, I want these tools to help me interpret complex information, so I can apply my own expertise. Even if an AI system performs well in optimized development settings, real-world implementation exposes new complexities and limitations. Identifying when and how these limitations and failures occur is a time-consuming process for team members. These operational realities underscore the importance of communication and coordination when integrating AI into existing team processes and intuitions, especially in high-stakes environments.

The rapid integration of generative AI in the workplace has heightened awareness of these factors, and this book arrives just in time to comprehensively tackle them and offer unique perspectives about human–AI teaming that you won't find in other resources. Instead of purely theoretical perspectives or technical guidance, the authors combine empirical research and case studies to offer practical insights for human–AI teams. As an interdisciplinary researcher, I am especially impressed by the diverse backgrounds, fields, and experiences of the authors. This breadth has allowed them to cover the most pressing topics in human–AI teaming and produce a breadth of coverage unattainable by more homogenous teams.

The book's emphasis on real-world applications should empower organizations to not only implement AI but also foster a culture of collaboration that elevates human intelligence alongside artificial capabilities. Readers will find details and actionable strategies that allow them to navigate the interplay between technology, human behavior, and organizational culture in an increasingly automated world. It also provides an in-depth review of the requirements for building trust and maximizing the potential of human–AI teams to improve outcomes and organizational resilience.

Figuring out where, how, and when to integrate which type of AI into teams is difficult. The conventional wisdom has been to allocate tasks by "letting the system do what it does best, and the human do what it does best," but the authors point out that the rapid advancement of tools like AI agents makes such coordination even more challenging. Expanding beyond the technical capabilities of AI and robotics, the authors also cover a dizzying array of practical, societal, and ethical factors that teams need to stay on top of, including intellectual property, informed consent, upskilling, security, and surveillance. For each of these concerns, the book provides a thorough analysis and reminds the reader about the importance of recognizing and communicating system limitations and clarifying the level of autonomy within the human–AI team.

Much of the current discussion around AI is dominated by concerns about economic and workforce shifts. The authors dive into this topic from the outset by exploring the ongoing debate about whether AI is a tool or a teammate, landing on the need for AI to always be human-centered and in support of humans rather than to replace or diminish them. Their thoughtful exploration of these themes and the role of humans in the human–AI team is carried throughout the book and positions it as an essential guide for anyone seeking to understand and effectively navigate the evolving discourse on human–AI teaming. It will undoubtedly be the definitive guide to human–AI teaming for years to come.

Reva Schwartz

ACKNOWLEDGMENTS

We are grateful to various professional communities that have provided enabling environments for discussing, learning about, and debating these topics, particularly the Organizational Teams and Technology Research Society (OTTRS) out of the University of Maryland, College Park (https://ottrs.info.umd.edu) and the Interdisciplinary Network for Group Research (INGRoup, https://ingroup.net/), which is how we met. Not all of our colleagues in these institutions had time to write chapters, but we are grateful to them, nonetheless. We would like to thank in particular OTTRS past and present members Wei Ai, Susan Campbell, Marine Carpuat, Melissa Carraway, Breana Carter, Joel Chan, Luis Cortes, Hal Daumé, Kimberly Do, Ciara Fabian, Ge Gao, Sharon Glazer, N. Sharon Hill, Xiaodi (Sara) Hu, Noel Kuriakos, Paris Lane, Polly O'Rourke, Jay Patel, Deborah Shapiro, Snehesh Shrestha, Connie Siebold, Josh Strauss, Sarah Vahlkamp, Stephanie Valencia Valencia, Susan Winter, and Siyi Zhu, as well as the various speakers in the speaker series who sparked lively conversations on this and related topics. INGRoup colleagues include Steve Zaccaro, who suggested we put this book together and gave us comments on an earlier draft of the Conclusion, and others who have been active in this area such as Sydney Bergowski, Anita Blanchard, Nancy Cooke, Steve Fiore, Alexandra Harris-Watson, Lindsay Larson, Marissa Shuffler, and Anita Williams Woolley. We appreciate Ben Shneiderman for his wisdom and inspiration to always push for human-centered design and also for acting as a necessary foil for us to refine our thinking with precision regarding any issue involving AI and teams. We are also grateful for our colleagues in our institutions at the College of Information at the University of Maryland, College Park, and at the MITRE Corporation for providing engaging intellectual environments. Of course, we are grateful to our chapter authors for bringing their disciplinary and expert perspectives to this book. Last but not least, we would like to thank our patient families: Susannah's husband, Christopher Hatty, and daughter, Dalia R. H. Paletz, and Samantha's husband, Samuel Canter, and son, Seth Harrison Canter, and our respective parents for their support for this book.

Work on this book was accomplished under U.S. Army Research Office Grant Number W911NF-20-1-0214 and Cooperative Agreement Number W911NF-25-2-0001. The views, opinions, findings, conclusions, and recommendations contained in this document are those of the authors and should not be interpreted as representing the official policies, either expressed or implied, of the Army Research Office, the U.S. Government, the University of Maryland, or the MITRE Corporation. The U.S. Government is authorized to reproduce and distribute reprints for Government purposes notwithstanding any copyright notation herein.

CHAPTER 1

INTRODUCTION: ARTIFICIAL INTELLIGENCE IN TEAMS*

Susannah B. F. Paletz[a] and Samantha R. Dubrow[b]

[a]*College of Information, University of Maryland, College Park, USA*
[b]*The MITRE Corporation, McLean, VA, USA*

ABSTRACT

Advances in artificial intelligence (AI) and related technologies have stormed into workplaces and education. This book presents a variety of chapters from different disciplinary perspectives. The chapters draw on extant or new research, and they theorize on different roles that AI could play in teams. This introduction defines AI and teams and discusses one of the key current debates about whether AI can ever be a teammate or must be a tool. While we provide guidelines on these issues, we allowed the chapter authors to approach those questions from their own disciplinary perspectives. We also describe some ways in which AI can influence teams and teams' influence on AI and summarize the key sections of this book: trust and AI in teams, AI and team processes, AI and team cognition, AI in teams in context, and reflections on AI in teams.

Keywords: Artificial intelligence; teams; future of work; multidisciplinary; human–AI teams; human–agent teams; human–autonomy teams; augmentation

*Approved for public release. Distribution unlimited 25-01892-2.

AI in Teams: Research on Managing Groups and Teams, Volume 21, 1–14

ISSN: 1534-0856/doi:10.1108/S1534-085620260000021002

INTRODUCTION: AI IN TEAMS

It is a cliche for books on AI to begin with the complaint that the state of the technology has advanced quickly between the beginning and end of writing the book and from submission to publication. This book fully embodies the cliche. When we proposed this book in Fall 2023, chatGPT had just arrived. As of fall 2025, Gemini, Claude, Perplexity, Copilot, and others compete for market share; Google search has an AI Overview before showing search results; mammogram results are regularly offering an optional AI diagnosis in conjunction with doctor diagnoses; and nearly every application on computers and smartphones has some sort of built in AI feature. By summer 2026, companies will have achieved even more impressive advances in AI, as well as new integrations (or invasions) of AI into existing products and processes. Human *teams*, meanwhile, are historically and persistently ubiquitous in both work and leisure (Mathieu et al., 2019). This book addresses how different types of AI agents, both physically embodied and digital, influence the work of teams.

The current wave of AI has both a real and perceived impact on work and education (e.g., Chiang, 2024; Ivanova, 2025; Litwin, 2023; Liu, 2023; Ruddick, 2025; Tang et al., 2023; Zheng, 2025; Zhou, 2025). The considered societal impact of the development, use, and recovery from AI is growing (Shah & Bender, 2024), be it from the increase in energy required to create and maintain AIs (e.g., de Vries, 2023), the political and psychological costs of creation (e.g., extraction and exploitation, Crawford, 2021; e.g., having to review hate speech and violent images, Rowe, 2023), bias being built into algorithms (e.g., Buolamwini & Gebru, 2018; Fayola et al., 2023; Ferrer et al., 2021), the potential positive impacts of AI on productivity and creativity (e.g., Liu et al., 2025; Wang & Fan, 2025), and the potential negative impacts of AI use on human skills, also called de-skilling (e.g., Budzyń et al., 2025; Kosmyna et al., 2025).

AI is in our phones, our appliances, our schools, our offices, and more, fulfilling a variety of roles with varying degrees of obviousness. A great deal has been written about AI: how we can design and use it effectively, including human-centered design perspectives (e.g., Shneiderman, 2020, 2022; Steckman et al., 2025; Zhang & Reicherts, 2025); how AI affects individuals and society as a whole (e.g., Buolamwini & Gebru, 2018; Crawford, 2021; Major & Shah, 2020; National Academies of Sciences, Engineering, and Medicine, 2024; Noble, 2018); and legal and policy approaches to AI (e.g., Cwik et al., 2024; National Institute of Standards and Technology [NIST], U.S. Department of Commerce, 2023). There have been an increasing number of academic articles about human–agent teams (HATs) (also commonly referred to as human–AI teams, human–robot teams, human–machine teams, etc.), but most of that research has focused on designing and integrating agents to work with teams with little consideration for the human team dynamics affected by the insertion of agents.

We hope that this book in your hands (or on your screen, or the AI summary of the book that you are reading) provides something new while building on current thinking. This book focuses on AI in teams (Carter et al., in press; Fiore, 2025; Myers et al., 2024; National Academies of Sciences, Engineering, and Medicine, 2021). What roles can AI play in human teams, and what roles *should* AI play in human teams? How does, or could, using an AI change human teamwork and influence team behaviors? How does this evolving technology and these impacts change our perceptions of humans and AI? What are the future considerations for integrating AI into teams? In this exciting and dynamic time, the purpose of this book is to engage various disciplines in a conversation of how AI is affecting teamwork. Leading scholars whose research has implications for how we should grapple with AI for productive, satisfying, and ethical teamwork have provided chapters discussing the various aspects of this problem. This book draws on expertise from psychology (applied, social, industrial/organizational, experimental, educational), management, computer science, cognitive science, robotics (including healthcare robotics), education, communication, sociology, human–computer interaction, human factors, information science, systems engineering, and military science. The intended audience for this book includes team research scholars who want to engage in learning about the potential impacts and roles of AI, and AI scholars who want to learn about how AI can be designed for teams.

While we welcomed dissenting opinions from the authors, the book starts from the idea that AI will play a role in human teams, regardless of whether the AI technology in question is true "artificial intelligence," whether one considers an AI a teammate now or in a hypothetical future, and whether AI is a tool (either in addition to or instead of a teammate, or on some kind of continuum). One commonality in this book is that the authors take seriously that AI should be human-centered (Shneiderman, 2022; Winter, 2024). Technology is often developed to serve the needs of organizations rather than individual workers, but we increasingly see movements to create technology, including AI, to support the needs of individual humans (Winter, 2024). This book adds to that perspective that AI should also be designed to serve *teams* of humans.

TERMINOLOGY: WHAT IS A TEAM, AN AI, AND AN HAT?

Before discussing HATs, we need to define a team. Various researchers (e.g., Guzzo & Dickson, 1996; Hackman, 2012; Kozlowski & Ilgen, 2006; Salas et al., 1992) have identified teams, particularly work teams, as a type of group that has members with differentiated roles, who interact, and have interdependent tasks and shared goals. Many teams also have a definable life span (beginning and end, Salas et al., 1992). In addition, teams have boundaries such that members and non-members can be identified. Some scholars argue that a team must have a minimum of three people because the dynamics of three-person teams are inherently more complex than dyads, whereas others argue for a minimum of two in order to include small teams such as pilots in planes (Kozlowski & Ilgen, 2006; Salas et al., 1992). The specific maximum number of humans in a team is often not discussed, above and beyond that the team should be the right size appropriate to the work (O'Neill et al., 2023). Chapters in this book address teams of a variety of sizes. Due to the focus on team dynamics affected by AI, most chapters discuss teams that have two or more humans and/or two or more agents.

What is an AI? Loosely speaking, an AI is some kind of software, including a robot, designed to perform tasks associated with what is considered to be some aspect of human intelligence, such as learning, reasoning, or generalization (Copeland, 2025). Winter (2024) points out that this anthropomorphizing language lacks precision. For instance, what is deemed an AI might have the technological capability of data pattern matching, but this capability is not exactly the same as human intelligence or learning. Relatedly, "synthetic teammates" are generally defined as "artificially intelligent systems capable of interacting with humans to produce desired results" (Myers et al., 2024, p. 380).

Some of the confusion and conflict about AI stems from the term referring to different specific technologies with different features, costs, impacts, biases, and strengths (Narayanan & Kapoor, 2024). Narayanan and Kapoor (2024) make the analogy that discussions about AI are as if instead of distinguishing between bicycles, cars, trucks, and rockets, we only had one word – "vehicles." AI systems, be they rule-based systems, supervised or unsupervised learning systems, reinforcement learning systems, hybrid systems, generative AI, or others, have different applications and types of human involvement in their creation (Jarrahi & Glaser, 2025). Related literature and conferences include the fields of human–machine teaming and human–robot interaction. However, not all machines are AI, and not all AI are robots or embodied machines. We examine AI in any form: the authors of these chapters approach the different kinds of AI as relevant to their foci. These include anything currently termed AI, such as large language models (LLMs), generative AI (genAI), natural language processing, and more.

For this book, we choose to use the term human–agent teams or human–agent teaming (HATs). That said, the terminology is always evolving. Scholars also use HATs to mean human–autonomy teams or teaming (e.g., Myers et al., 2024; O'Neill et al., 2022, 2023), and more recently, we see "human-AI teams" or "human-AI teaming" (e.g., Fiore, 2025; National Academies of Sciences, Engineering, and Medicine, 2021). In the U.S. military, the terminology of "human-AI teaming" is widely used to refer to a single human and a single AI. We chose HATs because the level of AI autonomy can vary due to research questions and/or practical requirements and design of the AI. In other words, we do not presume a specific level of autonomy of either the human or the AI. Shneiderman (2020), for instance, argues for a two-dimensional structure with the levels of autonomy for the human and the AI are separate, such that both human and AI autonomy can be high. The two-versus-three person minimum distinction may be important for HATs. Some scholars currently argue that a HAT would require at least one AI that can interact, for whatever definition of interaction, with at least two humans (e.g., Carter et al., in press; see also Sebo et al., 2020). The National Academies of Sciences, Engineering, and Medicine (NAS, 2021), however, argues that a HAT requires "two heterogeneous entities, each with their own roles and responsibilities" (p. 19). O'Neill and colleagues (2022, 2023) similarly argue that a HAT is when there is at least one human and one autonomous agent that are interdependent and have a shared goal. For the purposes of this book, we allow any of these related definitions: at least one human and one AI with enough autonomy to "count" for the chapter authors as a teammate; interdependent and interacting with each other, with their own distinct roles, but goals shared across the team; and in a group where members are perceived as inside the team rather than outside or not members. This definition, which suits the needs of this book, does not deny the many reasons why many scholars argue that AI can never be a teammate.

THE TEAMMATE VERSUS TOOL DEBATE

One question being vigorously debated is whether an AI could – now or in the future – qualify as a teammate. This debate tends to be framed as a dichotomy: an AI is either a tool or a teammate. Some scholars argue that an AI can never be a teammate, and any attempts to characterize different AI technologies in that way are, at best, anthropomorphizing in a mistaken attempt to increase acceptance of AI, or, at worst, using a poor metaphor that interferes with designing AI (e.g., Shneiderman, 2022). In arguing against the teammate classification, Shneiderman (2022) and others note that computers and software *are not* and *cannot* be responsible parties, legally or ethically. And yet, DARPA (the U.S. Defense Advanced Research Projects Agency) funded a program on Artificial Social Intelligence for Successful Teams, with the goal of developing artificial social intelligence that would be necessary for AI to work as an appropriate teammate (e.g., Fiore, 2025; Williams et al., 2022). For an AI to effectively support teamwork, this program proposed, it should have a theory of mind such that it could anticipate and understand human behavior from a human's perspective (Williams et al., 2022).

Other researchers study the question of perceptions of AI based on different characterizations directly (Larson & Harris-Watson, forthcoming). Drawing on earlier literature regarding the role of technology in human lives, we suspect the distinction can be fuzzier than many scholars would prefer. Some ways of conceptualizing human–AI interactions in the past have included "centaur" teams, in which humans use an AI in an interdependent way (e.g., as with Centaur Chess, see Cooke et al., 2023). Relevant here is the concept of shared cognition with and within sociotechnical systems (Hutchins, 1995). In a sociotechnical system, a human's memory, knowledge, and attention can all be extended and augmented by the technical part of the system (e.g., flight information; pdfs of virtual piles of articles stored in a searchable database) which is made by and used by groups of humans. Thus, the line between a tool that augments and a teammate depends in part on what a teammate really is.

Interestingly, in the current team science literature, "teammate" is rarely (if ever) clearly defined, even when "team" is. As noted previously, a team is "a distinguishable set of two or more people who interact, dynamically, interdependently, and adaptively toward a common and valued goal/objective/mission, who have each been assigned specific roles or functions to perform, and who have a limited life-span of membership" (Salas et al., 1992, p. 4). One could simply identify those "people" to include non-human agents: an agent teammate would similarly need to hold a differentiated role, interact, be interdependent with others in the team, have shared goals, and be perceived as inside the team. In its current and future forms, AI often serves as a tool, but could potentially be considered a teammate when contributing to transition, action, and interpersonal processes (Marks et al., 2001; O'Neill et al., 2023). Steve Zaccaro (personal communication, July 19, 2025; Zaccaro, 2025), for example, argues that an AI is a teammate if contributes not only to tasks and action processes interdependently (e.g., systems monitoring, coordination) but also to transition processes (e.g., goal specification, mission planning) and interpersonal processes (e.g., conflict management, affect management; Marks et al., 2001).

We agree that there are presumptions of what makes a human a teammate that need to be made explicit for an AI to be a teammate (Carter-Browne et al., 2021). For instance, we (and others) assume that agency and responsibility over one's own actions are necessary to be perceived and to actually be a teammate, even though there are situations where human teammates may have low autonomy, as with students, trainees, or people in very low-status positions (Carter-Browne et al., 2021; Newton et al., 2024; O'Neill et al., 2023). Current AI is considered to have a level of agency, in general, somewhere between humans and other technology, and trust in AI may be influenced by perceptions of its agency (Vanneste & Puranam, 2024). Harris-Watson and Larson (2025) examined perceptions of an AI when it was characterized as a teammate or tool. AI teammates were assumed to have more agency than when it was labeled as a tool. Importantly, they also examined how being characterized as a teammate affects perceptions of *conscious experience* of the AI, which then was positively related to affective trust. They concluded that labels between tool and teammate could be helpful in appropriately understanding the role of an AI in the context of a team.

We agree with several of the arguments put forth by the National Academies of Sciences, Engineering, and Medicine's (NAS, 2021) report on human–AI teaming: (1) human–AI teaming is a step beyond simple human–AI interaction, in terms of numbers (one human and one AI vs. more), complexity, and other characteristics of teams (e.g., interaction, interdependence); (2) for AI, animal teammates are a better analogy than human teammates, although there are differences (see Lum et al. (2026)'s chapter in this volume, as well as Cooke et al., 2023; Darling, 2022; Kapalo et al., 2016; Lum & Phillips, 2024); (3) accordingly, one *can* discuss an AI teammate without presuming humanness to the AI; and (4) discussions of HATs do not mean anthropomorphizing an AI is necessary or desired, AI designed for HATs should still be human-centered, and humans should or could still have appropriate levels of autonomy. Thus, we considered, but discarded, the idea of clearly defining a tool-to-teammate spectrum for this book. Due to the interdisciplinary nature of the book, we wanted to allow the chapter authors to come to their own conclusions about the tool to teammate spectrum. Most chapters skip the "tool" or "teammate" debate altogether, and many choose to focus on the verb "teaming" rather than on the noun "team."

In other words, several chapters argue that agents can act/engage in teamwork as a verb, regardless of whether they are technically qualified as teammates. Agents can *contribute* to teamwork processes (e.g., communication, leadership), teamwork emergent states (e.g., shared situation awareness), and teamwork outcomes (e.g., innovation, performance). For instance, a human teammate can have shared cognition leveraging the capabilities of an AI (or other tool or representation of information) without needing it to be a teammate.

That noted, we agree that AI should be designed to help individuals (Winter, 2024), individual workers (Begerowski et al., 2023), and teams. AI should be human-centered (NAS, 2021; Shneiderman, 2022), regardless of whether different specific AI fulfill team roles or are perceived as teammates. There are also moral and practical concerns with AI as teammates. So far, people in general do not attribute full moral agency to AI technologies, but the degree to which people attribute moral agency (and grant moral concern as targets) to AI depends on a range of swiftly changing factors (e.g., anthropomorphization, social functions; Ladak et al., 2024). Systems can fail due to a variety of problems with design, maintenance, regulation, and interacting and multiple factors, without the immediate operators (consumers or workers) being the direct cause (Elish, 2019). Nevertheless, perceptions of AI as teammates should not absolve humans of their own individual or collective agency or morality (Shneiderman, 2022). There are also practical reasons that it may be important to consider something a teammate (or not) that may be different from academic definitions. For example, human life is the most delicate part of military operations. There are times when military teams may choose to destroy or leave a drone, such as when it is headed toward the wrong target, because otherwise it might cause the human team to get detected. In these cases and more, humans and agents need to be considered differently. Even outside emergency situations, there are ethical and legal considerations in business for how AI versus humans are selected, recognized, compensated, and blamed. We agree that it is important not to dehumanize humans in an attempt to characterize AI as teammates or anthropomorphize them (Bender, 2024; Kwan & Fiske, 2008).

In 2025, people in the workplace are being laid off and replaced with AI. Recently, some companies have brought people back to work upon realizing that the AI cannot, in fact, replace their human workers (e.g., Ivanova, 2025). Professional organizations such as the American Psychological Association (APA) have rules regarding the use of LLMs, specifically generative AI: APA dictates that an AI cannot be named as an author on an APA scholarly paper, AI use must be disclosed in methods sections and cited, and the full output of an AI used must be uploaded as supplemental material (APA, 2023). The publisher of this book, Emerald Publishing, similarly has strict rules about what is and is not allowed in terms of AI (Emerald Publishing, 2025). In other words, for the same reasons that it is important not to anthropomorphize AI, it may be important in some situations to not consider AI as an equal teammate even if it is contributing to teamwork processes, states, and outcomes. Some kinds of AI may in time or even now may be considered teammates, and some never will.

AI INFLUENCES ON TEAMS, AND TEAMS INFLUENCE ON AI

Regardless of the teammate versus tool debate, and regardless of whether specific AI technologies are built to work in human teams, AI will have influence on human teams. The current (fall 2025) most relevant debates are about the unanticipated effects of AI on human cognition and productivity. Rather than how to trust AI in general, the question is how to trust different, specific AI appropriately – neither overly trusting nor overly distrusting – and how to build AI that is worthy of trust (e.g., NIST, 2023). Does the use of LLMs and/or generative AI interfere with human information seeking processes and information interpretation (Shah & Bender, 2022)? Or, can some improve learning productivity (Wang & Fan, 2025)? With regards to creativity, can AI use help overcome cognitive fixedness (Liu et al., 2025) and improve creativity, specifically for higher skilled employees (Jia et al., 2024) or for general topics (but not for domain-specific topics, Fukumura & Ito, 2025)? While there are currently debates about whether generative AI can "scheme" (covertly pursue alternate goals; Meinke et al., 2025; Summerfield et al., 2025), an established limitation of LLMs is that information generated can be inaccurate because the goal and function of the technology is to closely mimic human language, not to fact check (Bender & Hanna, 2025; Hicks et al., 2024; Narayanan & Kapoor, 2024).

Current research is also examining whether relying on AI to augment decision making can lead to a degradation of skills, such as detecting fewer adenomas with colonoscopies (Budzyń et al., 2025) and deskilling in writing essays after months of using an LLM (Kosmyna et al., 2025). This research is in its infancy, with some papers being reported in the news before peer review (e.g., Kosmyna et al., 2025). Still, the concerns are valid. We lack a deep or nuanced understanding of the effects of different AI technologies on individual cognition and affect, team processes, or societies as their use becomes widespread. This widespread use is sometimes voluntary but also has been deployed without request, such as when Google search now has its "AI Overview" dominating the top of a search result. A greater understanding of the tradeoffs and both immediate and distal effects of the different technologies and use cases is necessary. Even perceptions of increased efficiency and when and how to use critical thinking can change when using generative AI (Lee et al., 2025). The next few years will see research on these topics and more.

What the current research tends to ignore is the effects of AI use on teams or on humans embedded in teams. Understanding AI from a teaming perspective is likely important in any scenario when the AI has an interdependent role with one or more humans and is perceived as a teammate, rightly or wrongly, even as a non-human one. Different configurations of AI and humans could exist: one AI affecting many people; many AI, including with different functions, influencing many people; and, depending on the perceptions of the AI, many AI and a single person. This last case presumes perceived teammate qualities of the different AI; otherwise, it is simply a person with their set of helpful technologies.

In addition to different configurations, there are different immediate (proximal) and downstream (distal) effects of AI on human team members. Take this example involving team cognition, one human team member could assume another knows something because of what a useful (or faulty) AI communicates. More specifically, one of us (Paletz) has a friend, a historian at Western Michigan University, who created a "party game" where different versions of generative AI are asked to state the academic's most notable works. For Paletz, chatGPT 3.5 emitted only fake citations, claiming that Paletz had published in the *Atlantic*, *The New York Times*, and similar outlets on the topics of gender and race. She had never published in those outlets or those articles, nor had anyone else with the family name Paletz. ChatGPT 4.0, however, relayed many articles she had genuinely published, and even the incorrect citations captured a similar pattern of names with her coauthors and topics (e.g., it claimed she had published an article on humor and conflict that did not exist but sounded in her area of expertise). Using Claude in 2025, while not all her notable works were covered, each citation was accurate. A teammate of Paletz's trying to understand her background in an attempt to develop a transactive memory system of a team's expertise would have been wildly incorrect in using chatGPT 3.5, close enough for a general idea with 4.0, and accurate with Claude (with some omissions). But, even with 4.0, the specific articles were not entirely correct, if specific references were necessary. Using chatGPT to develop a shared knowledge of who knows what would have resulted in minor to severe inaccuracies.

So far, this discussion ignores the effects of humans on AI. In addition to the usual effects of humans on technology (e.g., design, maintenance, and refinement), one hopes that humans will have effects on AI as teammates. If AI learns (for some definitions of learning), this means that humans can teach, either deliberately or inadvertently, with benevolence and/or malevolence in mind. The issue of trust in AI is huge and the topic of many, many papers (e.g., NIST, 2023). Our book has two chapters on trust from sufficiently different perspectives that they complement rather than overlap with each other. As with any kind of technology, overreliance and underreliance issues are meaningful in the use and appropriate adoption of a technology but are not the only issues. Beyond trust, technology needs to be qualified to do the job as designed, whatever it may be, and will affect how humans anticipate the behavior of an AI and gauge uncertainty around the likelihood of different AI behaviors.

IN THIS BOOK

Much more work is needed to understand HATs in particular, and it is foolish to ignore the several decades of research on human teams when designing AI (Carter et al., in press; Cooke et al., 2023; NAS, 2021; O'Neill et al., 2022, 2023). Thus, for this book on this topic, we draw on the expertise of team scholars across several disciplines. The questions revolving around AI in teams are interdisciplinary, and so this is an interdisciplinary book. While the majority of the authors come from the disciplines of psychology (industrial/organizational, social, applied, experimental) and management (e.g., organizational behavior), many scholars wrote their chapters in multidisciplinary teams with computer scientists and/or roboticists. Other chapters come from perspectives from human–computer interaction, human factors, military science, information science, and systems engineering, as well as domains such as healthcare robotics and educational psychology. Similarly, the chapter authors hail from different countries and institutions.

The book is divided into the following sections:

- *AI, Teams, and Trust*, which is two chapters on trust: one by Webb and Hunt (2026) and then Wildman et al. (2026);
- *AI and Team Processes*, specifically discussions of the potential roles of AI in team meetings with Allen et al. (2026), and team creativity with Medeiros et al. (2026);
- *AI and Team Cognition*, including a chapter on AI supports for dynamic hybrid teams with Fouse et al. (2026), and HATs for knowledge workers with Kane et al. (2026);
- *AI in Context*, a collection of four chapters on different aspects of AI as supports, tools, teammates, or objects of design in: human–robot action medical teams with Jamshad et al. (2026), professional designers with Clark and Graff (2026), participatory design and children with AI by Bonsignore et al. (2026), and the challenges of instituting AI in the battlefield by Canter (2026);
- *Reflections on AI in Teams*, in which Lum et al. (2026) tackle considerations of human–animal, human–agent, and human–animal–agent teams; then, we (Paletz and Dubrow) conclude by summarizing the themes of the book and what is missing from the literature so far.

While most of these chapters are literature reviews that shape new descriptive and/or prescriptive theory (as is normal in a collection like this), other chapters take an empirical approach. Some are small empirical studies: Jamshad et al. (2026)'s that involve observation and interviews of teams going through escape rooms, Clark and Graff (2026)'s interviews in a design company, and Bonsignore et al. (2026)'s participatory design cases. Fouse et al. (2026) draw on their own company's reports, cognitive task analyses, and projects to come to conclusions about how AI could be helpful to complex hybrid teams. Finally, Canter (2026) uses a historical case analysis to discuss the potential integration of AI on soldier teams based on previous introductions of technology onto the battlefield.

We find this area of research and theorizing incredibly exciting. While a great deal is understood about human teamwork and, separately, how humans approach or accept technology, these new AI technologies offer new challenges, opportunities, and ways of working in teams. Different AIs have the potential to challenge our assumptions about how teams work. This area of research is wide open. It is our hope that this book inspires, informs, and asks new questions.

REFERENCES

Allen, J., Grabowski, M., Thiese, M. S., & Eden, M. (2026). Artificial intelligence (AI) in the team meeting landscape. In S. B. F. Paletz & S. Dubrow (Eds.) *AI in teams* (pp. 59–77). Emerald Publishing.

American Psychological Association. (2023, November). *APA journals policy on generative AI: Additional guidance*. Retrieved June 20, 2025, from https://www.apa.org/pubs/journals/resources/publishing-tips/policy-generative-ai

Begerowski, S. R., Hedrick, K. N., Waldherr, F., Mears, L., & Shuffler, M. L. (2023). The forgotten teammate: Considering the labor perspective in human-autonomy teams. *Computers in Human Behavior*, *145*, 107763. https://doi.org/10.1016/j.chb.2023.107763

Bender, E. M. (2024). Resisting dehumanization in the age of "AI". *Current Directions in Psychological Science*, *33*(2), 114–120. https://doi.org/10.1177/09637214231217286

Bender, E. M., & Hanna, A. (2025). *The AI con: How to fight big tech's hype and create the future we want*. HarperCollins.

Bonsignore, E., Nanduri, D. K., Blinder, E., Lin, Y.-H., Dwivedi, U., Guha, M. L., Tare, M., & Kacorri, H. (2026). Participatory AI: Children and families co-designing and collaborating with AI systems. In S. B. F. Paletz & S. Dubrow (Eds.), *AI in teams* (pp. 173–197). Emerald Publishing.

Budzyń, K., Romańczyk, M., Kitala, D., Kołodziej, P., Bugajski, M., Adami, H. O., Blom, J., Buskiewicz, M., Halvorsen, N., Hassan, C., Romańczyk, T., Holme, O., Jarus, K., Fielding, S., Kunar, M., Pellise, M., Pilonis, N., Kamiński, M. F., Kalager, M., Bretthaver, M., & Mori, Y. (2025). Endoscopist deskilling risk after exposure to artificial intelligence in colonoscopy: A multicentre, observational study. *Lancet Gastroenterology and Hepatology*. https://doi.org/10.1016/S2468-1253(25)00133-5

Buolamwini, J., & Gebru, T. (2018). Gender shades: Intersectional accuracy disparities in commercial gender classification. *Proceedings of Machine Learning Research*, *81*, 1–15.

Canter, S. (2026). "It's your turn to carry the AI, soldier!" Artificial intelligence and the challenges of introducing new technologies to tactical military teams. In S. B. F. Paletz & S. Dubrow (Eds.), *AI in teams* (pp. 199–214). Emerald Publishing.

Carter, B. M., Paletz, S. B. F., Campbell, S. G., O'Rourke, P., Carraway, M. J., Vahlkamp, S. H., & Schwartz, J. (in press). There is no "AI" in teams: A multi-disciplinary framework for AIs to work in human teams. In B. Bonner & M. Baumann (Eds.), *Research handbook on group decision making. Research handbooks on social psychology series*. Edward Elgar Publishing.

Carter-Browne, B. M., Paletz, S. B. F., Campbell, S. G., Carraway, M. J., Vahlkamp, S. H., Schwartz, J., & O'Rourke, P. (2021). *There is no "AI" in teams: A multi-disciplinary framework for AIs to work in human teams* (p. 94). University of Maryland Applied Research Laboratory for Intelligence and Security. https://www.arlis.umd.edu/sites/default/files/2022-03/No_AI_In_Teams_FinalReport%20(1).pdf

Chiang, T. (2024, August 31). Why A. I. isn't going to make art. *The New Yorker*. https://www.newyorker.com/culture/the-weekend-essay/why-ai-isnt-going-to-make-art

Clark, M. A., & Graff, D. (2026). AI and design collaboration: Not a full member (yet). In S. B. F. Paletz & S. Dubrow (Eds.), *AI in teams* (pp. 153–171). Emerald Publishing.

Cooke, N. J., Cohen, M. C., Fazio, W. C., Inderberg, L. H., Johnson, C. J., Lematta, G. J., Peel, M., & Teo, A. (2023). From teams to teamness: Future directions in the science of team cognition. *Human Factors*, *66*(6), 1669–1680. https://doi.org/10.1177/00187208231162449

Copeland, B. J. (2025, June 18). Artificial intelligence. *Encyclopedia Britannica*. Retrieved June 18, 2025, from https://www.britannica.com/technology/artificial-intelligence/Methods-and-goals-in-AI

Crawford, K. (2021). *Atlas of AI: Power, politics, and the planetary costs of artificial intelligence*. Yale University Press.

Cwik, C. H., Suarez, C. A., & Thomson, L. L. (2024). *Artificial intelligence: Legal issues, policy, and practical strategies*. American Bar Association.

Darling, K. (2022). *The new breed: What our history with animals reveals about our future with robots*. Holt Paperbacks.

de Vries, A. (2023). The growing energy footprint of artificial intelligence. *Joule*, *7*, 1–4.

Elish, M. C. (2019). Moral crumple zones: Cautionary tales in human-robot interaction. *Engaging Science, Technology, and Society*, *5*, 40–60. https://doi.org/10.17351/ests2019.260

Emerald Publishing. (2025). *Publishing ethics*. Emerald Group Publishing. https://www.emeraldgrouppublishing.com/publish-with-us/ethics-integrity/research-publishing-ethics#ai

Fayola, M. M., Tal, I., Connolly, R., Saber, T., & Bendechache, M. (2023). Ethics and trustworthiness of AI for prediction the risk of recidivism: A systematic literature review. *Information*, *14*, 426.

Ferrer, X., van Nuenen, T., Such, J., Coté, M., & Criado, N. (2021). Bias and discrimination in AI: A cross-disciplinary perspective. *IEEE Technology and Society Magazine*, *40*, 72–80.

Fiore, S. M. (2025). Social science and social AI: Developing artificial social intelligence to support teams. In *The International FLAIRS Conference Proceedings* (Vol. 38). https://doi.org/10.32473/flairs.38.1.139096

Fouse, A., Ganberg, G., Bruni, S., Volkova, S., Orbis, K. L., & Klinefelter, Z. (2026). AI-powered dynamic hybrid teaming. In S. B. F. Paletz & S. Dubrow (Eds.), *AI in teams* (pp. 99–116). Emerald Publishing.

Fukumura, K., & Ito, T. (2025). *Can LLM-powered multi-agent systems augment human creativity?* Evidence from brainstorming tasks. Collective Intelligence 2025, San Diego, CA.

Guzzo, R. A., & Dickson, M. W. (1996). Teams in organizations: Recent research on performance and effectiveness. *Annual Review of Psychology*, *47*, 307–338.

Hackman, J. R. (2012). From causes to conditions in group research. *Journal of Organizational Behavior*, *33*, 428–444.

Harris-Watson, A. M., & Larson, L. E. (2025, July 19). What's in a name? Framing AI roles for successful human-AI teaming. Exploring human-AI team dynamics: Core constructs and assessment strategies [Symposium]. *The 20th annual interdisciplinary network for group research (INGRoup) conference*. Rotterdam, Netherlands.

Hicks, M. T., Humphries, J., & Slater, J. (2024). ChatGPT is bullshit. *Ethics and Information Technology*, *26*, 38. https://doi.org/10.1007/s10676-024-09775-5

Hutchins, E. (1995). How a cockpit remembers its speeds. *Cognitive Science*, *19*, 256–288.

Ivanova, I. (2025, May 9). As Klarna flips from AI-first to hiring people again, a new landmark survey reveals most AI projects fail to deliver. *Fortune*. Retrieved May 15, 2025, from https://fortune.com/2025/05/09/klarna-ai-humans-return-on-investment/

Jamshad, R., Simkins, S., & Riek, L. D. (2026). Proactive robots in human-robot action teams. In S. B. F. Paletz & S. Dubrow (Eds.), *AI in teams* (pp. 137–151). Emerald Publishing.

Jarrahi, M. H., & Glaser, V. (2025). Not all AI systems are created equal: A typology of AI systems' performance and affordance. *Proceedings of the 58th annual Hawaii international conference on systems sciences* (HICSS) (pp. 5449–5458). http://dx.doi.org/10.24251/HICSS.2025.655

Jia, N., Luo, X., Fang, Z., & Liao, C. (2024). When and how artificial intelligence augments employee creativity. *Academy of Management Journal*, *67*(1), 5–32. https://doi.org/10.5465/amj.2022.0426

Kane, A. A., Diep, M. M., Porter, A. A., & Paletz, S. B. F. (2026). Operationalizing and optimizing human-agent teaming for knowledge work. In S. B. F. Paletz & S. Dubrow (Eds.), *AI in teams* (pp. 117–133). Emerald Publishing.

Kapalo, K. A., Phillips, E., & Fiore, S. M. (2016). The application and extension of the human-animal team model to better understand human-robot interaction: Recommendations for further research. *Proceedings of the Human Factors and Ergonomics Society Annual Meeting*, *60*(1), 1225–1229. https://doi.org/10.1177/1541931213601286

Kosmyna, N., Hauptmann, E., Yuan, Y. T., Situ, J., Liao, X.-H., Beresnitzky, A. V., Braunstein, I., & Maes, P. (2025). *Your brain on ChatGPT: Accumulation of cognitive debt when using an AI assistant for essay writing task*. https://arxiv.org/pdf/2506.08872

Kozlowski, S. W. J., & Ilgen, D. R. (2006). Enhancing the effectiveness of work groups and teams. *Psychological Science in the Public Interest*, *7*(3), 77–124.

Kwan, V. S. Y., & Fiske, S. T. (2008). Missing links in social cognition: The continuum from nonhuman agents to dehumanized humans. *Social Cognition*, *26*, 125–128.

Ladak, A., Loughnan, S., & Wilks, M. (2024). The moral psychology of artificial intelligence. *Current Directions in Psychological Science*, *33*(1), 27–34. https://doi.org/10.1177/09637214231205866

Larson, L. E., & Harris-Watson, A. M. (forthcoming). Preparing for a new era of teamwork: Strategies for teaming with AI. In I. Hernandez, G. Yankov, & I. Thompson (Eds.), *Artificial intelligence for I-O psychologists: Research and applications*. Oxford University Press.

Lee, H.-P., Sarkar, A., Tankelevitch, L., Drosos, I., Rintel, S., Banks, R., & Wilson, N. (2025). *The impact of generative AI on critical thinking: Self-reported reductions in cognitive effort and confidence effects from a survey of knowledge workers*. CHI '25, Yokohama, Japan. https://doi.org/10.1145/3706598.3713778

Litwin, A. S., (2023, September 29). Hollywood's deal with screenwriters just rewrote the rules around A.I. *The New York Times*. https://www.nytimes.com/2023/09/29/opinion/wga-strike-deal-ai-jobs.html

Liu, J. (2023, October 3). JPMorgan CEO Jamie Dimon says AI could bring a 3½-day workweek. *CNBC*. https://www.cnbc.com/2023/10/03/jpmorgan-ceo-jamie-dimon-says-ai-could-bring-a-3-day-workweek.html

Liu, Y., Kay, M., Green, A., & Beaty, R. (2025). Sketching with generative AI: Verbal but not visual inspiration mitigates cognitive fixations. In D. Barner, N. R. Bramley, A. Ruggeri, & C. M. Walker (Eds.), *Proceedings of the 47th annual conference of the cognitive science society* (pp. 5975–5981).

Lum, H. C., Evans, S., Jayakumar, R., Inderberg, L. H., & Suresh, S. (2026). Human-animal team modeling for more effective human-agent teaming design. In S. B. F. Paletz & S. Dubrow (Eds.), *AI in teams* (pp. 217–236). Emerald Publishing.

Lum, H. C., & Phillips, E. K. (2024). Understanding human-autonomy teams through a human-animal teaming model. *Topics in Cognitive Science*, 16, 554-567. https://doi.org/10.1111/tops.12713

Major, L., & Shah, J. (2020). *What to expect when you're expecting robots: The future of human-robot collaboration*. Basic Books.

Marks, M. A., Mathieu, J. E., & Zaccaro, S. J. (2001). A temporally based framework and taxonomy of team processes. *Academy of Management Review*, *26*, 356–376.

Mathieu, J. E., Gallagher, P. T., Domingo, M. A., & Klock, E. A. (2019). Embracing complexity: Reviewing the past decade of team effectiveness research. *Annual Review of Organizational Psychology and Organizational Behavior*, *6*, 17–46.

Medeiros, K., Marrone, R., & Reiter-Palmon, R. (2026). A time-saving dishwasher: AI's role in team creative processes. In S. B. F. Paletz & S. Dubrow (Eds.), *AI in teams* (pp. 79–96). Emerald Publishing.

Meinke, A., Schoen, B., Scheurer, J., Balesni, M., Shah, R., & Hobbhahn, M. (2025, January 14). *Frontier models are capable of in-context scheming*. arXiv. https://doi.org/10.48550/arXiv.2412.04984

Myers, C. W., Cooke, N. J., Gorman, J. C., & McNeese, N. J. (2024). Introduction to the emerging cognitive science of distributed human-autonomy teams. *Topics in Cognitive Science*, *16*, 377–390. https://doi.org/10.1111/tops.12744

Narayanan, A., & Kapoor, S. (2024). *AI snake oil: What artificial intelligence can do, what it can't, and how to tell the difference*. Princeton University Press.

National Academies of Sciences, Engineering, and Medicine. (2021). *Human-AI teaming: State of the art and research needs*. The National Academies Press. https://doi.org/10.17226/26355

National Academies of Sciences, Engineering, and Medicine. (2024). *Artificial intelligence and the future of work*. The National Academies Press. https://doi.org/10.17226/27644

National Institute of Standards and Technology, U. S. Department of Commerce (NIST). (2023). *Artificial intelligence risk management framework (AI RMF 1.0)* [NIST AI 100-1]. https://www.nist.gov/itl/ai-risk-management-framework

Newton, O. B., Saadat, S., Song, J., Fiore, S. M., & Sukthankar, G. (2024). EveryBOTy counts: Examining human-machine teams in open source software development. *Topics in Cognitive Science*, *16*, 450–484. https://doi.org/10.1111/tops.12613

Noble, S. U. (2018). *Algorithms of oppression: How search engines reinforce racism*. New York University Press.

O'Neill, T. A., Flathmann, C., McNeese, N. J., & Salas, E. (2023). Human-autonomy teaming: Need for a guiding team-based framework? *Computers in Human Behavior*, *146*, 107762. https://doi.org/10.1016/j.chb.2023.107874

O'Neill, T. A., McNeese, N. J., Barron, A., & Schelbe, B. (2022). Human-autonomy teaming: A review and analysis of the empirical literature. *Human Factors*, *64*(5), 904–938. https://doi.org/10.1177/0018720820960865

Rowe, N. (2023, August 2). 'It's destroyed me completely': Kenyan moderators decry toll of training of AI models. *The Guardian*. https://www.theguardian.com/technology/2023/aug/02/ai-chatbot-training-human-toll-content-moderator-meta-openai

Ruddick, C. (2025, August 12). *The incompatibilities between generative AI and art: Q&A with Ted Chiang*. The Center for Digital Humanities @Princeton. https://cdh.princeton.edu/blog/2025/08/12/ted-chiang/

Salas, E., Dickinson, T. L., Converse, S. A., & Tannenbaum, S. I. (1992). Toward an understanding of team performance and training. In R. W. Swezey & E. Salas (Eds.), *Teams: Their training and performance* (pp. 3–29). Ablex Publishing.

Sebo, S., Stoll, B., Scassellati, B., & Jung, M. F. (2020). Robots in groups and teams: A literature review. *Proceedings of the ACM on Human-Computer Interaction*, *4*(CSCW2), 1–36. Article 176. https://doi.org/10.1145/3415247

Shah, C., & Bender, E. M. (2022). Situating search. *CHIR '22, Proceedings of the 2022 conference on human information interaction and retrieval* (pp. 221–232). Regensburg, Germany. https://doi.org/10.1145/3498366.3505816

Shah, C., & Bender, E. M. (2024). Envisioning information access systems: What makes for good tools and a healthy web? *ACM Transactions of the Web*, *18*(3), Article 33. https://doi.org/10.1145/3649468

Shneiderman, B. (2020). Human-centered artificial intelligence: Reliable, safe & trustworthy. *International Journal of Human-Computer Interaction*, *36*(6), 495–504. https://doi.org/10.1080/10447318.2020.1741118

Shneiderman, B. (2022). *Human-centered AI*. Oxford University Press.

Steckman, L., Iyer, N., Kim, B., Lyons, J., Cappuccio, M., Gaffley, M. R., Phillips, E., Sousa, S., & Van Kleek, M. (2025). *Challenges and opportunities in the responsible use of AI and human-computer interaction*. CHI EA '25, Yokohama, Japan.

Summerfield, C., Luettgau, L., Dubois, M., Kirk, H. R., Hackenburg, K., Fist, C., Slama, K., Ding, N., Anselmetti, R., Strait, A., Giulianelli, M., & Ududec, C. (2025, July 4). *Lessons from a chimp: AI 'scheming' and the quest for ape language*. arXiv. https://doi.org/10.48550/arXiv.2507.03409

Tang, P. M., Koopman, J., Mai, K. M., De Cremer, D., Zhang, J. H., Reynders, P., Ng, C. T. S., & Chen, I-H. (2023). No person is an island: Unpacking the work and after-work consequences of interacting with artificial intelligence. *Journal of Applied Psychology*, *108*(11), 1766–1789. https://doi.org/10.1037/apl0001103

Vanneste, B. S., & Puranam, P. (2024). Artificial intelligence, trust, and perceptions of agency. *Academy of Management Review*. https://doi.org/10.5465/amr.2022.0041

Wang, J., & Fan, W. (2025). The effect of ChatGPT on students' learning performance, learning perception, and higher-order thinking: Insights from a meta-analysis. *Humanities & Social Sciences Communication*, *12*, Article 621. https://doi.org/10.1057/s41599-025-04787-y

Webb, N., & Hunt, E. R. (2026). Active trust management for successful human-robot teaming: Moving from a trust repair to a trust satisficing perspective. In S. B. F. Paletz & S. Dubrow (Eds.), *AI in teams* (pp. 17–37). Emerald Publishing.

Wildman, J. L., Carroll, M., Thayer, A. L., Carmody, K., Nguyen, D., Akib, M., Addis, A., Fickle, C., & Robbins-Roth, V. (2026). Trust in human-agent teams: Temporal, multilevel, and multimodal perspectives. In S. B. F. Paletz & S. Dubrow (Eds.), *AI in teams* (pp. 39–56). Emerald Publishing.

Williams, J., Fiore, S. M., & Jentsch, F. (2022). Supporting artificial intelligence with theory of mind. *Frontiers in Artificial Intelligence*, *5*, 750763. https://doi.org/10.3389/frai.2022.750763

Winter, S. J. (2024). The road less taken: Pathways to ethical and responsible technologies. In H. Werthner, C. Ghezzi, J. Kramer, J. Nida-Rümelin, B. Nuseibeh, E. Prem, & A. Stanger (Eds.), *Introduction to digital humanism* (pp. 267–281). Springer. https://doi.org/10.1007/978-3-031-45304-5_18

Zaccaro, S. (2025, July 19). What is a teammate? An interactive discussion [Interactive panel]. *20th Annual interdisciplinary network for group research (INGRoup) conference*. Rotterdam, Netherlands.

Zhang, Z. T., & Reicherts, L. (2025). *Augmenting human cognition with generative AI: Lessons from AI-assisted decision-making*. CHI '25 T4T Workshop, Yokohama, Japan.

Zheng, K. (2025). You don't need to prove yourself: A raciolinguistic perspective on Chinese international students' academic language anxiety and ChatGPT use. *Linguistics and Education*, *86*, 101406. https://doi.org/10.1016/j.linged.2025.101406

Zhou, Y. (2025, July 28). How AI is impacting 700 professions – And might impact yours. *The Washington Post*. https://www.washingtonpost.com/opinions/interactive/2025/ai-jobs-layoffs-tech/

PART 1

AI, TEAMS, AND TRUST

CHAPTER 2

ACTIVE TRUST MANAGEMENT FOR SUCCESSFUL HUMAN–ROBOT TEAMING: MOVING FROM A TRUST REPAIR TO A TRUST SATISFICING PERSPECTIVE

Nicola Webb and Edmund R. Hunt

University of Bristol, UK

ABSTRACT

Integrating mobile robots into human teams promises significant capability improvements for tasks such as searching hazardous environments. Unlike existing teleoperated robots, future robot systems will increasingly be endowed with some level of artificial intelligence (AI), giving them a degree of autonomy in how they pursue mission goals. This autonomy could make a human–agent (robot) team more effective but also put inter-agent trust under strain if robots make a mistake, or (appear to) pursue task priorities that conflict with the team's best interest. During a mission, agents' trust states are anticipated to vary according to the situation as understood by each teammate (trustor). If component-level (agent) or system-level trust falls below sufficient levels for cooperative tasks to be completed, it could critically affect mission success. We argue that active trust management *will be an important precondition for the success of human–robot teams (HRTs, a subcategory of human–agent teams (HATs) with embodied agents), especially in dynamic, high-risk environments. We present a trust satisficing perspective which acknowledges and*

AI in Teams: Research on Managing Groups and Teams, Volume 21, 17–37

Published under exclusive licence by Emerald Publishing Limited
ISSN: 1534-0856/doi:10.1108/S1534-085620260000021005

attempts to account for the fluctuating, multi-faceted, and context-dependent nature of trust and trust requirements even under normal operating conditions. Our outline of a trust management framework for human–robot teaming includes online measurement of proxy metrics for trust, closed-loop adaptation of robot behavior and variable autonomy to give space for human responsibility in situations requiring value judgments. We refer to a recent experimental exploration of "swift trust" and a novel behavioral trust metric for HRT, and we highlight issues for further investigation.

Keywords: Human–robot teaming; mobile robots; trust management; high risk environments; variable autonomy; search and rescue

Robot technologies are recognized as having important potential for use in high-risk environments, for instance in emergency services work, such as search and rescue or post-disaster survey scenarios. This is due to the challenging conditions facing workers in such situations and the possibility of reducing personal safety risks while enhancing effectiveness (Delmerico et al., 2019). In the future, robots are anticipated to have a certain level of autonomy – beyond teleoperation – as they work alongside humans in HRTs. We focus on HRTs as a distinct subcategory of HATs, where the agents are physically embodied in the mission environment and can interact with humans through non-verbal communication (e.g., dynamic use of space through time; joint attention through gaze). The question of how to achieve high HAT (HRT) performance is an ongoing and growing subject of research, and establishment and maintenance of trust is regarded as a central element of the answer (e.g., Chen & Barnes, 2014; De Visser et al., 2020; Huang et al., 2021). In this chapter, we outline elements of an active trust management framework in HRT, whereby trust can be measured and managed online during a mission so that the mission can have its best chance of success. First, we briefly describe our approach to trust in HRTs, the sorts of high-stakes environments we are focused on with deployment of mobile robots, and the way such environments put trust under strain even in the absence of obvious event-based ruptures in inter-agent trust. While much HRT research has focused on trust repair (e.g., Baker et al., 2018; Kox et al., 2021), we see this research as one component of the broader trust management challenge.

DYNAMIC TRUST AND TRUST REQUIREMENTS

A recent review by Malle and Ullman (2021) suggests that trust is multidimensional, incorporating both performance aspects (which are central in the human–automation literature) and moral aspects (which are more often studied in the human–human trust literature). For our research project, "Satisficing Trust in

Human-Robot Teams" (funded by UK EPSRC, 2023–26), we have taken the model of Lewis and Marsh (2022), which considers trust to comprise three main components: capability, predictability, and integrity. Integrity effectively covers the moral component identified by Malle and Ullman (2021). As recently noted by Schroepfer and Pradalier (2023), trust is a challenging concept to define and has, therefore, spawned a diversity of definitions reflecting the disciplinary diversity of human–robot interaction (HRI) research. Broadly, though, trust tends to be conceptualized either with respect to the internal trust state of the trustor (a "psychological" approach) or with respect to situated behaviors and interaction with various external factors (a "sociological" approach). The approach we propose here focuses more on the latter approach, attempting to define "trust" in a way that is interpretable, and hence usable, by both humans and robots (Hunt et al., 2023), though it includes scope for psychophysical proxy trust metrics (Figs. 2.1 and 2.2). For a practical operationalization of trust concepts, one might identify a set of factors that are associated with high, or at least sufficient, trust between individuals in an HRT (Hancock et al., 2021), ideally in a format that is meaningful to both HRT members (Hunt et al., 2023). Notwithstanding preexisting trust relationships between members of an HRT, we expect trust to vary according to the developing situation encountered by each teammate (Hunt et al., 2023). Huang et al. (2021) use the term distributed dynamic team trust (D2T2), "to include both interpersonal factors and technical factors related to trust in human-AI-robot teaming along a dynamic timeline, all of which are typically missing in traditional dyadic trust research" (Huang et al., p. 302). Wildman et al. (2026, Chapter 3 in this volume) also emphasize the critical importance of better understanding the temporal dynamics of trust. Moreover, beyond the immediate HRT on the mission, there is likely to be a command hierarchy and a variety of other stakeholders (e.g., Huang et al., 2021; Schroepfer et al., 2024). These other human stakeholders may also require trust satisficing actions by the mission participants, and so our framework includes space for these actors as well. In our active trust management framework, we try to consider relevant factors as control inputs to an autonomous system able to estimate and *satisfice* trust levels over the course of a mission and perhaps use them as the basis of explanation of robot decisions for the humans. For instance, in Webb et al. (2024), we examined a possible behavioral metric for trust (inter-agent movement synchronization) that could be estimated online during deployment and used as such a control input. Notably, this behavioral metric is distinctive to embodied agents, as an example of the unique considerations of HRT we focus on here.

We have outlined aspects of our overall approach in Hunt et al. (2023), where we consider categories of metrics for which each member of a team is able to acquire information ("When," "Where," "Who," "What," and "Why"). We enumerate some of the different ways teammates (human or robot) can acquire this information, with a view to modeling trust in a way that is mutually intelligible between humans and robots, as far as possible. Without this transparency, there is greater likelihood of members being viewed as unreliable or misunderstood (Sanders et al., 2014). The metrics are similarly applicable, except for "Why," where values inform human choices. In Hunt et al. (2023), we question whether autonomous value alignment for robots in high-risk environments is plausible, given that interpretation and expression of values in morally sensitive situations (such as those commonly confronted by emergency or defense workers) is a human responsibility. Thus, we see in our framework that the ongoing responsibility to maintain the value alignment of the robot goals and tasks with the teams' values (construed in its broadest sense, beyond team members "on the ground" to include command hierarchy, political decision-makers, etc.) lies with the human team members, notwithstanding attempts to somehow program a sense of values into robots before deployment. Apart from trust levels being dynamic, our perspective also highlights that *trust requirements* are dynamic and driven by the demands of the mission environment. Thus, for example, while trust between a human and a robot may be sufficient for the dyad to carry out a task in one set of circumstances, in another context – such as the aforementioned morally sensitive situation – trust may need to be higher before cooperation is possible. Thus, "satisficing trust" does not mean merely repairing or restoring impaired trust but also boosting it to sufficient levels as the mission requirements and situation evolve in unpredictable ways (Hunt et al., 2023). Moreover, it may also include reducing trust *requirements* to meet the situation as it stands, by using variable autonomy to hand (temporarily) a greater degree of control to human teammates, to augment capabilities with expert operation or to reassign tasks, for instance.

We discuss the importance of a Concept of Operations (CONOPS) for variable autonomy in more detail in Section "Determine a Concept of Operations (CONOPS) for Variable Autonomy" and we suggest that determining this CONOPS is likely to increase system-level trust in the HRT in advance of deployment. This increase in trust is because it will aid in the creation of shared mental models; enhance predictability; manage expectations and reduce uncertainty; clarify roles and responsibilities; and provide a basis for accountability and learning. Wildman et al. (2024) recently put forward a perspective that trust is dynamic and event-based, suggesting research should explore discontinuous changes in trust in response to events such as agent- and human-enacted trust violation and repair. Indeed, much trust research has focused on the possibility and effectiveness of trust repair after damage to trust has occurred (e.g., Baker et al., 2018). While we agree that discontinuous changes in trust are clearly important, they do not amount to the full picture of situated trust dynamics. As we describe in our outline framework in this chapter, factors like changing proximity, situation awareness, and the ability to direct values-based task and goal choices are also going to dynamically shape trust within the HAT at the component and system level. As such, we see trust change in HRT (HAT) as comprising both discontinuous and continuous elements, which together need to be monitored and responded to by a range of actors for missions to be successful.

AD HOC TEAMS AND SWIFT TRUST

In Milivojevic et al. (2024), HRT is considered in the context of mobile ad hoc teams, where the trust between team members is likely to be provisional. While development of trust in the longer term is rightly seen as an important element to successful HATs in many contexts, decrements in trust could be particularly problematic in teams that have formed on an ad hoc basis (Ribeiro et al., 2021). Provisional trust might occur quite often in emergency scenarios where team members may not have previously worked together, where a certain degree of "swift trust" will need to be assumed to give team members the necessary confidence in each other to cooperate (Meyerson et al., 1996). Much research on HAT trust has been focused on agent dyads (e.g., a human trustor and a robot trustee), with relatively little work done on real experiments with multiple, mobile robots. This includes research on a one human, two-robot constellation. Therefore, Milivojevic et al. (2024) sought to understand the development of swift trust in HRT in scenarios such as search by teams of firefighters each operating more than one robot. The findings of that experimental study inform the framework proposed here, such that all elements are not assumed to be available: for instance, psychophysical measurements such as eye tracking, which can be used as a proxy trust measure, obviously cannot be acquired without sensorized human team members; gaze behaviors such as fixation duration, gaze coordinates, pupil dilation, and eye openness have been shown to indicate one's trust toward an autonomous agent (Hulle et al., 2024).

In our approach to trust satisficing – maintaining a "good enough" level of trust – we envisage that each team member will form estimates of teammates' capability, predictability, and integrity as task performance is observed directly or reported by other teammates (Hunt et al., 2023). As robotics continues to mature as a technology, people will encounter an ever-increasing variety of robots, provisioned in larger multi-robot teams, and thus may have little opportunity to build up a long-term trusting relationship with specific individual robots, which foregrounds the importance of the swift trust perspective on HRT. Haring et al. (2021) outline the components of swift trust in an HRT context, which include environmental factors, imported information, individual trust tendencies, and surface-level cues. Imported information refers to pre-existing knowledge that users bring to the ad hoc team, which can include category-based stereotypes associated with the trustee (e.g., stereotypes about their occupation), or from trusted third-party information such as certifications or group memberships (Haring et al., 2021; Wildman et al., 2012). In the case of robots, relevant imported information could include prior interactions with the provider of the robot (e.g., the fire service or military branch) rather than the specific technology at hand.

In the following sections, we introduce our trust management framework, commenting on individual elements and giving examples.

ACTIVE TRUST MANAGEMENT: AN OUTLINE FRAMEWORK

Our proposed active trust management framework is shown in Fig. 2.1. We divide the chart into three phases (top): pre-mission (before the HRT is deployed), on-mission, and post-mission. A more detailed view of the on-mission phase is

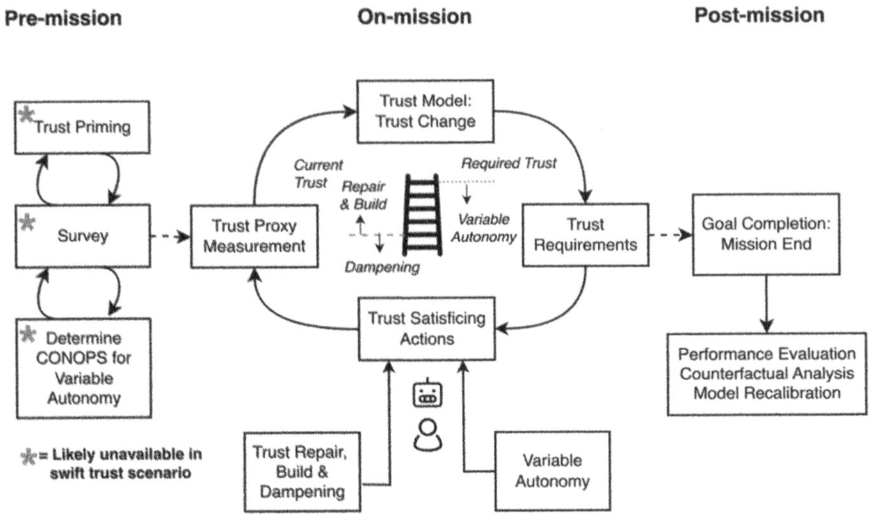

Fig. 2.1. A Flow Diagram Depiction of the Stages of Our Active Trust Management Concept, Which Begins Before Deployment. Depending on Whether the Mission Is Routine or Ad Hoc, the "Swift Trust" Demand Will Shape the Possibility of Including All Elements. "Satisficing Trust" Can Involve Raising Trust Levels (at the Dyad, Team, or System Levels) Through Actions to Repair or Build It, Dampening It Prudently If Agent Capabilities Are Becoming a Poor Match for the Task, and/or Lowering Required Trust, by Taking Greater Control of the Robot Through Variable Autonomy (i.e., Lowering the Autonomy Level).

shown in Fig. 2.2. As marked by an asterisk, some elements are unlikely to be feasible in a "swift trust" context, that is, when an ad hoc HRT forms, for example, in an emergency when human team members must work with an unfamiliar type of robot.

Pre-mission

In the first phase of the framework, we envisage that human team members can be surveyed for self-reported trust levels in the robot(s) to be used in the mission. Such a survey can be used for trust priming, which essentially focuses on increased transparency as to how the robot or system of robots makes decisions. This transparency is an important aspect of trust calibration (Lee & See, 2004; Wang et al., 2016) and ensuring initial over- or under-trust is avoided. The CONOPS for how the HRT will control the robots' level of autonomy for different tasks and situations should also be developed in advance of mission deployment, and it will be informed by the level of trust in the robots and shape trust priming approaches. Depending on how much time is available pre-deployment, these three elements could be iterated to a high level of refinement.

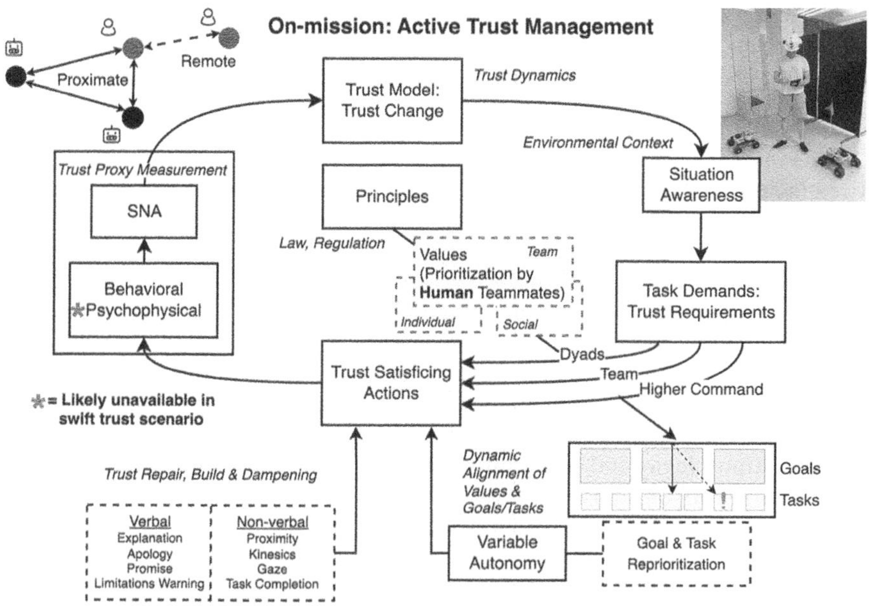

Fig. 2.2. This Diagram Illustrates the Central Feedback Loop of the On-mission Phase of Active Trust Management, Where Trust Is Continually Measured, Modeled, and Acted Upon to Meet Dynamic Mission Requirements. An Important Aspect of HRT Trust Satisficing Is the Continued Dynamic Alignment of the Robot and Human Goals and Tasks with Humans' Individual, Team, and Social Values, Which Requires Periodic Goal and Task Reprioritization; This Need for Dynamic Value Alignment Provides Additional Motivation for a Variable Level of Autonomy Whereby Users Can Intervene with Robot Goal and Task Choices Where Necessary. A Non-exhaustive Variety of Trust Repair and Build Methods Are Shown.

Trust Survey

Assuming a mission is routine, the human team members will know in advance which robot platforms are being used. This advanced knowledge means that baseline levels of trust can be established before deployment through (rapid) survey instruments. Self-reported measures, such as questionnaires, are a common method for assessing trust. One notable example is the 14-item Trust Perception Scale developed by Schaefer in 2016. This scale is designed to capture individuals' subjective trust perceptions across various contexts, providing insights into how trust is established and maintained in HRIs. However, relying solely on self-report measures can be problematic. Chita-Tegmark et al. (2021) consider different trust measures and investigate which items in the questionnaires are suitable for robots and interactions. They found people have differing mental models of robots, and so one must be mindful not to make assumptions regarding how users will anthropomorphize robots, for instance, which will affect how they will trust them. They also found that people can define words differently and may find some survey questions ambiguous. Such limitations could be partly mitigated through consistent pre-survey briefing and instructions and definition of terms.

Trust Priming

Creating a foundational level of trust before initiating teamwork is essential for fostering effective collaboration among team members. One effective approach to building this trust is known as *trust priming*, which involves taking deliberate steps to shape users' mental models of an AI or robot in a way that increases the likelihood of positive outcomes (Pataranutaporn et al., 2023). Trust priming differs from priming in a more traditional sense, which involves the activation of an existing mental model as opposed to altering them. A key component of trust priming is ensuring that all team members have a clear understanding of how a robot or automated system makes its decisions, often by providing insights into the algorithms, logic, and data that inform the robot's actions through training. Before setting out on a mission, team members can be trained on the agents' abilities and setting expectations about where an agent may fail. The timescale over which this understanding is best achieved (e.g., hours, days, or weeks prior) is an important question for future research. When team members are informed about a robot's decision-making process, they are more likely to feel confident in the robot's capabilities, increasing their trust in both the technology and one another.

Enhanced understanding not only boosts trust but also contributes to improved overall decision-making and performance within the team. When team members are aware of what to expect from the robot, it allows them to align their goals and collaborate more seamlessly. For example, Pataranutaporn et al. (2023) found that priming individuals with information about AI agents (an LLM-based chatbot in their case) can influence mental models and hence shape perceptions of trustworthiness, empathy, and performance, which in an HAT or HRT context could favor more effective teamwork. As Pataranutaporn et al. (2023) note, "sociotechnical imaginaries" can have an important narrative influence in shaping shared mental models about what endeavor the human–AI (robot) team is embarked upon. This term refers to the feedback loop between humans' imagination of the future and present social reality. To attempt a simple example in the HRT search and rescue case, a human user's imagination that a robot is a loyal friend like a trained dog will not correspond to the engineering reality of its simple OODA loops (observe–orient–decide–act). More than that, the human's imagination of his or her place within a technological vanguard, and that future vision's attendant norms and values, will shape behavior in the present situation. Therefore, trust priming could include deliberate actions to understand and recalibrate sociotechnical imaginaries, recognizing the broader social context for how people engage in "algorithmic reading" (Finn, 2018).

Determine a CONOPS for Variable Autonomy

The Concept of Operations (CONOPS) for how the HRT will work together on the mission, particularly in complex and ethically charged environments, should specifically address the use of variable autonomy to ensure that robots function in accordance with relevant human values (individual, team, and social) and appropriate to the level of trust in them. For instance, when the mission environment creates dilemmas such as continuing to pursue a goal-related task (e.g., surveil a target building) or assist the evacuation of a civilian, an autonomous robot should ideally escalate the decision to a human teammate. The CONOPS would define the specific responsibilities of the human team members, including not only supervision and possible teleoperation but also the extent of their moral and legal responsibility for the robots' actions. It would define a clear spectrum of autonomy, ranging from full autonomy for well-understood and defined tasks (e.g., search a building), to supervised autonomy or full teleoperation for more complex or morally fraught situations. Critically, it should specify (to some level of precision) the conditions under which the level of autonomy will change, especially if the expectation is that the system itself should trigger this change according to quantifiable thresholds.

Triggers to change autonomy level will interact with the level of trust in the robot actors. For example, in situations with low trust and high moral consequence (e.g., an unreliable drone navigating near civilians), the CONOPS would mandate a shift to a lower level of autonomy – either from proactive human intervention or through the autonomy itself handing back control. In a situation of high trust and low moral consequence (e.g., a slow rover mapping an empty building) the CONOPS might permit full autonomy. The CONOPS would also define how and what information the robots communicate to their human teammates – so they can maintain situation awareness – including when to explicitly signal uncertainty or when to flag up a morally fraught situation (c.f. Verhagen et al., 2024). Finally, it would contain explicit rules of engagement making clear what robot actions are permissible, interaction protocols (with the robot's environment, other robots, and humans), and operational constraints (physical and logical limits), such that the human teammates understand where their own and others' responsibility lies (immediate users, commanders, technicians, manufacturers, etc.). In the case where humans are working with unfamiliar robots in an ad hoc team, establishing this CONOPS before deployment will be highly constrained, and in that regard, some kind of standardization of approach within application domains (e.g., emergency services, defense) may be highly valuable.

On-mission

A more detailed view of the on-mission phase of active trust management is shown in Fig. 2.2. In the on-mission phase, we envisage an ongoing loop of trust proxy measurement (e.g., Hu et al., 2016), trust modeling, awareness of changing trust requirements, and, where necessary or recommended, trust satisficing actions by the robot or human team members, either individually or as a concerted (sub)team. We first consider trust metrics that are more focused on the individual or dyad (behavioral and psychophysical) and then the system-level (social network analysis, SNA). In our framework, we do not include survey popups as a measure (noted in Huang et al., 2021) because while these could be useful for experimental calibration of unobtrusive trust metrics, they would be unwelcome in a real mission deployment, at least in high-risk contexts.

Behavioral Trust Metrics

Behavioral measures are frequently employed to evaluate trust, drawing from a range of observable indicators. One significant aspect of these measures is team performance assessment (Kohn et al., 2021), which involves analyzing how effectively team members – both human and robotic – collaborate to achieve common goals. Metrics such as the accuracy of task completion, quality of outcomes, and overall team productivity are critical for understanding the functioning of the team as a cohesive unit. Another important aspect of behavioral measures is the evaluation of decision-making and response times. These metrics offer insight into how swiftly decisions are reached and how quickly team members react to changes or challenges during tasks. Shorter decision times in the context of interdependent tasks can reflect higher levels of trust, as team members are likely to feel more confident in each other's abilities. Furthermore, the extent to which team members depend on a robot and the frequency of human interventions during tasks can reveal underlying trust dynamics. A higher reliance on robotic support coupled with fewer interventions may indicate a robust level of trust in the robot's capabilities. In Hunt et al. (2023), we relate these to capability and predictability, per the Lewis and Marsh (2022) model.

Nonverbal or implicit communication is important for increasing the transparency and understandability of a robot's internal state, for improving task performance, and for recovering from errors quickly (Breazeal et al., 2005). Nonverbal communication is a core aspect of human–human communication (Urakami & Seaborn, 2023) and thus understanding the range of nonverbal cues that might be afforded, by design or incidentally, by robot behavior is an important opportunity for HRT. In particular, proxemics and kinesics are important modalities for HRI (Saunderson & Nejat, 2019).

In Webb et al. (2024), we considered what observable behavioral changes in movement characteristics can be identified during an HRT mission, which might be markers of (impaired) implicit communication and hence be used as indicators of trust development. In an experimental study with 22 participants, we tracked whole-body movement dynamics of team members (one human and two robots) in an extensive test environment of approximately 200 square meters using an ultrasound tracking system. Using pre- and post-mission trust surveys (Schaefer, 2016), we found a correlation between trust change and movement synchronization between the human and the most used of the two robots. We posit that in the experimental condition with the deliberate interruption to explicit communications, there was a (variable amount of) damage to the participants' trust in the robots, especially the one they were using at the time of interruption. One participant was quoted speaking of the loss of communication: "[The robot] didn't come to help us. No. If that was a real gas leak, I'd be dead. ... Once you've broken the trust, there is no trust." This loss of trust, in turn, is hypothesized to have impaired participants' capacity for subsequent implicit communication after communications had been restored, specifically coordination, for which movement synchrony is a key indicator. We suggest that synchrony can also build trust, which would favor improved communications. In this view, trust acts as a mediating factor between reliable communication and the ability to achieve behavioral synchrony (a distinct construct in social psychology, communications studies, and elsewhere). Qualitative interviews with participants indicated that robot proximity was an important factor in which robot they preferred to use and that a robot staying nearby over time made it "part of the team." On the other hand, when communications were interrupted, the robot being nearby and yet remaining unresponsive aggravated participants' feelings of frustration (Webb et al., 2024). Beyond the opportunity for such a behavioral trust metric to indicate the need for trust repair, we also propose that it could be used as an "early warning signal" for when trust levels might be slipping, but not in an obvious event-based way (e.g., an identifiable mistake by a robot).

Cha et al. (2018) surveyed nonverbal signaling methods for non-humanoid robots, which are the type nearly always deployed in realistic security, defense, and emergency scenarios. Their goal was to "support varying levels of interaction while increasing transparency of a robot's internal state" (Cha et al., 2018, p. 214). They identified different levels of interaction, starting with mere "coexistence" (where humans are bystanders or observers), rising to "coordination" (coordinating actions in time or space, for greater efficiency or conflict prevention), and then describing the highest level of interaction as "collaboration" (actively working toward a shared goal by communicating such that actions are complementary). In our study (Webb et al., 2024), involving two rovers that purposefully navigate around the perimeter of the experimental space until the user calls them to help, we identified all three such levels of interaction. Users could watch the robots as they "autonomously" search the room (coexistence), walk alongside or nearby a robot with mutual care between the human and robot not to collide with each other (coordination), and also stand alongside a robot for a simulated joint search task (collaboration). We suggest that each of these three increasing levels of interaction is likely to have an increasing impact on trust levels, for better or worse, depending on if the interaction is successful, and that there is likely to be a relationship between decreasing social distance and these higher levels of interaction occurring. We propose that there is significant opportunity for HRT research to identify related indicators of effective ongoing nonverbal communication and use them for active trust management as we outline here. In our future experiments, we will also consider alternative, non-intrusive measures of trust instead of self-reported trust: for instance, by asking the participants to explicitly choose to delegate a sub-task to the robot or to perform it themselves, thus using robot reliance as a proxy trust measure. With respect to robot design, the availability of other forms of minimal, nonverbal communication suited to non-humanoid robots (Cha et al., 2018), such as indicator lights or sounds, could also be used to increase the legibility of the robots' state and mitigate the trust damage that can occur in the absence of explanation when human–robot teaming dynamics are disrupted.

Psychophysical Trust Metrics

Psychophysical measures of trust provide a physiological perspective on trust, typically using invasive physical measures, which are unlikely to be available in ad hoc teams (where "swift trust" will need to be established). Ajenaghughrure et al. (2020) provide a review of various approaches. Electroencephalograms (EEG) are used to monitor electrical activity in the brain, offering insights into cognitive processes that underpin trust. Certain EEG channel activations have been found to correspond to events in a trustworthiness scenario between humans and agents (Wang et al., 2018). Electrocardiograms measure the electrical signals of the heart, which can be indicative of emotional responses linked to trust or mistrust. Waytz et al. (2014) propose that the higher the trust in an agent, the lower the heart rate increase and startle response when faced with an accident involving the agent. Electrodermal activity is another valuable psychophysical measure, as it assesses changes in the sympathetic nervous system related to sweat gland activity. This measure can indicate levels of arousal or anxiety during interactions, providing a deeper understanding of the emotional state of team members. Additionally, eye-tracking technology serves as an effective tool to analyze participants' focal points during interactions, revealing how attention is directed and whether it shifts in response to different stimuli. Patterns in gaze behavior can be telling of trust or mistrust, as individuals may exhibit specific visual cues, such as increased fixation duration, when feeling secure or uncertain (Hergeth et al., 2016).

SNA-based Trust Metrics

SNA can be used to capture trust networks between team members, commanders, and other stakeholders (Huang et al., 2021), which in principle can enable network-based metrics for emergent, system-wide trust (Walliser et al., 2023). It could also be used to estimate trust attitudes of focal individuals. One approach to trust evaluation is described by Gong et al. (2020) based on linear uncertainty theory. Their model allows for computation of the "recommended trust" between agents in a complex network, whereby the transitivity of trust (if A trusts B, and B trusts C, then A is likely to trust C) points toward trust between agents that do not have direct interaction experience. Such an approach permits estimation of trust relationships between the wide range of stakeholders present in a real-world HRT/HAT deployment and accounts for incomplete information using uncertainty modeling. Trust estimates from the various agents' trust models (next subsection) can thus be input into such a network analysis, to produce a range of proxy measures, for example, team and system-level trust that are fed back as evidence into future individual trust model estimates in an iterative manner. For instance, the "recommended trust" value calculated by the SNA for a pair of agents (A, C) could become an evidence node in agent A's BBN for its trust in C, supplementing its own direct experience.

Trust Modeling and Trust Change Detection

Using time series of trust measurements, trust change can be monitored via a dual system of trust models for each robot (agent). This dual system distinguishes between a robot's own trust *in others* (a "trust-out" model) and its inference of others' trust *in itself* (a "trust-in" model). These models can be maintained in either a distributed (across agents) or centralized manner (e.g., an off-site server), depending on factors like available communications. We have previously considered (Hunt et al., 2023) how trust levels (which are hidden or "latent" variables) could be inferred using a Bayesian Belief Network (BBN): this methodology has previously shown its utility for modeling distributed situation awareness (Yusuf & Baber, 2022). Under this dual trust modeling framework, each robot (agent) would maintain two BBN models: a "trust-out" BBN producing estimates of its trust in all other relevant agents and a separate "trust-in" BBN for inferring the trust those agents (humans, other robots, and AI agents) hold in it. These distinct models are necessary as each direction of trust is inferred from different tangible evidence. Trust estimates would be shared locally to nearby agents or directly to a central command center that would have oversight of the trust levels between agents over time. In a BBN model for trust, the system of HRT members, command hierarchy, and even other stakeholders, such as engineers and managers (e.g., Ho et al., 2017), could be modeled using a graph. The BBN graph $G(N, E)$ comprises N, a set of nodes connected by causal directional edges, E. Each node represents an element of component-level trust with a defined number of states (e.g., goal achieved or not achieved, agent location in different zones, agent reputation positive or negative). Trust proxy measures (e.g., psychophysical, behavioral, SNA-based measures, c.f. Fig. 2.2) would be included in the BBN model after thresholding continuous values into discretized states. To provide an example with an SNA measure, the average degree of the communication network over a window of time could provide evidence for the latent (hidden) variable of team cohesion, which one might posit is related to team-level trust. For a given team size, for example, a five-agent team, the average degree could be thresholded into states "dense," "nominal," and "sparse," with "sparse" being defined as less than 1.5 for a five-agent team (for instance). Similarly, a behavioral metric like human–robot movement synchrony could be thresholded into states such as "synchronized," "nominal," and "asynchronous," providing another observable evidence node for the latent trust variable. States have associated probabilities, that is, between 0% and 100%, to reflect the assumption that each agent is estimating the chance that the respective states have materialized (this allows for noisy or partial observations). Probabilities are then updated based on mission information or learned over time (Yusuf & Baber, 2022). In this way, the trust elements (e.g., goals, tasks, reputation, etc.) can be modeled using BBN nodes with assigned probabilities and causal relationships based on the operating mission context (see further discussion in Hunt et al., 2023). The dual trust-out, trust-in perspective significantly enhances autonomous response capabilities. Via a trust model, be it based on a BBN or otherwise, if a fall in trust is detected – at the level of agent dyads, the team or at a higher command or stakeholder level – trust satisficing actions may be prompted or otherwise commanded from an array of strategies. For example, a trust level decrement in a robot's "trust-in" model (e.g., decreased task delegation by a human teammate; closer human monitoring of the robot; more manual overrides; lower physical proximity indicating discomfort; expressions of verbal frustration), could prompt trust repair behaviors. A decrement in "trust-out" for a certain teammate (e.g., actions relating to integrity, such as violating applicable regulations) might trigger risk mitigation behaviors, for example, such as enhanced behavioral monitoring.

Situation Awareness

An important aspect of active trust management will be maintaining sufficient situation awareness, that is, an understanding of the mission environment and its various elements, and how they are changing over time as the HRT and other third parties interact with it (Endsley, 2023; Ezenyilimba et al., 2023). Limited situation awareness may lead to a loss of trust if a robot teammate acts in a way that is not understood by human teammates (Webb et al., 2025); it will also make allocation of responsibility more challenging (Waterson et al., 2025). Pertinent information will be gathered via the trust measurements mentioned in the prior subsections, including the spatial positions and communications of team members and their physiological state. For instance, the level of risk in the environment might be revealed by heart rate measurements. Other information will also be relevant beyond the immediate trust metrics, such as the presence of other actors identified via reconnaissance (e.g., satellites). Good situation awareness will allow insight into the changing trust requirements of the various members of the extended HRT.

Task Demands and Trust Requirements

As the mission continues and the HRT pursues its goals, various tasks and subtasks will need to be completed. To the best of the team's ability, given its level of situation awareness, it will need to assign humans and robots to these tasks, which will require a certain level of trust between them at the component and system level. Here, we come to the notion of "satisficing trust." Where the relevant trust levels are insufficient, or at risk of becoming insufficient given the estimated trajectory of trust change, trust satisficing actions may be prompted.

Trust Satisficing Actions

Trust satisficing actions may be led from the bottom up (self-organized with the initiative of individual agents, i.e., triggered by the dual trust models of robots or AI agents, or the action of human teammates) or from the top down (instructed through the command hierarchy, e.g., from a remote command center). The choice of trust satisficing action could be prioritized according to empirical studies of their efficacy (e.g., Baker et al., 2018). While trust satisficing actions will typically be enjoined to the robot team members (i.e., to improve trust attitudes of relevant human teammates toward them), it is possible that human team members may need to take some action to improve the trust of their robot teammates in them as well, depending on their actions and the dynamic environmental context. We have previously introduced the notion of a "Ladder of Trust" (Baber et al., 2023), as a metaphor for how allocation of function among team members could be dynamic, with tasks potentially being reassigned according to the level of trust agents have in each other to reach the necessary rung on the ladder. Apart from event-driven trust violation and repair events (e.g., Wildman et al., 2026, Chapter 3 in this book), we identify that variable autonomy (i.e., the human or robot taking, or handing over, greater decision-making control) is an important part of our trust satisficing perspective. Even with a constant level of trust in robot teammates, a dynamic situational context is highly likely to present variable trust requirements that may exceed what an autonomous agent (robot) can (or should) obtain, thus favoring a switch from full to assisted autonomy, for example.

We consider that an important aspect of trust satisficing includes value-driven goal and task reprioritization, because humans retain a vital responsibility to align robot behavior with values (individual, team, social) in the situated context of the mission. This ongoing requirement for value alignment implies the need for some level of variable autonomy, as otherwise autonomous robots are unlikely to be able to satisfactorily resolve morally fraught situations. The trust requirement for a robot to act autonomously in certain situations will be too high to satisfice, and therefore, a human will have to either assume greater supervision or teleoperation or otherwise complete the task themselves. In this regard, Verhagen et al. (2024) have discussed "meaningful human control" and variable autonomy, whereby a robot is able to identify when it is a "morally sensitive situation" and reallocate the decision to a human operator. At the center of the trust management loop (Fig. 2.2) are codified principles – applicable laws and regulations – that impose constraints and obligations on behavior. These principles inform values, which are moral in character, but the expression of values in terms of the choice of goal and acceptable outcomes for the HAT mission is context-specific. Although HAT leaders will deploy missions with goals and associated tasks in mind, sometimes these must be adapted online. As we suggest in Hunt et al. (2023), "values can fill the gap where legal principles fail to provide guidance. For example, acting according to social values would be to defuse a bomb even if that means a loss of human life, where such action saves the lives of many others… Principles command; values recommend; goals direct" (p. 1).

For both robot and human team members, we reflect that a range of "verbal" (text or speech) and nonverbal trust repair actions are available. Verbal strategies are a well-studied method of repairing trust after a violation. A review by Esterwood and Robert (2022) highlights mixed findings in this area. Apologies, for instance, tend to be more effective when delivered closer to the trust violation event, but their effectiveness diminishes with time. Denials and explanations also show varying degrees of success, with explanations being less effective when the trust violation is severe. Wildman et al. (2026, Chapter 3 in this volume) provide a summary of some recent research on explanation-based trust repair. Promises are often examined in conjunction with apologies and explanations, but their independent impact remains inconsistent. No repair measure has shown to be superior; however, more research is needed, especially in regard to the timing of strategy deployment. Non-verbal behaviors play a critical role in trust repair as well. Proximity and synchronized movement patterns could contribute to rebuilding trust: as noted in our earlier discussion of Webb et al. (2024), moving together through shared spaces could foster a sense of cohesion and companionship in HRTs. Gaze behaviors also influence trust dynamics. Zhang et al. (2024) found that increased gaze fixation occurs when trust is violated, leading humans to visually scan their environment more actively in an effort to reassess the robot's reliability. Successful task completion is another key factor: Guo and Yang (2021) found that observing a robot successfully complete tasks over time leads to an increase in trust from human collaborators (also, van den Brule et al., 2014).

While trust repair, build, and maintenance have received most research attention, we also recognize that "over-trust," leading to over-reliance (Lee & See, 2004), may be an issue in HRTs. As such, "trust dampening" actions can also be available to team members; de Visser et al. (2020) list candidate methods for this, including providing timely warnings about a robot (or indeed, a human's) potential limitations in certain emerging contexts (e.g., when a task is potentially too challenging for its capabilities). In this regard, situation awareness of the dynamic mission environment (previous subsection) is likely to be a decisive factor in initiating trust dampening actions.

Overall, recent research findings collectively underscore the importance of addressing both verbal and non-verbal elements to build, maintain, repair, and, where necessary, dampen trust in collaborative HRTs. Notwithstanding the effectiveness of trust manipulation strategies, the availability of variable autonomy (by user initiative or system handover) is a vital enabler when trust levels fail to meet evolving trust requirements.

Post-mission

In the post-mission phase, depending on the series of actions taken and other factors, the mission will end with some degree of success (or failure). We include trust model recalibration and counterfactual analysis (CFA) of the trust satisficing actions as an important part of the mission debrief. These rely on logged time series of agent actions, environment state, and trust metrics and BBN trust estimates, which may be more complete after the mission if disparate agents had only partial knowledge of each other's data. Time permitting, additional data could be obtained through surveys and interviews of human team members on how their trust levels varied during the mission. Based on each agent's chosen actions (e.g., the disuse or overreliance on a robot teammate), the accuracy of the estimated trust relationships can be reviewed with a view to calibrating how the different trust metrics (sensor-based proxies, SNA, etc.) are weighted in a multi-modal, BBN-based trust estimation architecture. CFA considers the effectiveness of the trust satisficing actions taken in bolstering trust to a sufficient level – or reducing trust requirements in the case of variations in autonomy level – in the context of all the other actions taken by the HRT, other stakeholders, and third parties. The CFA simulates alternative courses of action ("what if?" questions) to consider if the action recommendations were the most effective available. While an ad hoc HRT might find it difficult to immediately carry out a post-mission analysis in a fraught situation, it could be done over a longer time horizon, provided mission data are retained. A formal, written CONOPS (Section "Determine a CONOPS for Variable Autonomy") will also serve as a baseline against which the HRT's performance can be evaluated.

For instance, if something goes wrong on the mission, the CONOPS can help diagnose the failure – whether technical fault, a team member operating outside their defined role, or a shortcoming in the CONOPS itself. The use of the CONOPS can be instrumental in transforming the collection of individual agents into a coherent system that can build more resilient, long-term trust.

CONCLUSION

HRTs are already being deployed in high-stakes environments for missions such as search and rescue. It is widely recognized that maintaining sufficient trust between members of the extended team, including the humans and robots on the ground, remote commanders, and other stakeholders, is a vital part of ensuring the team's success and robotic technology's ongoing adoption (Robinette et al., 2017). We have presented the outline of an active trust management framework, identifying and describing important elements of that framework with respect to a trust satisficing perspective that recognizes the need for distributed, dynamic trust to be "good enough" for the goals at hand (Hunt et al., 2023). This approach goes beyond a reactive, trust-repair-based strategy to proactively sense when trust might be slipping or trust requirements may have shifted. As part of this approach, we explicitly include space for aligning robot behavior with human values, by retaining control over robot actions in sensitive or otherwise fluid situations with variable autonomy, allowing prohibitive trust requirements to be overcome by human intervention. A thorough CONOPS for this variable autonomy is an important foundation for HRT mission success. Our approach to trust measurement focuses on behavioral and psychophysical proxy metrics, and SNA to quantify individual and emergent system-level trust relationships (e.g., Gong et al., 2020), although further research is still required to firm up the evidence base for these (Huang et al., 2021; Webb et al., 2024). We also allow for ad hoc teaming and its need for "swift trust" (Haring et al., 2021; Milivojevic et al., 2024). Given a longer-term opportunity to prepare an HRT for mission deployment, trust priming and the broader social context of sociotechnical imaginaries can also be tactfully addressed. Our active trust management framework reiterates the opportunity to undertake a more subtle trust calibration (Lee & See, 2004) that forms adaptive shared mental models among team members. We look forward to a future where robots (and AI) are successfully integrated into robust and resilient HRTs, for widespread social benefit.

ACKNOWLEDGMENT

We acknowledge support from the £1.2M UK EPSRC grant "Satisficing Trust in Human-Robot Teams" (2023–26, reference EP/X028569/1).

REFERENCES

Ajenaghughrure, I. B., Sousa, S. D. C., & Lamas, D. (2020). Measuring trust with psychophysiological signals: A systematic mapping study of approaches used. *Multimodal Technologies and Interaction, 4*(3), 63. https://doi.org/10.3390/mti4030063

Baber, C., Waterson, P., Milivojevic, S., Maynard, S., Hunt, E. R., & Yusuf, S. (2023). Incorporating a ladder of trust into dynamic allocation of function in human-autonomous agent collectives. *14th Organisational design and management conference (ODAM) 2023*. arXiv preprint. https://doi.org/10.48550/arXiv.2408.10654

Baker, A. L., Phillips, E. K., Ullman, D., & Keebler, J. R. (2018). Toward an understanding of trust repair in human-robot interaction: Current research and future directions. *ACM Transactions on Interactive Intelligent Systems (TiiS), 8*(4), 1–30. https://doi.org/10.1145/3181671

Breazeal, C., Kidd, C. D., Thomaz, A. L., Hoffman, G., & Berlin, M. (2005, August). Effects of nonverbal communication on efficiency and robustness in human-robot teamwork (pp. 708–713). *2005 IEEE/RSJ international conference on intelligent robots and systems*. https://doi.org/10.1109/IROS.2005.1545011

Cha, E., Kim, Y., Fong, T., & Mataric, M. J. (2018). A survey of nonverbal signaling methods for non-humanoid robots. *Foundations and Trends in Robotics, 6*(4), 211–323. http://doi.org/10.1561/2300000057

Chen, J. Y., & Barnes, M. J. (2014). Human–agent teaming for multirobot control: A review of human factors issues. *IEEE Transactions on Human-Machine Systems, 44*(1), 13–29. https://doi.org/10.1109/THMS.2013.2293535

Chita-Tegmark, M., Law, T., Rabb, N., & Scheutz, M. (2021, March). Can you trust your trust measure?. *Proceedings of the 2021 ACM/IEEE international conference on human-robot interaction* (pp. 92–100). https://doi.org/10.1145/3434073.3444677

Delmerico, J., Mintchev, S., Giusti, A., Gromov, B., Melo, K., Horvat, T., Cadena, C., Hutter, M., Ijspeert, A., Floreano, D., Gambardella, L. M, Siegwart, R., & Scaramuzza, D. (2019). The current state and future outlook of rescue robotics. *Journal of Field Robotics, 36*(7), 1171–1191. https://doi.org/10.1002/rob.21887

de Visser, E. J., Peeters, M. M. M., Jung, M. F., Kohn, S., Shaw, T. H., Pak, R., & Neerincx, M. A. (2020). Towards a theory of longitudinal trust calibration in human–robot teams. *International Journal of Social Robotics, 12*(2), 459–478. https://doi.org/10.1007/s12369-019-00596-x

Endsley, M. R. (2023). Supporting human-AI teams: Transparency, explainability, and situation awareness. *Computers in Human Behavior, 140*, 107574. https://doi.org/10.1016/j.chb.2022.107574

Esterwood, C., & Robert, L. P. (2022). A literature review of trust repair in HRI. *2022 31st IEEE international conference on robot and human interactive communication (RO-MAN)* (pp. 1641–1646). IEEE. https://doi.org/10.1109/RO-MAN53752.2022.9900667

Ezenyilimba, A., Wong, M., Hehr, A., Demir, M., Wolff, A., Chiou, E., & Cooke, N. (2023). Impact of transparency and explanations on trust and situation awareness in human–robot teams. *Journal of Cognitive Engineering and Decision Making, 17*(1), 75–93. https://doi.org/10.1177/15553434221136358

Finn, E. (2018). *What algorithms want: Imagination in the age of computing*. MIT Press.

Gong, Z., Wang, H., Guo, W., Gong, Z., & Wei, G. (2020). Measuring trust in social networks based on linear uncertainty theory. *Information Sciences, 508*, 154–172. https://doi.org/10.1016/j.ins.2019.08.055

Guo, Y., & Yang, X. J. (2021). Modeling and predicting trust dynamics in human–robot teaming: A Bayesian inference approach. *International Journal of Social Robotics, 13*(8), 1899–1909. https://doi.org/10.1007/s12369-020-00703-3

Hancock, P. A., Kessler, T. T., Kaplan, A. D., Brill, J. C., & Szalma, J. L. (2021). Evolving trust in robots: Specification through sequential and comparative meta-analyses. *Human Factors, 63*(7), 1196–1229. https://doi.org/10.1177/0018720820922080

Haring, K. S., Phillips, E., Lazzara, E. H., Ullman, D., Baker, A. L., & Keebler, J. R. (2021). Applying the swift trust model to human-robot teaming. In C. S. Nam & J. B. Lyons (Eds.), *Trust in human-robot interaction* (pp. 407–427). Academic Press. https://doi.org/10.1016/B978-0-12-819472-0.00017-4

Hergeth, S., Lorenz, L., Vilimek, R., & Krems, J. F. (2016). Keep your scanners peeled: Gaze behavior as a measure of automation trust during highly automated driving. *Human Factors*, *58*(3), 509–519. https://doi.org/10.1177/0018720815625744

Ho, N. T., Sadler, G. G., Hoffmann, L. C., Lyons, J. B., & Johnson, W. W. (2017). Trust of a military automated system in an operational context. *Military Psychology*, *29*(6), 524–541. https://doi.org/10.1037/mil0000189

Hu, W.-L., Akash, K., Jain, N., & Reid, T. (2016). Real-time sensing of trust in human-machine interactions. *IFAC-PapersOnLine*, *49*(32), 48–53. https://doi.org/10.1016/j.ifacol.2016.12.188

Huang, L., Cooke, N. J., Gutzwiller, R. S., Berman, S., Chiou, E. K., Demir, M., & Zhang, W. (2021). Distributed dynamic team trust in human, artificial intelligence, and robot teaming. In C. S. Nam & J. B. Lyons (Eds.), *Trust in human-robot interaction* (pp. 301–319). Academic Press. https://doi.org/10.1016/B978-0-12-819472-0.00013-7

Hulle, N., Aroca-Ouellette, S., Ries, A. J., Brawer, J., Von Der Wense, K., & Roncone, A. (2024, August). Eyes on the game: Deciphering implicit human signals to infer human proficiency, trust, and intent. *2024 33rd IEEE international conference on robot and human interactive communication (ROMAN)* (pp. 453–460). IEEE. https://doi.org/10.1109/RO-MAN60168.2024.10731204

Hunt, E. R., Baber, C., Sobhani, M., Milivojevic, S., Yusuf, S., Musolesi, M., Waterson, P., & Maynard, S. (2023). Steps towards satisficing distributed dynamic team trust. *Proceedings of the AAAI Symposium Series*, *2*(1), 18–25. https://doi.org/10.1609/aaaiss.v2i1.27644

Kohn, S. C., De Visser, E. J., Wiese, E., Lee, Y. C., & Shaw, T. H. (2021). Measurement of trust in automation: A narrative review and reference guide. *Frontiers in Psychology*, *12*, 604977. https://doi.org/10.3389/fpsyg.2021.604977

Kox, E. S., Kerstholt, J. H., Hueting, T. F., & de Vries, P. W. (2021). Trust repair in human-agent teams: The effectiveness of explanations and expressing regret. *Autonomous Agents and Multi-Agent Systems*, *35*(2). https://doi.org/10.1007/s10458-021-09515-9

Lee, J. D., & See, K. A. (2004). Trust in automation: Designing for appropriate reliance. *Human Factors*, *46*(1), 50–80. https://doi.org/10.1518/hfes.46.1.50_30392

Lewis, P. R., & Marsh, S. (2022). What is it like to trust a rock? A functionalist perspective on trust and trustworthiness in artificial intelligence. *Cognitive Systems Research*, *72*, 33–49. https://doi.org/10.1016/j.cogsys.2021.11.001

Malle, B. F., & Ullman, D. (2021). A multi-dimensional conception and measure of human-robot trust. In C. S. Nam & J. B. Lyons (Eds.), *Trust in human-robot interaction: Research and applications* (pp. 3–25). Elsevier. https://doi.org/10.1016/B978-0-12-819472-0.00001-0

Meyerson, D., Weick, K. E., & Kramer, R. M. (1996). Swift trust and temporary groups. In R. M. Kramer & T. R. Tyler (Eds.), *Trust in organizations: Frontiers of theory and research* (pp. 166–195). SAGE Publications. https://doi.org/10.4135/9781452243610.n9

Milivojevic, S., Sobhani, M., Webb, N., Madin, Z., Ward, J., Yusuf, S., Baber, C., & Hunt, E. R. (2024, September 17–18). Swift trust in mobile ad hoc human-robot teams. *Proceedings of the second international symposium on trustworthy autonomous systems* (pp. 1–10). Austin TX, United States. https://doi.org/10.1145/3686038.3686057

Pataranutaporn, P., Liu, R., Finn, E., & Maes, P. (2023). Influencing human–AI interaction by priming beliefs about AI can increase perceived trustworthiness, empathy and effectiveness. *Nature Machine Intelligence*, *5*(10), 1076–1086. https://doi.org/10.1038/s42256-023-00720-7

Ribeiro, J. G., Faria, M., Sardinha, A., & Melo, F. S. (2021, September 7–9). Helping people on the fly: Ad hoc teamwork for human-robot teams. In *Progress in artificial intelligence: 20th EPIA conference on artificial intelligence, EPIA 2021, virtual event* (pp. 635–647). Springer International Publishing. https://doi.org/10.1007/978-3-030-86230-5_50

Robinette, P., Howard, A. M., & Wagner, A. R. (2017). Effect of robot performance on human–robot trust in time-critical situations. *IEEE Transactions on Human-Machine Systems*, *47*(4), 425–436. https://doi.org/10.1109/THMS.2017.2648849

Sanders, T. L., Wixon, T., Schafer, K. E., Chen, J. Y., & Hancock, P. A. (2014, March). The influence of modality and transparency on trust in human-robot interaction. *2014 IEEE international inter-disciplinary conference on cognitive methods in situation awareness and decision support (CogSIMA)* (pp. 156–159). IEEE. https://doi.org/10.1109/CogSIMA.2014.6816556

Saunderson, S., & Nejat, G. (2019). How robots influence humans: A survey of nonverbal communication in social human–robot interaction. *International Journal of Social Robotics, 11*(4), 575–608. https://doi.org/10.1007/s12369-019-00523-0

Schaefer, K. E. (2016). Measuring trust in human robot interactions: Development of the "trust perception scale-HRI". In *Robust intelligence and trust in autonomous systems* (pp. 191–218). Springer US. https://doi.org/10.1007/978-1-4899-7668-0_10

Schroepfer, P., Gründling, J. P., Schauffel, N., Oehrl, S., Pape, S., Kuhlen, T. W., & Pradalier, C. (2024, March). Navigating real-world complexity: A multi-medium system for heterogeneous robot teams and multi-stakeholder human-robot interaction. *Proceedings of the 2024 ACM/IEEE international conference on human-robot interaction* (pp. 630–638). https://doi.org/10.1145/3610977.3634932

Schroepfer, P., & Pradalier, C. (2023, August). Why there is no definition of trust: A systems approach with a metamodel representation. *2023 32nd IEEE international conference on robot and human interactive communication (RO-MAN)* (pp. 1245–1251). https://doi.org/10.1109/RO-MAN57019.2023.10309503

Urakami, J., & Seaborn, K. (2023). Nonverbal cues in human–robot interaction: A communication studies perspective. *ACM Transactions on Human-Robot Interaction, 12*(2), 1–21. https://doi.org/10.1145/3570169

van den Brule, R., Dotsch, R., Bijlstra, G., Wigboldus, D. H., & Haselager, P. (2014). Do robot performance and behavioral style affect human trust? A multi-method approach. *International Journal of Social Robotics, 6*, 519–531. https://doi.org/10.1007/s12369-014-0231-5

Verhagen, R. S., Neerincx, M. A., & Tielman, M. L. (2024). Meaningful human control and variable autonomy in human-robot teams for firefighting. *Frontiers in Robotics and AI, 11*, 1323980. https://doi.org/10.3389/frobt.2024.1323980

Walliser, J. C., de Visser, E. J., & Shaw, T. H. (2023). Exploring system wide trust prevalence and mitigation strategies with multiple autonomous agents. *Computers in Human Behavior, 143*, 107671. https://doi.org/10.1016/j.chb.2023.107671

Wang, M., Hussein, A., Rojas, R. F., Shafi, K., & Abbass, H. A. (2018, November). EEG-based neural correlates of trust in human-autonomy interaction. *2018 IEEE symposium series on computational intelligence (SSCI)* (pp. 350–357). IEEE. https://doi.org/10.1109/SSCI.2018.8628649

Wang, N., Pynadath, D. V., & Hill, S. G. (2016, March). Trust calibration within a human-robot team: Comparing automatically generated explanations. In *2016 11th ACM/IEEE international conference on human-robot interaction (HRI)* (pp. 109–116). IEEE. https://doi.org/10.1109/HRI.2016.7451741

Waterson, P., Baber, C., Hunt, E., Milivojevic, S., Maynard, S., & Musolesi, M. (2025). Function allocation for responsible artificial intelligence: How do we allocate trust and responsibility? In *Contemporary ergonomics & human factors 2025* (pp. 277–283). Chartered Institute of Ergonomics & Human Factors. https://ergonomics.org.uk/asset/028A90A5%2DE1A9%2D4003%2DAF6BFDAF0660222A/

Waytz, A., Heafner, J., & Epley, N. (2014). The mind in the machine: Anthropomorphism increases trust in an autonomous vehicle. *Journal of Experimental Social Psychology, 52*, 113–117. https://doi.org/10.1016/j.jesp.2014.01.005

Webb, N., Huang, Z., Milivojevic, S., Baber, C., & Hunt, E. R. (2025, September 10–12). When robots say no: temporal trust recovery through explanation. *Proceedings of the 17th international conference on social robotics + AI (ICSR '24)*. Naples, Italy.

Webb, N., Milivojevic, S., Sobhani, S., Madin, Z. R., Ward, J. C., Yusuf, S., Baber, C., & Hunt, E. R. (2024, October 23–26). Co-movement as an indicator of trust development in human-robot teams. *Proceedings of the 16th international conference on social robotics + AI (ICSR '24)*. Odense, Denmark. https://doi.org/10.1007/978-981-96-3522-1_11

Wildman, J. L., Carroll, M., Thayer, A. L., Carmody, K., Nguyen, D., Akib, M., Addis, A., Ficke, C., & Robbins-Roth, V. (2026). Trust in human-agent teams: Temporal, multilevel, and multimodal perspectives. In S. B. F. Paletz & S. R. Dubrow (Eds.), *AI in teams* (pp. 39–56). Emerald Publishing.

Wildman, J. L., Nguyen, D., Thayer, A. L., Robbins-Roth, V. T., Carroll, M., Carmody, K., Ficke, C., Akib, M., & Addis, A. (2024). Trust in human-agent teams: A multilevel perspective and future research agenda. *Organizational Psychology Review*, *14*(3), 373–402. https://doi.org/10.1177/20413866241253278

Wildman, J. L., Shuffler, M. L., Lazzara, E. H., Fiore, S. M., Burke, C. S., Salas, E., & Garven, S. (2012). Trust development in swift starting action teams: A multilevel framework. *Group & Organization Management*, *37*(2), 137–170. https://doi.org/10.1177/1059601111434202

Yusuf, S. M., & Baber, C. (2022). Formalizing distributed situation awareness in multi-agent networks. *IEEE Transactions on Human-Machine Systems*, *52*(6), 1166–1175. https://doi.org/10.1109/THMS.2022.3142109

Zhang, Y., Yadav, A., Hopko, S. K., & Mehta, R. K. (2024, March). In gaze we trust: comparing eye tracking, self-report, and physiological indicators of dynamic trust during HRI. *Companion of the 2024 ACM/IEEE international conference on human-robot interaction* (pp. 1188–1193). https://doi.org/10.1145/3610978.3640649

CHAPTER 3

TRUST IN HUMAN–AGENT TEAMS: TEMPORAL, MULTILEVEL, AND MULTIMODAL PERSPECTIVES

Jessica L. Wildman[a], Meredith Carroll[a], Amanda L. Thayer[a], Kendall Carmody[a], Daniel Nguyen[a], Mohammed Akib[a], Arianna Addis[a], Cherrise Ficke[b] and Valerie Tuccillo Robbins-Roth[a]

[a]*Florida Institute of Technology, USA*
[b]*Aptima, Inc., USA*

ABSTRACT

Although much research has explored trust within what are sometimes referred to as human–agent teams (HATs), this research has largely been focused on when and why a single human develops trust toward a single collaborating agent. There has been less attention paid to trust in more complex, heterogeneous HAT settings. Yet, the future of human–agent teaming in organizations likely includes such complex teams comprised of multiple humans working with multiple types of automated agents in diverse roles such as transport, surveillance, search and rescue, and decision support. The purpose of this chapter is to summarize findings from our prior work and to outline key future research directions stemming from those findings, organized around three key perspectives: temporal, multilevel, and multimodal. Example findings include that the average of a human's trust toward their multiple agent teammates as individual

AI in Teams: Research on Managing Groups and Teams, Volume 21, 39–56

Published under exclusive licence by Emerald Publishing Limited
ISSN: 1534-0856/doi:10.1108/S1534-085620260000021007

referents is not equivalent to trust measured toward the HAT as a referent, that trust violations committed by one agent in an HAT can impact the trust held toward other non-violating agents in the HAT, that trust in a violating agent is most effectively repaired when the larger team as a whole engages in trust repair efforts, and that the connection of self-reported trust and unobtrusive metrics requires a constellation-based, multimodal approach. Overall, this chapter will highlight the importance of advanced temporal perspectives, multilevel theory, and multimodal measurement approaches for effectively studying trust in HATs.

Keywords: Trust; trustworthiness; agent; AI; robot; teams

INTRODUCTION

The age of highly intelligent technological systems, such as robots performing sophisticated tasks such as search and rescue, surveillance, or even leading and directing humans, is rapidly approaching. These accelerating technological shifts have increased the prevalence of HATs and created a compelling need for research aimed at optimizing collaboration and mission performance within HATs. One key factor for success in HATs is the ability for human team members to develop appropriate levels of trust in agents (Klein et al., 2004). Although trust in HATs has been the focus of much academic study, this research is heavily focused on identifying which agent characteristics determine one human's trust toward that agent. This research has demonstrated that trust in an agent varies greatly depending on an individual agent's role, appearance, and location (e.g., physical, virtual, or embedded; Glikson & Woolley, 2020). There is much less research attention focused on trust in more complex, distributed, heterogeneous, multi-agent teams (Wildman et al., 2024).

Furthermore, research on trust in HATs has not been carefully integrated with the literature on human–human trust and trust in teams. There is a need to understand how trust is calibrated across multiple referents within heterogeneous multi-agent teams, including across differing team members and the team overall. In such heterogeneous settings, there may be spillover effects from interactions with the individual teammates that could impact trust in other agent teammates and the team as a whole. Furthermore, a key challenge in studying trust in HATs is the lack of frequent interactions and communications, which makes assessment of dynamic team processes and levels of trust more difficult. Although some studies have utilized behavioral and physiological measures of trust such as taking manual control of the agent or the gaze patterns of the humans (Walker et al., 2019), more focus is needed on the systematic development and validation of unobtrusive measures of operator trust in HATs, especially across levels and referents.

Accordingly, this chapter summarizes the methods and findings from a three-year research effort aimed at examining trust in heterogeneous HATs from an explicitly temporal, multilevel, and multimodal perspective. Our findings highlight the importance of multilevel theory, advanced temporal perspectives, and multimodal measurement approaches for more effectively studying, and ultimately managing, trust in HATs. It should be noted that, as compared to the previous chapter on trust (Webb & Hunt, Chapter 5), our chapter is more descriptive in that it provides a summary of basic research findings regarding how trust is naturally developed, violated, and restored within heterogeneous HATs. Webb and Hunt take a more prescriptive approach in outlining a proposed trust management framework intended to improve the active measurement and management of trust in human–robot teams.

KEY DEFINITIONS

The terminology used to describe the technologies that interact with humans varies across the literature, with terms such as autonomy, artificial intelligence (AI), agent, robot, and automation sometimes being used interchangeably despite having distinct meanings. The current work utilizes definitions drawn primarily from the social science disciplines including human factors, cognitive sciences, and applied psychology. Within these fields, automation refers to technology that executes predefined tasks when prompted but does not act independently (Parasuraman et al., 2000). Autonomy, in contrast, denotes a system's ability to operate independently, adapting to its environment and making decisions without human input (Chen & Barnes, 2014). AI encompasses systems capable of learning and adapting over time, but not all autonomous systems are necessarily AI-driven (Russell & Norvig, 2020). Agents are commonly understood as autonomous technologies that operate with some degree of independence and interdependence with human teammates (O'Neill et al., 2023). For the purposes of the current work, our focus is on HATs, which we define as teams, composed of at least one human and one autonomous agent, who work interdependently toward shared goals.

In discussing trust, we distinguish between trust as a psychological state and reliance on a system as a behavior. Trust, as we conceptualize it, is an internally held, attitudinal state reflecting a willingness to be vulnerable based on positive expectations (Fulmer & Gelfand, 2012; Rousseau et al., 1998). Trust as an attitude differs from reliance, which is a behavioral concept referring to the extent to which a human depends on an agent's actions or recommendations. Ross et al. (2008) define reliance in human–agent interaction research as the behavioral tendency to use automation in place of manual control. In this context, reliance is often framed as a decision-making process, in which a human chooses whether or not to use an agent or engage with an agent's recommendations. Although trust and reliance are causally related, we emphasize that they are conceptually distinct. Reliance can occur with or without trust, driven by factors such as necessity, constraints, or habit, rather than positive expectations of the agent. Thus, our research examined trust, defined as an internally held attitudinal psychological state, as it was directed at each of the agents and the team as a whole, in a simulated HAT comprised of one human participant and four agents.

RESEARCH CONTEXT

As part of a funded three-year effort, we first completed a systematic review and synthesis of the multidisciplinary social science literature surrounding trust development, violation, and repair in HATs. We conducted a search using key terms related to HATs such as human–agent, human–robot, and human–machine, as well as terms related to trust such as trust, trustworthiness, and repair. The initial search resulted in 399 articles that were uploaded, organized, and tagged in a Zotero database. Those were reviewed for relevance and a final set of 167 articles (139 empirical, 21 theoretical, 4 meta-analyses, and 3 reviews) were coded using an extensive coding spreadsheet for relevant information such as key methods, results, task descriptions, and team characteristics. Based on this systematic review, we identified several gaps in the existing literature and designed our work to begin to address some of these gaps. Specifically, much previous research has focused on teams that consisted of one human working with one agent (e.g., Hancock et al., 2011; Kaplan et al., 2021). Although we acknowledge that most formal definitions of teams do define them to include a collective of two or more individuals working together toward a shared goal (e.g., Salas et al., 2005), our work focuses on a more complex team context that includes multiple agents working together. Furthermore, we apply a multilevel theoretical lens (Kozlowski & Klein, 2000) to examine trust within that team context.

Our review suggests that prior research tends to look at agents as tools, whereas we seek to position them as teammates. Additionally, most prior research has manipulated aspects of an agent being trusted, such as anthropomorphism and reliability, whereas we build upon this foundation of work and adopt a temporal and event-based perspective to focus on specific trust violation and repair events. Prior research has begun to scratch the surface on understanding the role of time in HATs, but we explicitly examine trust trajectories developed and measured over seven points in time for multiple different targets of trust. Finally, previous research has heavily relied on self-report measures of trust and "use" of the agent as the primary reflection of trust, whereas we broaden our measurement toolkit to consider other unobtrusive and behavioral indicators of trust from a multimodal perspective.

In order to examine HATs from a multilevel and unobtrusive perspective, we needed a simulated environment for experiments that allowed for human participants to be working together with multiple, interdependent agents toward a shared goal. As such, we conceptualized a novel HAT task paradigm and worked with the Air Force Research Laboratory's Gaming Research Integration for Learning Laboratory (GRILL) to develop our own custom experimental testbed, the Multi-Agent Team Trust Emergence Research, or MATTER, testbed. This laptop-computer-based simulation, which was built using Unreal Engine, mimics an urban search and rescue type scenario in which the human participant works with four agent-based teammates (i.e., two ground robots and two aerial drones) to search and clear routes within a post-conflict town. In order to clear routes, the team members must (1) find and defuse improved explosive devices (IEDs), (2) rescue trapped civilians, and (3) report, but not engage in combat with, any remaining enemies. The human is responsible for patrolling their own route through town while also collaborating with two sub-teams, each consisting of one ground robot and one aerial drone that are responsible for patrolling their own routes as well. Each team member type has a unique role and thus the teams are interdependent. The human is the only team member that has the ability to defuse IEDs once found, the two aerial drones are the only team members that can search high areas such as rooftops and second floor windows, and the two ground robots are the only team members that can clear rubble from blocked areas. All of these functions are required to clear the IEDs, civilians, and enemies identified along each route. Thus, the team members must call on one another for help with these specific tasks as they progress through the landscape and encounter these various objectives. The testbed includes a communications log in which the human participant can receive requests from the agents for help (i.e., to defuse a found IED), request agents for help (i.e., to search a rooftop or clear rubble blocking an entrance), and monitor what is happening with other agents. The human participant can also review each agent's performance statistics at any time and can either nudge them to perform more quickly if they are falling behind or nudge them to slow down and be more careful if they are making mistakes.

Using the MATTER testbed, years two and three of our funded effort focused on experimental data collection. In year two, we conducted a trust violation experiment involving almost 200 participants in which one or more of the agents made a mistake (i.e., a competence-based trust violation) that resulted in the loss of civilian life within the simulation. The violation manipulation was communicated via a written message in the communication log and a loud alert sound. In year three, we conducted a trust repair experiment involving 150 participants in which one agent, a ground-based automated vehicle named Rocky, made two consecutive mistakes, followed by various trust repair interventions. The five trust repair conditions manipulated which agent(s) enacted trust repair: violating agent repairs, same type of agent on different team repairs, different types of agent on different team repairs, the full team repairs, or no repair. All repair interventions consisted of the assigned parties communicating within the communication log the following verbiage: *Agent(s) has/have automatically run diagnostics after ROCKY's earlier failures and identified that ROCKY's driver was missing updates. ROCKY'S driver has now been updated to prevent further errors.*

In both experiments, we utilized multiple types of measures to assess trust toward the various agents within the team as well as the team as a whole: self-report surveys, behavioral measures, and physiological measures. We used a single-item measure in the form of a brief pop-up survey that asked the participant how much they trust each of the four agents, and the team as a whole, to do what is expected of them, on a scale ranging from (1) not at all to (5) a great deal. This measure was administered before the mission and every 10 minutes after that to allow us to study trust trajectories over time. Four main behavioral indicators of trust were also captured throughout the participants' time in the simulation, including (1) team monitoring, as measured by how frequently a participant accessed an individual agent's statistics page, which included number of houses the agent has visited, and objects missed or identified; (2) assistance requested, which is the number of times a participant called a specific agent for aid; (3) nudge positive, which is the number of times the participant requested the agent search more houses more quickly on their route; and (4) nudge negative, which is the number of times the participant requested the agent search houses more carefully and slowly on their route. For the purposes of this chapter, all results reported utilize self-report surveys and behavioral measures. If referring to "trust" in the results, we are referencing the quantitative scores between one and five obtained via the self-report items regarding trust, whereas results using the behavior measures will explicitly refer to the four trust-related behaviors of monitoring, assistance, nudge positive, and nudge negative.

In the sections that follow, we summarize three overarching issues, identified through the process of conducting this research, that are critical to the effective study of trust within HATs: (1) temporal considerations, (2) multilevel considerations, and (3) multimodal considerations. For each of these themes, we provide an overview of our research findings and outline suggested future research directions.

TEMPORAL PERSPECTIVES ON TRUST IN HATs

Given that trust development, violation, and repair are explicitly conceptualized as unfolding processes that occur over time (e.g., Lewicki & Brinsfield, 2017), it is crucial that research on trust in HATs considers such temporal elements in a nuanced and explicit way. As discussed in Wildman et al. (2024), trust is a very dynamic emergent state that changes in response to interactions between its team members, and those changes can in some cases be quite dramatic when triggered by salient trust-related events. For example, prior research has found that trust generally increases steadily over time in response to perceptions of consistent performance (Yu et al., 2019), but that the upward increase of trust can be disrupted by perceived events such as trust violation and trust repair acts.

Taking a temporal perspective in research can mean many things, but for our work examining trust in HATs, it meant an emphasis on examining not just what factors contribute to a human's trust in an agent at any single "snapshot" in time, but instead tracking trust more carefully over time from the beginning to the end of a performance episode to consider how the trajectory of trust changes and reacts to relevant events over time. It also meant we took an event-based perspective (Morgeson et al., 2015) to examine not just trust development, but how the enactment of trust violation and repair events throughout a performance episode may influence and interrupt the trajectory of trust development over time.

Temporal Perspectives: Our Findings

Number of Violations

One of our primary research questions was focused on the extent to which frequency of violations committed by different agents within a HAT impacts the trajectory of a human's trust in those agents over time. Therefore, our year two study directly manipulated the frequency of violations by having one of the agents within the team make one mistake at the 29-minute mark or two mistakes, both at the 29-minute and 35-minute marks, within the roughly one-hour performance episode. These mistakes reflect one or two incorrect actions in the midst of dozens of correct actions. The relative frequency of mistakes to correct actions was determined in part based on a goal of establishing the agents as overall reliable while also engaging in strong enough violations to elicit noticeable changes in trust. We then investigated the difference between violation frequency conditions by comparing the slope of trust loss. As a first step in studying violation frequency, we examined one versus two violations committed by the same agent, but we acknowledge that future research is necessary to explore beyond just two violations. Our results suggest a steeper initial loss of self-reported trust toward the violating agent in the condition with one violation than the condition with two violations (Fig. 3.1). Since the rate of trust loss was calculated using different timeframes, the conditions were not directly comparable, potentially influencing the observed differences. Another analysis compared trust lost over the entire mission ranging from Time 1 to Time 6, accounting for trust lost after the violation as well as natural trust recovery that often takes place after a violation. This analysis suggested more trust loss in the condition with two violations as compared to the condition with one. In fact, the pattern of trust changes over time suggests that trust recovers back to nearly the level it was pre-violation when there is only one violation. However, the occurrence of a second violation prevented trust from recovering to this level. Next, the natural trajectory of trust restoration, meaning the upward trajectory of trust in the absence of any explicitly enacted trust repair tactics, was examined. An analysis compared the overall trust restoration slopes, operationalized as the upward change in trust after the violation (i.e., Time 3 to Time 6) for the one violation condition, and the upward change in trust after the violations (i.e., Time 4 to Time 6) for the two-violation condition. Our findings suggest significant differences between the two conditions, with the overall restoration slope after one violation being significantly steeper than the restoration slopes after two violations. This finding suggests that there might be a cumulative effect of repeated trust violations that inhibits natural trust restoration to pre-violation levels, though future research examining three or more violations is needed to explore if this pattern continues at higher frequencies.

In sum, our findings regarding the frequency of violations suggest that after a single violation, self-reported trust in the violating agent immediately decreased but recovered relatively quickly, ultimately stabilizing above pre-violation levels. However, following the occurrence of two consecutive violations, trust in the violating agent declined significantly and did not recover to baseline levels before the end of the performance episode.

Timing of Violations

Another temporally oriented research question was the impact of the timing of violations on reactions to those violations. To study how violation timing affects trust, we looked at early-, middle-, and late-mission violations. More specifically,

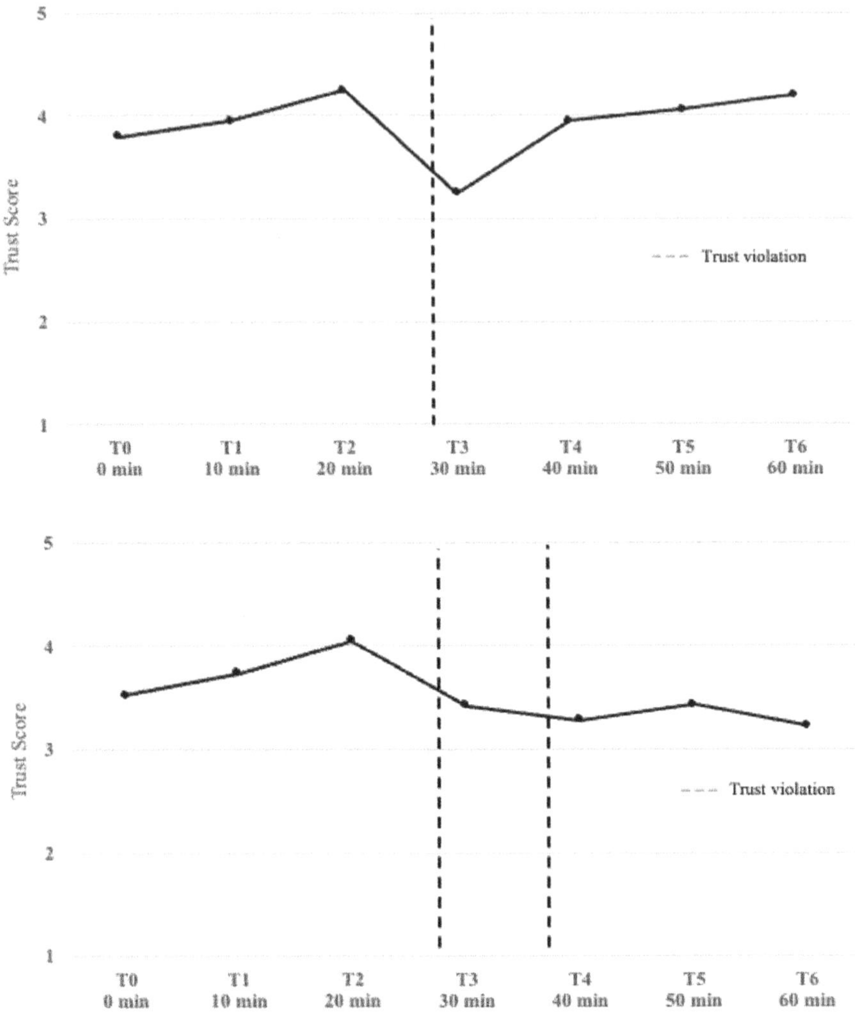

Fig. 3.1. Trust in Violating Agent (Rocky) Trajectories Over Time for One Versus Two Violations.

we compared self-reported trust dissolution and restoration slopes across conditions in which a single trust violation occurred quite early within the performance mission (i.e., after 10 minutes), at a midpoint in the mission (i.e., after 30 minutes), and near the end of the mission (i.e., after 50 minutes). Results suggest a significant impact of violation timing on the slope of trust loss toward the violating agent, such that a trust violation occurring early within the performance mission resulted in a less steep dissolution slope as compared to a trust violation occurring at a midpoint in the mission or late in the mission, suggesting that later violations lead to a steeper decline in trust. This finding is in line with recent research that has found what is called the "peak-end rule," in which, above a certain level of reliability, trust levels are higher later in time and consequently, trust violations have a bigger impact later in time because you have more trust to lose (Wang et al., 2023).

To dig deeper into this pattern of results, we examined trust levels just before and just after the violation across different timing conditions. We found a significant difference across conditions in trust levels just before the violation, suggesting that trust continued to build at a steady rate until the violation occurred, with later violations corresponding to higher pre-violation trust levels. However, directly after the violation, we found there was no significant difference in trust levels between conditions, suggesting that regardless of when during the performance episode the violation took place, trust dropped to roughly the same level post-violation. This could suggest a potential threshold of trust that individuals tend to revert to following a violation. In other words, while it appears that in the absence of violations, trust builds steadily, there may be a consistent level to which it falls after a transgression.

Regarding differences in natural restoration (i.e., upward increase in scores in the absence of explicit trust repair attempts) of trust following violations at different times, results suggest a significant effect of timing, with a trust violation occurring at the midpoint of the mission resulting in a steeper restoration slope than a trust violation occurring later in the mission. Trust violations occurring early in the mission did not differ significantly in restoration slope compared to midpoint and late conditions. This suggests that violations that occur somewhere near the midpoint of the mission resulted in faster natural trust restoration as compared to a violation occurring before the last 10 minutes of this mission. However, we must acknowledge that the nature of the experimental paradigm makes it difficult to determine if the lack of trust restoration late in the mission is simply reflective of lack of remaining time and opportunity to continue restoring trust.

Temporal Perspectives: Future Research

The research findings described above only begin to hint at the temporal complexities inherent in understanding trust in complex, heterogeneous HATs. There exist many fruitful avenues for future research to continue to explore. One obvious starting point, as mentioned previously, is the fact that our study only compared one versus two violations and three different potential timing conditions. It is quite possible that our findings may not hold or apply when considering much higher frequencies or relative proportions of trust violations out of possible performance episodes. They may also not hold for other in-between timing of events (i.e., all of the possibilities between early, midpoint, and late). Furthermore, there is likely an interaction between frequency and timing of trust violation events that could change their nature and impact as well. Future research is needed to explore the impact of high frequency trust violations within HATs, and related questions such as how many trust violations may constitute a threshold beyond which trust recovery is no longer possible, or at which point the user abandons use of the agent teammate or abandons progress toward the mission entirely.

Another area in which there is a need for more explicitly temporal research, as discussed in detail in Wildman et al. (2024), is the possible existence and nature of different types or forms of trust that may develop over time within HATs. Whereas the human–human trust literature has long posited and examined forms of trust that are theorized to develop and change over time such as calculus-, knowledge-, and identification-based trust (Lewicki & Bunker, 1995), no such frameworks exist for trust in HATs. Is it possible for humans to eventually develop deeper bonds such as identification-based trust with agents or toward the HAT as a higher-level society entity? Or are HATs relegated to more cognitively oriented forms of trust such as calculus- and knowledge-based alone, no matter how long the relationship between human and agent? Or are these not the right terms for discussing the gradual development of trust within HATs at all? There is a need for further theorizing and empirical research regarding temporal forms of trust in HATs.

Another area ripe for exploration is what might be coined the "when" of trust in HATs. In other words, understanding what impacts trust, and what trust subsequently impacts, within HATs, requires the researcher to think carefully about when these phenomena are occurring, what temporal form of these phenomena are at play, and when and how these constructs are being measured. For example, it has been demonstrated that higher trust in teams, including HATs, relates to desirable outcomes such as team performance (De Jong et al., 2016; McNeese et al., 2021; Morrissette & Kisamore, 2020). However, when trust in agent teammates is not calibrated appropriately, either in terms of over trusting unreliable AI or having excessive skepticism toward capable agents, it can lead to inefficiencies, reduced system adoption, or even safety risks (Glikson & Woolley, 2020). These findings underscore the importance of designing HATs that foster appropriate trust calibration, ensuring that human agent collaboration is both effective and sustainable (de Visser et al., 2020). However, research has not fully grappled with what might be most predictive of outcomes in the team: trust as measured at a certain snapshot in time, the average of one's trust in an agent or the team over an entire performance episode, or the average of one's trust for some specific time frame within a performance episode? Combining temporal and event-based perspectives may be an effective strategy for identifying the most predictive combination of variables. For instance, trust measured over a brief period of time following key events (e.g., trust violation, trust repair) could be more predictive of reliance behavior or performance that is also measured over some specific span of time, rather than trust averaged over the entire performance episode, or measured at any given single point in time. What we know now is that much of the research simply is not considering the "when" of trust in HATs at a granular enough level to answer these or similar questions.

MULTILEVEL PERSPECTIVES ON TRUST IN HATs

To more directly address the nested nature of individual and dyadic phenomena housed within a group context, contemporary teams research has argued for the adoption of an explicitly multilevel theoretical perspective (Kozlowski & Klein, 2000). Multilevel theory acknowledges and describes both top-down influences and bottom-up emergent processes that inherently occur with higher-level social entities. Of particular relevance to studying trust in HAT settings, multilevel theoretical assertions about bottom-up emergent processes suggest that individuals' behaviors and dyadic interactions among pairs of teammates that are enacted within higher-level social entities (e.g., teams, organizations) can influence the attitudes, cognitions, and behaviors toward (a) other individuals within that entity and (b) the higher-level social entity itself. Multilevel theory also suggests that the lower-level elemental content in teams (e.g., individual team member attitudes, cognitions, behaviors) co-develop and interact over time to manifest as higher-level phenomenon (e.g., team trust) at the team-level through emergence processes that range on a continuum from compositional (i.e., similarity and convergence across members) to compilational (i.e., variability and divergence across members). On the compositional end of the emergence spectrum, it is assumed that the lower-level elemental contents are isomorphic, meaning they are conceptually similar enough in type and amount that they combine through repeated interactions into a highly similar, shared phenomenon at the team level. In the case of trust within a HAT, this would mean it is assumed that all team members hold similar types and amounts of trust toward one another and toward the team. On the compilational end of the emergence spectrum, it is assumed that lower-level elemental contents are different in type and amount, and therefore, that the emergent phenomenon at the team level will be non-isomorphic – that is, varied, or patterned – in nature. In the case of trust in HATs, this would mean that team members may hold differing amounts of trust toward one another and the team.

Multilevel Perspectives: Our Findings

Trust Across Referents

One of our hypotheses that take an explicitly multilevel perspective on trust in HATs is that we generally expect that self-reported trust toward individual agents in a HAT and self-reported trust toward the HAT as a whole will be related, but distinct, concepts. This argument is based on prior human–human team research which has conceptualized trust in individual referents and trust in larger intact social systems as distinguishable concepts (Fulmer & Gelfand, 2012). Additionally, when considering a person's trust in another individual, that is a judgment that is typically driven by perception of the trustee only, whereas when forming a judgment about one's team, the self is included as part of that social entity and, therefore, trust in that social entity may be in some part influence by one's self-perceptions. We, therefore, expected that averaging the participant's self-reported trust scores in each of the four agents in our simulation would be highly, but not perfectly, correlated with directly asking how much the participants trusted their team as a whole. When correlating the average of a participant's trust toward all four individual agents with the participant's trust reported toward the team as a whole, correlations ranged between 0.75 and 0.83. Based on precedents set regarding empirical redundancy (Le & Pan, 2021), this suggests these measures are not empirically redundant concepts. In other words, our findings support the argument that trust in the team and combined trust in individual agents are related but not equivalent concepts.

Adjacency Effect

Another multilevel phenomenon we explored was the concept of spillover of trust loss between agents of different types within the team, following a scripted trust violation event. Specifically, we studied the impact of subgrouping agents by subteam and subtype. To study this, we assigned one of the ground vehicles as the first trust violator across three conditions and manipulated the second violator, who in the first condition was another ground vehicle on a different subteam (i.e., same type, different team), in the second condition, was a drone on the same subteam (i.e., different type, same subteam), and in the third condition, was a drone on a different subteam (i.e., different type and different subteam). Not surprisingly, we found that trust in the violating agent dropped significantly after they committed either the first or second violation. Additionally, we found an interesting phenomenon that we have termed the "adjacency effect," in which trust is lost in an agent who did not directly engage in any violation in only one situation: when the second violating agent is both a different type of agent and on a different subteam than the original violator. We speculate that when the second violating agent shares something in common with the first violating agent, whether that is being the same type or on the same subteam, trust loss is not generalized to other agents because the violations are seen as an issue isolated to agents of that type or that subteam. However, when the second violating agent is not connected to the first violator in any direct way, the problem is seen as more widespread, and therefore loss of trust ripples out to other unrelated teammates, even if they did not yet commit a violation.

Full Team Repair

In year three, our research questions focused on whether the source of a trust repair attempt impacted the effectiveness of that repair. We collected data with 161 participants in a between-groups experiment in which participants all experienced two trust violations, by the same agent (Rocky), back-to-back midway through the mission. Following this violation, a trust repair was attempted by different agents, which varied based on condition. In the first condition, the violating agent attempted a repair. In the second condition, the same type of agent (i.e., another ground-based automated vehicle) on a different team attempted repair. In the third condition, a different type of agent (i.e., an automated aerial vehicle) on a different team attempted repair. In the fourth condition, the entire team attempted repair, and the fifth condition was a control condition in which no repair was attempted. For all conditions that included a repair attempt, this repair was enacted by sending a message in the communication log with the following verbiage: *Agent(s) has/have automatically run diagnostics after ROCKY's earlier failures and identified that ROCKY's driver was missing updates. ROCKY'S driver has now been updated to prevent further errors.* Examining the trajectories of trust over time across these five conditions, we found that in all cases, we saw a significant loss of trust in the violating agent in response to the violations, followed by a natural restoration prior to the repair attempt. We also observed that without a repair attempt, the restoration of trust becomes asymptotic (i.e., trust scores stop increasing and stay relatively constant) after about 10 minutes. However, with a repair attempt, we see restoration (i.e., upward change in trust) continue until the last 10 minutes of the mission, with the greatest restoration being when the entire team attempts repair. In fact, results showed that when the entire team repaired, there was a significantly steeper slope in the 10 minutes following repair compared to no repair.

This quantitative finding was reinforced by qualitative data that were collected as well: we asked participants, "Was there any attempt from specifically the autonomous agents on your team to correct the issue after the mistake(s)?" and if they selected yes, "Please explain in detail what your teammate(s) did to repair the mistake and how you felt when a teammate(s) tried to repair the mistake(s)." Unexpectedly, but very interestingly, the source of the repair attempt influenced whether the participant perceived that a repair attempt had been made. When the violating agent (i.e., Rocky) alone attempted repair, approximately one-third of participants reported they did not perceive a repair had occurred. However, when agent teammates other than the violating agent itself attempted repair, almost all of the participants perceived that a trust repair had been initiated. Thus, it appears full team repair may be a more effective strategy even when a single agent commits a violation.

Multilevel Perspectives: Future Research

There are many research questions that remain in terms of the multilevel nature of trust in HATs. One particular example is that most HAT research has primarily considered trust from human team members' perspectives. Less research has emphasized the nature of agents' trust in their human teammates, agents' trust in other agent teammates, and human trust in other human teammates within the context of working in a heterogeneous HAT. Research has underexplored just about every relationship and level of trust within HATs other than the single dyadic perspective. There are many questions to ask in terms of what influences and settings might lead to the development of more compositional (i.e., shared and convergent) trust in HATs versus more compilational (i.e., varied and divergent) trust in HATs, and what it means to say that an agent trusts a human or another agent. Finally, what is the nature and form of emergent, higher-level trust in HATs if that emergent property is formed from the combination of trust held by both humans and agents? Can higher-level team trust actually exist in HATs, and if it exists, how can it be measured and aggregated most appropriately?

Another series of future research questions stem from our findings of the adjacency effect and trust repair. In general, our findings suggest that there is a need to explore how trust violation and repair function beyond the dyadic context within HATs. We found that trust violation and repair enacted by one agent can impact the trust held in other agents, but what are the implications of more than one team member simultaneously or jointly violating or repairing trust? What happens if a violation occurs and is attributed to a subgroup of the team made up of a combination of humans and agents? What are the implications of these types of events in terms of appropriately calibrating trust and performance within HATs? There are many combinations of trust violation and repair enacted by different referents at different points over time that may result in very different trajectories of trust development and mission performance.

MULTIMODAL MEASUREMENT PERSPECTIVES ON TRUST IN HATs

Key to the ability to study trust in teams is the ability to measure trust in this context. The predominant approach to assessing team emergent states and trust, more specifically, has been through self-report survey methodologies. However, self-reported trust measures suffer from several limitations including confounding with cognitive biases and social desirability (e.g., Arnold & Feldman, 1981; Taylor, 1961), inaccuracies due to retrospective assessments of abstract concepts (Podsakoff & Organ, 1986), assessment of trust as a static state rather than as a dynamic process of emergence (Kozlowski, 2015), and the impracticality of asking team members to pause activities to complete a survey. There is a clear need for innovative approaches to better capture trust and other team processes and emergent states, for both research and applied purposes. In particular, research suggests combining multiple measures may be key to painting a more accurate picture of trust (Schaefer, 2019). As a primary step toward developing a more theory-based and holistic approach to measuring trust in HATs, we utilized the Rational Approach to Developing Systems-based Measures (RADSM; Orvis et al., 2013). As described in more detail in Ficke et al. (2023), we began by identifying the construct of interest, which in this case was competence-based trust. Then, we developed a list of observable behaviors that could reflect competence-based trust within our simulated search and rescue scenario. Then, we identified the type of data available and how that data would be analyzed. Below, we describe some preliminary findings related to the captured behavioral indicators.

Multimodal Perspectives: Our Findings

As mentioned earlier, four main behavioral indicators of trust were captured throughout the participants' time in the simulation, including (1) team monitoring, which is how frequently a participant viewed an individual agent's statistics page, which included number of houses the agent has visited, and objects missed or identified; (2) assistance requested, which is the number of times a participant called a specific agent for aid; (3) nudge positive, which is the number of times the participant requested the agent search more quickly on their route; and (4) nudge negative, which is the number of times the participant requested the agent search more carefully on their route. As one of our primary goals is to develop a more multimodal assessment of trust that accounts for multiple behavioral indicators simultaneously, as an initial proof of concept, we regressed the behavioral indicators from this time period on self-reported trust scores for the respective times (see Carmody et al., 2024, for more details). While several different regression analyses were conducted, the basic finding was that somewhere between 7% and 13% of the variance in changes of self-reported trust were explained collectively by the combination of assistance requested, nudge positive, and nudge negative. Together, this provides support for the idea that simultaneously considering multiple indicators of trust may provide a more holistic picture of trust in HATs.

Multimodal Perspectives: Future Research

Some of the most insightful research questions that have arisen from our efforts to improve the multimodal measurement of trust come down to the challenges we faced in finding meaningful results. In other words, while our work has not yet clearly identified the right set of data and indicators to combine to reflect trust most accurately in HATs, it has inspired a number of important questions to guide better future research. For example, combining some of our temporal thinking with the idea of behavioral measures of trust, we have realized that there is very little theory or practical guidance in terms of how best to connect self-reported trust measures to more dynamic behavioral data. For example, we know that theoretically and empirically, trust is related to monitoring behavior (e.g., De Jong & Elfring, 2010). However, what are the most appropriate time spans across which to capture, aggregate, and correlate these concepts if we want to understand the relationship between trust and behaviors in HATs? Could the lack of concordance between self-reported trust and other multimodal indicators of trust in some cases be due to a mismatch in the temporal conceptualizations surrounding these variables? For example, does a self-reported measure of trust captured before a trust violation occurs still relate to monitoring behaviors or other constellations of unobtrusive data after a trust violation, or does the occurrence of that event change the causal relationship between trust and monitoring? Might it actually be the change in trust scores that then becomes more related to more unobtrusive indicators of trust?

Overall, we suggest that the development of multimodal unobtrusive measures of trust would benefit from taking a diagnostician's approach. In other words, HAT researchers need to think of the unobtrusive measurement of trust the way a doctor may think of a constellation of symptoms. A doctor may suspect you have influenza not based on body temperature alone, but because you have a combination of a fever, body aches, a runny nose, and fatigue, all several days after exposure to others who were ill. In the same way, we suggest that measuring trust in HATs unobtrusively will not be achieved effectively by looking at any single indicator, but by identifying the constellation of symptoms (e.g., increased heart rate, heightened monitoring behavior, reduced reliance, eye gaze focused on particular aspects of the environment, all after a particular event occurs) that might indicate key trust-related events such as a perceived trust violation.

CONCLUSION

The technology and capabilities underlying intelligent systems and agents is improving quickly, as is the research examining the interactions and effectiveness of HATs. Over the past three years, we have explored emerging research questions regarding how trust is developed, violated, and repaired in complex, heterogeneous HATs. We have found evidence of several interesting phenomenon including that trust toward one's HAT as a higher-level social entity is not equivalent to the average of one's trust in all of the agents within that HAT, that trust violations may be more severe when occurring later within the team's mission, and that the actions of one agent during a performance mission can impact a human's trust in another unrelated agent. Our work has also illuminated several research areas that seem ripe for future focus. First, we emphasize the inherently temporal nature of HAT interactions, and the need for HAT research to take a more theoretically nuanced, higher resolution approach to understanding the role of time and temporal issues. Second, we urge more researchers to adopt an explicitly multilevel theory perspective when considering HATs, such that research more carefully examines not just a single human's trust in a single agent or a homogenous swarm of agents, but instead takes a more compilational approach to consider all dyadic relationships within a HAT, potential sub-groups, and higher-level emergence of trust. Third, we echo calls for more cutting-edge unobtrusive measurement of trust and other constructs within HATs but emphasize that effective measures will likely need to take a multimodal approach that considers the constellation of various streams of data including eye tracking, physiological response, and behavioral data, rather than trying to find any single proxy measure of trust. We hope the findings and future research directions discussed in this chapter will spur new and innovative thinking regarding the future of HAT research and practice.

ACKNOWLEDGMENTS

This material is based upon work supported by the Air Force Office of Scientific Research under award number FA9550-21-1-0294. Any opinions, findings, conclusions, or recommendations expressed in this material are those of the authors and do not necessarily reflect the views of the United States Air Force. We would also like to thank the Air Force Research Lab's Gaming Research Integration for Learning Lab (GRILL) for support in the development of the Multi-Agent Team Trust Emergence Research (MATTER) computer-based testbed.

REFERENCES

Arnold, H. J., & Feldman, D. C. (1981). Social desirability response bias in self-report choice situations. *Academy of Management Journal*, *24*(2), 377–385. https://doi.org/10.5465/255848

Carmody, K., Sharma, V., Addis, A., Nguyen, D., Ficke, C., Thayer, A., Wildman, J., & Carroll, M. (2024). Behave yourself! Behavioral indicators of trust in human-agent teams. *Proceedings of the Human Factors and Ergonomics Society Annual Meeting*, *68*(1), 323–328. https://doi-org.portal.lib.fit.edu/10.1177/10711813241276485

Chen, J. Y., & Barnes, M. J. (2014). Human–agent teaming for multirobot control: A review of human factors issues. *IEEE Transactions on Human-Machine Systems*, *44*(1), 13–29. https://doi.org/10.1109/thms.2013.2293535

De Jong, B. A., & Elfring, T. (2010). How does trust affect the performance of ongoing teams? The mediating role of reflexivity, monitoring, and effort. *Academy of Management Journal*, *53*(3), 535–549. https://doi.org/10.5465/amj.2010.51468649

De Jong, B. A., Dirks, K. T., & Gillespie, N. (2016). Trust and team performance: A meta-analysis of main effects, moderators, and covariates. *Journal of Applied Psychology*, *101*(8), 1134–1150. https://doi.org/10.1037/apl0000110

de Visser, E. J., Peeters, M. M. M., Jung, M. F., Kohn, S., Shaw, T. H., Pak, R., & Neerincx, M. A. (2020). Towards a theory of longitudinal trust calibration in human–robot teams. *International Journal of Social Robotics*, *12*(2), 459–478. https://doi.org/10.1007/s12369-019-00596-x

Ficke, C., Addis, A., Nguyen, D., Carmody, K., Thayer, A., Wildman, J., & Carroll, M. (2023). Measuring trust in a simulated human agent team task. *AHFE International*. https://doi.org/10.54941/ahfe1003560

Fulmer, C. A., & Gelfand, M. J. (2012). At what level (and in whom) we trust. *Journal of Management*, *38*(4), 1167–1230. https://doi.org/10.1177/0149206312439327

Glikson, E., & Woolley, A. W. (2020). Human trust in artificial intelligence: Review of empirical research. *Academy of Management Annals*, *14*(2), 627–660. https://doi.org/10.5465/annals.2018.0057

Hancock, P. A., Billings, D. R., Schaefer, K. E., Chen, J. Y. C., de Visser, E. J., & Parasuraman, R. (2011). A meta-analysis of factors affecting trust in human-robot interaction. *Human Factors*, *53*(5), 517–527. https://doi.org/10.1177/0018720811417254

Kaplan, A. D., Kessler, T. T., Brill, J. C., & Hancock, P. A. (2021). Trust in artificial intelligence: Meta-analytic findings. *Human Factors*, *65*(2), 337–359. https://doi.org/10.1177/00187208211013988

Klein, G., Woods, D. D., Bradshaw, J. M., Hoffman, R. R., & Feltovich, P. J. (2004). Ten challenges for making automation a "team player" in joint human-agent activity. *IEEE Intelligent Systems*, *19*(06), 91–95. https://doi.org/10.1109/mis.2004.74

Kozlowski, S. W. (2015). Advancing research on team process dynamics. *Organizational Psychology Review*, *5*(4), 270–299. https://doi.org/10.1177/2041386614533586

Kozlowski, S. W. J., & Klein, K. J. (2000). A multilevel approach to theory and research in organizations: Contextual, temporal, and emergent processes. In K. J. Klein & S. W. J. Kozlowski (Eds.), *Multilevel theory, research, and methods in organizations: Foundations, extensions, and new directions* (pp. 3–90). Jossey-Bass/Wiley.

Le, H., & Pan, L. (2021). Examining the empirical redundancy of organizational justice constructs. *Organizational Behavior and Human Decision Processes*, *165*, 21–44. https://doi.org/10.1016/j.obhdp.2021.03.004

Lewicki, R. J., & Brinsfield, C. (2017). Trust repair. *Annual Review of Organizational Psychology and Organizational Behavior*, *4*(1), 287–313. https://doi.org/10.1146/annurev-orgpsych-032516-113147

Lewicki, R. J., & Bunker, B. B. (1995). Trust in relationships: A model of development and decline. In B. B. Bunker & J. Z. Rubin (Eds.), *Conflict, cooperation, and justice: Essays inspired by the work of Morton Deutsch* (pp. 133–173). Jossey-Bass/Wiley.

McNeese, N. J., Demir, M., Chiou, E. K., & Cooke, N. J. (2021). Trust and team performance in human–autonomy teaming. *International Journal of Electronic Commerce*, *25*(1), 51–72. https://doi.org/10.1080/10864415.2021.1846854

Morgeson, F. P., Mitchell, T. R., & Liu, D. (2015). Event system theory: An event-oriented approach to the organizational sciences. *Academy of Management Review*, *40*(4), 515–537. https://doi.org/10.5465/amr.2012.0099

Morrissette, A. M., & Kisamore, J. L. (2020). Trust and performance in business teams: A meta-analysis. *Team Performance Management*, *26*(5/6), 287–300. https://doi.org/10.1108/TPM-02-2020-0012

O'Neill, T. A., Flathmann, C., McNeese, N. J., & Salas, E. (2023). 21st Century teaming and beyond: Advances in human-autonomy teamwork. *Computers in Human Behavior*, *147*, 1–4. https://doi.org/10.1016/j.chb.2023.107865

O'Neill, T., McNeese, N., Barron, A., & Schelble, B. (2020). Human–autonomy teaming: A review and analysis of the empirical literature. *Human Factors: The Journal of the Human Factors and Ergonomics Society*, *64*(5), 904–938. https://doi.org/10.1177/0018720820960865

Orvis, K. L., DeCostanza, A. H., & Duchon, A. (2013). Developing systems-based performance measures: A rational approach. *The interservice/industry training, simulation and education conference* (I/ITSEC, no. 1).

Parasuraman, R., Sheridan, T. B., & Wickens, C. D. (2000). A model for types and levels of human interaction with automation. *IEEE Transactions on Systems, Man, and Cybernetics – Part A: Systems and Humans*, *30*(3), 286–297. https://doi.org/10.1109/3468.844354

Podsakoff, P. M., & Organ, D. W. (1986). Self-reports in organizational research: Problems and prospects. *Journal of Management*, *12*(4), 531–544. https://doi.org/10.1177/014920638601200408

Ross, J. M., Szalma, J. L., Hancock, P. A., Barnett, J. S., & Taylor, G. (2008). The effect of automation reliability on user automation trust and reliance in a search-and-rescue scenario. *Proceedings of the Human Factors and Ergonomics Society Annual Meeting*, *52*(19), 1340–1344. https://doi-org.portal.lib.fit.edu/10.1177/154193120805201908

Rousseau, D. M., Sitkin, S. B., Burt, R. S., & Camerer, C. (1998). Not so different after all: A cross-discipline view of trust. *Academy of Management Review*, *23*(3), 393–404. https://doi.org/10.5465/amr.1998.926617

Russell, S. J., & Norvig, P. (2020). Artificial intelligence: A modern approach. In S. Russell & P. Norvig (Eds.), *Artificial intelligence* (3rd ed.). https://doi.org/10.1017/S0269888900007724

Salas, E., Sims, D. E., & Burke, C. S. (2005). Is there a "big five" in teamwork? *Small Group Research*, *36*(5), 555–599. https://doi-org.portal.lib.fit.edu/10.1177/1046496405277134

Schaefer, K., Baker, A., Brewer, R., Patton, D., Canady, J., & Metcalfe, J. (2019). Assessing multi-agent human-autonomy teams: US Army Robotic Wingman gunnery operations. In M. S. Islam & T. George (Eds.), *Micro- and nanotechnology sensors, systems, and applications XI* (p. 82). SPIE. https://doi.org/10.1117/12.2519302

Taylor, L. R. (1961). Aggregation, variance and the mean. *Nature*, *189*(4766), 732–735. https://doi.org/10.1038/189732a0

Walker, F., Wang, J., Martens, M. H., & Verwey, W. B. (2019). Gaze behaviour and electrodermal activity: Objective measures of drivers' trust in automated vehicles. *Transportation Research Part F: Traffic Psychology and Behaviour*, *64*, 401–412. https://doi.org/10.1016/j.trf.2019.05.021

Wang, K., Lu, J., Ruan, S., & Qi, Y. (2023). Continuous error timing in automation: The peak-end effect on human-automation trust. *International Journal of Human–Computer Interaction*, *40*(8), 1832–1844. https://doi.org/10.1080/10447318.2023.2223954

Wildman, J. L., Nguyen, D., Thayer, A. L., Robbins-Roth, V. T., Carroll, M., Carmody, K., Ficke, C., Akib, M., & Addis, A. (2024). Trust in human-agent teams: A multilevel perspective and future research agenda. *Organizational Psychology Review*, *14*(3), 373–402. https://doi.org/10.1177/20413866241253278

Yu, K., Berkovsky, S., Taib, R., Zhou, J., & Chen, F. (2019). Do I trust my machine teammate?: An investigation from perception to decision. *Proceedings of the 24th international conference on intelligent user interfaces* (pp. 460–468). https://doi.org/10.1145/3301275.3302277

PART 2

AI AND TEAM PROCESSES

CHAPTER 4

AI IN THE TEAM MEETING LANDSCAPE

Joseph A. Allen[a], Marvin Grabowski[b], Matthew S. Thiese[a] and Emilee Eden[a]

[a]*University of Utah, USA*
[b]*University of Hamburg, Germany*

ABSTRACT

Artificial intelligence (AI) is increasingly shaping workplace collaboration, with profound implications for how team meetings are conducted and experienced. This chapter explores the growing role of AI in meetings, highlighting both current applications and future potential. AI technologies now support a wide range of functions – from live transcription and real-time translation to emotion detection, bias monitoring, and intelligent virtual assistants (IVAs). These tools aim to enhance meeting productivity, inclusivity, and decision quality. At the same time, their integration introduces new challenges related to data privacy, transparency, informed consent, and algorithmic bias. We critically examine these ethical concerns, emphasizing the need for clear communication, robust consent protocols, and governance mechanisms that ensure responsible AI deployment. We outline the hidden nature of many AI tools and the importance of making AI presence visible and understandable to meeting participants. Building on these insights, the chapter outlines key research directions, including experimental investigations into AI-assisted moderation, qualitative studies of emotional AI perception, and longitudinal analyses of AI-generated feedback on team learning. We call for the development of standardized metrics, greater diversity in training datasets, and broader adoption of

AI in Teams: Research on Managing Groups and Teams, Volume 21, 59–76

Published under exclusive licence by Emerald Publishing Limited
ISSN: 1534-0856/doi:10.1108/S1534-085620260000021010

explainable AI (XAI) to build trust and accountability. By integrating technical innovation with ethical foresight, this chapter offers a roadmap for understanding and guiding the evolving role of AI in workplace meetings – ensuring it enhances, rather than undermines, human collaboration and organizational effectiveness.

Keywords: AI; meetings; teams; AI application; intelligent virtual assistants; modality; meeting summary; AI ethics

The emergence of AI, including the availability of large language models and other algorithms and applications, has rocked nearly every industry (Cardon et al., 2023), ushering in an era where organizations and workers are leveraging rapidly changing technologies to automate repetitive tasks, analyze data, spur innovation, and more. Given the rapid and widespread adoption of AI technologies, it is unsurprising that team meetings – a ubiquitous component of organizational life worldwide – are already being transformed by AI and are likely to experience even more significant changes as the technology matures.

WHY MEETINGS MATTER AND HOW THEY ARE CHANGING

Team meetings are defined as scheduled work-related interactions of more than two individuals and provide the basis for social interactions in the workplace (Allen & Lehmann-Willenbrock, 2023). The core purpose of most workplace team meetings is to discuss work-related topics, brainstorm ideas, resolve conflicts, prepare, and/or make decisions (e.g., Lehmann-Willenbrock et al., 2018). Serving as the central venue for interaction with colleagues, team meetings leverage team productivity and, subsequently, provide organizational benefit at large (Blanchard & Allen, 2023; Lehmann-Willenbrock et al., 2018). Team members communicate with each other and share common sense in a social unit (Moreland, 2010). Concretely, team members exchange social signals via verbal communication and non-verbal multimodal behavior (Lehmann-Willenbrock & Hung, 2024). In principle, successful team meetings depend on the active involvement of all members, who fill various roles, including leaders, moderators, facilitators, or regular attendees (for an overview of key features of team meetings, see Allen & Lehmann-Willenbrock, 2023).

But meetings, for all their importance, also present challenges. For one, workers spend a lot of time in meetings or preparing for meetings. The typical mid-level manager in a large organization spends approximately 75% of their working hours on meeting-related activities (Mroz et al., 2018; Reed & Allen, 2022). Researchers, meanwhile, have consistently shown that people do not like meetings (Perlow et al., 2017), and that workers rate meetings as poor uses of their time (Kauffeld & Lehmann-Willenbrock, 2012), despite meetings being useful in helping people accomplish their work (Allen & Lehmann-Willenbrock, 2023).

Even before the recent leap of AI into the public consciousness, meetings were changing. Hastened by the COVID-19 pandemic and the increasing flexibility of work locations, there have been significant shifts in the ways meetings are conducted, with virtual meetings, hybrid meetings, and immersive meetings offering alternatives to the traditional face-to-face meeting implementation. Meanwhile, AI has begun to spur the next transformation for meetings, with several virtual meeting platforms incorporating AI-related tools into their systems, creating human–agent teams in nearly every workplace meeting (McKendrick, 2024). Because of these new features, speculation abounds as to the implications of the integration of AI into meetings.

The purpose of this chapter is to review what we currently know about AI and human–agent teams in workplace meetings while providing a theoretically driven guide for future research in this domain. We begin with an overview of meeting modalities (i.e., face-to-face meetings, virtual meetings, hybrid meetings, and immersive meetings) and discuss how they relate to different perspectives on AI, before going on to outline specific areas of application for AI in meetings. We hope that by demonstrating the existing and potential use of AI in workplace meetings, we will inspire researchers and scholars to further investigate just how much technology is impacting human–agent and human–human collaboration, invention, and performance. Furthermore, we discuss key issues related to privacy and accuracy that plague the use of AI in meetings and will impact how research is performed. In doing so, we demonstrate the challenge of even knowing when AI is present in meetings and discuss opportunities for future inquiry.

HOW HAS MEETING MODALITY SHIFTED TO INCLUDE AI?

As previously noted, how people meet shifted dramatically as a result of the COVID-19 pandemic (Reed & Allen, 2021). The shift allowed new technology to enter workplace meetings, including AI, and we discuss each common modality here as it pertains to the use of AI in team meetings.

Face-to-face Meetings

Face-to-face meetings are the original and most common form of team meetings. Typically, meeting participants come together in an office space while physically sitting in the same room as each other. Face-to-face meetings are subject to various psychological mechanisms that differ from technology-mediated meeting platforms. The exchange of social cues takes place in the most natural way and without any technological requirements (for an overview, see Allen & Lehmann-Willenbrock, 2023). In addition, early studies indicate that differences in individuals' social and organizational status can impact decision-making in face-to-face contexts (Dubrovsky et al., 1991). High-status members can dominate the meeting and take on a perceived dominant role in the room.

While the benefits of AI being used to participate in and contribute to teams are already acknowledged (Jora et al., 2022), the widespread integration of AI in face-to-face meetings is still in its infancy. AI cannot connect directly in face-to-face meetings without a technical interface. As such, meeting assistant applications need to be compatible with the technology used in the meeting. Therefore, the use of AI in face-to-face meetings primarily relates to coordination in advance of the meeting or the transcription or evaluation of a meeting recording (Hefer et al., 2023).

Virtual Meetings

Virtual meetings leverage remote communication technologies to facilitate communication and collaboration across distances, such as through conference calls and video conferences (e.g., Microsoft Teams or Zoom; see Karl et al., 2022). Employees and managers value the fact that they can join meetings from their home offices or elsewhere (Pass & Ridgway, 2022). However, traditional low-immersive 2D video conferencing platforms, such as Zoom and Microsoft Teams, often struggle to convey nonverbal and social cues effectively, as meeting participants are only visible via a small tile of their faces. The rich social exchange that naturally occurs in face-to-face meetings is typically disrupted in virtual meetings (Karl et al., 2022). For example, being on camera for an extended period can lead to stress mitigating the overall meeting experience. As a result, the effectiveness and productivity of virtual meetings are often compromised (e.g., Shockley et al., 2021). Virtual meeting software has the technical requirements to be linked directly to AI (without external hardware, as would be necessary in face-to-face meetings; see Hefer et al., 2023). AI could enhance interaction in virtual meetings. For example, AI applications in speech recognition, emotion analysis, or notetaking can be implemented directly via the technologies utilized to host the virtual meeting (Behn et al., 2024).

Hybrid Meetings

As organizations transition from entirely virtual meetings necessitated by the COVID-19 pandemic, there is a notable rise in flexible schedules and remote work positions driven by employee preferences (Bloom et al., 2024), paving the way for hybrid meetings. Hybrid meetings have become increasingly popular over the last few years and have the potential to impact the future of workplace meetings irreversibly by redefining norms around participation and collaboration across physical and virtual environments (Wigert & Argawal, 2022). Hybrid meetings include both co-located on-site and virtual participants with at least three people attending (Neumayr et al., 2021). The exact modalities for hybrid meetings may vary – for example, whether or not virtual participants actually turn on their cameras to show their faces. Due to potential imbalances in participation and influence between on-site and remote attendees, hybrid meetings pose challenges for both meeting leaders and employees. These imbalances can create faultlines, divisions within the group based on mode of attendance, that affect cohesion, trust, and effective collaboration (Straube & Kauffeld, 2020). Meeting leaders must balance the needs and requirements of both on-site and virtual meeting attendees. Both forms of participation in a hybrid meeting could potentially be supported by AI depending on its interface. It remains to be seen whether virtual participants can be better involved via specific applications or whether the leadership style in hybrid meetings can be supported via AI.

3D Immersive Meetings

Advancements in emerging system technologies such as extended reality (XR) enable more-natural and immersive group meetings, potentially surpassing traditional low-immersive 2D virtual interactions (Steinicke et al., 2020). 3D immersive virtual meetings, often referred to in the context of the "Metaverse," hold substantial potential for innovative learning and fruitful group dynamics (Grabowski et al., 2024a). Meeting participants are immersed in the 3D interaction space via head-mounted displays as a "figurative door" into the metaverse. In 3D immersive meetings, XR technologies allow users to create and interact through personalized avatars as a new medium of communication (Grabowski et al., 2024b). Avatars reproduce three-dimensional motions such as hand gestures in real time, enabling embodied interaction in the fully immersive space from different locations (Kim et al., 2023). Enhanced immersion generally increases the user's subjective feeling of being in the meeting space with others, leading to a meeting being perceived as successful (Han et al., 2023). More recently, developments in augmented reality (AR) and lightweight smart glasses extend these experiences by blending digital elements with the physical environment, offering more flexible forms of participation (Crogman et al., 2025).

Further improvements in XR and AI may enhance the real-time analysis and synthesis of multimodal social signals, interactive meeting analytics, and feedback. These technologies could also enable intelligent virtual agents to assist meeting leaders or act as facilitators or moderators.

CURRENT AI USAGE IN MEETINGS

In recent years, the integration of AI technologies into workplace processes has revolutionized how employees and organizations conduct meetings. From enhancing efficiency to fostering inclusivity and aiding decision-making processes, AI-driven solutions have become pivotal in transforming traditional meeting paradigms (Przegalinska et al., 2025). This section explores the current applications of AI in meetings, such as real-time language translation, bias detection, meeting moderation, and the inclusion of IVAs. Additionally, AI can empower proactive meeting management through agenda preparation and performance tracking, offering personalized insights and recommendations for more productive and engaging meetings. By delving into these advancements, we uncover how AI enhances and redefines the dynamics of workplace meeting interactions.

Intelligent Virtual Assistants

Preliminary research highlights the importance of developing a more detailed perspective on the effects of AI on users of these emerging technologies (Anthony et al., 2023). IVAs are software systems that carry out a range of tasks and services and play a crucial role in providing support in meetings. Whether taking on active or passive roles, IVAs support administrative activities like notetaking and creating to-do lists to be discussed later, providing support audio and visual data such as converting spoken dialog into live transcripts or extracting and summarizing text from presentations using optical character recognition, or summarizing meeting contexts (for an overview, see Hefer et al., 2023). At the interface of AI and XR, IVAs can be integrated as anthropomorphic virtual characters resembling the avatars used by meeting participants (Weidner et al., 2023). The acceptance of such IVAs depends on the quality and implementation of adaptive learning algorithms, natural language processing (NLP), and emotional intelligence. Initial findings indicate that IVAs can at least partially fulfill the requirements and perspectives of meetings (Hefer et al., 2023). In the following, we will discuss various practical use cases of AI usage in meetings.

Live Translator

One of the most impactful applications of AI in modern meetings is its capability for real-time language translation. As organizations become increasingly globalized, the need for seamless communication across linguistic boundaries has never been more critical. AI-powered live translation solutions have emerged as a transformative tool, facilitating fluid conversations and ensuring participants can contribute effectively regardless of their native language. These AI systems employ advanced NLP algorithms to instantly interpret spoken words and transcribe them into the preferred language of each participant (Kolhar & Alameen, 2021; Sutandijo & Qomariyah, 2023; Xiao, 2020). By breaking down language barriers, these technologies not only promote inclusivity but also streamline decision-making processes and foster a more collaborative and productive meeting environment (Hassan, 2024; Mehendale et al., 2024). In fact, given the potential for language barriers to induce challenges for teams in terms of trust and other factors (Tenzer et al., 2014), these tools may prove useful to further enhancing team cohesion for multinational and multicultural teams.

Bias Detection

In addition to real-time translation, AI can play a crucial role in detecting and mitigating biases during meetings. Unconscious biases can subtly influence decision-making processes, potentially hindering diversity and inclusivity within organizational discussions (Fuller & Murphy, 2020). AI-powered bias detection algorithms can analyze interactions within meetings, including speech patterns, facial expressions, and participation dynamics (patterns, behaviors, and interactions among participants), to identify patterns indicative of bias (Chen et al., 2024). By flagging these patterns in real-time, AI allows facilitators and participants to intervene and ensure fair and equitable participation. These technologies can contribute to fostering a more-inclusive workplace culture by raising awareness of biases and promoting mindful team member interactions.

Meeting Moderation/Leadership

AI's role in meeting moderation and leadership is increasingly pivotal as organizations seek efficient ways to manage collaborative sessions. For example, there are several AI-powered tools that use real-time analytics to monitor engagement, track speaking time, and identify patterns that may indicate bias or participation imbalance. IVAs equipped with AI functionalities can assume roles traditionally held by human moderators to facilitate smoother interactions and guide discussions toward predefined meeting goals (Hefer et al., 2023). These assistants can manage agendas, time allocations, and participant contributions, ensuring meetings stay on track and productive (Chen et al., 2024; Chu et al., 2023). They can also summarize and record key meeting points to maintain accurate records of decisions made (Hefer et al., 2023). Therefore, AI-driven meeting moderation not only optimizes efficiency but also enhances the quality of decision-making by fostering inclusive and purposeful discussions.

Meeting Performance Tracking & Recommendations

Beyond facilitating the flow and dynamics of meetings, AI-driven performance tracking capabilities offer valuable insights that can significantly enhance team collaboration and individual development. By analyzing meeting interactions, AI systems can assess various metrics such as participation levels, contribution frequency, and engagement patterns. These insights enable personalized feedback and recommendations tailored to each participant (Afzaal et al., 2021; Khan et al., 2021; Tong et al., 2021). Additionally, by aggregating data over time, these systems can provide longitudinal insights into team dynamics and performance trends. As AI continues to evolve, its ability to deliver specific and actionable performance analytics promises to redefine how organizations optimize their meeting outcomes and develop professional growth.

POTENTIAL ROLES OF AI IN TEAM MEETINGS

The integration of AI into team meetings has introduced transformative possibilities for enhancing collaboration, productivity, and emotional well-being. In this section, we explore potential uses rather than existing uses of AI in meetings that could enhance a worker's experience inside of the meeting room. These capabilities hold significant potential for creating more dynamic and supportive environments to conduct team meetings.

Using AI to detect emotions of meeting participants, for instance, can enhance the quality and effectiveness of interactions by providing rich information to meeting attendees. AI systems can analyze facial expressions, vocal tones, and body language in real-time to assess the emotional states of meeting participants

(Chu et al., 2023; Nazer et al., 2023). This feedback could enable facilitators to recognize signs of stress, frustration, or disengagement among team members, allowing for timely interventions to address issues before they escalate. For example, if AI detects, and signals to the meeting leader, that several participants are showing signs of confusion or frustration, the meeting leader can pause to clarify points or encourage a more inclusive discussion. By leveraging AI to monitor emotional cues, organizations can improve meeting communication, team cohesion, and meeting outcomes.

AI can also be utilized to code (annotate) and analyze interactions between participants in real-time. For instance, AI can identify key themes, track who speaks most frequently, and assess the sentiment of the conversations, providing a comprehensive overview of the meeting dynamics (Khan et al., 2021). This automated analysis can save time and promote consistency, potentially reducing some forms of human error or bias introduced by subjective interpretation (Khan et al., 2021; Shemshack et al., 2021). However, AI systems are themselves susceptible to biases embedded in their training data, particularly when those datasets are limited, unrepresentative, or fail to capture the diversity of real-world interactions. When training sets do not reflect the linguistic, cultural, or behavioral variation of user populations, the outputs of AI analysis may perpetuate or amplify pre-existing biases. This issue is further complicated by coder drift, not only in human annotators but also in AI models whose fixed training data may fail to accommodate evolving communication patterns, emerging language, or context-specific nuances.

The presumed objectivity of AI can obscure these limitations, especially if systems are not periodically retrained or validated against newer datasets. Therefore, while AI tools offer considerable advantages, they should be deployed with caution, accompanied by regular audits, transparent documentation, and possibly hybrid models that incorporate human oversight to interpret ambiguous or context-sensitive interactions.

ETHICAL CONSIDERATIONS WHEN USING AI IN TEAM MEETINGS

While AI offers numerous benefits, such as real-time translation, bias detection, and meeting moderation, it also raises a broad spectrum of ethical concerns. These concerns include not only data security and privacy but also informed consent, algorithmic transparency, fairness, potential for bias and discrimination, and the risks associated with emotional surveillance or manipulation. This section aims to provide an overview of these key ethical challenges associated with AI integration in team meetings, drawing on current literature to highlight both risks and mechanisms for the mitigation of these challenges.

Data Security and Confidentiality

The integration of AI systems in meetings necessitates access to extensive data, encompassing audio, video, and text-based interactions. Protecting the security and integrity of these data is paramount to prevent unauthorized access and potential breaches. Meetings often involve the discussion of sensitive information, ranging from strategic business plans to personal employee data, which can be vulnerable if AI systems lack robust security measures (Nazer et al., 2023). Comprehensive data protection involves implementing advanced encryption protocols and secure storage solutions, mitigating the risks associated with data breaches. Furthermore, adherence to data privacy regulations, such as the General Data Protection Regulation and other relevant frameworks, is crucial in maintaining the confidentiality and integrity of the data processed by AI systems in meetings. Secure access controls are also essential, limiting data access to authorized personnel only and preventing potential breaches. Regular audits and assessments of AI systems are crucial to identify vulnerabilities and ensure compliance with security standards (Nazer et al., 2023). By conducting periodic security evaluations, organizations can proactively address potential risks and implement necessary updates to enhance system integrity.

Consent and Autonomy

The deployment of AI in meetings requires obtaining explicit consent from all participants to respect their autonomy and privacy rights. It is essential for individuals to be fully informed about how their data will be collected, stored, and utilized. Transparent communication regarding the data-handling processes ensures that participants are aware of the scope and purpose of AI integration within the meeting environment. Without clear and informed consent, the use of AI can inadvertently infringe upon participants' privacy, leading to ethical and legal implications (Fuller & Murphy, 2020). To address these concerns, organizations should implement robust and transparent consent mechanisms, providing participants with comprehensive details about the AI's functionalities and data-usage policies as well as the option to opt out of AI-enabled meetings. Furthermore, regular reviews and updates of policies are necessary to adapt to evolving AI capabilities and regulatory requirements.

Transparency and Explainability

AI algorithms frequently function as "black boxes," posing significant challenges for users in understanding the decision-making processes. This opacity can engender mistrust and raise concerns about the fairness and impartiality of AI interventions (Chen et al., 2024). To mitigate these issues, it is imperative that AI systems used in meetings are designed to be explainable, offering clear insights into how they process data and arrive at conclusions. Transparency in AI operations fosters trust among users, ensuring that technologies used in meetings are perceived as fair and reliable. By making the inner workings of AI systems more comprehensible, organizations can demystify the decision-making process, promoting a sense of accountability and ethical responsibility (Akhtar et al., 2024; Balasubramaniam et al., 2022). Implementing XAI not only addresses potential biases and inaccuracies but also empowers meeting participants to engage more confidently with AI technologies. Bias is a meaningful concern in AI integration and is discussed further below. This approach is essential for maintaining a balanced and transparent meeting environment where AI actions are scrutinized and validated by human oversight.

Additional Ethical Implications

There are additional ethical implications of AI in meetings encompassing various aspects, including bias, discrimination, and emotional manipulation. AI systems can inadvertently perpetuate biases present in training data, leading to unfair treatment of certain individuals or groups (Chu et al., 2023). Integrating ethical considerations into the development and deployment of AI systems is paramount to ensure their responsible use in meetings. This process should involve rigorous testing to identify and mitigate any biases within the algorithms to prevent discriminatory outcomes and ensure fairness.

For instance, it may be necessary to regulate emotional detection and fully understood before implementation. The European Union has implemented stringent regulations regarding the use of AI for emotion detection, emphasizing the need for transparency, data protection, and ethical considerations (European Commission, 2024). These laws require organizations to ensure that AI systems respect individuals' privacy rights and are used in a manner that is both transparent and accountable.

These ethical considerations carry important implications for team leaders and facilitators, who are often responsible for selecting, implementing, and managing AI tools during meetings. Leaders must not only understand the capabilities of AI systems but also remain vigilant about their limitations and potential risks. They play a key role in ensuring transparency with participants, securing informed consent and fostering an environment where AI enhances, rather than undermines, trust. Leaders should be trained to interpret AI-generated insights critically, rather than relying on them unquestioningly, and to intervene when algorithms produce outputs that may reflect or reinforce bias. Ultimately, ethical leadership requires balancing the efficiency gains of AI with a commitment to inclusivity, fairness, and the protection of individual rights within the team setting.

The future of AI in team meetings lies in balancing technological advancements with ethical and privacy considerations. Research and development should focus on creating AI systems that enhance meeting productivity while safeguarding participants' privacy and autonomy. Collaborative efforts among technologists, ethicists, and legal experts are necessary to establish frameworks that guide the ethical use of AI in meetings.

KNOWING WHEN AI IS IN THE ROOM AND WHEN IT'S NOT

One of the significant challenges that teams face is determining when AI is actively participating in meetings. Many AI tools operate unobtrusively in the background of meetings, performing essential tasks such as note-taking, transcription, and participant monitoring without overtly indicating their presence. For instance, AI features like noise cancelation, auto-framing, and voice recognition enhance meeting quality seamlessly and efficiently, often without users being explicitly aware of their operation (Sharma & Dash, 2023). These background functionalities ensure a smoother and more-productive meeting experience by reducing distractions and enhancing audio and visual clarity. However, this invisibility can make it challenging for meeting participants to discern when AI is actively engaged (TechRadar, 2024), raising both technical and ethical considerations. Addressing these complexities requires a multifaceted approach that includes clear communication, robust technical solutions, and adherence to ethical standards.

The visibility and impact of AI tools can vary significantly depending on the meeting format. In virtual meetings, AI tools are often deeply embedded in the platform infrastructure, making functions like transcription, emotion recognition, or engagement tracking more seamless but also more opaque to participants. In face-to-face meetings, AI tools may be more conspicuous – for example, in the form of smart cameras, voice assistants, or external recording devices – making their presence easier to detect but potentially more intrusive. Hybrid meetings introduce unique complexities, as AI may interact differently with in-room and remote participants, raising concerns about equitable treatment and consistent data capture across modalities. Therefore, the ethical and practical implications of AI use – such as consent, transparency, and access – must be tailored to the specific meeting context, with team leaders playing a key role in communicating how AI is being deployed in each format. From a technical perspective, organizations can implement features that signal AI activity in a subtle yet effective manner. For example, meeting software could include visual indicators, such as icons or notifications, that alert participants when AI functionalities like transcription, note-taking, or participant monitoring are active. These indicators should be designed to be non-disruptive yet noticeable enough to keep participants informed. Additionally, providing access logs that detail AI activity during the meeting can offer participants a clear record of AI engagement, enhancing transparency.

Beyond signaling AI activity during a meeting, it is essential to obtain informed, proactive consent from participants before AI functionalities are activated – particularly for features that involve recording, transcription, or the use of data for model training. Consent should not be implied or buried in platform terms of service but should instead be explicit, clear, and context-specific. For example, participants should be notified in advance if their speech, behavior, or biometric data (e.g., facial expressions) may be recorded or used to improve AI algorithms. This consent process should be accompanied by a concise explanation of how the data will be stored, who will have access to it, and whether it will be anonymized or retained long-term. Integrating these consent procedures into meeting invitations or platform onboarding flows can help ensure that participation is fully voluntary and ethically sound. Moreover, this approach reinforces confidentiality expectations, fostering a more transparent and respectful meeting environment.

Platforms such as Zoom and Microsoft Teams have been continuously integrating AI-driven features like transcription, meeting summaries, and smart recordings to enhance virtual meeting experiences (Koenecke et al., 2020). While these tools offer convenience, they also raise important considerations about participant consent and data privacy. For instance, when a meeting host enables transcription or recording features, participants typically receive a notification indicating that the session is being recorded. However, participants often cannot decline these features without leaving the meeting, effectively limiting their ability to opt out while remaining engaged.

Zoom's AI Companion, for example, provides functionalities such as meeting summaries and smart recordings. When activated, participants are notified, but their continued participation is considered as implied consent, with limited options to refuse without exiting the meeting. Similarly, Microsoft Teams has implemented policies requiring explicit consent for features like transcription and recording. Administrators can configure settings to ensure that all participants must agree before these features are activated, promoting transparency and user control.

These scenarios underscore the importance of clear communication and consent mechanisms when deploying AI features in virtual meetings. Organizations should establish policies that respect participant autonomy, ensuring that individuals are fully informed about AI functionalities and have the ability to provide or withhold consent without compromising their participation. Hosts can require participants to authenticate their identity before joining, making it easier to identify and manage AI tools labeled as bots in the waiting room. This process not only enhances security but also ensures that only authorized participants, whether human or AI, gain access to the meeting. By leveraging these features, meeting hosts can maintain better control over the meeting environment, preventing unauthorized AI interventions and ensuring a secure and organized virtual meeting space. Additionally, these measures help in maintaining the integrity of the meeting content, as authenticated participants are more accountable for their contributions. Such protocols are essential in fostering a trustworthy and reliable virtual meeting experience, where the presence and role of AI can be effectively managed and monitored.

On the ethical front, it is crucial to establish and communicate clear policies regarding AI use in meetings. Organizations should ensure that all participants are fully informed about the AI tools being utilized, including the specific tasks they perform and how data are being handled. This can be achieved through comprehensive briefing sessions or detailed consent forms distributed prior to meetings. To be effective, consent mechanisms should prioritize clarity and brevity, avoiding dense or overly legalistic language; instead, organizations should aim for concise, accessible explanations that highlight key information about AI use in plain terms. Participants should have the opportunity to understand the scope of AI involvement and express their preferences or concerns, including the option to opt out if they feel uncomfortable. For example, organizations can describe the type and scope of AI use in meetings in their internal code of conduct to ensure transparency.

Fostering a culture of openness and trust in team meetings is essential. Regularly engaging with employees and stakeholders about the benefits and limitations of AI in meetings can help demystify the technology and alleviate concerns. Providing training on AI literacy can empower participants to better understand and interact with AI tools, reducing the perceived gap between human and AI contributions.

Ethical considerations also extend to ensuring that AI tools are designed and used in ways that respect participants' privacy and autonomy. This involves implementing rigorous data protection measures, such as encryption and secure storage, and regularly auditing AI systems to identify and mitigate biases or inaccuracies. Organizations should adhere to relevant data privacy regulations and ethical guidelines, ensuring that AI use aligns with broader societal values and legal requirements.

Incorporating user feedback mechanisms allows participants to voice their experiences and suggestions regarding AI use in meetings. This feedback is invaluable for continuous improvement and for when organizations are forcing breaches of confidentiality, helping refine AI tools and address any issues that may arise. By actively involving participants in the evaluation and development process, organizations can build a more inclusive and responsive AI ecosystem. We summarized four strategies for managing AI presence in Table 4.1.

Table 4.1. Four Strategies for Managing AI Presence.

Strategy	Description	Related Work
(1) Clear communication and transparency	To promote transparency, teams should clearly communicate which AI tools are in use and what functions they perform at the start of each meeting. Additionally, visual indicators or verbal cues can be integrated into meeting platforms to signal when AI is actively operating, helping participants stay informed and fostering trust	Akhtar et al. (2024)
(2) Using technological controls	Leveraging technological features such as authentication and waiting rooms for AI can help hosts manage and control AI presence in meetings. Hosts can then review and admit participants, including AI bots, more effectively	Hassan (2024), Harvard T.H. Chan School of Public Health (2024)
(3) Regular audits and reviews	Regular audits by the teams of AI tools and their activities can help organizations ensure compliance with privacy regulations and internal policies. Audits can identify any unauthorized AI activities and ensure that AI tools are used ethically and transparently	Mehendale et al. (2024) and Microsoft Community Hub (2024)
(4) Participant education	Educating meeting participants about AI tools and their functionalities can empower them to recognize and manage AI presence. Providing training on how to select AI tools and understand their impact on meetings can enhance overall awareness and control	Hefer et al. (2023) and Otter.ai (2024)

FUTURE DIRECTIONS

Given the forgoing review and analysis of current research and practice concerning AI in meetings, several possibilities for future research would enable the growth in our understanding of meetings, meeting science, and AI overall. First, researchers should consider evaluating the effectiveness of AI-driven meeting moderators in hybrid environments. As hybrid meetings present unique challenges – especially imbalances in participation between co-located and remote attendees – a study such as this would experimentally test whether AI-driven meeting moderators (e.g., IVAs managing agenda adherence, speaking time equity, and engagement prompts) improve meeting equity, decision quality, and satisfaction. A controlled field experiment could compare hybrid meetings with and without AI moderation across multiple organizations, using outcome measures such as contribution balance, perceived fairness, psychological safety, and meeting effectiveness. Metrics can be derived from both observational coding (Lehmann-Willenbrock & Hung, 2024) and participant surveys (Allen & Lehmann-Willenbrock, 2023). Moving forward, research of this nature will be key in legitimizing the AI "co-moderator" as a trusted meeting assistant, especially in diverse and distributed teams.

Second, researchers could explore human perceptions of emotion detecting AI in meetings. Specifically, emotion detection AI in meetings – analyzing tone, facial expression, and body language – is advancing rapidly, but ethical and perceptual challenges remain (Behn et al., 2024). A qualitative study using semi-structured interviews and thematic analysis could explore how participants react to feedback generated by emotional AI tools during and after meetings. Topics would include perceived accuracy, emotional impact, trust in AI, and concerns over surveillance or manipulation. The study would help inform the design of emotionally intelligent AI tools that are socially acceptable and ethically aligned with user expectations (Behn et al., 2024; Chu et al., 2023). It would also support the development of transparency frameworks aligned with recent EU AI Act principles (European Commission, 2024).

Third, using a mixed-methods design, researchers could investigate the longitudinal impact of AI meeting analytics on team learning and adaptation. For instance, building on the promise of AI to generate feedback and behavioral insights, this study would examine how teams adapt over time when exposed to regular AI-generated analytics (e.g., participation patterns, talk ratios, decision clarity, and sentiment tracking). A mixed-methods longitudinal design could involve tracking teams over several months, using pre/post surveys to assess team learning, cohesion, and reflexivity, complemented by content analysis of meeting transcripts and AI dashboards. Interviews would provide contextual understanding of how teams internalize and act on AI feedback. This research would offer critical insight into the conditions under which AI tools become integrated into team routines and foster developmental learning (Afzaal et al., 2021; Tong et al., 2021).

The Future of AI in Meetings Research

To meaningfully advance the integration of AI into workplace meetings, the next five years should focus on several key priorities grounded in both technological development and ethical implementation. First, there is a pressing need to create standardized performance metrics for AI systems used in meetings, including indicators such as transcription accuracy, engagement monitoring precision, and bias detection efficacy (Chen et al., 2024; Hefer et al., 2023). Without consistent benchmarks, evaluating and comparing tools across platforms and contexts remains difficult, limiting both transparency and trust in these systems. In tandem with standardization, researchers and developers must expand the diversity of training datasets used to build AI algorithms. Many AI models have been trained on data that underrepresent linguistic, cultural, and demographic diversity, leading to inaccuracies and reinforcing systemic biases, especially in cross-cultural or multilingual meeting environments (Nazer et al., 2023; Simultrans, 2024). Expanding these datasets to better reflect real-world variation is critical to ensure fair and equitable AI performance.

Additionally, promoting the development and adoption of XAI is essential for making algorithmic decision-making more transparent to meeting participants and leaders (Arrieta et al., 2020; Dwivedi et al., 2023). XAI can help users understand how AI-generated outputs – such as participation summaries, emotional assessments, or task recommendations – are derived, fostering trust and improving user interaction with AI systems (Tong et al., 2021). Alongside these technical developments, robust governance frameworks must be established to guide the responsible use of AI in meetings. These frameworks should combine technical safeguards (e.g., encryption, authentication) with human oversight to ensure ethical compliance, data protection, and user consent (European Commission, 2024; Fuller & Murphy, 2020).

Finally, researchers should prioritize conducting field trials across diverse sectors – such as healthcare, education, and technology – to examine the generalizability and real-world impact of AI meeting tools. These trials can provide critical insights into sector-specific needs, uncover unintended consequences, and offer evidence-based recommendations for refining AI applications (Afzaal et al., 2021; Anthony et al., 2023). Together, these five directions form a roadmap for responsibly harnessing AI's potential in meetings while preserving human values and enhancing collaborative work. Meeting science must evolve in tandem with AI development to ensure that human–agent collaboration enhances rather than disrupts the psychological, communicative, and ethical dimensions of workplace meetings.

REFERENCES

Akhtar, M. A. K., Kumar, M., & Nayyar, A. (2024). Transparency and accountability in explainable AI: Best practices. In M. A. Akhtar, M. Kumar, & A. Nayyar (Eds.), *Towards ethical and socially responsible explainable AI: Challenges and opportunities* (pp. 127–164). Springer Nature.

Allen, J. A., & Lehmann-Willenbrock, N. (2023). The key features of workplace meetings: Conceptualizing the why, how, and what of meetings at work. *Organizational Psychology Review*, *13*(4), 355–378. https://doi.org/10.1177/20413866221129231

Anthony, C., Bechky, B. A., & Fayard, A. L. (2023). "Collaborating" with AI: Taking a system view to explore the future of work. *Organization Science, 34*(5), 1672–1694. https://doi.org/10.1287/orsc.2022.1651

Arrieta, A. B., Díaz-Rodríguez, N., Del Ser, J., Bennetot, A., Tabik, S., Barbado, A., & Herrera, F. (2020). Explainable Artificial Intelligence (XAI): Concepts, taxonomies, opportunities and challenges toward responsible AI. *Information Fusion, 58*, 82–115. https://doi.org/10.1016/j.inffus.2019.12.012

Balasubramaniam, N., Kauppinen, M., Hiekkanen, K., & Kujala, S. (2022, March). Transparency and explainability of AI systems: Ethical guidelines in practice. In *International working conference on requirements engineering: Foundation for software quality* (pp. 3–18). Springer International Publishing. https://doi.org/10.1016/j.infsof.2023.107197

Behn, O., Leyer, M., & Iren, D. (2024). Employees' acceptance of AI-based emotion analytics from speech on a group level in virtual meetings. *Technology in Society, 76*, Article 102466. https://doi.org/10.1016/j.techsoc.2024.102466

Blanchard, A. L., & Allen, J. A. (2023). The entitativity underlying meetings: Meetings as key in the lifecycle of effective workgroups. *Organizational Psychology Review, 13*(4), 458–477. https://doi.org/10.1177/20413866221101341

Bloom, N., Han, R., & Liang, J. (2024). Hybrid working from home improves retention without damaging performance. *Nature, 630*, 920–925. https://doi.org/10.1038/s41586-024-07500-2

Cardon, P. W., Ma, H., & Fleischmann, C. (2023). Recorded business meetings and AI algorithmic tools: Negotiating privacy concerns, psychological safety, and control. *International Journal of Business Communication, 60*(4), 1095–1122. https://doi.org/10.1177/23294884211037009

Chen, F., Wang, L., Hong, J., Jiang, J., & Zhou, L. (2024). Unmasking bias in artificial intelligence: A systematic review of bias detection and mitigation strategies in electronic health record-based models. *Journal of the American Medical Informatics Association, 31*(5), 1172–1183. https://doi.org/10.1093/jamia/ocae060

Chu, C. H., Donato-Woodger, S., Khan, S. S., Nyrup, R., Leslie, K., Lyn, A., Shi, T., Bianchi, A., Abbasgholizadeh Rahimi, S., & Grenier, A. (2023). Age-related bias and artificial intelligence: A scoping review. *Humanities and Social Sciences Communications, 10*(1), Article 510. https://doi.org/10.1057/s41599-023-01999-y

Crogman, H. T., Cano, V. D., Pacheco, E., Sonawane, R. B., & Boroon, R. (2025). Virtual reality, augmented reality, and mixed reality in experiential learning: Transforming educational paradigms. *Education Sciences, 15*(3), Article 303. https://doi.org/10.3390/educsci15030303

Dubrovsky, V. J., Kiesler, S., & Sethna, B. N. (1991). The equalization phenomenon: Status effects in computer-mediated and face-to-face decision-making groups. *Human-Computer Interaction, 6*(2), 119–146. https://doi.org/10.1207/s15327051hci0602_2

Dwivedi, R., Dave, D., Naik, H., Singhal, S., Omer, R., Patel, P., & Ranjan, R. (2023). Explainable AI (XAI): Core ideas, techniques, and solutions. *ACM Computing Surveys, 55*(9), 1–33. https://doi.org/10.1145/3561048

European Commission. (2024). *AI act*. https://digital-strategy.ec.europa.eu/en/policies/regulatory-framework-ai

Fuller, P., & Murphy, M. (2020). *The leader's guide to unconscious bias: How to reframe bias, cultivate connection, and create high-performing teams*. Simon and Schuster.

Grabowski, M., Lehmann-Willenbrock, N., Rings, S., Blanchard, A., & Steinicke, F. (2024a). Group dynamics in the Metaverse: A conceptual framework and first empirical insights. *Small Group Research, 55*(5), 763–804. https://doi.org/10.1177/10464964241274120

Grabowski, M., Steinicke, F., Rings, S., & Lehmann-Willenbrock, N. (2024b). Exploring immersive student meetings in the metaverse: Experiential learning and emergent group entitativity. In D. Liu, R. Huang, A. H. S. Metwally, A. Tlili, & E. Fan Lin (Eds.), *Application of the metaverse in education* (Smart Computing and Intelligence, pp. 105–123). Springer. https://doi.org/10.1007/978-981-97-1298-4_8.

Han, E., Miller, M. R., DeVeaux, C., Jun, H., Nowak, K. L., Hancock, J. T., Ram, N., & Bailenson, J. N. (2023). People, places, and time: A large-scale, longitudinal study of transformed avatars and environmental context in group interaction in the metaverse. *Journal of Computer-Mediated Communication, 28*(2), zmac031. https://doi.org/10.1093/jcmc/zmac031

Harvard, T. H. Chan School of Public Health. (2024). *How to effectively manage AI meeting assistants (aka: bots) in your Zoom sessions*. https://www.hsph.harvard.edu

Hassan, A. (2024). The impact of artificial intelligence on organizational communication. In A. M. A. Musleh Al-Sartawi & A. I. Nour (Eds.), *Artificial intelligence and economic sustainability in the era of industrial revolution 5.0* (Studies in Systems, Decision and Control, Vol. 528, pp. 793 –807). Springer. https://doi.org/10.1007/978-3-031-56586-1_58.

Hefer, L., Gal, U., & Hsu, C. (2023). AI meeting assistants, views of organisational meetings and potential implications to productivity. *ACIS 2023 Proceedings, 112*. https://aisel.aisnet.org/acis2023/112

Jora, R. B., Sodhi, K. K., Mittal, P., & Saxena, P. (2022, March). Role of artificial intelligence (AI) in meeting diversity, equality and inclusion (DEI) goals. In *Proceedings of the 2022 8th International Conference on Advanced Computing and Communication Systems (ICACCS)* (pp. 1687–1690). IEEE https://doi.org/10.1109/ICACCS54159.2022.9785266

Karl, K. A., Peluchette, J. V., & Aghakhani, N. (2022). Virtual work meetings during the COVID-19 pandemic: The good, bad, and ugly. *Small Group Research, 53*(3), 343–365. https://doi.org/10.1177/10464964211015286

Kauffeld, S., & Lehmann-Willenbrock, N. (2012). Meetings matter: Effects of team meetings on team and organizational success. *Small Group Research, 43*(2), 130–158. https://doi.org/10.1177/1046496411429599

Khan, I., Ahmad, A. R., Jabeur, N., & Mahdi, M. N. (2021). An artificial intelligence approach to monitor student performance and devise preventive measures. *Smart Learning Environments, 8*, 1–18. https://doi.org/10.1186/s40561-021-00161-y

Kim, D. Y., Lee, H. K., & Chung, K. (2023). Avatar-mediated experience in the metaverse: The impact of avatar realism on user-avatar relationship. *Journal of Retailing and Consumer Services, 73*, Article 103382. https://doi.org/10.1016/j.jretconser.2023.103382

Koenecke, A., Nam, A., Lake, E., Nudell, J., Quartey, M., Mengesha, Z., Toups, C., Rickford, J. R., Jurafsky, D., & Goel, S. (2020). Racial disparities in automated speech recognition. *Proceedings of the National Academy of Sciences of the United States of America, 117*(14), 7684–7689. https://doi.org/10.1073/pnas.1915768117

Kolhar, M., & Alameen, A. (2021). Artificial intelligence based language translation platform. *Intelligent Automation & Soft Computing, 28*(1), 1–9. https://doi.org/10.32604/iasc.2021.014995

Lehmann-Willenbrock, N., & Hung, H. (2024). A multimodal social signal processing approach to team interactions. *Organizational Research Methods, 27*(3), 477–515. https://doi.org/10.1177/10944281231202741

Lehmann-Willenbrock, N., Rogelberg, S. G., Allen, J. A., & Kello, J. E. (2018). The critical importance of meetings to leader and organizational success: Evidence-based insights and implications for key stakeholders. *Organizational Dynamics, 47*(1), 32–36. https://doi.org/10.1016/j.orgdyn.2017.07.005

McKendrick, J. (2024). AI may be able to reduce the scourge of meetings. *Forbes*. https://www.forbes.com/sites/joemckendrick/2024/03/13/ai-may-be-able-to-reduce-the-scourge-of-meetings/

Mehendale, G., Kale, C., Khatri, P., Goswami, H., Shah, H., & Bagul, S. (2024). Multilingual meeting management with NLP: Automated minutes, transcription, and translation. In H. Sharma, V. Shrivastava, A. K. Tripathi, & L. Wang (Eds.), *Communication and intelligent systems. ICCIS 2023* (Lecture Notes in Networks and Systems, Vol. 968, pp. 291–303). Springer.

Microsoft Community Hub. (2024). *Get more out of hybrid meetings with Teams Rooms and Copilot*. https://techcommunity.microsoft.com

Moreland, R. L. (2010). Are dyads really groups? *Small Group Research, 41*(2), 251–267. https://doi.org/10.1177/1046496409358618

Mroz, J. E., Allen, J. A., Verhoeven, D. C., & Shuffler, M. L. (2018). Do we really need another meeting? The science of workplace meetings. *Current Directions in Psychological Science, 27*(6), 484–491. https://doi.org/10.1177/0963721418776 3

Nazer, L. H., Zatarah, R., Waldrip, S., Ke, J. X. C., Moukheiber, M., Khanna, A. K., & Mathur, P. (2023). Bias in artificial intelligence algorithms and recommendations for mitigation. *PLOS Digital Health, 2*(6), Article e0000278. https://doi.org/10.1371/journal.pdig.0000278

Neumayr, T., Saatci, B., Rintel, S., Klokmose, C. N., & Augstein, M. (2021). *What was hybrid? A systematic review of hybrid collaboration and meetings research*. arXiv preprint, Article 2111.06172. https://doi.org/10.48550/arXiv.2111.06172

Otter.ai. (2024). *Increasing productivity in meetings with an AI meeting assistant*. https://www.otter.ai

Pass, S., & Ridgway, M. (2022). An informed discussion on the impact of COVID-19 and 'enforced' remote working on employee engagement. *Human Resource Development International, 25*(2), 254–270. https://doi.org/10.1080/13678868.2022.2048605

Perlow, L. A., Hadley, C. N., & Eun, E. (2017). Stop the meeting madness: How to free up time for meaningful work. *Harvard Business Review, 95*(4), 62–69.

Przegalinska, A., Triantoro, T., Kovbasiuk, A., Ciechanowski, L., Freeman, R. B., & Sowa, K. (2025). Collaborative AI in the workplace: Enhancing organizational performance through resource-based and task-technology fit perspectives. *International Journal of Information Management, 81*, Article 102853. https://doi.org/10.1016/j.ijinfomgt.2024.102853

Reed, K., & Allen, J. A. (2021). *Suddenly virtual: Making remote meetings work*. Wiley.

Reed, K., & Allen, J. A. (2022). *Suddenly hybrid: Managing the modern meeting*. Wiley.

Sharma, P., & Dash, B. (2023). Active noise cancellation in Microsoft teams using AI & NLP powered algorithms. *International Journal of Computer Science and Information Technology, 15*(1), 31–42. https://doi.org/10.5121/ijcsit.2023.15103

Shemshack, A., Kinshuk, & Spector, J. M. (2021). A comprehensive analysis of personalized learning components. *Journal of Computers in Education, 8*(4), 485–503. https://doi.org/10.1007/s40692-021-00188-7

Shockley, K. M., Gabriel, A. S., Robertson, D., Rosen, C. C., Chawla, N., Ganster, M. L., & Ezerins, M. E. (2021). The fatiguing effects of camera use in virtual meetings: A within-person field experiment. *Journal of Applied Psychology, 106*(8), 1137–1155. https://doi.org/10.1037/apl0000948

Simultrans. (2024). *The risks of AI translation: Learning from Microsoft's controversy*. https://www.simultrans.com/blog/the-risks-of-ai-translation-learning-from-microsofts-controversy#:~:text=AI%20translation%20is%20not%20perfect,in%20Microsoft's%20AI%2Dgenerated%20news

Steinicke, F., Lehmann-Willenbrock, N., & Meinecke, A. L. (2020). A first pilot study to compare virtual group meetings using video conferences and (immersive) virtual reality. In P. Willemsen & G. Bruder (Eds.), *SUI'20: Proceedings of the 2020 ACM symposium on spatial user interaction (Article 19)*. Association for Computing Machinery. https://doi.org/10.1145/3385959.3422699

Straube, J., & Kauffeld, S. (2020). Faultlines during meeting interactions: The role of intersubgroup communication. In A. L. Meinecke, J. A. Allen, & N. Lehmann-Willenbrock (Eds.), *Managing meetings in organizations. Research on managing groups and teams* (pp. 163–183). Emerald Publishing Limited. https://doi.org/10.1108/S1534-085620200000020008

Sutandijo, V. J., & Qomariyah, N. N. (2023). Artificial intelligence based automatic live stream chat machine translator. *Procedia Computer Science, 227*, 454–463. https://doi.org/10.1016/j.procs.2023.10.546

TechRadar. (2024). *AI-enabled meetings – What's in store for the future of work?* https://www.techradar.com

Tenzer, H., Pudelko, M., & Harzing, A. W. (2014). The impact of language barriers on trust formation in multinational teams. *Journal of International Business Studies, 45*(5), 508–535. https://doi.org/10.1057/jibs.2013.64

Tong, S., Jia, N., Luo, X., & Fang, Z. (2021). The Janus face of artificial intelligence feedback: Deployment versus disclosure effects on employee performance. *Strategic Management Journal, 42*(9), 1600–1631. https://doi.org/10.1002/smj.3322

Weidner, F., Boettcher, G., Arboleda, S. A., Diao, C., Sinani, L., Kunert, C., Gerhardt, C., Broll, W., & Raake, A. (2023). A systematic review on the visualization of avatars and agents in AR & VR displayed using head-mounted displays. *IEEE Transactions on Visualization and Computer Graphics, 29*(5), 2596–2606. https://doi.org/10.1109/TVCG.2023.3247072

Wigert, B., & Argawal, S. (2022, August 31). *Returning to the office: The current, preferred and future state of remote work*. Gallup. https://www.gallup.com/workplace/397751/returning-office-current-preferred-future-state-remote-work.aspx

Xiao, G. (2020). Research on multilingual intelligent translation system based on artificial intelligence technology. In *Proceedings of the 2020 IEEE 3rd International Conference on Information Systems and Computer Aided Education (ICISCAE)* (pp. 419–424). IEEE. https://doi.org/10.1109/ICISCAE51034.2020.9236858

CHAPTER 5

A TIME-SAVING DISHWASHER: AI'S ROLE IN TEAM CREATIVE PROCESSES

Kelsey E. Medeiros[a], Rebecca L. Marrone[b] and Roni Reiter-Palmon[c]

[a]*Department of Management, The University of Nebraska at Omaha, USA*
[b]*The Centre for Change and Complexity in Learning (C3L), University of South Australia, Australia*
[c]*Psychology Department, University of Nebraska at Omaha, USA*

ABSTRACT

Initial reports on the use of artificial intelligence (AI) tools for creativity suggested that a revolution of AI-generated creativity had arrived. As time and research progressed, however, it became apparent that AI's capabilities had been over-hyped, with many concluding that AI lacked the capabilities to successfully engage in creativity autonomously. More recently, generative AI (gen AI) has emerged as a useful teammate or support in the creative process. Through the lens of creative problem solving, this chapter discusses AI's creative capabilities and how teams can use AI tools to facilitate creativity. Furthermore, this chapter discusses three creative problem-solving processes – problem definition, idea generation, idea evaluation – and emerging ideas for how teams can incorporate AI tools to enhance performance in each process. Overall, we suggest that AI's primary benefit to team creative problem-solving processes is by providing support through prompts and structure, as well as through fast-paced analysis. Based on this conclusion, the chapter concludes

AI in Teams: Research on Managing Groups and Teams, Volume 21, 77–94

ISSN: 1534-0856/doi:10.1108/S1534-085620260000021013

with several suggestions for how teams can incorporate AI into their creative process from both a process and people perspective.

Keywords: Artificial intelligence; team creativity; creative problem solving; problem definition; idea generation; idea evaluation

A lot of people like to cook, but nobody likes to do the dishes. Let's find the things we can do to allow you to cook. But let's use AI for the dishes. (Rodney Lam, 2024, CEO of Daily Paper)

The dawn of ChatGPT and similar gen AI tools marked a new age for teams working on creative endeavors. Many in the media proselytized the creative power of AI tools such as ChatGPT and Dall-E (e.g., Baxter, 2024). The result was a looming presence of AI as an independent creative entity with little to no need for human input. In an article hypothesizing the effects of gen AI tools in the creative realm, De Cremer et al. (2023) argued that AI tools were "threatening to upend this special status [creativity as a human masterpiece] and significantly alter creative work" (p. 2). The authors suggested three potential outcomes, including that "machines monopolize creativity" (p. 2), suppressing the need for team creativity altogether.

In early days, it appeared that this may be the case. In one instance, an AI-generated painting sold for $432,500 at a Christie's Auction House sale (Preece & Çelik, 2023) indicating the potential significant value of AI-generated "creative" work. Scholarly empirical research also initially supported this hypothesis (Chen & Ding, 2023; Stevenson et al., 2022) showing that ChatGPT outperformed human participants, scoring in the top percentile on common tasks used to assess creativity-related thinking (i.e., the Alternative Uses Task: Guilford, 1967; the Divergent Association Task: Olson et al., 2021).

As the dialog around AI's potential to outpace the creativity of human teams advanced, critiques of initial research findings emerged. The primary critique of this early work lies in the conflation of creativity with a specific process – divergent thinking (the production of multiple solutions; Guilford, 1950) – rather than the multi-faceted and team-based nature through which creative work occurs. More specifically, creativity is scientifically understood through the lens of creative problem solving, or the production of useful and novel solutions to new, complex, and ill-defined problems (Mumford & Gustafson, 1988) and involves a series of complex processes (e.g., Mumford et al., 1991).

Scholarly arguments focused on a process perspective generally suggest that AI is not capable of successfully performing them independently (at least not yet). For example, in a discussion of the "creativity" of DALL-E-2, Marrone et al. (2024) argued that the work of DALL-E-2 is still primarily driven by human input. DALL-E-2, like ChatGPT and other gen AI tools, responds to human prompts, or the instructions provided to an AI-tool to obtain a response. The more specific the prompts provided, the better (or more novel) the output from the tool. From a creative problem-solving perspective, this finding suggests that the better a human is at defining a problem, the better the AI tool can respond.

But importantly, the AI tool is not defining the problem itself. Other researchers have drawn similar conclusions regarding the dependency of AI on human influence (e.g., Cropley et al., 2023; Medeiros et al., 2023). Marrone et al. (2024) noted that generative AI is typically classified into two broad categories: narrow (or weak) AI and general (or strong) AI. Narrow AI refers to systems developed and trained to perform a specific task, whereas general AI encompasses systems with broader human-like cognitive abilities, enabling them to solve problems independently of human input (Sajja, 2021). Our focus will remain on present-day AI, which fits within the narrow AI category, meaning the systems considered are confined to performing singular, predefined tasks. Through this lens, AI is best considered a teammate in the creative process.

In a recent survey conducted by the In-House Agency Leaders Club, a group focused on bringing together individuals working in in-house marketing and creative operations teams across the UK, Europe, and North America, found that 80% of members surveyed agreed that "AI's role in creativity will be primarily as an assistant to human creative teams" (Burgoyne, 2024). One way in which survey respondents believed AI would assist was through the automation of mundane tasks. A similar sentiment was reported by Rodney Lam (2024), CEO of Daily Paper, a Dutch fashion brand. His team raised the issue of a reduction in jobs and, in particular, a reduction in jobs for those historically underrepresented in the fashion industry. Over time, however, Lam (2024)'s team adopted the vision summarized by the opening quote – AI can take on the mundane tasks, freeing the team to "cook." This philosophy ultimately argues that AI is not a replacement for creativity, but a teammate in the creative problem-solving process.

The question then becomes: how can AI best support humans in the pursuit of creative solutions to today's problems? This chapter will help answer this question and provide both theoretical and practical arguments for what gen AI is capable of, as well as "how to" best collaborate with AI to maximize creative output. To do so, we first summarize AI's current capabilities regarding three specific processes: problem definition, idea generation, and idea evaluation. We will then provide practical suggestions to leverage AI in creative teams, as well as potential pitfalls to avoid when doing so.

GEN AI'S CURRENT CREATIVE PROBLEM-SOLVING CAPABILITIES

Problem Definition

An Overview

A hallmark feature of creative problem solving is the ill-defined and novel nature of the problem at hand (Mumford & Gustafson, 1988). Inherently, this characteristic requires that a team exert cognitive effort to understand, or define, the problem. As such, problem definition refers to the identification of goals and objectives, as well as establishing a structure to guide subsequent processes and activities (Mumford et al., 1994).

Effective problem definition is crucial for the success of teams working on creative efforts. Studies indicate that individuals or teams who spend more time in the problem-definition phase often produce more creative and innovative solutions (Abdulla et al., 2020; Reiter-Palmon & Murugavel, 2018). It has also been suggested that teams, especially newly formed teams, spend significant time clarifying the problem to ensure that all team members have a similar understanding (Leone et al., in press). Additionally, large differences in understanding the problem between team members can contribute to creativity of the solutions, but only if team members integrate the different perspectives (Cronin & Weingart, 2007). Effective problem definition involves iterative refinement, where problem solvers gather information, redefine the problem space, and adjust their goals as new insights are gained. This iterative nature is critical when dealing with complex, dynamic problems that require adaptive thinking and the ability to shift perspectives.

AI's Problem Definition Capabilities

AI has shown promise as a teammate in problem definition, especially in data-rich and complex environments. Current AI models, particularly those using natural language processing (NLP) and machine learning, can analyze large datasets, extract patterns, and generate insights that help clarify the parameters of a problem (Vajjala et al., 2020). For instance, AI systems can summarize existing literature or data streams, providing human problem solvers with a clearer understanding of the problem space, thus aiding in the identification of relevant variables and constraints (Bolaños et al., 2024). However, while gen AI can support the identification of patterns or generate possible interpretations of data, its capacity to fully define a problem is limited by its reliance on pre-defined training data and the problem spaces it has been exposed to. Unlike human teams who can draw on tacit knowledge, contextual understanding, and emotional intelligence, AI lacks the innate flexibility to address highly ambiguous, novel problems that may have little precedent in historical data (Boden, 2016). Furthermore, in some cases, problems are found and identified while others would merely view them as errors (see, for example, the case of the identification of Penicillin when Alexander Flemming noticed an area where bacteria failed to grow around an invading fungus after he returned from vacation. A series of investigative steps later, this led to his discovery of the important drug (Gaynes, 2017). As a result, AI's problem definition often relies on human input to refine and validate the understanding of problem goals, especially in creative or strategic decision-making processes.

While current AI large language models (LLMs) can support creative and strategic decision-making processes through data analysis and simulations – such as predicting the potential impact of different problem definitions – they inherently lack the capacity for genuine problem finding, a key aspect of human creativity. As highlighted by Runco (2023), true creative problem finding requires intrinsic motivation and autonomy, elements that AI cannot replicate. LLMs can assist with identifying and exploring defined problem spaces but must be directed toward these tasks, as they lack the ability to independently discover and frame problems. Therefore, in human–AI teams, AI contributes computational power and data-driven insights, while human problem solvers provide the creative thinking and contextual interpretation that AI lacks. Cropley et al. (2023) extended this distinction using the example of Mary Jacob's invention of the bra, arguing that AI tools such as ChatGPT would fail to inherently understand the discomfort of a corset and thus not recognize a problem. As such, although AI may be able to identify gaps or trends that point to potential problems, it requires a human team to recognize the uniquely human experience that creates new problems to solve.

How to Use AI as an Effective Teammate in Problem Definition

Given current gen AI capabilities – described by Marrone et al. (2024) as narrow in scope – AI can assist in the process of problem definition, but only to a limited extent. We suggest two potential roles for AI in a team's problem definition process. First, teams could ask AI agents to report on specific emerging gaps or trends. The humans in the team could then lend their uniquely human experience to interpret those gaps and trends to identify the specific problem at hand. Note, however, that the human teammates must already have a clear sense of potential gaps or trends to request information. Research on prompts shows that people often lack the style-specific vocabulary necessary for effective prompting (Oppenlaender et al., 2024). These authors suggest specific training on effective prompt writing may improve creative outputs and production. Prompt writing can, therefore, be seen as an emerging skill that should be actively encouraged to help individuals maximize the effectiveness of their prompts – and, in turn, the capabilities of the AI. Work by Knoth et al. (2024) suggests that higher quality prompts predicted the quality of the LLM output. They further suggest that prompts require an interaction between the person and the LLM, with the prompts being refined based on the output and the review of the person generating the prompt.

Second, once the human teammates identify a problem, they could ask AI tools such as ChatGPT to elaborate or restate that problem. This process would allow human teammates to obtain a broader perspective from the information available to AI (World Economic Forum, 2023). However, appropriate prompting should be used, as current models of gen AI lack the specific information needed for prediction (Wang et al., 2023).

Idea Generation

Overview of Idea Generation

Idea generation refers to the production of solutions to the problem at hand. This process is most commonly associated with creativity and has historically been misconstrued as the only process for creative problem solving (Cropley, 2016). As a result, idea generation is the most studied process. At the team level, idea generation often takes the form of brainstorming (Osborn, 1953).

Research on face-to-face brainstorming consistently demonstrates that brainstorming in groups is less effective than brainstorming on one's own (Paulus & Kenworthy, 2019). Much of the ineffectiveness of team brainstorming in the traditional sense stems from an anxiety about sharing ideas, a lack of anonymity, and production blocking, or the loss of ideas due to speaking time as each member shares their ideas (Diehl & Strobe, 1991; Diehl & Stroebe, 1987). When teams have high psychological safety, the anxiety and lack of anonymity are likely less of a concern. However, production blocking remains problematic. Other research has identified issues such as unrelated discussions and moving on from a discussion too quickly as to why brainstorming in a team is particularly ineffective (Dugosh et al., 2000; Oxley et al., 1996). As a result, Paulus and Kenworthy (2019) suggested the use of trained facilitators to keep the team on task and help focus and guide the sessions. Research has also demonstrated improvements in idea generation through alternative processes including virtual, anonymous brainstorming sessions and brainwriting, or the sharing of ideas on paper rather than verbally (e.g., Dennis & Williams, 2003; VanGundy, 1995).

AI's Idea Generation Capabilities

Research on AI's idea generation capabilities reveals that AI can streamline individual brainstorming, making it more effective and efficient than relying solely on human effort (Boussioux et al., 2024; Meincke et al., 2023). AI can help alleviate cognitive load (Garbuio & Lin, 2021), relax or emphasize constraints of mental models (Verganti et al., 2020), and expand users' perspectives. While some researchers argue that AI can generate more effective and novel ideas than humans (e.g., Chen & Ding, 2023; Stevenson et al., 2022), we contend that the effectiveness of these ideas is inherently limited by the scope of knowledge on which the LLM is trained. The training data introduce inherent biases and constraints, which can limit the model's ability to generate truly original knowledge. Therefore, effective idea generation requires more than just generating ideas – it involves a deeper, more nuanced process.

Emerging research on the use of AI to stimulate idea generation has provided mixed results. Most of these studies have examined AI facilitating idea generation with a single individual, rather than in a team context. However, they provide initial insights on how AI could be used in this capacity for teams. Some studies have demonstrated that AI may be particularly beneficial for those who are typically below average in creativity (Doshi & Hauser, 2024; Haase & Hanel, 2023). However, others have found that high performers benefit more from collaboration with AI than low performers (Jia et al., 2024). Others have shown that using AI as an exemplar of idea generation promotes similar levels of idea generation in humans when compared to exemplars from humans (e.g., Medeiros et al., 2025). However, this same research also demonstrated that when AI provided low creative ideas, subsequent idea generation by human participants suffered. Other researchers have seen more harmful effects, revealing increased productivity with the use of AI at the expense of novelty (Doshi & Hauser, 2024; Niloy et al., 2023). This emerging work suggests that there are boundaries regarding when AI is an effective teammate and who it will be effective with, but the results remain murky.

How to Use AI as an Effective Teammate in Idea Generation
Eric Gunther, the cofounder of the digital design firm SOSO, argued that we should move away from "human–computer interaction, to a framework of AI 'sparking, strengthening, and supporting' human-to-human interactions" (Werner, 2024). In line with the emerging research, this perspective suggests that expert teams who are highly creative (e.g., research and development; marketing) should leverage AI tools to provide structural support in their idea generation sessions, rather than as a co-idea generator. Practically, this means that these highly creative teams could use AI tools in a coaching capacity, to provide challenging prompts and spark debate. From a brainstorming perspective, AI could be used to facilitate conversations, noting when the team diverges from the topic at hand and by providing stimulating prompts that encourage sustained idea generation. Additionally, gen AI can be instructed to take on different personas based on demographic variables such as gender, age, race, and education and help provide responses based on those personas' perspectives (Laverghetta et al., 2024). This may provide the team with missing perspectives and ideas.

For teams who are not necessarily working in creative domains and, therefore, may not be as skilled in creativity, using AI tools as co-generator may be more beneficial, particularly as the technology advances. For example, asking ChatGPT for ideas on how to solve a particular problem may be a useful approach. However, given anchoring bias, which suggests that initial ideas can substantially direct subsequent processing (Tversky & Kahnemah, 1974), we would recommend that teams follow a more traditional brainstorming path before introducing ChatGPT. Specifically, we suggest teams (1) engage in idea generation individually, (2) share and generate ideas collectively as a team, (3) ask ChatGPT for its ideas, (4) include ChatGPT ideas with the other ideas, and (5) discuss and evaluate the ChatGPT ideas along with other potential ideas (as discussed in the next section). Additionally, gen AI may be able to assist these teams in suggesting ways to elaborate on ideas and how to combine ideas to create more effective and novel ideas.

Idea Evaluation

Overview of Idea Evaluation
After generating ideas, it is important for teams to evaluate the novelty and usefulness of the proposed ideas, as well as consider the extent to which proposed ideas solve the problem at hand and forecast the potential consequences of implementing those ideas (Mumford et al., 2002). Given that not all ideas that are generated can be implemented, the idea evaluation process is important for identifying which ideas are worth progressing and implementing. Furthermore, Cropley (2006) noted that if ideas are not sufficiently evaluated, there are two potential negative consequences: (1) teams may select an idea that lacks novelty and thereby miss a key market opportunity (feasibility bias; Paulus et al., 2018) or (2) teams may select a novel idea that is not, in fact, feasible or useful, leading to failures of production or in the market (reckless variability; Cropley et al., 2006). Additionally, as demonstrated in a laboratory experiment, teams may end

up selecting ideas that are neither creative nor effective, with 25% to 45% of teams selecting less than optimal solutions (Reiter-Palmon et al., 2018). Thus, it is essential that teams effectively evaluate their ideas.

Research on effective idea evaluation has largely explored methods for improving the process in teams such as on emphasizing both quality and novelty and improving the cognitive processes associated with effective idea evaluation. Regarding the first, Reiter-Palmon et al. (2018) found that providing a detailed rubric to guide the evaluation process resulted in the selection of ideas that were higher in originality. Importantly, there was no effect regarding the quality of ideas, meaning that providing structure to the evaluation process resulted in participants selecting more solutions with the same level of feasibility compared to when they were provided no or little structure. Using structural tools to aid in the idea evaluation process was also emphasized by Puccio et al. (2007), when they argued that using a structured strategy in the idea evaluation process would benefit team creativity. Specifically, they argued that these tools were essential for helping teams move beyond their initial evaluation, which often favors feasibility over novelty, and to instead think critically and deeply about the ideas presented.

Regarding team evaluative processes, one cognitive process frequently discussed is forecasting. Forecasting refers to the consideration of downstream consequences – both short and long term (Mumford et al., 2002). Multiple studies have demonstrated the positive impact of forecasting during idea evaluation on subsequent creative performance (Berg, 2016; Lonergan et al., 2004; Lubart, 2001; Mumford et al., 2001). For example, Berg (2016) asked creators and managers to evaluate the potential of new circus acts and compared these forecasts to thousands of evaluations by circus goers. Results from this study showed that creators were more effective at evaluating ideas compared to managers. Berg suggested that the creator advantage lies in the need for both divergent and convergent thinking when forecasting. Forecasting is, in some respects, a form of idea generation – considering multiple future alternatives (divergent thinking) – while also considering if ideas meet the requirements of the problem at hand (convergent thinking). The importance of one's role in idea evaluation was echoed by Mueller et al. (2018), who found that those asked to take on a decision-making role (compared to an advisory role) were more likely to evaluate ideas differently and to select less risky and less creative ideas.

AI's Idea Evaluation Capabilities

Initial research on AI's idea evaluation capacity provides promising results. Several studies have demonstrated that current LLMs (i.e., ChatGPT's) AI produces similar evaluations to humans across both criteria of usefulness and novelty (e.g., Beaty & Johnson, 2020; Bell et al., 2023; Christensen et al., 2018; Just et al., 2024; Marrone et al., 2022). For example, Marrone et al. (2022) developed an algorithm to assess mathematical creativity in students, finding that the algorithm was as reliable as human raters. These results led Marrone et al. (2024) to propose that one of AI's strengths is the ability to provide faster feedback on ideas than a human team.

It is important to note, however, that AI consistently demonstrates the same biases as humans due to humans being the source of the tools' training data (Buolamwini & Gebru, 2018; Mehrabi et al., 2021). As such, AI should not be seen as a magic bullet that will necessarily improve and reduce bias in the idea selection process. Rather, at present, AI tools can produce similar results to that of human teams.

How to Use AI as an Effective Teammate in Idea Evaluation

Based on research conducted by Paulus and colleagues (e.g., Paulus & Yang, 2000; Paulus et al., 2006), Puccio and Cabra (2011) outlined several practical strategies for improving idea evaluation including evaluating ideas using a methodological, structured approach and employing outside experts to ensure that all evaluative criteria and problem parameters have been addressed. AI is a perfect match for providing this kind of structural support for idea evaluation. Specifically, AI can provide a structured guide for evaluating the solutions at hand and make notes of the evaluations made. Additionally, AI can serve as an "outside evaluator" to provide feedback on how the available ideas meet the required criteria. For instance, one could use gen AI such as ChatGPT to consider whether ideas meet particular criteria for creativity.

AI may also serve as a teammate in some of the cognitive processes important to idea evaluation. AI may be able to forecast potential outcomes if specific criteria are specified. For instance, team could ask an AI tool to forecast the success of a particular product given current market conditions, and perhaps to consider how those forecasts would change if certain market conditions were altered. Given its processing power, it will be able to provide this information at a rate faster than its human teammate can calculate it.

However, it is critical to remember that AI is not all-knowing-agent and, similar to the human brain, is limited by biases and boundaries. For instance, just as business leaders did not include COVID-19 when completing their business forecasts for 2020 in 2019, neither would AI have incorporated it into the forecast. Furthermore, as discussed regarding problem identification, AI cannot understand human feeling and needs (although it can be programmed to recognize human emotion, it does not, at present, truly feel it). As such, it will not be capable of considering these factors. Finally, given that forecasting requires divergent thinking, in which AI is not currently skilled, AI should not be relied on for the generative aspects of forecasting without clear direction from the team. AI may be best thought of as a structural support to the idea evaluation process that can also provide supplementary analysis to support evaluation processes at a faster rate.

Human–AI Teaming in Creative Problem Solving

Conclusions from emerging research suggest that AI is best conceptualized as a structural tool in the creative process rather than as a sole creator. Returning to the analogy presented in the opening quote, we can think of AI as the commercial dishwasher of the creative process. Commercial dishwashers clean dishes

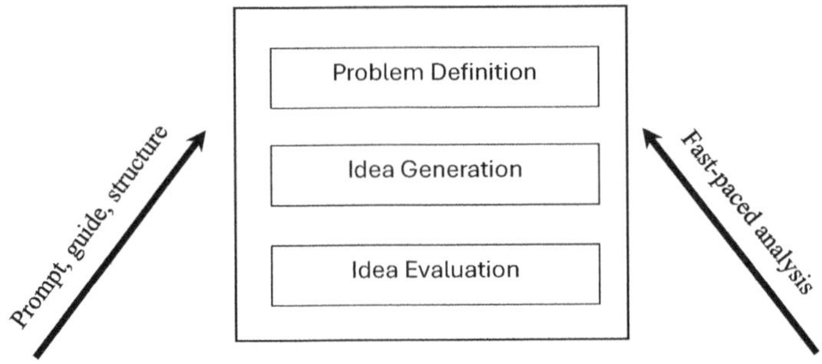

Fig. 5.1. AI Support in Creative Efforts.

extremely quickly (compared to domestic dishwashers or humans), and they do their job highly effectively. They allow restaurants to speed up the pace of service on a busy night and serve mouthwatering dishes from the chefs without worrying whether or not the plates are available. In this same way, AI serves as the high-speed support for creative teams, allowing teams to generate and implement novel ideas more quickly. Important to this analogy, however, is the human role in loading and unloading the dishwasher! As such, we suggest that teams engaged in creative problem solving should consider the following two primary principles for using AI to support their work: (1) prompt, guide, structure and (2) fast-paced analysis. A summary of how AI can help support the creative process is depicted in Fig. 5.1.

INCORPORATING AI FROM A PROCESS PERSPECTIVE

Regarding prompts, guides, and structure, we suggest that creative teams focus on how AI can support their creative work. An example unrelated to divergent thinking is in the refinement and optimization phase of product development. Here, LLMs can play a role in offering structured guidance on refining existing concepts to better align with practical constraints, such as manufacturing capabilities or user preferences. For instance, in product design, after a team has generated initial concepts, AI can help evaluate and optimize these designs based on specific criteria like material efficiency, cost-effectiveness, or ergonomic considerations. It can simulate different design variations and highlight potential areas for improvement or redesign, such as suggesting adjustments for better weight distribution in a physical product or identifying elements that could be simplified for easier production.

By doing this, AI guides the design team through a structured process of iteration, ensuring that their ideas not only meet creative aspirations but also align with technical and practical constraints. This allows the team to focus on refining the user experience or aesthetic aspects of the product while AI handles the more systematic analysis, providing concrete suggestions for optimization. This example showcases AI's ability to support a structured and efficient refinement process, enabling human teams to achieve a balance between creativity and functionality. Furthermore, within this phase, AI can provide a framework for creative teams to organize their thoughts and ideas. It can help in categorizing and mapping out problem spaces, highlighting key themes and relationships among different elements. This structured support allows teams to better manage the complexity of creative challenges, helping to maintain focus while exploring multiple avenues.

Another advantage of an AI teammate in the creative process is the speed with which it can conduct analysis or supply additional information. Forecasting outcomes and collecting information can take a significant amount of time and cognitive energy. Offloading these types of tasks frees up time and space to engage in more human-driven activities. For example, the Chief Innovation Officer at Embryo, a Digital Marketing Agency, reported using AI tools to: "pre-filter industry news: to get rid of duplicates, puff pieces and listicles. We then use AI to read articles for us, giving us a detailed synopsis so that we know whether to spend time reading the full article or not" (May, 2024). Additionally, AI may be used to quickly visualize products in a way that was previously impossible or slow. For example, an article in *Creative Boom* (May, 2024) discussed the speed with which creative agencies can prototype their proposed advertisements and work to clients, allowing for an arguably better evaluation process. The article used the examples of Poppins Agency and UsTwo, which both used AI image generators to protype their proposed work. They stated, "This saves the client spending a lot of money on something before they know it's going to work" (May, 2024, para. 12). This is further underscored by Clark and Graff (2026) in their case study of the software company, that prototyping is a key task for AI.

When discussing speed, however, it is important to recognize that not all processes in creative problem solving should be sped up. For instance, research repeatedly shows that teams should commit large amounts of time and cognitive effort to understanding the problem at hand, as well as generating and evaluating ideas (Reiter-Palmon & Linnell, 2023). Paulus and Brown (2007) argued that teams should dedicate multiple meetings across multiple days to the generation and evaluation processes to ensure these processes are effective.

INCORPORATING AI FROM A TEAM-DYNAMICS PERSPECTIVE

From a team-dynamics perspective, psychological safety is an essential element for teams wanting to engage in creative problem solving (Hunter et al., 2007). This remains true and is perhaps even more important when AI is introduced to the process. While AI would not require feeling psychologically safe in a team environment, human team members would still need to. One of the reasons psychological safety is important for teams engaged in creative problem solving is the need for team members to feel comfortable both sharing ideas and critiquing those ideas (Edmondson, 1999). When AI is introduced as a structural support, teams may choose to offload certain "dishwashing" responsibilities that can influence these processes. It is important that teams develop a collective mental model around the use of AI as a tool in the process and how the information or work it produces will be used. To do so, however, a team needs the psychological safety to freely share their views of AI and its utility for the project.

By fostering psychological safety and understanding individual reactions to AI, teams can strike a balance where human expertise and AI-generated insights work together effectively. This approach ensures that AI is seen as a tool for empowerment, helping team members leverage its capabilities without losing sight of their own creative strengths. Ultimately, focusing on the people aspect of AI integration can lead to greater acceptance of AI and more effective use of its potential in creative problem solving, leading to a collaborative environment where both human and AI contributions are valued. In addition, team members need to be able and willing to critically review the contributions of team members and the AI.

Additionally, it is important to consider the impact on the team's creative process more generally. For example, if a team chooses to speed up the creative process by using AI to search for relevant information rather than conducting a manual search, the effects on cognition and the team dynamic are currently unknown. Given the importance of allowing teams the necessary time to think and develop their ideas, it is unclear whether speeding up some of these processes will impact the development of ideas more holistically and if so, what the effect would be. Additionally, spending time searching for information, or another offloaded process, may be important for developing team shared mental models and other dynamics such as psychological safety and cohesion. As such, leaders and teams should monitor potential changes in their processes and dynamics and intentionally emphasize the development of important team dynamics.

FUTURE RESEARCH DIRECTIONS

The present chapter outlines several suggestions for how gen AI can support teams in the creative process. Although suggestions are drawn from a rich literature on the creative process, as well as the emerging research on AI and creativity, much remains scientifically unknown about AI and the creative process, especially in teams. Studies that have explored this impact have typically examined trust of AI (e.g., Marmolejo-Ramos et al., 2025). Only a few studies have looked at the effect of gen AI on team performance (Shaikh & Cruz, 2022; Zhang et al., 2021). As such, there is ample opportunity and need for researchers and practitioners to engage in a systematic and deliberate research agenda to understand how to best leverage AI technology for creative problem solving. We provide a few suggestions for advancing this agenda.

First, while many of the suggestions presented in this chapter are extrapolated from research, they have not necessarily been directly tested. Therefore, we suggest that researchers begin by investigating the claims discussed here. Researchers should examine the degree to which AI can be used to provide structure, guides, and prompts in problem definition, idea generation, and idea evaluation to improve creative performance. The boundaries and interactive effects of this structure should similarly be tested. For instance, can AI provide too much structure such that it then decreases creativity? Or, are there particular team or organizational characteristics that reduce (or enhance) the effectiveness of this structure?

Second, the present chapter only discussed three processes involved in team creative problem solving. Previous research, however, suggests that there may be up to eight distinct processes including information gathering, concept selection, concept combination, implementation planning, and solution monitoring (Mumford et al., 1991). Therefore, there is a need to stretch the discussion beyond problem definition, idea generation, and idea evaluation to understand how AI can be used to facilitate creative problem solving. For instance, information gathering may be a process particularly conducive to the introduction of AI. Sitting in between problem identification and idea generation, information gathering refers to the directed collection of information relevant to the problem at hand (Mumford et al., 1991). If given clear direction and parameters by its human teammates, then AI should be able to quickly and successfully complete this step. This should, in turn, free up time for the humans to engage in other creative processes. In theory, offloading this process to AI would then allow the human teammates to dedicate more cognitive resources and time to complex thinking activities.

Third, although AI *can* take on some processes, it is important to ask if it *should*. This point is particularly true as AI continues to advance in its capabilities and as laws and regulations catch up with its implementation. Research should consider the consequences of adding AI into the creative process. For example, researchers (Gerlich, 2025) have suggested that the cognitive offloading of specific tasks may influence subsequent processing. For instance, if the humans in the team offload the primary forecasting effort to AI, how does that influence their processing of the information and the evaluation and selection of ideas to advance? More research is needed to fully understand these types of consequences of introducing AI into the creative process.

Fourth, we emphasize the need to better understand the AI–human teaming experience. Although AI may be effective at some of these processes, it is not clear how humans feel about having AI as a teammate. Initial research suggests a general public distrust of AI (Dwork & Minow, 2022). However, that same distrust may not carry over to those who are more familiar with how AI functions (Marmolejo-Ramos et al., 2025). For creative teams who work closely with AI, they may trust it and its contributions. However, more research is needed on the important team, and uniquely human, dynamics such as feelings of trust, psychological safety, and satisfaction.

Fifth, and finally, research should explore the role of AI specifically in a creative team context. Research to date has largely focused on how individuals respond to and interact with AI, as well as how AI influences individual cognition. How AI fits into the development of and changes in a shared mental model is unclear. Other important factors such as how to build trust and cohesion also remain unknown. Therefore, we suggest that in addition to the individual-level research, researchers should also explore AI–human creativity in teams specifically.

CONCLUSION

Although AI currently lacks the capability to engage in the creative process autonomously, it still offers several benefits for teams. Specifically, AI can provide structure to a team's creative problem-solving process, as well as reduce the time spent on analysis processes. This view provides multiple avenues for using AI to improve a team's creative process, but caution is warranted as AI is a quickly evolving technology and research in this area remains limited. In its current state, however, AI appears well-suited to take on the dishwashing to help teams create and innovate.

REFERENCES

Abdulla, A. M., Paek, S. H., Cramond, B., & Runco, M. A. (2020). Problem finding and creativity: A meta-analytic review. *Psychology of Aesthetics, Creativity, and the Arts*, *14*(1), 3–14. https://doi.org/10.1037/aca0000194

Baxter, C. (2024). AI art: The end of creativity or the start of a new movement? *BBC*. https://www.bbc.com/future/article/20241018-ai-art-the-end-of-creativity-or-a-new-movement

Beaty, R. E., & Johnson, D. R. (2020). Automating creativity assessment with SemDis: An open platform for computing semantic distance. *Behavior Research Methods*, *53*, 757–780. https://doi.org/10.3758/s13429-020-01453-w

Bell, J. J., Perscher, C., Tellis, G. J., & Füller, J. (2023). Can AI help in ideation? A theory-based model for idea screening in crowdsourcing contests. *Marketing Science*, *43*(1), 54–72. https://doi.org/10.1287/mksc.2023.1434

Berg, J. M. (2016). Balancing on the creative highwire: Forecasting the success of novel ideas in organizations. *Administrative Science Quarterly*, *61*(3), 433–468. https://doi.org/10.1177/0001839216642211

Boden, M. A. (2016). *AI: Its nature and future*. Oxford University Press.

Bolaños, F., Salatino, A., Osborne, F., & Motta, E. (2024) Artificial intelligence for literature reviews: Opportunities and challenges. *Artificial Intelligence Review*, *57*(259). https://doi.org/10.1007/s10462-024-10902-3

Boussioux, L., Lane, J. N., Zhang, M., Jacimovic, V., & Lakhani, K. R. (2024). The crowdless future? Generative AI and creative problem-solving. *Organization Science*, *35*(5), 1571–1955. https://doi.org/10.1287/orscs.2023.18430

Buolamwini, J., & Gebru, T. (2018). Gender shades: Intersectional accuracy disparities in commercial gender classification. *Proceedings of the Conference on Fairness, Accountability, and Transparency*, *81*, 77–91. https://proceedings.mlr.press/v81/buolamwini18a.html?mod=article_inline&ref=akusion-ci-shi-dai-bizinesumedeia

Burgoyne, P. (2024, May 6). How in-house agencies are adopting AI. *Creative Review*. https://www.creativereview.co.uk/how-in-house-agencies-are-adopting-ai/

Chen, H., & Ding, N. (2023). *Probing the creativity of large language models: Can models produce divergent semantic association?* PsyArXiv https://doi.org/10.48550/arXiv.2310.11158

Christensen, K., Scholderer, J., Hersleth, S. A., Naes, T., Kvaal, K., Mollestad, T., Veflen, N., & Risvik, E. (2018). How good are ideas identified by an automatic idea detection system? *Creativity and Innovation Management*, *27*(1), 23–31. https://doi.org/10.1111/caim.12260

Clark, M. A., & Graff, D. (2026). AI and design collaboration: Not a full member (yet). In S. Paletz & S. Dubrow (Eds.), *AI in teams* (pp. 153–171). Emerald Publishing.

Cronin, M. A., & Weingart, L. R. (2007). Representational gaps, information processing, and conflict in functionally diverse teams. *Academy of Management Review*, *32*(3), 761–773. https://doi.org/10.5465/amr.2007.25275511

Cropley, A. (2006). In praise of convergent thinking. *Creativity Research Journal, 18*(3), 391-404. https://doi.org/10.1207/s15326934crj1803_13

Cropley, A. (2016). The myths of heaven-sent creativity: Toward a perhaps less democratic but more down-to-earth understanding. *Creativity Research Journal*, *28*(3), 238–246. https://doi.org/10.1080/10400419.2016.1195614

Cropley, D. H., Medeiros, K. E., & Damadzic, A. (2023). The intersection of human and artificial creativity. In D. Henriksen & P. Mishra (Eds.), *Creative provocations: Speculations of the future of creativity, technology, & learning, creativity theory in action* (Vol. 7). https://doi.org/10.1007/978-3-031-14549-0_2

De Cremer, D., Bianzino, N. M., & Falk, B. (2023, April 13). How generative AI could disrupt creative work. *Harvard Business Review*. https://hbr.org/2023/04/how-generative-ai-could-disrupt-creative-work

Dennis, A. R., & Williams, M. L. (2003). Electronic brainstorming: Theory, research, and future directions. In P. B. Paulus & B. A. Nijstad (Eds.), *Group creativity: Innovation through collaboration* (pp. 160–178). Oxford University Press.

Diehl, M., & Strobe, W. (1991). Productivity loss in idea-generating groups: Tracking down the blocking effect. *Journal of Personality and Social Psychology*, *61*(3), 392–403. https://doi.org/10.1037/0022-3514.61.3.392

Diehl, M., & Stroebe, W. (1987). Productivity loss in brainstorming groups: Toward the solution of a riddle. *Journal of Personality and Social Psychology*, *53*(3), 497–509. https://doi.org/10/1037/0022-3514.53.3.497

Doshi, A. R., & Hauser, O. P. (2024). Generative AI enhances individual creativity but reduces the collective diversity of novel content. *Science*, *10*(28). https://doi.org/10.1126/sciadv.adn5290

Dugosh, K. L., Paulus, P. B. Roland, E. J., & Yang, H. C. (2000). Cognitive stimulation in brainstorming. *Journal of Personality and Social Psychology*, *79*(5), 722–735. https://doi.org/10/1037//0022-3514.79.5.722

Dwork, C. & Minow, M. (2022). Distrust of artificial intelligence: Sources and responses from computer science law. *Daedalus, 151*(2), 309-321. https://doi.org/10.1162/daed_a_01918.

Edmondson, A. C. (1999). Psychological safety and learning behavior in work teams. *Administrative Science Quarterly*, *44*(2), 350–383. https://doi.org/10.2307/2666999

Garbuio, M., & Lin, N. (2021). Innovative idea generation in problem finding: Abductive reasoning, cognitive impediments, and the promise of artificial intelligence. *Journal of Product Innovation Management*, *38*(6), 701–725. https://doi.org/10.1111/jpim.12602

Gaynes, R. (2017). Th discovery of Penicillin – New insights after more than 75 years of clinical use. *Emerging Infectious Diseases*, *23*(5), 849–853. https://doi.org/10.3201/eid2305.161556

Gerlich, M. (2025). AI tools in society: Impacts on cognitive offloading and the future of critical thinking. *Societies*, *15*(6), 1–28. https://doi.org/10.3390/soc15010006

Guilford, J. P. (1950). Creativity. *American Psychologist*, *5*, 444–454.

Guilford, J. P. (1967). *The nature of human intelligence*. McGraw-Hill.

Haase, J., & Hanel, P. H. P. (2023). Artificial muses: Generative artificial intelligence chatbots have risen to human-level creativity. *Journal of Creativity*, *33*(3), 100066. https://doi.org/10.1016/j.yjoc.2023.100066

Hunter, S. T., Bedell, K. E., & Mumford, M. D. (2007). Climate for creativity: A quantitative review. *Creativity Research Journal*, *19*(1), 69–90. https://doi.org/10.1080/10400410709336883

Jia, N., Luo, X., Fang, Z., & Liao, C. (2024). When and how artificial intelligence augments employee creativity. *Academy of Management Journal*, *67*(1). https://doi.org/10.5465/amj.2022.0426

Just, J., Ströhle, T., Fuller, J., & Hutter, K. (2024). AI-based novelty detection in crowdsourced idea spaces. *Innovation: Organization & Management*, *26*(3), 359–386. https://doi.org/10.1080/14479338.2023.2215740

Knoth, N., Tolzin, A., Janson, A., & Leimeister, J. M. (2024). AI literacy and its implications for prompt engineering strategies. *Computers and Education: Artificial Intelligence*, *6*, 100225. https://doi.org/10.1016/j.caeai.2024.100225

Lam, R. (2024, September). Never miss with a moment: How one fashion brand met YouTube trends with AI. *Think with Google*. https://www.thinkwithgoogle.com/intl/en-emea/marketing-strategies/automation/daily-paper-ai-videos/

Laverghetta Jr, A., Luchini, S., Linnell, A., Reiter-Palmon, R., & Beaty, R. (2024, October). The creative psychometric item generator: A framework for item generation and validation using large language models [Conference presentation]. *CREAI 2024: Workshop on artificial intelligence and creativity Santiago de Compostela*, Spain.

Lonergan, D., Scott, G. M., & Mumford, M. D. (2004). Evaluative aspects of creative thought: Effects of appraisal and revision standards. *Creativity Research Journal, 16*(2–3), 231–246. https://doi.org/10.1080/10400419.2004.9651455

Lubart, T. (2001). Models of the creative process: Past, present, and future. *Creativity Research Journal, 13*(3–4), 195–308. https://doi.org/10.1207/S15326934CRJ1334_07

Marmolejo-Ramos, F., Marrone, R., Korolkiewicz, M., Garbiel, F., Siemens, G., Joksimovic, S., Yamada, Y., Mori, Y., Rahwan, T., Sahakyan, M., Sonna, B., Meirmanov, A., Bolatov, A., Som, B., Ndukaihe, I., Arinze, N. C., Kundrát, J., Skanderová, L., Ngo, V., ... & Tejada, J. (2025). Factors influencing trust in algorithmic decision-making: An indirect scenario-based experiment. *Frontiers in Artificial Intelligence*, *7*, 1465606. http://doi.org/10.3389/frai.2024.1465605

Marrone, R., Cropley, D., & Medeiros, K. E. (2024). How does narrow AI impact human creativity? *Creativity Research Journal*, 1–11. https://doi.org/10.1080/10400419.2024.2378264

Marrone, R., Cropley, D. H., & Wang, Z. (2022). Automatic assessment of mathematical creativity using natural language processing. *Creativity Research Journal*, *35*(4), 661–676. https://doi.org/10.1080/10400419.2022.213209

Marrone, R., Zamecnik, A., Joksimovic, S., et al. (2024). Understanding student perceptions of artificial intelligence as a teammate. *Technology, Knowledge, and Learning*, *30*, 1847–1869. https://doi.org/10.1007/s10758-024-09780-z

May, T. (2024, February 27). Special report: How design agencies are actually using AI in 2024. *Creative Boom*. https://www.creativeboom.com/features/special-report-how-design-agencies-are-using-ai-in-2024/

Medeiros, K. E., Cropley, D., Marrone, R., & Reiter-Palmon, R. (2025). Human-AI co-creativity: Does ChatGPT make us more creative? *The Journal of Creative Behavior*, *59*(2), e70022. https://doi.org/10.1002/jocb.70022

Medeiros, K. E., Marrone, R. L., Joksimovic, S., Cropley, D. H., & Siemens, G. (2023). Promised and realities of artificial creativity. In R. Reiter-Palmon & S. T. Hunter (Eds.) *Handbook of organizational creativity* (pp. 275–289). Academic Press. https://doi.org/10.1016/B978-0-323-91841-1.00010-5

Mehrabi, N., Morstatter, F., Saxena, N., Lerman, K., & Galstyan, A. (2021). A survey on bias and fairness in machine learning. *ACM Computing Surveys*, *54*(6), 1–35. https://doi.org/10.1145/3457607

Meincke, L., Girotra, K., Nave, G., Terwiesch, C., & Ulrich, K. T. (2023). *Ideas are dimes a dozen: Large language models for idea generation in innovation.* SSRN. https://papers.ssrn.com/sol3/papers.cfm?abstract_id=4526071

Mueller, J., Melwani, S., Loewenstein, J., & Deal, J. D. (2018). Reframing the decision-makers' dilemma: Towards a social context model of creative idea recognition. *Academy of Management Journal, 65*(1). https://doi.org/10.5465/amj.2013.0887.

Mumford, M. D., Feldman, J. M., Hein, M. B., & Nagao, D. J. (2001). Tradeoffs between ideas and structure: Individual versus group performance in creative problem solving. *Journal of Creative Behavior*, *35*(1) 1–23. https://doi-org.leo.lib.unomaha.edu/10.1002/j.2162-6057.2001.tb01218.x

Mumford, M. D., & Gustafson, S. B. (1988). Creativity syndrome: Integration, application, and innovation. *Psychological Bulletin, 103*(1), 27–43. https://doi.org/10.1037/0033-2909.103.1.27

Mumford, M. D., Longergan, D. C., & Scott, G. (2002). Evaluating creative ideas: Processes, standards, and context. *Inquiry: Critical Thinking Across the Disciplines*, *22*(1), 21–30. https://doi.org/10.5840/inquiryctnews20022213

Mumford, M. D., Mobley, M. I., Uhlman, C. E., Reiter-Palmo, R., & Doares, L. M. (1991). Process analytic models of creative capacities. *Creativity Research Journal*, *4*(2), 91–122. https://doi.org/10.1080/10400419109534380

Mumford, M. D., Reiter-Palmon, R., & Redmond, M. R. (1994). Problem construction and cognition: Applying problem representations in ill-defined domains. In M. A. Runco (Ed.), *Problem finding, problem solving, and creativity* (pp. 3–39). Ablex Publishing.

Mumford, M. D., Schultz, R. A., & Van Doorn, J. R. 2001). Performance in planning: Processes, requirements, and errors. *Review of General Psychology*, *5*(3), 213–240. https://doi.org/10.1037/1089-2680.5.3.213

Niloy, A. C., Akter, S., Sultana, N., Sultana, J., & Rahman, S. I. U. (2023). Is Chatgpt a menace for creative writing ability? An experiment. *Journal of Computer Assisted Learning*, *40*(2), 919–930. https://doi.org/10.1111/jcal.12929

Olson, J. A., Nahas, J., Chmoulevitch, D., Cropper, S. J., & Webb, M. E. (2021). Naming unrelated words predicts creativity. *Proceedings of the National Academy of Sciences*, *118*(25), e2022340118. https://doi.org/10.1073/pnas.2022340118

Oppenlaender, J., Linder, R., & Silvennoinen, J. (2024). Prompting AI art: An investigation into the creative skill of prompt engineering. *International Journal of Human–Computer Interaction*, 1–23. https://doi.org/10.1080/10447318.2024.2431761

Osborn, A. F. (1953). *Applied imagination: Principles and procedures of creative thinking*. Scribner.

Oxley, N. L., Dzindolet, M. T., & Paulus, P. B. (1996). The effects of facilitators on the performance of brainstorming groups. *Journal of Social Behavior and Personality*, *11*(4), 633–646.

Paulus, P. B., & Brown, V. R. (2007). Toward more creative and innovative group idea generation: A cognitive-social-motivational persepctive on brainstorming. *Social and Personality Psychology Compass, 1*(1), 248-265. https://doi.org/10.1111/j.1751-9004.2007.00006.x.

Paulus, P. B., Baruah, J., & Kenworthy, J. B. (2018). Enhancing collaborative ideation in organizations. *Frontiers in Psychology*, *9*. https://doi.org/10.3389/fpsyg.2018.02024

Paulus, P. B., & Kenworthy, J. B. (2019). Effective brainstorming. In P. B. Paulus & A. B. Nijstad (Eds.), *The Oxford handbook of group creativity and innovation* (pp. 287–305). Oxford Press.

Paulus, P. B., Nakui, T., & Putman, V. L. (2006). Group brainstorming and teamwork: Some rules for the road to innovation. In L. Thompson & H. Choi (Eds.), *Creativity and innovation in organizational teams* (pp. 69–86). Lawrence Erlbaum Associates.

Paulus, P. B., & Yang, H. C. (2000). Idea generation in groups: A basis for creativity in organizations. *Organizational Behavior and Human Decision Processing*, *82*, 76–87. https://doi.org/10.1006/obhd.2000.2888

Preece, C., & Çelik, H. (2023, May 31). AI can replicate human creativity in two key ways – But falls apart when asked to produce something truly new. *The Conversation*. https://www.christies.com/en/stories/a-collaboration-between-two-artists-one-human-one-a-machine-0cd01f4e232f4279a525a446d60d4cd1

Puccio, G. J., & Cabra, J. F. (2011). Idea generation and idea evaluation: Cognitive skills and deliberate practice. In M. D. Mumford's (Ed.), *Handbook of organizational creativity* (pp. 187–213). Elsevier.

Puccio, G. J., Murdock, M. C., & Mance, M. (2007). *Creative leadership: Skills that drive change*. Sage.

Reiter-Palmon, R., Kennel, V., dr Vreede, T., & de Vreede, G. (2018). The role of structure and instruction on creative idea evaluation and selection. In I. Lebuda & V. P. Glaveanu (Eds.), *The handbook of social creativity research* (pp. 209–224). Palgrave Press.

Reiter-Palmon, R., & Linnell, A. E. (2023). Team creativity and innovation: The effect of team creative cognition. In R. Reiter-Palmon & S. T. Hunter (Eds.), *Handbook of organizational creativity* (2nd ed., pp. 239–252). Academic Press. https://doi.org/10.1016/B978-0-323-91840-4.00023-2

Reiter-Palmon, R., & Murugavel, V. (2018). The effect of problem construction on team process and creativity. *Frontiers in Psychology*, *9*. https://doi.org/10.3389/fpsyg.2018.02098

Runco, M. A. (2023). AI can only produce artificial creativity. *Journal of Creativity*, *33*(3), 100063. https://doi.org/10.1016/j.yjoc.2023.100063

Sajja, P. S. (2021). Introduction to artificial intelligence. *Illustrated Computational Intelligence: Examples and Applications*, 1–25. https://doi.org/10.1007/978-981-15-9589-9_1

Shaikh, S. J., & Cruz, I. F. (2022). AI in human teams: Effects on technology use, members' interactions, and creative performance under time scarcity. *AI & Society, 28,* 1587–1600. https://doi.org/10.1007/s00146-021-01335-5.

Stevenson, C., Smal, I., Baas, M., Grasman, R., & van der Maas, H. (2022). *Putting GPT-3's creativity to the (alternative uses) test*. PsyArXiv. https://doi.org/10.48550/arXiv.2206.08932

Tversky, A., & Kahnemah, D. (1974). Judgment under uncertainty: Heuristics and biases. *Science*, *185*, 1124–1131. https://doi.org/10.1126/science.185.4157.1124

Vajjala, S., Majumder, B., Gupta, A., & Surana, H. (2020). *Practical natural language processing: A comprehensive guide to building real-world NLP systems*. O'Reilly Media.

VanGundy, A. B. (1995). Creativity in marketing. In J. Heilbrunn (Ed.), *Marketing encyclopedia: Issues and trends shaping the future* (pp. 31–39). NTC Business Books.

Verganti, R., Vendraminelli, L., & Iansitit, M. (2020). Innovation and design in the age of artificial intelligence. *Journal of Product and Innovation Management*, *37*(3), 212–227. https://doi.org/10.1111/jpim.12523

Wang, H., Fu, T., Du, Y., Gao, W., Huang, K., Liu, Z., Chandak, P., Liu, S., Van Katwyk, P., Deac, A., Anandkumar, A., Bergen, K., Gomes, C. P., Ho, S., Kohli, P., Lasenby, J., Leskovec, J., Liu, T.-Y., Manrai, A., ... & Zitnik, M. (2023). Scientific discovery in the age of artificial intelligence. *Nature*, *620*, 47–60. https://doi.org/10.1038/s41586-023-06221-2

Werner, J. (2024, March 20). Brainstorming with AI. *Forbes*. https://www.forbes.com/sites/johnwerner/2024/03/20/brainstorming-with-ai/

World Economic Forum. (2023, September 7). Forget problem-solving. In the age of AI, it's problem-finding that counts. *We Forum*. https://www.weforum.org/stories/2023/09/forget-problem-solving-in-the-age-of-ai-its-problem-finding-that-matters/

Zhang, R., McNeese, N. J., Freeman, G., Musick, G. (2021). "An ideal human": Expectations of AI teammates in human-AI teaming. *Proceedings of the ACM on human-computer interaction, 4*(CSCW3), 1–25. https://doi.org/10.1145/3432945.

PART 3

AI AND TEAM COGNITION

CHAPTER 6

AI-POWERED DYNAMIC HYBRID TEAMING

Adam Fouse, Gabriel Ganberg, Sylvain Bruni, Svitlana Volkova, Kara L. Orvis and Zachary Klinefelter

Aptima, Inc., USA

ABSTRACT

Organizations have long relied on teams to accomplish difficult tasks, and the nature of team membership has evolved and grown more complex. Given the current state of work, individuals may find themselves being members of many teams at once, and team membership may be dynamic, changing frequently as the work to be performed evolves. Teams may also be hybrid, with members geographically distributed across many locations, leading to reliance on technology not only for team communication and coordination but also for performing tasks within their teams. This chapter presents a vision for how artificial intelligence (AI) can change the nature of how these dynamic hybrid teams *perform work in these types of settings. We argue that a key function of AI in human–agent teams (HATs) is to act as an enabler of teamwork, acting as an artificial transactive memory system (ATMS) to address the challenges these teams face. In an ATMS, we can leverage AI to encode, store, and retrieve information about human and artificial team members, improve the flow of information between members, and help to increase productive collaboration. This chapter describes the types of teams and teamwork that this approach targets, the challenges faced by workers in these team settings, a general set of capabilities for AI systems designed to support these teams, and a*

AI in Teams: Research on Managing Groups and Teams, Volume 21, 97–114

Published under exclusive licence by Emerald Publishing Limited
ISSN: 1534-0856/doi:10.1108/S1534-085620260000021015

specific approach that leverages AI to provide that support. Examples from different work domains ground these approaches. Finally, we identify risks and future work required to realize the vision.

Keywords: Human–agent teams; dynamic hybrid teams; artificial intelligence; transactive memory systems; teamwork; multi-agent systems; team cognition

INTRODUCTION

Organizations have long relied on teams to accomplish difficult tasks. Given the nature of complex work, members of organizations often belong to many teams simultaneously. For example, a civilian office worker may be on both a sales team and a product team. Similarly, an intelligence officer may belong to a collection management team (i.e., focused on creating intelligence gathering plans) and a leadership team (i.e., making decisions about insights inferred from the intelligence collected). In these settings, workers collaborate with colleagues who have vastly different expertise and experience, along significantly different workflows and timescales, for various purposes. Membership in teams may also change frequently as work evolves and different expertise is required. Team members may also be distributed across multiple locations and time zones, relying on technology for team communication and coordination, as more organizations utilize talent across large, distributed (mixed virtual and multi-site) settings. These types of teaming environments provide agility in how organizations conduct work but also bring challenges that can increase the effort required of team members. Mechanisms used by stable, co-located teams, such as physical proximity in open workspaces or availability and responsiveness norms, may not be possible or effective in these environments.

This chapter presents a vision for how AI can change the nature of how these types of teams perform work. Historically, team leaders or team members have been responsible for managing and monitoring the team to ensure good team performance (Zaccaro et al., 2001). Given recent advancements, AI-powered agents can also act as enablers of teamwork, operating both behind the scenes to provide support and visibly as agents that provide guidance and assistance. This chapter will describe the types of teams and teamwork that we aim to support, the challenges faced by workers in these team settings, a general set of capabilities for AI systems designed to support these teams, and a specific approach that leverages AI to provide that support. Examples from different work domains will ground these approaches. Finally, we identify risks and future work required to realize the vision.

CHARACTERISTICS OF DYNAMIC HYBRID TEAMS

Collective work has historically relied on teams of humans working together. Traditional human teams have been defined as "a distinguishable set of two or more people who interact, dynamically, interdependently, and adaptively toward a common and valued goal/objective/mission, who have been assigned specific roles or functions to perform, and who have a limited life-span of membership" (Salas et al., 2006, p. 4). The performance of these human teams is dependent on team state (e.g., their level of trust, cohesion, and shared mental models) and processes (how they work together; Marks et al., 2001). These states and processes are influenced by individual knowledge, skills, and abilities (KSAs) of team members, the tools available to the team, and the nature and context of the work being performed.

Human work teams vary by size (Horwitz, 2005), composition (Harvey et al., 2009), structure (Zheng et al., 2010), and other factors. It is well supported that team attributes affect team performance (e.g., Horwitz, 2005) and the requirements for team states and processes vary according to team characteristics. Therefore, it is often helpful to consider interventions for specific types of teams. This chapter will describe how AI can assist what we refer to as *dynamic hybrid teams*. These teams are dynamic in the sense that they are defined by fluid membership, and hybrid in the sense that they are physically distributed, requiring their work to be mediated by digital tools for communication and collaboration. HATs are one form of these teams, but dynamic hybrid teams may or may not include AI agents as team members; this definition also encompasses human-only teams (Morris et al., 2024). These teams are similar to the "4-D" teams described by Haas and Mortensen (2016).

Dynamic hybrid teams have a set of characteristics that make team performance particularly challenging. A primary feature of dynamic hybrid teams is dynamic membership. Unlike traditional teams that are often stable over the course of a project, dynamic hybrid teams frequently scale and adapt according to the changing needs of a project, with individuals joining or leaving throughout the team's lifespan. A related characteristic is the fact that team members often belong to multiple teams simultaneously. This can mean that each person serves in different roles across different projects, bringing varied expertise and perspectives to each team. Although multiple team membership increases the diversity of knowledge within teams and across organizations, it also introduces challenges related to coordination and competing priorities.

Geographical distribution is another feature of dynamic hybrid teams. Team members are often spread across various locations, working from different time zones and performing tasks at different times of the day. This dispersion can create challenges, particularly in terms of real-time collaboration and awareness of task status. As a result of geographic distribution, much of the work of dynamic hybrid teams is mediated by digital tools. Asynchronous work is supported via collaboration tools such as Microsoft Teams and Google Docs that allow multiple people to access documents from multiple locations. Tools such as Teams, Slack, and Zoom support synchronous communication via videoconferencing and asynchronous communication via text chat. Collaboration platforms, project management software, and shared digital workspaces help team members communicate, share information, and coordinate their efforts. This reliance on digital tools enables distributed teams to work together efficiently, but using these tools also adds extra cognitive demand on team members.

Although the focus of this chapter is on AI supporting teamwork, it is important to acknowledge that AI agents are becoming increasingly capable and can perform some tasks independently. AI tools can automatically synthesize and summarize content, perform data analysis, monitor for anomalies, and streamline workflows. Agentic forms of AI can perform these tasks autonomously and help make team task assignment decisions. Although the purpose of this chapter is not to address the design or implementation of taskwork-performing AI agents, the challenges we identify below may be amplified when AI team members are added to teams. The approach we describe addresses these challenges in human-only teams but may provide even greater benefit in HATs.

CHALLENGES OF DYNAMIC HYBRID TEAMS

Dynamic hybrid teams can suffer from issues related to team cognition (shared mental models on how to accomplish work) and coordination. Traditionally, team states and processes are managed by the team leader or team members (Zaccaro et al., 2001). Our efforts, however, focus on moving some of that management to AI tools and teammates.

First, we describe the challenges faced by such teams, which will be used to guide the ways by which AI can support team states and processes. To ground identification of these challenges in data, a team of human factors and software engineers conducted an analysis to identify, aggregate, and rank end-user requirements that could be supported through HATs. As part of this analysis, we identified 50 applied research projects in our company that addressed HATs across domains including military decision making, intelligence analysis (Bruni et al., 2023; Mullins et al., 2020), missile defense, drone operations (Bruni et al., 2011), and communications and tasking in intensive care units. The analysis drew on artifacts from these projects including the output of human factors analyses such as cognitive task analysis (CTA; Crandall, 2006), hybrid cognitive task analysis (hCTA; Nehme et al., 2006), and software prototypes or products. We then interviewed the staff of 29 of these 50 projects, including experts in human factors and cognitive engineering, design and user experience, and software engineering using a standardized questionnaire targeting project goals, AI agent(s), software implementation and testing, and general reflections on outcomes. All answers were recorded in a structured database and a comprehensive data analysis extracted insights in the form of user requirements and system capabilities (built, planned, or desired), which were mapped to generalized requirements for what an engineering instantiation would entail.

Through this data collection and analysis, we identified several challenges that are faced by dynamic hybrid teams. These challenges span team composition, team organization, and task execution.

Team Composition

Significant logistical challenges arise when attempting to select team members. Identifying individuals with the right expertise can be difficult because such information is often limited or fragmented across organizations (Hong & Page, 2024; Orvis & Zaccaro, 2008). Skillsets may not be centrally documented, complete, or up to date, making it challenging to assemble teams that align with project needs. Exacerbating the problem of identifying who has the skills to do the work is the difficulty in ascertaining individual availability, especially when individuals are part of multiple project teams tackling different projects with dynamic demands on time, making it unclear who has the capacity to take on new tasks.

Task Alignment

Once teams are formed, another challenge is assigning specific roles and tasks within the team (Feigh & Pritchett, 2014; IJtsma et al., 2019). Without prior experience working together, team members may not have a shared mental model of the knowledge and skills of their team members and may not know who is best suited to complete specific tasks. Familiarity within teams can be a critical asset, but when teams are assembled dynamically, familiarity may be difficult to achieve. Lack of team members' detailed understanding of each other's expertise can hinder task distribution. General descriptions of roles such as "data scientist" or "software developer" may not provide the granularity necessary to assign tasks that precisely match each team member's abilities. Recommendations for tasking may be based on limited or high-level information, which can sometimes lead to misaligned tasking.

Shared Cognition

The distributed nature of hybrid teams also makes it difficult to develop shared awareness of individual KSAs during planning and task execution (Andrews et al., 2023; Schelble et al., 2022). In co-located teams, members naturally develop an understanding of who knows what and who is responsible for what. This shared understanding across the team is called a transactive memory system. Robust transactive memory systems are more difficult to achieve in distributed teams and in teams with dynamic membership in which the lack of face-to-face interaction and informal communication channels hinders the natural development of shared knowledge about individual expertise. As teams grow and change dynamically, with members joining and leaving projects frequently, maintaining a clear sense of each member's role and expertise becomes increasingly complex. Maintaining awareness of information across multiple digital tools also presents a challenge. Hybrid teams often rely on a wide variety of platforms – such as email, chat applications, shared documents, issue trackers, and project management software – to communicate and coordinate. Information about project progress, task assignments, and team coordination is frequently spread across these tools, making it difficult to form a coherent picture of the team's status and plan. This fragmentation of communication can result in team coordination errors such as missed deadlines, duplicated efforts, or misunderstandings about who is responsible for certain tasks. Even when tools are used to aggregate information across platforms, staying informed about the overall status of the team's efforts remains a challenge.

AI Integration

Another significant challenge is the integration of AI systems as part of the team (Bruni, 2022; Bruni et al., 2023; Volkova et al., 2024). Human team members often have varying levels of experience with and understanding of what AI can and cannot do. This discrepancy can lead to inefficiencies, as some may overestimate AI's capabilities, assigning it tasks it cannot perform, while others may underutilize the technology (McDuff et al., 2025; Niraula et al., 2025; Tu et al., 2025). Furthermore, AI itself is dynamic, with its capabilities changing as models evolve or new datasets become available. As a result, human team members may struggle to keep pace with these changes, leading to mismatches between their expectations and what AI can deliver.

Balancing Competing Objectives

Finally, hybrid teams must balance short-term and long-term objectives, as well as individual and team-level goals (Kozlowski & Ilgen, 2006). In the short term, teams perform most effectively when they are composed of people who have worked together before and have familiarity with each other's skills. This allows them to execute tasks efficiently using their existing knowledge. However, long-term success requires that teams and individuals continue to learn and grow. Building teams that bring together new people and encourage the development of new skills can expand individual expertise and organizational networks, even though task performance may decrease in the short term as a result. Balancing these immediate and future objectives is a delicate challenge, one ignored by many automation-based team selection approaches.

SUPPORTING DYNAMIC TEAMING THROUGH ATMSs

Our approach utilizes an artificial transactive memory system (ATMS) as a foundation for developing a set of system-level capabilities to address the challenges faced by dynamic hybrid teams. The concept of ATMS draws on research on transactive memory systems in teamwork. In human teams, a transactive memory system exists across team members, providing shared awareness of individual knowledge and capabilities (e.g., Argote & Ren, 2012). The ATMS concept also builds on previous research suggesting that support for inter-member transactive team processes would be an effective role for AI agents (Gupta & Woolley, 2021). In an ATMS, we can leverage AI agents to encode, store, and retrieve information about team members (both human and artificial), improve the flow of information between members, and help to increase productive collaboration.

These automated systems should combine information about team members, the work to be accomplished, and the digital tools available as part of the system. Information about team members may be declarative, as in information that individuals manually specify about themselves in a profile (e.g., level of knowledge or skills), or inferred, such as skills that are represented in the work products that a team member produces. Information about work should include the specific tasks and their interdependencies; task-relevant information; and information about

Table 6.1. Dynamic Hybrid Team Challenges Addressed by ATMS.

Challenges of Dynamic Hybrid Teams	Capabilities Enabled by ATMS
Team composition	• Inference about the KSAs of organizational members based on their observed activity and stated experience • Incorporation of task-performing AI agents alongside human team members
Task alignment	• Reasoning over the KSAs of team members in combination with their availability
Shared cognition	• Observation of team member digital activities and identification of connections within tasks across team members
AI integration	• Incorporation of AI abilities into the same model for task alignment as for human KSAs
Balancing competing objectives	• Incorporation of task performance goals and desired skill development into team composition recommendations • User-editable guidance for tuning how this balance is achieved

available tools, how they can be applied, their level of automation, and how information can be conveyed from tools to team members. Table 6.1 presents a general set of ATMS capabilities and how they address the challenges of dynamic hybrid teams discussed above.

IMPLEMENTING AN ATMS

Implementations of some aspects of the general capabilities identified as part of an ATMS approach have been created before, such as in context-aware computing (Dey et al., 2001; Mullins et al., 2020). These approaches, which leveraged a combination of techniques such as graph analytics, machine learning, and statistical measures of relevance, show promise but have limitations (e.g., they require a significant quantity of data up-front, are brittle to new domains, and have limited transparency to end users). Furthermore, although graphical data representations tend to be more understandable to humans than many other computable representations (Gaur et al., 2021), they do not support seamless communication.

Key to the successful implementation of an ATMS is the adoption of data representations that both humans and AI can understand and act upon. Additionally, the system must be capable of recognizing and adapting to the dynamically changing contexts of team members, including moving between different levels of contextual abstraction. Recent advancements in natural language processing, including large language models (LLMs) and techniques for their application, enable the creation of systems with these features. These advancements allow for natural language to be used not only as a communication method but also as the common data representation, mirroring how humans work together. In the next section, we describe how LLMs and structured data representations can be combined in a multi-agent systems approach to implement an ATMS.

Application of LLMs and Structured Knowledge Graph Representations

LLMs enable communication with AI through natural language text and generally serve as context-driven performers of tasks (OpenAI, 2023). They generate written content and computer program code and can invoke additional actions through function calling, a specialized form of program generation and execution (Schick et al., 2023). LLMs can also support graceful adaptation to new domains with sparse data by leveraging pretrained foundation knowledge (Li et al., 2023), are trained on massive amounts of text data, and are fine-tuned on instruction-following tasks, which enable them to predict text sequences and perform sophisticated operations. Their effectiveness is closely tied to managing a "context window" – the amount of information they can retain at once while processing. Techniques such as prompt engineering can help prioritize and clarify key instructions for more precise outputs, yet challenges like hallucinations, where the LLM generates fictitious, incorrect, or nonsensical information, remain.

Retrieval augmented generation (RAG; Lewis et al., 2020) supports incorporation of team- and domain-specific knowledge as it becomes available by using search techniques, semantic similarity, and graph traversal to dynamically construct the LLM's context. RAG provides a dynamic method of managing context for LLMs by grounding responses in external data sources. It operates similarly to how a parent might respond to a child's question about why the sky is blue, that is, relying on their existing knowledge or quickly searching for the correct answer online before rephrasing it for the child. In this analogy, RAG performs this search step by retrieving relevant information to ground the generated response in accurate, up-to-date knowledge.

Knowledge graph-based RAG (KG-RAG) extends the basic RAG model by linking data at multiple levels of abstraction through a structured knowledge graph (Pan et al., 2024). In KG-RAG, nodes represent source data, such as team member profiles or task-relevant documents, and derived nodes capture task-specific summaries or insights derived from those sources, with explicit links back to their origins. When handling a query, the system retrieves nodes with the highest semantic relevance, often at a more abstract level, and then recursively traverses the graph to pull in the detailed source data linked to these summaries.

This recursive retrieval process allows KG-RAG to navigate seamlessly between different levels of abstraction, ensuring that both high-level insights and granular data are considered when generating a response. It mirrors the way episodic memories (specific experiences) are distilled into semantic memories (generalized knowledge) in human cognition, allowing for more nuanced and context-aware responses. This approach not only improves the breadth of knowledge retrieval but also ensures a more balanced synthesis by considering multiple layers of information connected through the graph.

Natural Language User Profiles

KG-RAG can enable instantiation of an ATMS through the implementation of natural language user profiles (Radlinski et al., 2022). These represent the KSAs and experience of users in the form of natural language text. Compared to previous work in the field of context-aware computing, which often relied on noisy observations that were instantiated as links and nodes within a graph (Mullins et al., 2020), natural language user profiles increase transparency because they are readable and editable by both humans and LLMs.

Existing work in natural language user profiles has focused on relatively well-defined tasks such as media recommendations (Friedman et al., 2023). In these cases, initial profiles can be generated from activity to summarize an individual's preferences in natural language, which the individual can then scrutinize and correct. This work suggests the use of a single profile that represents an individual, although there are two potential problems with using a single profile for dynamic hybrid teaming. First, an individual's role, tasks, and skills employed may vary greatly across tasks. For example, a user experience engineer may act as a visual designer in one setting and as a front-end software engineer in another. Second, a person's skills and interests may change over time but at multiple time scales. For example, a software engineer may have experience with a range of programming languages, approaches, and libraries, but only have active working knowledge of a particular subset.

To address these potential problems, we use layered or hierarchical user profiles, leveraging the connection inherent to the knowledge graph to combine profiles with general (e.g., skills and past work) and specific (e.g., role and tasking on a project) information. This approach supports the varied roles that people may play in a dynamic teaming environment and increases alignment between user needs and the support the system provides.

Multi-agent Systems Approach

To instantiate natural language user profiles across a team and create the ATMS capabilities listed in Table 6.1, we take a multi-agent systems approach in which multiple autonomous agents perform tasks independently, with the overall functioning of the system emerging from their coordination and communication. In the context of expanding LLM applications, multi-agent systems have gained prominence as a way to amplify the capabilities of individual agents through LLM-driven control flows (Wu et al., 2024).

Multi-agent systems also enable the use of specialized agents, each with distinct roles, that have access to specific tools or data or represent particular perspectives. Each individual agent performs its tasks sequentially, planning and executing steps in a specific order. However, tasks can be parallelized when subtasks are dispatched to multiple specialized agents that can complete them concurrently. By distributing tasks among specialist agents, the system becomes more efficient and accurate while ensuring that different viewpoints and methods are considered. This structure aligns with the adaptability and flexibility needed for dynamic hybrid teaming, where roles and tasks can change frequently, and teams must be able to integrate and process information from diverse sources quickly and effectively.

For an ATMS multi-agent system, different agent types play distinct roles to support dynamic teamwork: **Profile agents**, **Orchestrator agents**, and **Executor**

agents. Each agent interacts with human team members and other agents to ensure that tasks are assigned, coordinated, and executed effectively.

Profile agents are matched to individual users and are responsible for maintaining up-to-date natural language user profiles that contain structured, human-readable information about an individual's KSAs, past activities, past collaborators, and preferences. Profile agents can be queried by the users themselves or by Orchestrator agents, providing a key resource for decision making about team roles and task allocation.

Orchestrator agents coordinate team activities by leveraging both human and AI resources. They gather data from Profile agents to assess each team member's capabilities, preferences, and workloads. This enables them to identify the best individuals or AI agents for specific tasks. Orchestrator agents also structure teamwork based on predefined strategies or theories of team dynamics, ensuring that tasks and team structures are aligned for optimal performance. They also manage Executor agents, ensuring that the AI components of the team are effectively leveraged for task completion.

Executor agents perform the actual task execution, either autonomously or with human guidance. These agents handle tasks such as content generation, problem solving, or other AI-driven processes. Many commercially available LLM-based agents such as ChatGPT fit into this category. Executor agents can act on their own or follow instructions from human teammates or Orchestrator agents, pulling in relevant data, tools, and capabilities as needed.

ATMS multi-agent systems operate via continuous agent–agent communication whereby Profile, Orchestrator, and Executor agents exchange information to ensure task progress and proper coordination. Real-time inputs from operational environments, external databases, and ongoing activities feed into this communication loop, allowing the system to adapt dynamically to new information. As a result, tasks are efficiently distributed, leveraging both human expertise and AI capabilities, to achieve team objectives.

This approach to instantiation of an ATMS addresses the challenges noted in Table 6.1. Profile agents represent individual users and can be queried and reasoned over by Orchestrator agents to support team composition decisions. As new members join an existing team, or a new team is brought together, Orchestrator agents can support task alignment by reasoning over the information in profiles to identify the best fit within the team. Orchestrator agents can also recommend Executor agents that are available to take on or assist with tasks. As team members perform their tasks, Profile agents can provide information to other Profile agents about updated task status, which can then be used to provide relevant updates or recommend further discussion or collaboration for aligned tasks.

Profile Construction and Maintenance

A critical function of Profile agents is construction and maintenance of detailed natural language profiles for each user. This process begins with profile construction, which aggregates data from various sources including system interactions, team communications, external inputs, and profile information explicitly stated by users up-front. Profiles are divided into three sections: long-term (stable aspects of individual KSAs such as professional background and accumulated experience), role-specific (individual skills and capabilities in relation to a specific role within the team), and task-specific (current tasks the individual is performing and specific skills they are applying to those tasks). Profile sections are stored in a natural language format and dynamically updated through agents' activities and their interactions with team members. Profile agents continuously gather data from user interactions with systems, team communications, and task performance, which are stored as episodic information with logs of interactions and activities. Over time, profile agents summarize episodic memory to update the KSAs in each section, similar to how human memory uses episodic memory to form generalized autobiographical knowledge (Conway, 2005). Profile agents also periodically prompt users to update or reflect on their profiles, validating that updated profile information remains in alignment with users' own knowledge and preferences, and giving users an opportunity to manually contribute written information about themselves for incorporation within the overall profile.

This recursive process of reflection and update allows the system to maintain an accurate, up-to-date representation of each user's capabilities and preferences. These profiles are essential for Orchestrator agents to make precise task assignments and role identifications, ensuring that tasks are aligned with the most appropriate human or AI resource in the team. The system's use of hierarchical, layered profiles also supports the dynamic nature of hybrid teaming, in which roles and tasks evolve frequently.

POTENTIAL APPLICATIONS

The notional examples discussed below help illustrate how the ATMS approach to AI-enabled dynamic teaming works and provides benefit. For these examples, which are drawn from our experience, we address two team configuration categories: (1) Teams that consist of human teammates supported by an AI-enabled collaboration platform in which humans are the primary task performers and the AI mediates human teammate interactions and (2) teams that employ task-performing agents that can generate content, perform analyses, or create code. For the latter, AI agents can be represented within the system using the same approach, including representing the capabilities of agents using natural language and incorporating their abilities into team- and task-composition decisions.

Example 1: Intelligence Analysis

Intelligence analysts engage in integrative knowledge work. Researchers studying intelligence analysis and similar domains have described the work as a sensemaking process, with intersecting information foraging and sensemaking activity loops (Pirolli & Card, 2005). The activities involved in intelligence analysis include defining a problem, breaking it into component parts, searching for information to support or refute claims, developing hypotheses based on the information found, and drawing conclusions based on the strength of the evidence aligned with multiple hypotheses. Thorough analysis can rarely be performed by a single individual and often requires collaboration with other analysts who have expertise in specialized domains. Furthermore, modern intelligence collection generates a far greater quantity of information than analysts have the time and ability to analyze, resulting in information overload (Brueggemann, 2008), and the security required for intelligence analysis often results in information silos.

A team of intelligence analysts could be supported by an ATMS-based system that suggests not only relevant information, but also human and AI collaborators and resources, and understands how and when to form those connections. The system could queue the most relevant documents and identify excerpts based on user needs. As analysis proceeds, draft analytic products could be produced automatically. Finally, collaboration could be facilitated by recommending not only other human team members who have worked on similar problems (ideally those who have used different approaches) but also AI agents that may support work. For example, the Construct–Opine–Reconstruct–Approve (CORA) process (Kane et al., 2026) constructs teams of agents to support analysis processes, with feedback and approval provided by human team members. An ATMS-based system could support identification of agents and alignment with human analysts, and the outputs from CORA could serve to update profiles within the ATMS.

Example 2: Research and Development Organizations

Many organizations that perform research and development experience frictions like those in intelligence analysis, with individuals often being involved in multiple project-based efforts involving different subsets of people and inadequate mechanisms for knowledge sharing. In many cases, efficient work involves integration of knowledge about internal resources such as artifacts from past projects, external resources such as techniques from research literature, team members' tasking, and day-to-day changes in working documents (Davenport & Prusak, 1998).

To support these types of organizations, an ATMS-based system could develop an understanding of the work of a project team based on the artifacts associated with the project including proposals and reports, source code, and accessible conversations such as those in public channels in collaboration tools. This understanding could be combined with team member profiles to recommend relevant projects, staff with availability to support a project, and others who have worked on similar problems, and to notify employees of highly relevant information they may have missed.

Example 3: Medical Teams

Healthcare providers need to coordinate schedules and information, interact with patients at different times, and coordinate to provide quality care. Information may exist in numerous forms such as in electronic medical record systems and care may be constrained by provider availability, facility availability, and financial constraints such as insurance approvals. In settings such as hospitals, shift changes further exacerbate the need to coordinate information. In addition, medical teams experience numerous pain points in their interactions with the systems that they use to perform their work, such as critical data existing in many different forms and levels of importance, leading to cognitive overload and many different systems being used to manage care and enter and access information, leading to inefficient system management overhead and reduced time for direct patient engagement (Klerings et al., 2015; Reddy & Jansen, 2008).

To address these issues, an ATMS-based system could use information about staff tasking and schedules to recommend staff reallocation to minimize burnout and risk to patients, offload documentation and menial tasks, share relevant and understandable information proactively with patients, and automatically provide explanations of care plans.

Example 4: Disaster Response Teams

Disaster response often involves people from dozens of organizations coordinating in real time, responding to rapidly changing situations, and needing to exchange information (Waring et al., 2020). Response teams have many of the characteristics of dynamic hybrid teams in that they are often geographically dispersed, have members with limited familiarity with each other, rely on digital tools to aid in coordination, and may require new team members to be brought in and rapidly be brought up to speed.

To address these issues, an ATMS-based system could represent team members with information about their areas of expertise and experience. As new team members are added, tailored information could be provided to rapidly integrate them with existing team structures, and their benefits to the team could be highlighted to existing members. As new information becomes available from disparate sources, that information could be routed to team members based on their tasks and experience. Finally, information gaps could be proactively identified and highlighted to people on the team.

RISKS

Although the approach and implementation described in this chapter offer potentially significant advantages (Butler et al., 2023) for supporting the work of teams, they are not without risks (Burton et al., 2024). These risks are important to identify and mitigate if this approach to supporting dynamic hybrid teams is implemented and deployed in operational systems.

User Acceptance

The first category of risk is related to user acceptance. Users may perceive the data requirements for an ATMS, especially within a hierarchical corporate environment, as creating a "big brother" type of system, which may lead to resistance to system adoption. One mitigation is for the ATMS to have explicit and transparent data-access policies, indicating which information is accessed by the system and how it is incorporated. For example, a policy that treats ATMS access the same as team member access allows for consistent rules to be applied, such as inclusion of team-accessible messages but exclusion of direct messages between individual team members. Natural language user profiles also help to mitigate this risk by enabling users to understand how the information is used to represent them within the system. A second factor in acceptance lies in the social agency such systems modify. ATMS-based systems may impact the authority and reputation of some users, diminishing their agency in the task, workflow, team, and organization. These factors are objectionable to certain users, which can lead them to ignore the system and undermine its use.

Data Accessibility

After data access policies are defined, another risk comes from the need for data to be technically accessible. These types of systems are designed to operate in coordination with existing systems. Application programming interfaces (APIs) need to exist for data to be read and reasoned over, and organizational cybersecurity policies need to be defined to allow access. In addition, interaction with end users may take place through other tools so APIs and cybersecurity policies need to allow the system to communicate with and contribute information back to the team.

Data Security

Data security is another risk, both from the perspective of security restrictions and security of the data. Most organizations have data that are accessible to some employees but not others. Within government spaces, these restrictions may include data at multiple levels of classification. An ATMS may not have access to required information or may need to have special processing techniques in place to account for data access policies within an organization. Collecting and reasoning about data also introduce cybersecurity risks by creating additional points at which security could be compromised.

Team Member Impact

Risks also need to be considered part of the larger socio-technical system (Yu et al., 2023). Data collected and reasoned over by the system could be exploited by malign organizations to negatively impact the lives of the human team members. Furthermore, there are concerns that the added capabilities of AI systems could be used to eliminate jobs or worsen workers' experience such as via constant surveillance of work habits.

Cost

Finally, a risk to ATMS system implementation is cost. Although progress is steadily being made toward increasing the efficiency of large AI models and thus reducing costs, the added financial cost of such systems may be significant.

CONCLUSION

In this chapter, we have focused on how AI can support dynamic hybrid teams. These teams are characterized by dynamic membership, with members joining and leaving throughout the team's lifespan; by members that have membership in multiple teams; by being distributed geographically; and by the team's work being mediated by digital tools. We identified challenges faced by these teams and identified AI-enabled approaches that are primarily targeted at supporting their teamwork. Central to this approach is the concept of an ATMS in which information about the expertise, experience, and tasking of team members is inferred, represented, and reasoned over as part of the system. This approach is enabled by the creation of a multi-agent architecture that combines recent advancements in the development and applications of LLMs with techniques for incorporating structured data about the team and its tasks. This combination allows for vastly improved natural language understanding and alignment of system and human representations.

This chapter has presented a vision for this approach and existing or ongoing research, but future work is required to fully realize this vision. This includes implementation of the ATMS concept with actual data, precise definition of team orchestration approaches, and reasoning about team dynamics. Although the approach described in this chapter primarily focuses on asynchronous interaction, expanding it to include synchronous collaboration will further increase the types of team activity that could be supported. In addition, the ATMS approach needs to be tested in realistic environments.

The risks with this approach that we identified in this chapter are likely, but the degree to which they impact the effectiveness of a system and whether the mitigations of those risks work as anticipated can only be determined through experimentation and user testing.

Finally, this approach opens opportunities for future research, including investigating the impact of mission criticality on the value and use of AI to support such teams, researching the tradeoffs along dimensions such as synchronous versus asynchronous collaboration and proactive versus reactive support, identifying the impact of this approach on task-performing agent design, and exploring the transferability of AI support for such teams across domains.

ACKNOWLEDGMENTS

The authors would like to thank Jared Freeman for his guidance on this approach and comments on this manuscript.

REFERENCES

Andrews, R. W., Lilly, J. M., Srivastava, D., & Feigh, K. M. (2023). The role of shared mental models in human-AI teams: A theoretical review. *Theoretical Issues in Ergonomics Science*, *24*(2), 129–175.

Argote, L., & Ren, Y. (2012). Transactive memory systems: A microfoundation of dynamic capabilities. *Journal of Management Studies*, *49*(8), 1375–1382.

Brueggemann, C. E. (2008). *Mitigating information overload: The impact of context-based approach to the design of tools for intelligence analysts* [Doctoral dissertation, Naval Postgraduate School].

Bruni, S. (2022). Introducing PATI, the Pareto Analysis for Technology Insertion, a human-centered methodology to identify and prioritize innovation in complex systems. *Proceedings of the 13th international conference on applied human factors and ergonomics* (AHFE).

Bruni, S., Freiman, M., & Riddle, K. (2023). Beyond the tool vs. teammate debate: Exploring the sidekick metaphor in designing human-AI dyads. *Proceedings of the 14th international conference on applied human factors and ergonomics* (AHFE).

Bruni, S., Schurr, N., Cooke, N., Riordan, B., & Freeman, J. (2011). Designing a mixed-initiative decision-support system for multi-UAS mission planning. *Proceedings of the Human Factors and Ergonomics Society Annual Meeting*, *55*(1), 21–25.

Burton, J. W., Lopez-Lopez, E., Hechtlinger, S., Rahwan, Z., Aeschbach, S., Bakker, M. A., Becker, J. A., Berditchevskaia, A., Berger, J., Brinkmann, L., Flek, L., Herzog, S. M., Huang, S., Kapoor, S., Narayanan, A., Nussberger, A.-M., Yasseri, T., Nickl, P., Almaatouq, A., Hahn, U., Kurvers, R. H. J. M.… & Hertwig, R. (2024). How large language models can reshape collective intelligence. *Nature Human Behaviour*, *8*, 1643–1655.

Butler, J., Jaffe, S., Baym, N., Czerwinski, M., Iqbal, S., Nowak, K., Rintel, R., Sellen, A., Vorvoreanu, M., Hecht, B., & Teevan, J. (Eds.). (2023). *Microsoft new future of work report 2023*. Microsoft Research Tech Report MSR-TR-2023-34. https://aka.ms/nfw2023

Conway, M. A. (2005). Memory and the self. *Journal of Memory and Language*, *53*(4), 594–628.

Crandall, B. (2006). *Working minds: A practitioner's guide to cognitive task analysis*. MIT Press.

Davenport, T. H., & Prusak, L. (1998). *Working knowledge: How organizations manage what they know*. Harvard Business Press.

Dey, A. K., Abowd, G. D., & Salber, D. (2001). A conceptual framework and a toolkit for supporting the rapid prototyping of context-aware applications. *Human–Computer Interaction*, *16*(2–4), 97–166.

Feigh, K. M., & Pritchett, A. R. (2014). Requirements for effective function allocation: A critical review. *Journal of Cognitive Engineering and Decision Making*, *8*(1), 23–32.

Friedman, L., Ahuja, S., Allen, D., Tan, Z., Sidahmed, H., Long, C., Xie, J., Schubiner, G., Patel, A., Lara, H., Chu, B., Chen, Z., & Tiwari, M. (2023). *Leveraging large language models in conversational recommender systems*. arXiv. http://arxiv.org/abs/2305.07961

Gaur, M., Faldu, K., & Sheth, A. (2021). Semantics of the black-box: Can knowledge graphs help make deep learning systems more interpretable and explainable? *IEEE Internet Computing*, *25*(1), 51–59.

Gupta, P., & Woolley, A. W. (2021). Articulating the role of artificial intelligence in collective intelligence: A transactive systems framework. *Proceedings of the Human Factors and Ergonomics Society Annual Meeting*, *65*(1), 670–674.

Haas, M., & Mortensen, M. (2016). The secrets of great teamwork. *Harvard Business Review*, *94*(6), 70–76.

Harvey, M., Fisher, R., McPhail, R., & Moeller, M. (2009). Globalization and its impact on global managers' decision processes. *Human Resource Development International*, *12*, 353–370.

Hong, L., & Page, S. E. (2024). Individual selection criteria for optimal team composition. *Theory and Decision*, *96*(4), 607–626.

Horwitz, S. K. (2005). The compositional impact of team diversity on performance: Theoretical considerations. *Human Resource Development Review*, *4*, 219–245.

IJtsma, M., Ma, L. M., Pritchett, A. R., & Feigh, K. M. (2019). Computational methodology for the allocation of work and interaction in human-robot teams. *Journal of Cognitive Engineering and Decision Making*, *13*(4), 221–241.

Kane, A. A., Diep, M. M., Porter, A. A., & Paletz, & S. B. F. (2026). Operationalizing and optimizing human-agent teaming for knowledge work. In S. B. F Paletz & S. B. Dubrow (Eds.), *AI in teams* (pp. 117–133). Emerald Publishing.

Klerings, I., Weinhandl, A. S., & Thaler, K. J. (2015). Information overload in healthcare: Too much of a good thing? *Zeitschrift für Evidenz, Fortbildung und Qualität im Gesundheitswesen*, *109*(4–5), 285–290.

Kozlowski, S. W. J., & Ilgen, D. R. (2006). Enhancing the effectiveness of work groups and teams. *Psychological Science in the Public Interest, 7*(3), 77–124.

Lewis, P., Perez, E., Piktus, A., Petroni, F., Karpukhin, V., Goyal, N., Kuttler, H., Lewis, M., Yih, W., Rocktaschel, T., Riedel, S., & Kiela, D. (2020). Retrieval-augmented generation for knowledge-intensive NLP tasks. *Advances in Neural Information Processing Systems, 33*, 9459–9474.

Li, Y., Wu, Y., Li, J., & Liu, S. (2023). Prompting large language models for zero-shot domain adaptation in speech recognition. 2023 *IEEE automatic speech recognition and understanding workshop* (ASRU) (pp. 1–8).

Marks, M. A., Mathieu, J. E., & Zaccaro, S. J. (2001). A temporally based framework and taxonomy of team processes. *Academy of Management Review, 26*(3), 356–376.

McDuff, D., Schaekermann, M., Tu, T., Palepu, A., Wang, A., Garrison, J., Singhal, K., Sharma, Y., Azizi, S., Kulkarni, K., Hou, L., Cheng, Y., Liu, Y., Mahdavi, S. S., Prakash, S., Pathak, A., Semturs, C., Patel, S., Webster, D. R., … Natarajan, V. (2025). Towards accurate differential diagnosis with large language models. *Nature, 642*(8067), 451–457. https://doi.org/10.1038/s41586-025-08869-4

Morris, M. R., Bernstein, M. S., Bigham, J. P., Bruckman, A. S., & Monroy-Hernández, A. (2024). Is human-AI interaction CSCW? *Companion publication of the 2024 conference on computer-supported cooperative work and social computing* (pp. 95–97). https://doi.org/10.1145/3678884.3689134

Mullins, R., Fouse, A., Ganberg, G., & Schurr, N. (2020). Practice makes perfect: Lesson learned from five years of trial and error building context-aware systems. *53rd Hawaii international conference on systems science* (pp. 1–10).

Nehme, C. E., Scott, S. D., Cummings, M. L., & Furusho, C. Y. (2006). Generating requirements for futuristic heterogeneous unmanned systems. *Proceedings of the Human Factors and Ergonomics Society Annual Meeting, 50*(3), 235–239.

Niraula, D., Cuneo, K. C., Dinov, I. D., Gonzalez, B. D., Jamaluddin, J. B., Jin, J. J., Luo, Y., Matuszak, M. M., Ten Haken, R. K., Bryant, A. K., Dilling, T. J., Dykstra, M. P., Frakes, J. M., Liveringhouse, C. L., Miller, S. R., Mills, M. N., Palm, R. F., Regan, S. N., Rishi, A., … El Naqa, I. (2025). Intricacies of human–AI interaction in dynamic decision-making for precision oncology. *Nature Communications, 16*(1), 1138. https://doi.org/10.1038/s41467-024-55259-x

OpenAI. (2023). *GPT-4 technical report*. arXiv. https://arxiv.org/abs/2303.08774

Orvis, K. L., & Zaccaro, S. J. (2008). Team composition and member selection. *The handbook of high performance virtual teams: A toolkit for collaborating across boundaries* (pp. 243–264).

Pan, S., Luo, L., Wang, Y., Chen, C., Wang, J., & Wu, X. (2024). Unifying large language models and knowledge graphs: A roadmap. *IEEE Transactions on Knowledge and Data Engineering, 36*(7), 3580–3599.

Pirolli, P., & Card, S. (2005). The sensemaking process and leverage points for analyst technology as identified through cognitive task analysis. *Proceedings of International Conference on Intelligence Analysis, 5*, 2–4.

Radlinski, F., Balog, K., Diaz, F., Dixon, L., & Wedin, B. (2022). On natural language user profiles for transparent and scrutable recommendation. *Proceedings of the 45th international ACM SIGIR conference on research and development in information retrieval* (pp. 2863–2874).

Reddy, M. C., & Jansen, B. J. (2008). A model for understanding collaborative information behavior in context: A study of two healthcare teams. *Information Processing & Management, 44*(1), 256–273.

Salas, E., Rosen, M. A., Burke, C. S., Goodwin, G. F., & Fiore, S. M. (2006). The making of a dream team: When expert teams do best. In K. A. Ericsson, N. Charness, P. Feltovich, & R. R. Hoffman (Eds.), *Cambridge handbook of expertise and expert performance* (pp. 439–456). Cambridge University Press.

Schelble, B. G., Flathmann, C., McNeese, N. J., Freeman, G., & Mallick, R. (2022). Let's think together! Assessing shared mental models, performance, and trust in human-agent teams. *Proceedings of the ACM on Human-Computer Interaction, 6*(GROUP), 1–29.

Schick, T., Dwivedi-Yu, J., Dessì, R., Raileanu, R., Lomeli, M., Hambro, E., Zettlemoyer, L., Cancedda, N., & Scialom, T. (2023). Toolformer: Language models can teach themselves to use tools. *Advances in Neural Information Processing Systems, 36*, 68539–68551.

Tu, T., Schaekermann, M., Palepu, A., Saab, K., Freyberg, J., Tanno, R., Wang, A., Li, B., Amin, M., Cheng, Y., Vedadi, E., Tomasev, N., Azizi, S., Singhal, K., Hou, L., Webson, A., Kulkarni, K., Mahdavi, S. S., Semturs, C., … Natarajan, V. (2025). Towards conversational diagnostic artificial intelligence. *Nature*, *642*(8067), 442–450. https://doi.org/10.1038/s41586-025-08866-7

Volkova, S., Rebensky, S., Cassani, L., McCormack, B., Fouse, A., Bruni, S., Ganberg, G., & Orvis, K. (2024). Compound AI ecosystem: Agents and tools to improve training and learning. *Interservice/industry training, simulation and education conference 2024*.

Waring, S., Alison, L., Shortland, N., & Humann, M. (2020). The role of information sharing on decision delay during multiteam disaster response. *Cognition, Technology & Work*, *22*(2), 263–279.

Wu, Q., Bansal, G., Zhang, J., Wu, Y., Li, B., Zhu, E., Jiang, L., Zhang, X., Zhang, S., Liu, J., Awadallah, A. H., White, R. W., Burger, D., & Wang, C. (2024). AutoGen: Enabling next-gen LLM applications via multi-agent conversations. *First conference on language modeling*.

Yu, X., Xu, S., & Ashton, M. (2023). Antecedents and outcomes of artificial intelligence adoption and application in the workplace: The socio-technical system theory perspective. *Information Technology & People*, *36*(1), 454–474.

Zaccaro, S. J., Rittman, A. L., & Marks, M. A. (2001). Team leadership. *The Leadership Quarterly*, *12*(4), 451–483.

Zheng, W., Khoury, A. E., & Grobmeier, C. (2010). How do leadership and context matter in R&D team innovation? A multiple case study. *Human Resources Development International*, *13*, 265–283.

CHAPTER 7

OPERATIONALIZING AND OPTIMIZING HUMAN–AGENT TEAMING FOR KNOWLEDGE WORK

Aimée A. Kane[a], Madeline M. Diep[b], Adam A. Porter[c] and Susannah B. F. Paletz[c]

[a]*Duquesne University, USA*
[b]*Fraunhofer USA Center Mid-Atlantic, USA*
[c]*University of Maryland, USA*

ABSTRACT

Research suggests that artificial intelligence (AI) will not completely replace human knowledge workers in the near-term future (Woodruff et al., 2024; World Economic Forum, 2025). Rather, recent AI developments will support and augment human capabilities. Knowledge work involves dynamically novel, collaborative tasks that require workers to make sense of large amounts of new information, to draw on deep domain expertise, and to continually update their situational awareness (of, say, a complex adversary or business competitor, its goals, and its actions), while accounting for unavoidably incomplete knowledge due to information overload and potentially inaccurate assumptions about the quality of one another's contributions (Kane et al., 2018, 2023, 2025). Given the complexity and open-ended nature of knowledge work, AI will be most effective when providing critical input to workers, rather than by trying to independently "solve" the key problem, whether that be determining the risk of an adversary's troop movement or the wisdom of opening a new business venture.

AI in Teams: Research on Managing Groups and Teams, Volume 21, 115–131

ISSN: 1534-0856/doi:10.1108/S1534-085620260000021018

Thus, the fundamental challenge we explore in this contribution is understanding how human–agent teams (HATs) performing knowledge work can most effectively structure their work. This chapter presents our conceptual framework for HAT orchestration and motivates the creation of testbeds to facilitate in the operationalization of this framework.

Keywords: Human–agent teaming; knowledge work; human-in-loop machine learning algorithms; team assembly and composition; task typologies; information challenges

INTRODUCTION

Over the last century, many countries have transformed their economies from being organized around land, labor, and capital to being organized around knowledge. Today's global knowledge society is characterized by increasing use of rapidly advancing digital technologies, globalization, and more educated populations. The management thinker, Peter Drucker, argued that the transformation of the United States' (U.S.) economy began in 1944 with the GI Bill of Rights, which "gave every American soldier returning from World War II the money to attend a university" (Drucker, 1992, p. 1). Right around this time, the U.S. Department of Labor's Bureau of Labor Statistics cooperated with the Veterans Administration to develop the first Occupational Outlook Handbook (OOH). The 1974 edition highlighted a decline in employment tied to the land, noting that "agriculture (farming), which until the late 1800's employed more than half of all workers in the economy, employed only 4 percent, or 3.5 million workers, in 1972" (Bureau of Labor Statistics, 1974, p. 18). The decline in individuals employed in agricultural occupations coincided with advances in mechanization, feeds, and fertilizers. Indeed, as Drucker (1992) noted "land, labor, and capital – the economist's traditional factors of production – do not disappear, but they become secondary" (p. 2).

Today, this trend continues. As of June 2025, the majority of employed Americans (137.8 million individuals) worked in service-providing industries, including professional and business services, information, education, and healthcare (Bureau of Labor Statistics, 2025a). A high proportion of these jobs may be considered forms of knowledge work. Broadly speaking, knowledge work involves employees applying specialized knowledge to solve conceptual tasks and tackle non-routine problems to provide services or develop products (Drucker, 1992; Woodruff et al., 2024). In other words, knowledge work as described here does not simply involve the heavy use of information but entails the application of expertise to novel situations and tasks. Business professionals, for example, develop expertise in strategic planning, marketing, supply chain, finance, or accounting, while information professionals develop engineering expertise in computer memory development, lithography, and software (Dokko et al., 2014). Military intelligence analysts specialize in pulling together information about foreign actors and their capabilities and intentions, including geographic regions, languages, communication signals, and other sources (Kane et al., 2023, 2025). Educational professionals specialize in the natural sciences, engineering, social science, art, and the humanities (Wuchty et al., 2007). Healthcare professionals often specialize in distinct areas of expertise, including immunology, cancer, endocrinology, infectious disease, psychiatry, and urology (Mayo, 2022; Salazar et al., 2011).

Presciently, Drucker (1992) suggested that the knowledge economy transformation would take decades and would change work profoundly. The rise of teaming is a key change in the nature of knowledge work, which had in prior decades been more of a solo enterprise, with lawyers, physicians, and many business professionals working alone (Bureau of Labor Statistics, 1974, pp. 117, 142, 226, 233). For example, the 1974 version of the OOH, noted that "persons planning to become bank officers should like to work independently" (p. 117), while the 2025 version highlighted that today's equivalent, financial managers, "often work on teams" (Bureau of Labor Statistics, 2025b). Drucker (1992) foresaw that such teaming would become commonplace, noting that the "tension between specialists with specialized knowledge and performance as a team" (p. 2) would need to be navigated in organizations.

The society in which contemporary knowledge workers operate is increasingly volatile, uncertain, complex, and ambiguous (VUCA), a term developed by the military (Edmondson, 2019). Knowledge work in the intelligence community has grown increasingly complex post 9/11 and with the explosion of data (Gartin, 2019). The high velocity, variety, and volume and indeterminate and mixed value and veracity (also known as the Vs of big data) of digital information has rapidly grown, increasing the information processing demands on knowledge workers (Jin et al., 2015; Owais & Hussein, 2016). Knowledge workers increasingly report that they turn to computer agents (otherwise known as artificial intelligence or AI) for help dealing with their on-the-job information processing demands (Lee et al., 2025; Woodruff et al., 2024).

This chapter starts by providing an overview of contemporary collaborative knowledge work, followed by a discussion about HATs and the challenges associated with human–agent teaming on knowledge worker teams. It then introduces a conceptual framework for orchestrating human–agent teaming for conducting knowledge work, discusses research questions and future directions, and concludes with the main takeaways.

CONTEMPORARY COLLABORATIVE KNOWLEDGE WORK

Few of the most high-value tasks encountered by knowledge workers are simple enough to be solved by one specialist. Rather, most require professionals to come together as a team and collaboratively integrate their specialized knowledge. In addition to domain knowledge about a product or service, developing new business products and services often requires a team bringing distinct knowledge from multiple business functions (e.g., marketing expertise to reach interested customers and accounting expertise to budget and track progress; Lazar et al., 2022). Innovating computer memory devices involves boundary spanning between specialist teams focused on new materials development, software interface development, lithography, and device testing among others (Dokko et al., 2014). In military intelligence, determining whether and why an adversary nation may be amassing troops near an ally nation's border requires collaboration among analysts with specialized knowledge regarding the region and the nations involved, as well as languages experts and experts in the communication signals and sources (Kane et al., 2023, 2025).

The shift from individual knowledge work to team knowledge work can also be seen in academia and healthcare. The production of high-impact academic knowledge, which was arguably once the purview of lone scientists, has increasingly become a collective endeavor in social science as well as in science and engineering (Wuchty et al., 2007). Complex medical diagnosis increasingly involves collaboration among nursing staff, generalist physicians, and sub-specialist physicians, among others (Mayo, 2022). Medical breakthroughs require bringing together experts from diverse topic areas, such as immunology and oncology, with basic as well as translational and clinical expertise (Salazar et al., 2011).

To better understand the activities that comprise collective knowledge work, it is instructive to review the McGrath (1984) circumplex model of group tasks. The model arranges group tasks into eight types, specifically planning, creativity, intellective, decision making, cognitive conflict, mixed motive, contests/battles/competitive, and performance/psycho-motor. McGrath arrayed these tasks along the circumplex to differentiate cooperation from conflict as well as to separate behavioral and conceptual work. Generating ideas and plans (Type 1: Planning Tasks and Type 2: Creativity Tasks), which exemplify the cooperation dimension, appear opposite from resolving conflicts of viewpoints and interests (Type 5: Cognitive Conflict Tasks and Type 6: Mixed Motive Tasks). Performance tasks and conflicts of power (Type 7: Contests/Battles/Competitive Tasks and Type 8: Performance/Psycho-Motor Tasks), which exemplify behavioral work, are opposite from the conceptually focused problem-solving and decision-making tasks (Type 3: Intellective Tasks and Type 4: Decision-Making Tasks), which can be considered quintessential knowledge work.

Developing a healthcare product or figuring out why troops are massing at an adversary nation's border are problem-solving tasks for which the correctness of one's solution or approach may be determined by facts, logic, or expert review (Type 3: Intellective Tasks). However, teams in business do not jump directly to product development; likewise, military intelligence analysis teams do not start with a threat assessment. As McGrath et al. (1993) illustrated in their studies of undergraduate student teams, knowledge work involves multiple group task types. Knowledge worker teams come together to generate ideas and plans (Type 1: Planning Tasks and Type 2: Creativity Tasks), negotiate to resolve conflicting viewpoints and interests (Type 5: Cognitive Conflict Tasks and Type 6: Mixed Motive Tasks), solve problems with correct answers and make decisions on issues where there is no clear "right" answer (Type 3: Intellective Tasks and Type 4: Decision-Making Tasks). These tasks largely correspond to the conceptual side of the McGrath (1984) circumplex and can be contrasted to the performances and psycho-motor execution tasks, such as landing a plane or manufacturing a product, that appear on the behavioral side of the circumplex.

Effective collaboration is essential to knowledge work. It has long been apparent that collaboration requires assembling a set of individuals who collectively have the resources needed to tackle their joint work (Steiner, 1972). Over the past half century, researchers have continued to explore team composition, finding that a key driver of team effectiveness is whether the team has the right mix of knowledge, skills, abilities, and other characteristics (KSAOs; Bell et al., 2018). Yet, resources alone are not enough. Teams engaged in knowledge-intensive tasks can benefit from members developing a transactive memory system, which involves specialization, knowledge of each other's expertise, and trust in one another's work such that each team member can focus on their own distinct areas of expertise (Argote et al., 2018; Kush, 2019; Lazar et al., 2022). See Fouse et al. (2026) for an examination of how AI can assist in the development of a transactive memory systems in dynamic teams where membership change occurs. Members also need to be motivated to expend their limited attention to consider and incorporate each other's ideas into their collective work (Dokko et al., 2014; Kane, 2010; Kane et al., 2005). To meet these demands, knowledge workers are increasing working as part of a HAT, which "involves one or more autonomous computerized agents collaborating with humans on interdependent tasks toward the achievement of a common goal" (O'Neill et al., 2023, abstract, p. 904).

KNOWLEDGE WORK AND HUMAN–AGENT TEAMING CHALLENGES

Effectively collaborating with autonomous agents for knowledge work requires HATs bring the right mix of KSAO to deal with the challenges inherent in the team's environment. Indeed, the idea that humans could collaborate with intelligent agents dates back at least to a NASA report from the early 1990s. This report details several aerospace challenges; noting "there is a need to provide intelligent support systems for flight operators to assist human operators in managing the complex, highly constrained aerospace environment" (Malin et al., 1991, pp. 3–6).

Today, the "five Vs" of Big Data (Jin et al., 2015) create information processing challenges for knowledge workers. Given powerful improvements in computing technologies, AI and machine learning (ML) are increasingly viewed as essential emerging technologies for addressing big data knowledge work challenges (Gartin, 2019; Lee et al., 2025; McNeese et al., 2015; Parameshwaran, 2024). Unfortunately, it is still unclear how best to operationalize this vision. From interviews with intelligence analysts, Kane et al. (2023) developed an inductive model of knowledge workers collaborating across shifts to process mission-critical information in 24/7 task environments. In our focal context of military intelligence, knowledge workers "need to sift through massive streams of data (e.g., surveillance images, reporting, social media) of varying veracity and relevance that are created day and night around the globe" (Kane et al., 2023, p. 3). The issue of inconsistent and unknown veracity is compounded because the data that analysts receive may be accurate, inaccurate, or intentionally falsified (Lowenthal, 2022). As noted by Kane et al. (2023), intelligence analysts often need to work in shifts to make sense of events unfolding in their area of responsibility, such as when there is a sudden explosion at a sports event, requiring knowledge of the who, what, how, and why as soon as possible.

Most of the HATs that have been researched, as of this writing, complete tasks located on the behavioral side of the McGrath (1984) group task circumplex rather than on the conceptual side of the circumplex where knowledge work resides (e.g., search and rescue HATs). In their systematic review of 74 HAT research articles, O'Neill et al. (2022) "found that the overwhelming majority of articles were military- or emergency-related simulations (n = 57). These articles largely involved command and control tasks including target identification, attacking, defending, navigation, and so on" (p. 918; e.g., flight simulations). According to McGrath (1984), execution tasks of this kind include competitive battles against adversaries (Type 7: Contests/battles/competitive tasks) and cooperative performances, such as landing a plane or manufacturing a product (Type 8: Performances/psycho-motor tasks). Such team execution tasks are relatively well-defined and highly repetitive, lending themselves to task analysis and the development of technological support. For example, one of the most widely studied HAT testbeds, the MIX, simulates an Operator Control Unit and Unmanned System Simulator in which humans collaborate with autonomous agents that assist with surveillance and target identification using unmanned vehicles (Wright et al., 2014). While these tasks involve skill and expertise, we do not consider them to be knowledge work, which centers around conceptual tasks and non-routine problems (Drucker, 1992; Woodruff et al., 2024).

Questions of HAT composition have also been explored in contest/battle/competitive game domains such as chess. For example, Zhang et al. (2023) paired up chess players and, using a two-by-two design, varied the teammate's expertise (gave high-quality or low-quality chess advice) and the teammate's identity (presented as another human or an AI agent). They found that participants were more willing to heed advice from the AI compared to the human teammate, but only the teammate's expertise (high > low) significantly affected the joint performance of the HAT (Zhang et al., 2023).

This work highlights the importance of composing HATs with AI agents whose expertise supports knowledge worker as they perform job tasks. While researchers have traditionally guided AI developers to let humans do what they are good at, and to let AI do what AI is good at (Parasuraman et al., 2000; Vaccaro et al., 2024), such advice can often be of little practical value. The advice to separate AI tasks from human tasks, depending on what each are best at, fails to consider the strategies, qualities, and complexity of assembling a team of AI agents to assist with the various conceptual tasks involved in knowledge work. In domains from intelligence analysis to healthcare, the number and types of potential AI tools are advancing so rapidly that knowledge workers are having trouble keeping up (Kolata, 2024). Accordingly, we believe a human-in-the loop computational approach is needed to assist knowledge workers in assembling teams of AI agents to assist with information processing tasks.

A CONCEPTUAL FRAMEWORK FOR KNOWLEDGE WORK HAT ORCHESTRATION

Given the non-triviality in composing HATs, we developed a framework for how humans and AI can work together efficiently and effectively – optimizing memberships, roles, and tasks – as a team in the context of knowledge work. Our approach to human–AI team orchestration is driven by several social and technical insights. First, we question the emerging perspective that AI will replace most workers, including knowledge workers (e.g., Berg, 2023; Dorr, 2025). Workers in industries associated with knowledge work (e.g., business, education, and law) questioned the job-replacement narrative and communicated an expectation that AI will largely assist with menial tasks that will be reviewed by humans (Woodruff et al., 2024). Corroborating this perspective, organizational leadership indicated that human–machine teaming is becoming increasingly prevalent and is expected to account for about a third of the tasks done by workers by 2030 (for details, see Financial Services Industry Profile, p. 257; Information and Technology Services Profile, p. 261; Medical and Health Services, p. 267; World Economic Forum, 2025).

We concur with those who suggest that AI needs to support and augment human capabilities (Agrawal et al., 2019; Ozmen Garibay et al., 2023; Zirar et al., 2023). We contend that AI will be most effective when providing helpful input to analysts, rather than trying to solve the analyst's problem. Thus, a fundamental challenge is to understand how human team members can most effectively enlist the help of AI agents to assist in information processing tasks. By applying McGrath's (1984) group task circumplex model of task types, we conclude that AI agents can assist knowledge workers with information processing tasks associated with resolving conflicts of viewpoints (Type 5: Cognitive Conflict Tasks), deciding issues that may have no right answer (Type 4: Decision-Making Tasks), and solving problems that may have a correct answer (Type 3: Intellective Tasks), but also broadly, generating plans and ideas (Type 1: Planning Tasks and Type 2: Creativity Tasks).

When doing knowledge work, human teams work best when they leverage the distinct KSAOs that different members bring to a problem such that work is distributed among teammates according to their unique expertise and capabilities (Argote & Kane, 2003; Bell et al., 2018; Kane, 2010; Kang et al., 2014; Ren & Argote, 2011). For task distribution to be implemented effectively, three conditions need to be met. First, the team comprises members whose KSAOs must match the configuration of subtask demands. As noted previously, transactive memory systems are key to team members knowing who knows what (e.g., Argote et al., 2018). Furthermore, team members need to understand the task and be able to match expertise to tasks (Dubrow, 2021). Second, taskwork is divided such that key subtasks are performed by at least one member with the requisite KSAOs. Third, members trust and rely on each other's taskwork rather than focus on another's subtask. These conditions emerge as members interact, incorporate feedback, reconstruct member-subtask assignments, and develop trust in teammates individually and the team as a whole (Ren & Argote, 2011).

Analogous to human teammates, the AI agents assisting a knowledge worker should each bring distinct, specialized value. In the setting of our focal context of intelligence analysis work, AI agents may be optimized for filtering out technically implausible information (from the point of view of their specific technical domain); others might be optimized for summarizing cultural clues to disambiguate the meaning of specific terms; others might provide machine translation for foreign languages; yet another might be optimized for flagging inconsistent, recently changed, or missing information and suggesting specific documents to the analyst for further review.

Deploying distinct capabilities as focused AI agents is likely to have many practical benefits as well. It can speed up individual AI agent creation, lead to AI agents optimized for specific domains, enable rapid experimentation with individual AI agents and AI agent teams, and support team learning and optimization over time. We believe that mixing and matching such AI agents and involving the human in determining that mix will greatly improve outcomes by (1) spurring human analysts to consider information from multiple perspectives and (2) by facilitating more effective, data-driven human/AI teams (Gomez-Zara, 2024). Applying McGrath's (1984) group task circumplex model, AI information processing assistance can support humans with resolving multiple viewpoints (Type 5: Cognitive Conflict Tasks), determining a path forward for issues without an objective answer (Type 4: Decision-Making Tasks), and arriving at a correct solution (Type 3: Intellective Tasks).

Our approach for human–AI teaming orchestration is built around a *Construct–Opine–Reconstruct–Approve* (CORA) process which will occur one or more times during an analysis task. The overall CORA process is illustrated in Fig. 7.1. CORA makes human-in-the-loop an inherent, rather than incidental, part of the process. To process highly dynamic, potentially massive streams of heterogeneous data, knowledge workers seek augmentation from AI agents. Focused AI agents with diverse KSAOs are available. Teams are orchestrated via the CORA process in which a system *constructs* AI agent–subtasks assignments, human analysts *opine*, the system *reconstructs*, and the human *approves* the AI agent–subtask assignments to be deployed. The recommended agent subtask (re)constructions are based on ML algorithms, such as reinforcement learning, and the human inputs provide feedback for improving ML matching algorithms.

The first step of the CORA process, *construct*, generates a recommended team of AI agents to triage data from multiple heterogeneous information sources such as articles, social media posts, other textual documents, audio files, maps, images, and videos. Each AI agent specifies the particular information source it

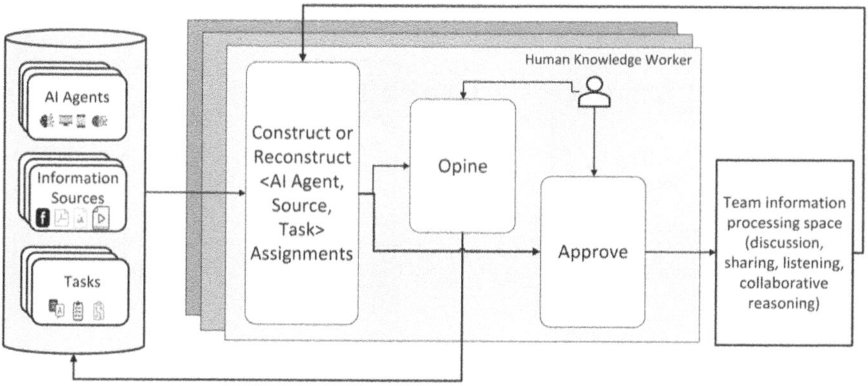

Fig. 7.1. Notational Overall CORA Team Orchestration Process.

can process, its skills/approaches, and/or domain expertise, such as filtering, summarizing, transcribing, image understanding, flagging missing information, and machine translation. Given an information source of that type, the AI agent also specifies one or more outputs that it can generate. Then, in this step, for taskwork to be completed, the recommended subtasks and corresponding AI-agent teammates are generated via ML processes. Such processes use active learning (Settles, 2010) to find documents requiring analyst attention and reinforcement learning (Kaelbling et al., 1996; Li, 2017; Sutton & Barto, 2018) to decide which AI agents to suggest to human analysts.

Reinforcement learning learns, given a state, which actions it should use. In the context of knowledge work HATs, the state is the current set of information sources, the progress the analyst has made with the sources, and the history of the AI agents applied to the sources. The goal of the reinforcement learning algorithm is to identify a policy, which indicates the action to take under a state that maximizes the cumulative reward. In knowledge work HAT orchestration, the reward design takes into account the diversity of the AI agents deployed and the human analyst preferences and capabilities. Specifically, we envision the following multi-objectives to be considered the reward: human satisfaction/rating, a matching score between the task and functionalities of the AI agents to the human analyst, and the diversity of the AI agents deployed. Support for such a human-in-the-loop approach can be found in a recent behavioral experiment examining algorithmic approaches to team formation. Specifically, human teams formed via a combination of member preferences and a diversity algorithm outperformed counterpart teams formed only via a diversity algorithm on a creativity task and also expressed greater satisfaction in the team (Gomez-Zara, 2024; Gomez-Zara et al., 2024).

The construct step results in the recommended AI agent–subtask assignments that are provided to the human analyst. These assignments are represented as a set of combinations of an AI agent, an information source, and a specific task. As detailed in Fig. 7.2, human analysts then *opine* on – review, update, or

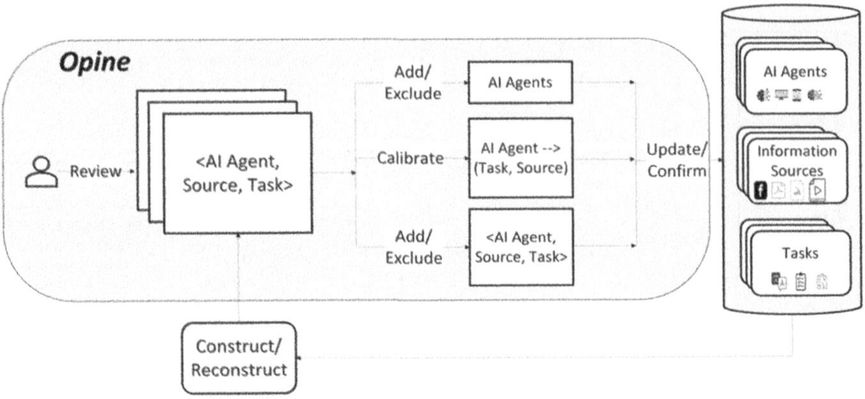

Fig. 7.2. Notational Opine Subprocess.

confirm – the recommended AI agent–subtask assignments. Human users are likely to increase their trust in an automated system when they have a say in how that system supports their work (e.g., the construction of their team, division of work, etc.). In a temperature monitoring experiment, Hellwig et al. (2023) varied whether a HAT system allowed human "voice" (some/none) to configure the number of temperature scales to be monitored. They found that voice led to higher perceptions of fairness, job satisfaction, and task performance.

The opining step may take place at the level of the recommended AI-agent capabilities, the information source types identified, and the subtasks to which the AI is deployed. For example, analysts may request AI agents not initially recommended in the construct step or request a specific AI agent for a subtask (e.g., a topic modeler, which is an AI for identifying main themes or topics, to sort documents into coherent piles). As shown in the middle of Fig. 7.2, analysts may exclude AI agents with redundant capabilities, such as a translator from a language the analyst speaks or summaries of documents the analyst has already read. In addition, analysts may calibrate how the AI teammates perform selected subtasks, such as by refining the output of topic models (e.g., splitting and merging topics or removing stop words as in Hu et al., 2014) or summaries (e.g., setting word count targets). Finally, analysts may add an AI agent to perform a task not yet assigned, such as requesting an AI summarize new information provided by teammates (Kane et al., 2025).

The next step is then to *reconstruct* the team of AI agents with inputs from the opine step. The activity is similar to the construct phase but now operates under a revised set of constraints and priorities defined during the opine phase. Subtasks deleted in the opine step will be omitted. New AI-agent capabilities identified by the human analysts will be crossed with information sources to generate new AI agent–subtask assignments. At this point, human analysts may *approve* the reconstructed assignments of AI-agent teammates and subtasks. Before approval, analysts may further refine subtasks or toggle setting configurable subtasks (e.g., topic models or summaries). Analysts preferring extensive changes may opt to revert back to the opine step and proceed until a reconstructed one is deemed satisfactory.

In addition to being focused, AI agents should also be independent and decentralized. AI agents should be independent, meaning that they are capable of making decisions, executing tasks, and adapting to changes in their environment based on their learned behavior. AI agents should be decentralized where they do not rely on a central system to manage or coordinate their actions; instead, they can collaborate or share information with other agents. Because the AI agents should be decentralized and designed to focus on specific tasks and information source types, any bleed over of one AI agent doing the work of another is avoided by design, although the AI agent may deploy an ensemble of ML models. For instance, one AI agent may identify the national origin of reports, while another does the same for social media, and others focus on transliteration, etc. In this sense, AI agents trust the work of other agents. Note, however, that one AI agent may override, challenge, or expand on the work of another AI agent in much the same way a supervisor or subject matter expert reviews work done by another person. In all cases, we envision the human analyst as the key high-level sensemaker, who ultimately decides which AI-agent output to use. This information can be fed back to use as an input in subsequent CORA processes.

Note that the CORA process occurs at two levels. The first level operates at the individual human analyst level, where a team of AI agents is orchestrated to support the specific need of a human analyst. However, a human analyst works with other human analysts as part of a team; therefore, the CORA process can also occur at the team level, involving multiple humans and multiple sets of AI agents, each tailored to support their respective human analyst. Within the team information processing space, each human analyst contributes their sensemaking – sharing insights, interpretations, and conclusions derived from their analysis. Their analysis can be refuted, confirmed, or refined by other team members through collaborative discussions and reasoning leading to the emergence of a new theory that becomes the starting point of the subsequent analysis. Through this process, the KSAO of each analyst or an AI agent can also be updated. For example, if the team discovers a team member has expertise in a specific aspect of the problem space, that member might be assigned to analyze a new set of information sources. As insights evolve, the team may need to reorganize the configuration of AI agents to better support the individuals or the team. This shift could necessitate deploying a different set of AI agents to provide the specialized support required for the evolving or new task.

This dual-level team orchestration using the CORA process – at the individual and team levels – enables a seamless integration of human and AI capabilities, fostering adaptability and enhancing the overall effectiveness of the analytical process.

DISCUSSION: OPEN QUESTIONS AND FUTURE DIRECTIONS

Operationalizing an effective CORA process in practice requires careful consideration of numerous factors, including developing a thorough understanding of human–AI agents' interaction dynamics to navigate the complexities of task orchestration – along with addressing the external and internal forces that influence them. To fully realize the potential of the CORA process, it is essential to explore how factors like individual differences and expertise of human knowledge workers and AI influence the ability to compose HATs for effective collaboration.

Future research could assess the impact of human knowledge workers' training, individual differences, and expertise on their ability in using the CORA process to effectively compose AI teams. With the availability of different AI agents with varying skills, knowledge workers need to be able to assess and evaluate each AI agents' skills and abilities. We can examine whether different levels of knowledge workers' experience (Argote & Kane, 2003) influence how they utilize the CORA process, such as, do the less experienced knowledge workers rely more on the construct step in the CORA process? Are knowledge workers with a higher Need for Cognitive Closure (Kruglanski & Webster, 1996) more likely to prematurely select, and not change, a particular composition, or too easily accept AI-generated reconstructions of the team?

Research should also examine how team composition strategies can optimize the joint performance of knowledge work HATs. Team size and expertise overlaps are theoretically and practically relevant aspects of composition worth investigating. With regard to team size, smaller teams are likely to enable humans to monitor AI agents' work in a way that builds trust and supports synthesis (Mueller, 2012), but larger teams are likely to provide a wider range of perspectives that could help overcome teammate inaccuracy blindness (Kang et al., 2014). Nonetheless, it remains an open empirical question whether humans will prefer a smaller or larger team of AI agents and what effect this has on the joint problem solving of the human–AI team.

Meanwhile, overlaps in the background expertise and function of the AIs in the HAT (low vs. high) may cause assembly and information integration challenges. The AI agents available at any point in time will vary in terms of their function (e.g., translators, summarizers) and expertise domains (e.g., cartel-relevant background knowledge, scientific findings regarding oil refineries), but they may also have overlap in function and expertise (e.g., all the language translation information is cartel-related). This kind of overlap relates to the human teaming concept of faultlines, which occur when the dimensions of diversity are overlapping (e.g., all the marketing employees are young women vs. the engineers are older men). Typically, teams with converging dimensions of diversity do not integrate information and encounter problem-solving issues (Thatcher & Patel, 2012). While the findings on human faultlines are based largely on social identity processes, there is some evidence that the effects may be due to broader categorization processes (Homan et al., 2007).

Additionally, researchers could also examine the effects of the quality of the AI agents. Each AI agent can be set to have varying levels of performance (accuracy, consistency), bias, and trustworthiness (transparency, explainability). In the context of interactions with teams of AI agents, human knowledge workers will need to process the outputs of multiple AI agents, which may sometimes overlap and/or depend on one another. It is important to understand if human knowledge workers are capable of detecting when an AI agent makes a mistake or is inherently biased, whether certain team composition strategies enhance or hinder the knowledge workers' ability to detect these issues, and how such awareness affects the humans' trust in and reliance on the individual and collective AI agents (and, therefore, how they may opine and approve their AI teammates within the CORA process). In the context of the type of problem-solving and decision-making tasks that make up knowledge work, we need to understand whether having multiple AI agents instead of one provides some degree of tolerance to small amounts of quality issues in the AI agents.

The theoretical insights in the CORA framework provide a foundation for systematic study. We join experts from the National Academies of Sciences, Engineering, and Medicine (2022) in advocating for the use of behavioral experiments and the development of human–AI testbeds (see also Paletz et al., 2025). To examine the CORA process and their impact on HAT's performance, decision-making, and cognitive load, researchers need to identify high-information load tasks that involve decision making and problem solving. Testbeds would also need to engage humans, bring in a set of AI agents with a diverse range of KSAOs, and support the orchestration of the HAT one or more times during an operation via the CORA process. Additionally, experimental infrastructures would also need to have features enabling researchers to: (1) test and evaluate approaches to compose AI agents and HAT in the working environments relevant to the knowledge workers (i.e., involving the triage of complex and heterogeneous data) and (2) flexibly, deeply, and systematically assess how knowledge workers develop and evolve mental models and collaborative sensemaking of information during their tasks and how those models change depending on different AI team compositions.

CONCLUSION

Collaborative knowledge work, such as intelligence analysis, is becoming increasingly complex due to the proliferation of big data (and their "five Vs" nature) and the VUCA landscape. AI has the potential to play a transformative role in this area, specifically in acting as teammates to knowledge workers, augmenting their capabilities and providing critical inputs to the workers. We introduced the CORA process which is the basis of our proposed framework for humans and AI agents to form a team and to efficiently tackle complex problems by taking advantage of their complementary strengths. Our proposed CORA process takes the idea of the human-in-the-loop seriously, making it an inherent part of the HAT. Further studies are needed to investigate the multitude of factors influencing the effectiveness of team orchestration in this context. New opportunities and challenges emerge from the rapid pace of advancements in AI technologies, where AI capabilities are growing – sometimes incrementally but other times dramatically such as seen with the Large Language Models. These advancements have the potential of creating novel ways for humans and AI to work together, transforming workflows and decision-making processes, as well as humans' perception of the AI themselves. All of these necessitate the need for flexible and scalable experimental testbeds to assess HATs in this ever-evolving landscape. Looking ahead, the instantiation of conceptual frameworks, such as ours, will be critical to foster productive, effective, and ethical HAT in knowledge work.

ACKNOWLEDGMENTS

Research was sponsored by the United States Government Army Research Office (ARO) grant # W911NF-20-1-0214. The views and conclusions contained in this document are those of the authors and should not be interpreted as representing the official policies, either expressed or implied, of the Army Research Office, the U.S. Government, Duquesne University, Fraunhofer USA Mid-Atlantic, or the University of Maryland. The U.S. Government is authorized to reproduce and distribute reprints for Government purposes notwithstanding any copyright notation herein.

REFERENCES

Agrawal, A., Gans, J. S., & Goldfarb, A. (2019). Artificial intelligence: The ambiguous labor market impact of automating prediction. *Journal of Economic Perspectives*, *33*(2), 31–50. https://doi.org/10.1257/jep.33.2.31

Argote, L., Aven, B. L., & Kush, J. (2018). The effects of communication networks and turnover on transactive memory and group performance. *Organization Science*, *29*(2), 191–206. https://doi.org/10.1287/orsc.2017.1176

Argote, L., & Kane, A. A. (2003). Learning from direct and indirect experience in organizations: The effects of experience content, timing, and distribution. In P. Paulus & B. Nijstad (Eds.), *Group creativity: Innovation through collaboration* (pp. 277–303). Oxford University Press.

Bell, S. T., Brown, S. G., Colaneri, A., & Outland, N. (2018). Team composition and the ABCs of teamwork. *American Psychologist*, *73*(4), 349–362. https://doi.org/10.1037/amp0000305

Berg, C. (2023, November 24). AGI is upon us at last – And what that will mean. *Medium*. https://cliff-berg.medium.com/agi-is-upon-us-at-last-and-what-that-will-mean-fd8ab565fce4

Bureau of Labor Statistics, U.S. Department of Labor. (1974). *Occupational outlook handbook*. https://fraser.stlouisfed.org/title/occupational-outlook-handbook-3964/occupational-outlook-handbook-1974-75-edition-499178?deep=true

Bureau of Labor Statistics, U.S. Department of Labor. (2025a). *Current Employment Statistics – CES (National). Employment and Earnings Table B-1. Employees on nonfarm payrolls by industry sector and selected industry detail, seasonally adjusted*. https://www.bls.gov/web/empsit/ceseeb1a.htm#ce_ee_table1a.f.p

Bureau of Labor Statistics, U.S. Department of Labor. (2025b). *Occupational outlook handbook*. Financial Managers. https://www.bls.gov/ooh/management/financial-managers.htm

Dokko, G., Kane, A. A., & Tortoriello, M. (2014). One of us or one of my friends: How social identity and tie strength shape the creative generativity of boundary-spanning ties. *Organization Studies*, *35*(5), 703–726. https://doi.org/10.1177/0170840613508397

Dorr, A. (2025, February 26). The painful truth about AI & robotics. *Rethinx*. https://www.rethinkx.com/blog/rethinkx/the-painful-truth-about-ai-and-robotics

Drucker. (1992). The new society of organizations. *Harvard Business Review*, *9*. https://hbr.org/1992/09/the-new-society-of-organizations
Dubrow, S. (2021). *Leadership transitions in teams* (Publication No. 28415609) [Doctoral dissertation, George Mason University]. ProQuest Dissertations & Theses Global.
Edmondson, A. C. (2019). *The fearless organization: Creating psychological safety in the workplace for learning, innovation, and growth*. Wiley.
Fouse, A., Ganberg, G., Bruni, S., Volkova, S., Orvis, K. L., & Klinefelter, Z. (2026). AI-powered dynamic hybrid teaming. In S. B. F. Paletz & S. Dubrow (Eds.), *AI in teams* (pp. 99–116). Emerald.
Gartin, J. W. (2019). The future of analysis. *Studies in Intelligence*, *63*(2), 1–5.
Gomez-Zara, D. (2024). Assigning or recommending you a team? The algorithmic effects on team formation and performance. *Academy of Management Proceedings*, *2024*(1), 12540. https://doi.org/10.5465/AMPROC.2024.275bp
Gomez-Zara, D., Kam, V., Chiang, C., DeChurch, L. A., & Contractor, N. S. (2024). *Augmenting team diversity and performance by enabling agency and fairness criteria in recommendation algorithms*. arXiv. https://doi.org/10.48550/arXiv.2410.0034
Hellwig, P., Buchholz, V., Kopp, S., & Maier, G. W. (2023). Let the user have a say – Voice in automated decision-making. *Computers in Human Behavior*, *138*, 107446. https://doi.org/10.1016/j.chb.2022.107446
Homan, A. C., van Knippenberg, D., Van Kleef, G. A., & De Dreu, C. K. W. (2007). Bridging faultlines by valuing diversity: Diversity beliefs, information elaboration, and performance in diverse work groups. *Journal of Applied Psychology*, *92*(5), 1189–1199.
Hu, Y., Boyd-Graber, J., Satinoff, B., & Smith, A. (2014). Interactive topic modeling. *Machine Learning*, *95*, 423–469. https://doi.org/10.1007/s10994-013-5413-0
Jin, X., Wah, B. W., Cheng, X., & Wang, Y. (2015). Significance and challenges of big data research. *Big Data Research*, *2*, 59–64. https://doi.org/10.1016/j.bdr.2015.01.006
Kaelbling, L. P., Littman, M. L., & Moore, A. W. (1996). Reinforcement learning: A survey. *Journal of Artificial Intelligence Research*, *4*, 237–285.
Kane, A. A. (2010). Unlocking knowledge transfer potential: Knowledge demonstrability and superordinate social identity. *Organization Science*, *21*(3), 643–660. https://doi.org/10.1287/orsc.1090.0469
Kane, A. A., Argote, L., & Levine, J. M. (2005). Knowledge transfer between groups via personnel rotation: Effects of social identity and knowledge quality. *Organizational Behavior and Human Decision Processes*, *96*(1), 56–71. https://doi.org/10.1016/j.obhdp.2004.09.002
Kane, A. A., Kiesier, S., & Kang, R. (2018). Inaccuracy blindness in collaboration persists, even with an evaluation prompt. *Proceedings of the 2018 CHI conference on human factors in computing systems*. (p. Article 494). Association for Computing Machinery. https://doi.org/10.1145/3173574.3174068
Kane, A. A., Paletz, S. B. F., Diep, M., Hajkowski, A., & Porter, A. (2025). Virtual collaborative analysis: Effects of two AI summarizers. *Small Group Research*, *56*(5), 821–863. https://doi.org/10.1177/10464964251361563
Kane, A. A., Paletz, S. B. F., Vahlkamp, S. H., Nelson, T., Porter, A., Diep, M., & Carraway, M. (2023). Intelligence analysis shift work: Sensemaking processes, tensions, and takeaways. *Proceedings of the Human Factors and Ergonomics Society Annual Meeting*. https://doi.org/10.1177/21695067231192569
Kang, R., Kane, A. A., & Kiesier, S. (2014). Teammate inaccuracy blindness: When information sharing tools hinder collaborative analysis. *CSCW '14: Proceedings of the 17th ACM conference on computer supported cooperative work & social computing* (pp. 797–806). https://doi.org/10.1145/2531602.2531681
Kolata, G. (2024, November 17). A.I. chatbots defeated doctors at diagnosing illness. *The New York Times*. https://www.nytimes.com/2024/11/17/health/chatgpt-ai-doctors-diagnosis.html
Kruglanski, A. W., & Webster, D. M. (1996). Motivated closing of the mind: "Seizing" and "freezing". *Psychological Review*, *103*(2), 263–283.
Kush, J. (2019). Conceptual and measurement issues for transactive memory systems: The indicators of TMS. *Group Dynamics: Theory, Research, and Practice*, *23*(2), 104–123. https://doi.org/10.1037/gdn0000101

Lazar, M., Miron-Spektor, E., Chen, G., Goldfarb, B., Erez, M., & Agarwal, R. (2022). Forming entrepreneurial teams: Mixing business and friendship to create transactive memory systems for enhanced success. *Academy of Management Journal*, *65*(4), 1110–1138. https://doi.org/10.5465/amj.2020.0393

Lee, H.-P., Sarkar, A., Tankelevitch, L., Drosos, I., Rintel, S., Banks, R., & Wilson, N. (2025, April 26–May 01). The impact of generative AI on critical thinking: Self-reported reductions in cognitive effort and confidence effects from a survey of knowledge workers. *Proceedings of the 2025 CHI conference on human factors in computing systems* (p. Article 1121). Association for Computing Machinery. https://doi.org/10.1145/3706598.3713778

Li, Y. (2017). *Deep reinforcement learning: An overview*. arXiv preprint arXiv:1701.07274.

Lowenthal, M. M. (2022). *Intelligence: From secrets to policy* (9th ed.). CQ Press.

Malin, J. T., Schreckenghost, D. L., Woods, D. D., Potter, S. S., Johanessen, L., Holloway, M., & Forbus, K. D. (1991). *Making intelligent systems team players: Case studies and design issues* (Vol. *1*). Human-computer interaction design (NASA Technical Memorandum 104738). https://ntrs.nasa.gov/api/citations/19910021399/downloads/19910021399.pdf

Mayo, A. T. (2022). Syncing up: A process model of emergent interdependence in dynamic teams. *Administrative Science Quarterly*, *67*(3), 821–864. https://doi.org/10.1177/00018392221096451

McGrath, J. E. (1984). *Groups: Interaction and performance*. Prentice Hall.

McGrath, J. E., Arrow, H., Gruenfeld, D. H., Hollingshead, A. B., & O'Connor, K. M. (1993). Groups, tasks, and technology: The effects of experience and change. *Small Group Research*, *24*(3), 406–420.

McNeese, N. J., Buchanan, V., & Cooke, N. J. (2015). The cognitive science of intelligence analysis. *Proceedings of the Human Factors and Ergonomics Society Annual Meeting*, *59*(1), 826–830. https://doi.org/10.1177/1541931215591250

Mueller, J. S. (2012). Why individuals in larger teams perform worse. *Organizational Behavior and Human Decision Processes*, *117*(1), 111–124. https://doi.org/10.1016/j.obhdp.2011.08.004

National Academies of Sciences, Engineering, and Medicine. (2022). *Human-AI teaming: State-of the-art and research needs*. The National Academies Press. https://doi.org/10.17226/26355

O'Neill, T. A., Flathmann, C., McNeese, N. J., & Salas, E. (2023). Human-autonomy teaming: Need for a guiding team-based framework? *Computers in Human Behavior*, 107762. https://doi.org/10.1016/j.chb.2023.107762

O'Neill, T. A., McNeese, N. J., Baron, A., & Schelble, B. (2022). Human-autonomy teaming: A review and analysis of the empirical literature. *Human Factors*, *64*(5), 904–938. https://doi.org/10.1177/0018 7208 20960865

Owais, S. S., & Hussein, N. S. (2016). Extract five categories CPIVW from the 9V's characteristics of big data. *International Journal of Advanced Computer Science and Applications*, *7*(3). https://doi.org/10.14569/IJACSA.2016.070337

Ozmen Garibay, O., Winslow, B., Andolina, S., Antona, M., Bodenschatz, A., Coursaris, C., Falco, G., Fiore, S. M., Garibay, I., Grieman, K., Havens, J. C., Jirotka, M., Kacorri, H., Karwowski, W., Kider, J., Konstan, J., Koon, S., Lopez-Gonzalez, M., Maifeld-Carucci, I., McGregor, S., Salvendy, G., Shneiderman, B., Stephanidis, C., Strobel, C., Holter, C. T., & Xu, W. (2023). Six human-centered artificial intelligence grand challenges. *International Journal of Human–Computer Interaction*, *39*(3), 391–437. https://doi.org/10.1080/10447318.2022.2153320

Paletz, S. B. F., Kane, A. A., Diep, M., Nelson, T. M., Porter, A., & Vahlkamp, S. H. (2025). Human-Agent Teaming on Intelligence Tasks (HATIT): A testbed for evaluating AI in intelligence analysis. *Proceedings of the association for information science and technology*, *62*, 483–494. https://doi.org/10.1002/pra2.1272 (pp. 474–485).

Parameshwaran, S. (2024). How early adopters of Gen AI are gaining efficiencies. *Knowledge at Wharton: A Business Journal from the University of Pennsylvania*. https://knowledge.wharton.upenn.edu/article/how-early-adopters-of-gen-ai-are-extracting-efficiencies/

Parasuraman, R., Sheridan, T. B., & Wickens, C. D. (2000). A model for types and levels of human interaction with automation. *IEEE Transactions on Systems, Man, and Cybernetics – Part A: Systems and Humans*, *30*(3), 286–297. https://doi.org/10.1109/3468.844354

Ren, Y., & Argote, L. (2011). Transactive memory systems 1985–2010: An integrative framework of key dimensions, antecedents, and consequences. *Academy of Management Annals*, *5*(1), 189–229. https://doi.org/10.1080/19416520.2011.590300

Salazar, M. R., Lant, T. K., & Kane, A. A. (2011). To join or not to join: An investigation of individual facilitators and inhibitors of medical faculty participation in interdisciplinary research teams. *CTS Clinical and Translational Science*, *4*(4), 274–278. https://doi.org/10.1111/j.1752-8062.2011.00321.x

Settles, B. (2010). *Active learning literature survey*. Computer Sciences Technical Report 1648, University of Wisconsin–Madison.

Steiner, I. D. (1972). *Group process and productivity*. Academic Press.

Sutton, R. S., & Barto, A. G. (2018). *Reinforcement learning: An introduction*. MIT Press.

Thatcher, S. M. B., & Patel, P. C. (2012). Group faultlines: A review, integration, and guide to future research. *Journal of Management*, *38*(4), 969–1009. https://doi.org/10.1177/0149206311426187

Vaccaro, M., Almaatouq, A., & Malone, T. (2024). When combinations of humans and AI are useful: A systematic review and meta-analysis. *Nature Human Behaviour*, *8*(12), 2293–2303. https://doi.org/10.1038/s41562-024-02024-1

Woodruff, A., Shelby, R., Kelley, P. G., Rousso-Schindler, S., Smith-Loud, J., & Wilcox, L. (2024). How knowledge workers think Generative AI will (not) transform their industries. *Proceedings of the 2024 CHI conference on human factors in computing systems* (p. Article 641). Association for Computing Machinery. https://doi.org/10.1145/3613904.3642700

World Economic Forum. (2025). *Future of jobs report* (p. 290). World Economic Forum. https://www.weforum.org/reports/the-future-ofjobs-report-2025/

Wright, J. L., Quinn, S. A., Chen, J. Y., & Barnes, M. J. (2014). Individual differences in Human-agent teaming: An analysis of workload and situation awareness through eye movements. *Proceedings of the Human Factors and Ergonomics Society*, *58*, 1410–1414.

Wuchty, S., Jones, B. F., & Uzzi, B. (2007). The increasing dominance of teams in production of knowledge. *Science*, *316*(5827), 1036. https://doi.org/10.1126/science.1136099

Zhang, G., Chong, L., Kotovsky, K., & Cagan, J. (2023). Trust in an AI versus a human teammate: The effects of teammate identity and performance on Human-AI cooperation. *Computers in Human Behavior*, *139*, 107536. https://doi.org/10.1016/j.chb.2022.107536

Zirar, A., Ali, S. I., & Islam, N. (2023). Worker and workplace artificial intelligence (AI) coexistence: Emerging themes and research agenda. *Technovation*, *124*, 102747. https://doi.org/10.1016/j.technovation.2023.102747

PART 4

AI IN CONTEXT

CHAPTER 8

PROACTIVE ROBOTS IN HUMAN–ROBOT ACTION TEAMS

Rabeya Jamshad[a], Susan Simkins[b] and Laurel D. Riek[a]

[a]*Computer Science and Engineering, University of California San Diego, USA*
[b]*Psychology, Pennsylvania State University, USA*

ABSTRACT

In action teams, members coordinate in fast-paced, uncertain conditions to achieve a common goal – for example, firefighters and emergency medical teams. In many contexts, action teams are under-resourced, which can impede their success. Well-designed and well-contextualized proactive robots, which take initiative to help their human teammates, may help teams achieve their goals. This chapter examines action teams, challenges in team coordination, and how robots can be designed to support these teams. We provide a brief overview of the literature covering proactive dialogue and action in human–robot teams. We then discuss a study we conducted with human–robot action teams to understand how robot initiative can be designed for dynamic environments. Our research informs the design of robots that are capable of proactively taking action to support team outcomes in uncertain, fast-paced environments.

Keywords: Action teams; robots; team dynamics; proactive robots; coordination; human–robot teaming

INTRODUCTION

One way people are able to overcome adversity is by collaborating in teams. In teams, people can combine their skills and contribute in different roles to

AI in Teams: Research on Managing Groups and Teams, Volume 21, 135–149

Published under exclusive licence by Emerald Publishing Limited
ISSN: 1534-0856/doi:10.1108/S1534-085620260000021020

accomplish tasks that may be overwhelming or impossible for any one individual. Examples of collaborative tasks include building structures and performing rescue operations to save lives. Success in teams is highly dependent on effective coordination (Rico et al., 2008), defined as the strategies and behavior patterns that align the actions of interdependent team members (Arrow et al., 2000).

Team coordination depends on many factors, including group potency (a shared belief that the team can be successful), cohesion (Jordan et al., 2002), leadership, trust, and communication. For example, in a study of firefighter teams, task cohesion was found to have a significant effect on whether accidents occurred in low- and high-risk situations (Fruhen & Keith, 2014).

In this chapter, we focus on teaming with robots, which are physically embodied agents, and human–robot interaction (HRI), which is a type of human–agent team (HAT). Specifically, we focus on HATs that are action teams with robots as team members. In action teams, members with specialized skills improvise and coordinate their actions in uncertain and dynamic environments (Edmondson, 2003). Examples of action teams include firefighters and healthcare workers in emergency medicine . The time-critical nature of action teams' work implies that they need to perform under constraints such as limited information and high workloads. Failures in action teams can lead to serious consequences, including irreparable harm and death.

One way to mitigate negative team outcomes in action teams is to foster robust team dynamics. Team dynamics refers to the "atmosphere within the team and the context in which it operates" (Proenca, 2007, p. 371). Robotics researchers have explored introducing robots into action teams, such as for assessing natural disasters, supporting search and rescue, and removing explosives (Murphy, 2017; Surmann et al., 2022; Wilk-Jakubowski et al., 2022). Robots can adopt several supportive roles, such as aiding in human decision making and reducing risk to team members by entering unsafe areas or adopting unsafe tasks.

Additionally, robots may be able to support team dynamics, such as by facilitating trust (Birmingham et al., 2020) and group engagement (Tennent et al., 2019). These ideas have been explored in multiple contexts, including acute care teams (Gombolay et al., 2018; Matsumoto et al., 2021; Taylor et al., 2019, 2024) and spacecraft maintenance teams (Ma et al., 2022).

However, robots may also negatively impact teams by interrupting team workflow, decreasing in-group identification, and interfering with inter-personal relationships (Jung et al., 2020; Mutlu & Forlizzi, 2008; Savela et al., 2021; Sebo, Dong et al., 2020). For example, introducing a robot in medical units modified the team's workflow, increased workload for some personnel, led to lower perceived quality of service and increased interruptions (Mutlu & Forlizzi, 2008). Therefore, it is important to design well-contextualized robots that can support team success and do not result in adverse outcomes for the team.

One robot behavior to consider is *initiative*, which specifies *when* a robot should help its teammates (Baraglia et al., 2016, 2017). Proactive robots can anticipate team needs and take initiative to support their teammates. There is evidence that people perceive robots that exhibit proactive behaviors as better teammates (Baraglia et al., 2016, 2017).

Despite increasing research in designing robots for teams and robot proactivity, there are still several key gaps. First, there is a dearth of research that has explored how proactive robots can support action teams. Prior work on robot proactive behaviors has mostly focused on dyadic interactions or has studied robot proactivity in constrained task contexts (van Den Broek & Moeslund, 2024). This gap limits our scientific understanding of how proactive behavior influences team performance and dynamics in uncertain, fast-paced environments.

Second, prior research on proactive robot behaviors has predominantly studied proactive speech and proactive action separately. This is a limitation, as both proactive speech and actions influence HRI, and studying them separately does not capture the complexity or joint influence of these interactions. Lastly, there is limited research on how proactive robots effectively interpret and respond to their teammates' verbal and nonverbal behaviors. This is problematic as appropriate proactive behavior by the robot should align with the task context and team dynamics to anticipate and support team needs.

In this chapter, we first discuss action teams and their teaming context. We then present research on how robots can support action teams. We also describe existing research on the design of proactive robots. We describe a study we conducted to investigate how teams in time-constrained contexts perceive proactive robot behaviors.

Our results provide insights into participants' experiences when teaming with a robot, as well as the observed teaming behaviors. This research supports our understanding of how robot behaviors affect action team dynamics and performance, as well as the perception of the robot. It also highlights how the dynamic and time-critical performance context of action teams influences the acceptance of robot behaviors. These insights can provide important considerations for designing robot behaviors to support action teams.

ACTION TEAMS

We define a team as a group of three or more individuals who interact socially, share a goal, and are interdependent (Reimer et al., 2017; Sebo, Stoll et al., 2020). In action teams, members have specialized skills and perform in time-critical, dynamic, and unpredictable environments (Kolbe et al., 2011; Krenz & Burtscher, 2021). These teams perform in contexts where tasks cannot be scheduled in advance. For example, firefighters respond to fires as they occur, and, despite extensive training for many different situations, firefighters cannot predetermine their specific tasks. This is characterized as the *epochality* of action teamwork (Krenz & Burtscher, 2021). Similarly, action teams also face *finality* of work such that the effects of the actions taken by the teams may be irreversible (e.g., the death of a patient; Krenz & Burtscher, 2021). Since action teams perform under uncertainty, it is important to consider how coordination occurs. In these teams, members must perform joint actions coordinated in space and time to complete interdependent tasks. They must also ensure effective information sharing to establish a shared understanding among team members (Rico et al., 2019).

Kolbe et al. (2011) proposed a two-dimensional model that describes coordination in action teams. On one dimension is the entity that is coordinated (*what*), that is, either action or information, and on the other dimension is the mechanism of coordination (*how*) which can be either explicit or implicit (Rico et al., 2008). Other research has also emphasized how action teams must share information to coordinate actions (Edmondson, 2003).

Teams have different requirements based on the nature of their tasks (e.g., safety-critical) (Kolbe et al., 2011). Also, team requirements can change depending on whether the teams are interdisciplinary or multiteam systems (groups of teams working interdependently to coordinate and to accomplish shared goals, while still working toward their own team-level goals; Zaccaro et al., 2020). These challenges can also lead to errors and conflicts between teams (Kolbe et al., 2011), which can be catastrophic in safety-critical contexts such as healthcare and firefighting. In our work, we look into how robot initiative impacts human–robot teaming in the dynamic, time- and safety-critical context of action teams.

ROBOTS IN HUMAN–ROBOT TEAMS

Types of Robots

Riek (2017, p. 68) defines robots as "physically embodied systems capable of enacting physical change in the world." These robots may have sensors such as cameras and microphones to understand the world around them. They may also have effectors, like a gripper, to interact with the physical environment. Robots can possess interactional interfaces, such as touch sensors and screens. The physical embodiment of robots, and their ability to interact with the world, distinguishes robots from software-only AI agents.

Robots can have different physical embodiments based on their intended capabilities and roles. Mobile robots are designed to transport objects from one place to another, for example in warehouses (Roach, 2022). Some robots are stationary manipulators that can be used to move or assemble objects in confined spaces, for example, in factories to assemble parts (Weber, 2023). Robots may also be embodied as mobile manipulators that can move around and pick and place objects. Mobile manipulators are being used in hospitals to perform object deliveries (Savage, 2022). Tabletop robots are small, stationary robots that can be used as personal assistants or to deliver cognitive rehabilitative therapies (Bouzida et al., 2024).

Designing Robots for Human–Robot Action Teams

There has been a growing interest in understanding how the introduction of robots influences dynamics in groups and teams (Sebo, Stoll et al., 2020). This interest is motivated by robots working in close proximity to people (and not just being in "robot-only" zones in cages). Thus, researchers have explored how to design technologies that support multi-party interaction, team dynamics, and in-group social identification (Gillet et al., 2024; Savela et al., 2021).

Prior research has considered how robots can support action teams in clinical settings. Taylor et al. (2019) studied how robots in these teams can be used to (1) reduce errors during procedures, (2) coordinate the spatial configuration of the team during a procedure, and (3) mitigate the negative consequence of power dynamics in clinical teams. Similarly, Matsumoto et al. (2023) considered how robots can be designed to better support clinicians who work under high cognitive load and are frequently interrupted. HRI researchers have also considered how robots can be designed to support teams in emergency situations, such as search and rescue (Murphy, 2017).

We also draw from the broader HRI literature to understand how robots can be effective in action teams. Robots must coordinate with their teammates in time and space to achieve team goals. To achieve this, robots can identify groups of people and track them in dynamic environments (Taylor & Riek, 2022). Furthermore, research by Iqbal et al. (2015) and Iqbal and Riek (2017) has shown how robots can temporally synchronize with their teammates and how the synchronization affects team coordination dynamics. Therefore, while there is still limited research on how robots can support action teams, there is a growing emphasis on understanding how to improve human–robot collaboration and how robots can team in dynamic contexts.

Proactive Robots in Human–Robot Teams

Proactivity is defined as taking the initiative to advance the current task, which can also support the achievement of social aims (Pandey et al., 2013). Being proactive can help individuals achieve positive outcomes for themselves, including improved performance at work (Zhang et al., 2021). In teams, however, proactivity has a curvilinear relationship with team performance (Zhang et al., 2021). It is initially positive but inflects as the mean level of proactive personality changes from low to high (Zhang et al., 2021). This finding suggests that proactivity is an important behavior to consider when planning for team success.

As a result, researchers have designed proactive robots that take the initiative to support their teammate(s). For example, Baraglia et al. (2016, 2017) found that proactivity in a robot improved team fluency and participants found their interaction with the proactive robot to be more natural compared to a reactive robot. Similarly, Huang et al. (2015) found that robot proactivity led to better team performance as opposed to reactive and adaptive robots (robots that adjusted to their teammate's availability) in handover tasks. Sirithunge et al. (2019) studied how a proactive robot evaluates the level of interest of an interaction partner to decide when and how to initiate interaction with its teammates. Their results suggest that the robot should respect people's personal space, not violate their expectations, and consider the interactants' task context as well as nonverbal cues when initiating interactions.

Robot support in the form of proactive explanations has been found especially useful. Proactive explanations by the robot increased the trust teammates placed in the robot (Zhu & Williams, 2020). In another study, a robot that proactively provided information about possible issues was trusted more and perceived as more intelligent than a reactive robot (LeMasurier et al., 2024).

Anticipatory actions are a well-researched way for robots to proactively interact with humans. Anticipatory actions can improve efficiency, perceived fluency of robot behavior and intelligence, and the robot's contribution to the team compared to a reactive robot (Hoffman, 2010; Hoffman & Breazeal, 2007, 2008). Similarly, methods for robots to anticipate and adapt to human teammates have improved team synchronization (Iqbal & Riek, 2017, 2021; Iqbal et al., 2015, 2016). A robot's anticipatory actions and strategy also influence people's decision-making (Newman et al., 2020). Other researchers have used temporal anticipation of object movement by robots to proactively support people with activities of daily living (Patel & Chernova, 2022; Patel et al., 2023). However, there are still gaps in our understanding of how proactive robots should be designed. First, most research has focused on dyadic interactions or studied robot proactivity using constrained tasks; this limits the applicability of their results to action teams. Second, in most prior work, proactive speech and proactive actions have been studied separately. To successfully interact with its teammates, a robot must exhibit proactive behavior in both speech and actions. Lastly, although prior work has reported negative consequences of proactive robot behaviors, it is unclear how inter-team dynamics and task context influence the perception of proactive robot behaviors. If poorly designed, proactive robots may worsen user experience (Huang et al., 2015), negatively impact trust in the robot (Kraus et al., 2022), reduce situational awareness (Zhang et al., 2015), be harder to use (Fink et al., 2014), and be perceived as interrupting and controlling (Haripriyan et al., 2024; Jamshad et al., 2024, 2026; Peng et al., 2019; Ramaraj et al., 2024).

UNDERSTANDING HUMAN–ROBOT ACTION TEAMS

Our work focuses on designing robots that can support action teams. In particular, we seek to understand how robot initiative impacts team performance and intra-team dynamics and how it is perceived by human teammates (Haripriyan et al., 2024; Jamshad et al., 2024, 2026; Ramaraj et al., 2024). This work contributes to the design of robots that can proactively collaborate in dynamic and time-constrained settings, potentially reducing people's workload and making their work safer.

Study Design

To investigate the effects of robot initiative on teaming, we conducted a within-subject, qualitative study in which teams of three people and a robot collaborated to complete two escape rooms. Participants either collaborated with a passive robot in the first escape room and then a proactive robot in the second escape room, or vice versa, depending on the experimental condition. After each escape room, team members participated in a semi-structured group interview and answered questions about their teaming experience with the robot. We collected video and audio recordings of teams as they completed the escape room. For more details about the study design, please refer to work by Jamshad et al., (2026).

In total, five teams of three people and a robot participated in our study. We counterbalanced the two escape rooms (medical- and hazard-themed) and the two robot behavior conditions (passive and proactive). However, due to four possible combinations (escape room–robot behavior) and five teams, we had two teams that experienced escape room–medical–passive robot (escape room–robot behavior) experimental conditions first. To participate in the study, individuals had to be fluent in English and be at least 18 years old. Five participants were 18–24 years old, nine were 25–34, and one was 35–44 years old. Seven identified as women, and eight as men. Each team member wore a different colored vest that researchers could match to their participant ID number. We referred to participants in our study by their team number and participant number (T#P#, e.g., T1P2). This study was declared exempt by the UC San Diego IRB.

Simulating Action Team Dynamics Through Escape Rooms

To simulate the time- and safety-critical contexts in which action teams perform, we designed two escape rooms inspired by two types of action teams (see Fig. 8.1). The first escape room was modeled on medical action teams which we call the escape room-medical (ER-M). The second escape room was modeled on hazard response action teams which we call the escape room-hazard (ER-H). In ER-M, teams completed tasks to provide care to a patient. In ER-H, teams completed tasks to secure an area after a chemical spill.

We designed the escape rooms according to the methodological guidelines by Cohen et al. (2020, 2021; Griggs et al., 2022). We first ran pilot studies to determine if the tasks supported interdependence between the teammates and the robot, were engaging, had clear goals, and could be completed within the time limit. Tasks in each escape room were designed through an iterative process.

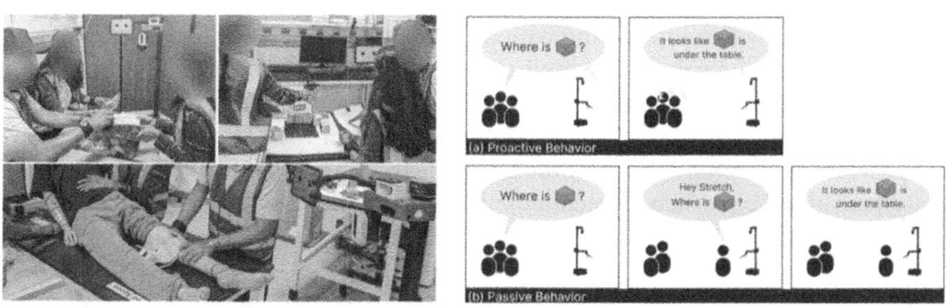

Fig. 8.1. (Left) Teams of Three People Collaborated with the Stretch Robot in the Escape Room Study. (Top Left to Bottom) Participants Completed an Icebreaker to Introduce Themselves and Become Familiar with the Stretch Robot. They Collaborated on Activities such as Solving Puzzles and Providing Care to a Patient. (Right) Design of Proactive and Passive Robot Behaviors. (a) The Proactive Robot Helped Whenever It Could. (b) The Passive Robot only Helped When Explicitly Requested by Its Teammates.

To provide a consistent experience to the participants, each of the three tasks across both escape room themes followed a similar task flow. In the first two tasks, teams had to complete challenges to either provide care to the patient in ER-M or secure the area from a chemical hazard in ER-H. In the third task, teams had to complete the challenges to make their escape. Teams were given 20 minutes to complete as many tasks as possible.

Each task consisted of several subtasks, designed to encourage teamwork between all team members (including the robot). For example, some subtasks that involved solving riddles to identify color or numeric codes were easier for human teammates to complete. Other subtasks required checking for toxins and deciphering encrypted codes. These subtasks were well-suited to the robot's capabilities and encouraged team members to collaborate with the robot.

Robot Design and Behavior

In this study, we used the Stretch robot (Kemp et al., 2022) in both escape rooms. This robot is a mobile manipulator, capable of moving around and fetching objects with its gripper. It is safe to use around people. We modified the robot's physical embodiment by adding additional hardware. We attached a tablet and a Bluetooth speaker to support audio communication and natural interaction with the team.

We employed a Wizard of Oz (WoZ) methodology (Riek, 2012) to control the robot. In a WoZ methodology, the robot is remotely controlled by a teleoperator (Wizard), but the participants are led to believe that the robot is autonomous. Participants were debriefed at the conclusion of the study that the robot was teleoperated. In our study, the Wizard controlled the robot using a bespoke Unity-ROS interface and an Xbox controller.

The interface allowed the Wizard to view camera streams from the cameras mounted on the robot. The Wizard also controlled the robot's speech using buttons on the interface. The audio was pre-recorded to constrain the verbal dialog used by Stretch when interacting with different teams for a consistent experience.

We designed the robot to exhibit two levels of robot initiative based on work by Baraglia et al. (2016). In the proactive condition, the robot had greater independence and control over its actions and helped out the team by taking actions or providing information whenever it could. In the passive condition, the robot only provided help when the team explicitly asked for it. Therefore, team members had greater control over the robot's actions in the passive condition.

Understanding Preferences of Robot Initiative in Human–Robot Action Teams

We wanted to understand what factors guided teams' perceptions of and preferences about robot initiative in time-constrained and dynamic teaming contexts. For this reason, we analyzed the group interviews using reflexive thematic analysis, which involves iteratively coding the data to generate themes (Braun & Clarke, 2006, 2021). Three researchers iteratively analyzed the interviews, with each interview being analyzed by two researchers. They met to discuss their codes and generate themes from the data.

Our analysis revealed that irrespective of the order in which teams interacted with the proactive or passive robot, teams were split in their preference between the two behaviors (Jamshad et al., 2024, 2026). Three teams preferred to interact with the proactive robot, whereas two teams preferred to interact with the passive robot. We found several factors that guided their preferences and derived design guidelines for the HRI community when integrating robots in dynamic, time-, and safety-critical collaboration contexts.

Teams that appreciated proactive robot behavior complemented its independence in completing tasks. The robot's proactive behavior also helped clarify the robot's capabilities to the team. Therefore, these teams found the proactive robot to be more helpful toward task progress and the team. On the other hand, teams that preferred the passive robot behavior appreciated that they were in control of the robot's actions and the task process. These teams also found that when they guided the verbal communication with the passive robot, it led to better quality of communication than with the proactive robot. They also shared that passive robot behavior was more appropriate based on their perceived capabilities of the robot.

Regardless of their preference for robot initiative, teams shared some common experiences. In general, teams reported that the robot should be capable of more naturalistic communication for effective collaboration. Some participants expressed trusting their human teammates more than the robot. For example, T4P3 said that they would not "ask [the robot] to save a human life or ask it any ethical or moral question without asking my teammates or trusting myself." In addition, teams also anthropomorphized the robot.

Our results highlight several important considerations for how a robot should take initiative in human–robot action teams. First, the robot's proactive behavior should be designed considering the perceived cost to the team. When the cost to the team is high, teams want more control over the robot and rely on their human teammates more than the robot. Second, it is important that the robot is capable of communicating with its teammates in a natural manner. While large language models (LLMs) can support this, we must carefully consider how to balance the need for fluent communication with accurate information since LLMs are prone to hallucination (William et al., 2024). Hallucination in LLMs occurs when the output generated by the LLM does not correctly represent the source data, leading to nonsensical or incorrect responses (Huang et al., 2025). This can be problematic in fast-paced decision-making contexts such as action teams. Lastly, given these concerns, it is important to consider whether proactive robots that appear as more independent and helpful may mislead people about their capabilities when they proactively share information that is not well-grounded in the team's performance context.

Understanding Human Behavior and Social Signals to Support Human–Robot Teaming

Through our research, we also wanted to understand how HRT may be affected by (1) the attitudes of human teammates toward the robot and (2) the robot's actions to assist its teammates (Haripriyan et al., 2024; Ramaraj et al., 2024).

To better understand these phenomena, we collected video data of the participants during the escape room. We followed a similar procedure for reflexive thematic analysis as described earlier (Braun & Clarke, 2006, 2021).

Our analysis showed that some participants expressed rapport-building behavior with the robot. For example, participants shared credit with the robot when working together to solve the escape room puzzles. In Team 5, when the robot helped its teammates locate an item they needed, T5P1 acknowledged it by saying, "Stretch told us." Participants also shared light moments as a team that were appreciative and inclusive of the robot. When Stretch responded with "No" to a participant's inquiry about whether the robot could help push an item, the team shared a laugh and T1P2 said "I love the way he [says] no." This suggests that participants were appreciative of the robot and thought of the robot as a part of their team even when the robot was unable to help them.

However, other participants did not perceive the robot as a part of the team and exhibited othering behaviors toward the robot. Participants in these teams had negative perceptions about the robot and doubted its ability to contribute. For example, when the robot stated, "I can help with that," T3P1 responded with "Can he?" Some participants therefore tried to micromanage the robot's movements to ensure the task was completed. These interactions between the robot and its teammates showed that these participants treated the robot as an outgroup member and doubted whether the robot could contribute to the team's goals.

This finding suggests that to support human–robot collaboration, it may not be enough to encourage participants to consider the robot as a part of the team. Instead, robot behaviors should be designed to build rapport with the team and minimize negative perceptions. One way to accomplish this may be for robots to engage in social behaviors appreciative of the team, for example, the robot may be designed to use positive affirmations to support team morale.

We also observed participants adapting their strategies and communication to collaborate better with the robot. For example, participants adapted the timing of their requests to the robot to account for the slow movement of the robot. When the robot failed to hand over an object to Team 1 due to a technical error, the participants modified their request and instead asked the robot to place the object on a table. These behaviors suggest that team members exerted effort to collaborate with the robot. The robot can capitalize on these adaptive behaviors of its teammates to understand their intent when they instruct or make requests to the robot.

Our analysis also showed that to better collaborate with the robot, some participants took on the role of the robot manager. In this role, they were responsible for coordinating with the robot by assigning tasks. However, this role was not always self-appointed, and in one instance a participant requested that another participant help coordinate with the robot. This role improvisation suggests that when people coordinate in teams with a robot, new roles may emerge, likely due to task interdependence between the humans and the robot. Therefore, it may become important to design robot behaviors that can support team members in these roles.

Another important finding of our analysis is the role of the robot's physical embodiment in setting its teammates' expectations of its abilities and intent. Since the robot in our study had a gripper, some participants expected that it should be able to pick any object in the environment. Participants were shocked when the robot said that it could not pick up a small object in the environment. Similarly, teams used the robot's body motion and sensors to obtain directional cues. However, this was also a source of confusion for some teammates as the movement of different sensors created ambiguity about the robot's focus of attention. Therefore, when designing robot embodiment, it is important to consider how (1) the embodiment may convey the robot's capabilities and limitations and (2) the robot's movement of its sensors may convey social cues and intent.

CONCLUSION AND OPEN CHALLENGES

Action teams perform in dynamic, safety-, and time-critical environments and coordinate their actions in space and time to achieve task success. This context requires that team members communicate effectively with each other to respond to evolving task needs. Robots are increasingly being introduced to teams where they can take over unsafe and repetitive tasks as well as support information collection and relaying. In these roles, robots will need to exhibit appropriate behaviors to be accepted by teammates and be beneficial to the team. However, understanding what these robot behaviors are and how they will influence intra-team dynamics is not an easy task. In our work, we studied proactive and passive robot behaviors using an escape room paradigm to understand (1) what factors influence team preference for proactive robots and (2) how robot behavior influences team dynamics. Our results suggest that we need to consider the cost to the team and quality of communication when designing how a proactive robot should take initiative.

Our work also highlighted that when robots interact with teams in time-critical contexts, we need to consider how that context affects people's attitudes toward the robot. First, our results revealed that people may have different attitudes toward the robot as some teams displayed othering behavior toward the robot, while other teams developed a rapport with the robot. Second, we found that participants adapted to the robot's abilities through workarounds and creating new roles such as the robot manager when teaming with the robot. Lastly, our findings illustrated that it is important to consider how a robot's intent is communicated both verbally and through non-verbal signals such as the robot's physical embodiment and motion.

While our research extends our understanding of how robot behaviors and action team contexts affect HRI, several challenges remain. As action teams perform in fast-paced environments, robots will need to continue to adapt their behaviors based on new task contexts. To achieve this, the robot will need to rapidly evaluate how it proactively prioritizes the help and information it provides to teammates. Another challenge is related to contextual awareness of robots in dynamic environments and how the robots can manage uncertainty and partial observations when reasoning about the world context. Correct reasoning about the world is essential if robots are to proactively assist teammates. Additionally, how a robot is onboarded into a team may impact the team's perceptions of the robot. If team members have negative perceptions of the robot, they may be unwilling to interact with it, resulting in poor human–robot action team dynamics. Furthermore, there is a need to understand how human–robot action team dynamics vary between short- and long-term interactions. Over longer periods of interaction, people's familiarity with the robot will change, affecting team dynamics and team workflows. Continued research is essential to unlock the potential of human–robot teaming, ensuring these collaborations are not only technically effective but also ethically sound, adaptable, and deeply aligned with human needs.

ACKNOWLEDGMENTS

Jamshad and colleagues acknowledge that the research was supported by the Office of Naval Research under Grant N000142212813.

REFERENCES

Arrow, H., McGrath, J. E., & Berdahl, J. L. (2000). *Small groups as complex systems: Formation, coordination, development, and adaptation*. Sage Publications.

Baraglia, J., Cakmak, M., Nagai, Y., Rao, R., & Asada, M. (2016). Initiative in robot assistance during collaborative task execution. *2016 11th ACM/IEEE international conference on human-robot interaction (HRI)* (pp. 67–74).

Baraglia, J., Cakmak, M., Nagai, Y., Rao, R. P., & Asada, M. (2017). Efficient human-robot collaboration: When should a robot take initiative? *The International Journal of Robotics Research*, *36*(5–7), 563–579.

Birmingham, C., Hu, Z., Mahajan, K., Reber, E., & Mataric´, M. J. (2020). Can I trust you? A user study of robot mediation of a support group. *2020 IEEE International conference on robotics and automation (ICRA)* (pp. 8019–8026).

Bouzida, A., Kubota, A., Cruz-Sandoval, D., Twamley, E. W., & Riek, L. D. (2024). Carmen: A cognitively assistive robot for personalized neurorehabilitation at home. *Proceedings of the 2024 ACM/IEEE international conference on human-robot interaction* (pp. 55–64).

Braun, V., & Clarke, V. (2006). Using thematic analysis in psychology. *Qualitative Research in Psychology*, *3*(2), 77–101.

Braun, V., & Clarke, V. (2021). One size fits all? What counts as quality practice in (reflexive) thematic analysis? *Qualitative Research in Psychology*, *18*(3), 328–352.

Cohen, T. N., Griggs, A. C., Kanji, F. F., Cohen, K. A., Lazzara, E. H., Keebler, J. R., & Gewertz, B. L. (2021). Advancing team cohesion: Using an escape room as a novel approach. *Journal of Patient Safety and Risk Management*, *26*(3), 126–134.

Cohen, T. N., Griggs, A. C., Keebler, J. R., Lazzara, E. H., Doherty, S. M., Kanji, F. F. & Gewertz, B. L. (2020). Using escape rooms for conducting team research: Understanding development, considerations, and challenges. *Simulation & Gaming*, *51*(4), 443–460.

Edmondson, A. C. (2003). Speaking up in the operating room: How team leaders promote learning in interdisciplinary action teams. *Journal of Management Studies*, *40*(6), 1419–1452.

Fink, J., Lemaignan, S., Dillenbourg, P., Re´tornaz, P., Vaussard, F., Berthoud, A., Mondada, F., Wille, F., & Franinovic´, K. (2014). Which robot behavior can motivate children to tidy up their toys? Design and evaluation of "ranger". *Proceedings of the 2014 ACM/IEEE international conference on human-robot interaction* (pp. 439–446).

Fruhen, L. S., & Keith, N. (2014). Team cohesion and error culture in risky work environments. *Safety Science*, *65*, 20–27.

Gillet, S., Vázquez, M., Andrist, S., Leite, I., & Sebo, S. (2024). Interaction-shaping robotics: Robots that influence interactions between other agents. *ACM Transactions on Human-Robot Interaction*, *13*(1), 1–23.

Gombolay, M., Yang, X. J., Hayes, B., Seo, N., Liu, Z., Wadhwania, S., Yu, T., Shah, N., Golen, T., & Shah, J. (2018). Robotic assistance in the coordination of patient care. *The International Journal of Robotics Research*, *37*(10), 1300–1316.

Griggs, A. C., Lazzara, E. H., Doherty, S. M., Keebler, J. R., Gewertz, B. L., & Cohen, T. N. (2022). Unlocking the methodology of escape rooms: Considerations for conducting applied escape rooms in research. *Simulation & Gaming*, *53*(6), 663–675.

Haripriyan, A., Jamshad, R., Ramaraj, P., & Riek, L. D. (2024). Human-robot action teams: A behavioral analysis of team dynamics. *2024 33rd IEEE International conference on robot and human interactive communication (ROMAN)* (pp. 1443–1448).

Hoffman, G. (2010, March). Anticipation in human-robot interaction. *AAAI Spring symposium: It's all in the timing*.

Hoffman, G., & Breazeal, C. (2007). Cost-based anticipatory action selection for human–robot fluency. *IEEE Transactions on Robotics*, *23*(5), 952–961.

Hoffman, G., & Breazeal, C. (2008). Achieving fluency through perceptual-symbol practice in human-robot collaboration. *Proceedings of the 3rd ACM/IEEE international conference on human robot interaction* (pp. 1–8).

Huang, C.-M., Cakmak, M., & Mutlu, B. (2015). Adaptive coordination strategies for human-robot handovers. *Robotics: Science and Systems*, *11*, pp. 1–10.

Huang, L., Yu, W., Ma, W., Zhong, W., Feng, Z., Wang, H., Chen, Q., Peng, W., Feng, X., Qin, B., & Liu, T., (2025). A survey on hallucination in large language models: Principles, taxonomy, challenges, and open questions. *ACM Transactions on Information Systems*, *43*(2), 1–55.

Iqbal, T., Gonzales, M. J., & Riek, L. D. (2015). Joint action perception to enable fluent human-robot teamwork. *2015 24th IEEE International symposium on robot and human interactive communication (RO-MAN)* (pp. 400–406).

Iqbal, T., Rack, S., & Riek, L. D. (2016). Movement coordination in human–robot teams: A dynamical systems approach. *IEEE Transactions on Robotics*, *32*(4), 909–919.

Iqbal, T., & Riek, L. D. (2017). Coordination dynamics in multihuman multirobot teams. *IEEE Robotics and Automation Letters*, *2*(3), 1712–1717.

Iqbal, T., & Riek, L. D. (2021). Temporal anticipation and adaptation methods for fluent human-robot teaming. *2021 IEEE International conference on robotics and automation (ICRA)* (pp. 3736–3743).

Jamshad, R., Haripriyan, A., Sonti, A., Simkins, S., & Riek, L. D. (2024). Taking initiative in human-robot action teams: How proactive robot behaviors affect teamwork. *Companion of the 2024 ACM/IEEE international conference on human-robot interaction* (pp. 559–562).

Jamshad, R., Haripriyan, A., Sonti, A., Simkins, S., & Riek, L. D., (2026). Human-robot action teams: How robot proactivity affects teamwork. *Computers in Human Behavior: Artificial Humans*, 100269.

Jordan, M. H., Feild, H. S., & Armenakis, A. A. (2002). The relationship of group process variables and team performance: A team-level analysis in a field setting. *Small Group Research*, *33*(1), 121–150.

Jung, M. F., DiFranzo, D., Shen, S., Stoll, B., Claure, H., & Lawrence, A. (2020). Robot-assisted tower construction – A method to study the impact of a robot's allocation behavior on interpersonal dynamics and collaboration in groups. *ACM Transactions on Human-Robot Interaction (THRI)*, *10*(1), 1–23.

Kemp, C. C., Edsinger, A., Clever, H. M., & Matulevich, B. (2022). The design of stretch: A compact, lightweight mobile manipulator for indoor human environments. *2022 International conference on robotics and automation (ICRA)* (pp. 3150–3157).

Kolbe, M., Burtscher, M., Manser, T., Ku¨nzle, B., & Grote, G. (2011). The role of coordination in preventing harm in healthcare groups: Research examples from anaesthesia and an integrated model of coordination for action teams in health care. *Coordination in Human and Primate Groups*, pp. 75–92.

Kraus, M., Wagner, N., Untereiner, N., & Minker, W. (2022). Including social expectations for trustworthy proactive human-robot dialogue. *Proceedings of the 30th ACM conference on user modeling, adaptation and personalization* (pp. 23–33).

Krenz, H. L., & Burtscher, M. J. (2021). Investigating voice in action teams: A critical review. *Cognition, Technology & Work*, *23*, 605–624.

LeMasurier, G., Gautam, A., Han, Z., Crandall, J. W., & Yanco, H. A. (2024). Reactive or proactive? How robots should explain failures. *Proceedings of the 2024 ACM/IEEE international conference on human-robot interaction* (pp. 413–422).

Ma, L. M., Ijtsma, M., Feigh, K. M., & Pritchett, A. R. (2022). Metrics for human-robot team design: A teamwork perspective on evaluation of human-robot teams. *ACM Transactions on Human-Robot Interaction (THRI)*, *11*(3), 1–36.

Matsumoto, S., Ghosh, P., Jamshad, R., & Riek, L. D. (2023). Robot, uninterrupted: Telemedical robots to mitigate care disruption. *Proceedings of the 2023 ACM/IEEE international conference on human-robot interaction* (pp. 495–505).

Matsumoto, S., Moharana, S., Devanagondi, N., Oyama, L. C., & Riek, L. D. (2021). Iris: A low-cost telemedicine robot to support healthcare safety and equity during a pandemic. *International conference on pervasive computing technologies for healthcare* (pp. 113–133).

Murphy, R. R. (2017). *Disaster robotics*. MIT Press.

Mutlu, B., & Forlizzi, J. (2008). Robots in organizations: The role of workflow, social, and environmental factors in human-robot interaction. *Proceedings of the 3rd ACM/IEEE international conference on human robot interaction* (pp. 287–294).

Newman, B. A., Biswas, A., Ahuja, S., Girdhar, S., Kitani, K. K., & Admoni, H. (2020). Examining the effects of anticipatory robot assistance on human decision making. *International conference on social robotics* (pp. 590–603).

Pandey, A. K., Ali, M., & Alami, R. (2013). Towards a task-aware proactive sociable robot based on multi-state perspective-taking. *International Journal of Social Robotics*, *5*, 215–236.

Patel, M. & Chernova, S. (2022). Proactive robot assistance via spatio-temporal object modeling. *arXiv preprint arXiv:2211.15501*.

Patel, M., Prakash, A., & Chernova, S. (2023). Predicting routine object usage for proactive robot assistance. *arXiv preprint arXiv:2309.06252*.

Peng, Z., Kwon, Y., Lu, J., Wu, Z., & Ma, X. (2019). Design and evaluation of service robot's proactivity in decision-making support process. *Proceedings of the 2019 CHI conference on human factors in computing systems* (pp. 1–13).

Proenca, E. J. (2007). Team dynamics and team empowerment in health care organizations. *Health Care Management Review*, *32*(4), 370–378.

Ramaraj, P., Haripriyan, A., Jamshad, R., & Riek, L. D. (2024). Analysis of social signals in human-robot action teams. In *HRI 2024 workshop on social signals for HRI (SS4HRI)*.

Reimer, T., Russell, T., & Roland, C. (2017). Groups and teams in organizations. *The international encyclopedia of organizational communication* (pp. 1–23).

Rico, R., Gibson, C. B., Sa´nchez-Manzanares, M., & Clark, M. A. (2019). Building team effectiveness through adaptation: Team knowledge and implicit and explicit coordination. *Organizational Psychology Review*, *9*(2–3), 71–98.

Rico, R., Sa´nchez-Manzanares, M., Gil, F., & Gibson, C. (2008). Team implicit coordination processes: A team knowledge-based approach. *Academy of Management Review*, *33*(1), 163–184.

Riek, L. D. (2012). Wizard of OZ studies in HRI: A systematic review and new reporting guidelines. *Journal of Human-Robot Interaction*, *1*(1), 119–136.

Riek, L. D. (2017). Healthcare robotics. *Communications of the ACM*, *60*(11), 68–78.

Roach, J. (2022). *The quest to deploy autonomous robots within amazon fulfillment centers*. Amazon Science. https://www.amazon.science/latest-news/the-quest-to-deploy-autonomous-robots-within-amazon-fulfillment-centers

Savage, N. (2022). Robots rise to meet the challenge of caring for old people. *Nature*, *601*(7893), 8–10.

Savela, N., Kaakinen, M., Ellonen, N., & Oksanen, A. (2021). Sharing a work team with robots: The negative effect of robot co-workers on in-group identification with the work team. *Computers in Human Behavior*, *115*, 106585.

Sebo, S., Stoll, B., Scassellati, B., & Jung, M. F. (2020). Robots in groups and teams: A literature review. *Proceedings of the ACM on Human-Computer Interaction*, *4*(CSCW2), 1–36.

Sirithunge, C., Ravindu, H., Bandara, T., Buddhika, A., Jayasekara, P., & Chandima, D. (2019). Situation awareness for proactive robots in HRI. *2019 IEEE/RSJ International conference on intelligent robots and systems (IROS)* (pp. 7813–7820).

Strohkorb Sebo, S., Dong, L. L., Chang, N., & Scassellati, B. (2020). Strategies for the inclusion of human members within human-robot teams. *Proceedings of the 2020 ACM/IEEE international conference on human-robot interaction* (pp. 309–317).

Surmann, H., Slomma, D., Grafe, R., & Grobelny, S. (2022). Deployment of aerial robots during the flood disaster in Erftstadt/Blessem in July 2021. *2022 8th International conference on automation, robotics and applications (ICARA)* (pp. 97–102).

Taylor, A., Lee, H. R., Kubota, A., & Riek, L. D. (2019). Coordinating clinical teams: Using robots to empower nurses to stop the line. *Proceedings of the ACM on Human-Computer Interaction*, *3*(CSCW), 1–30.

Taylor, A., & Riek, L. D. (2022). Regroup: A robot-centric group detection and tracking system. *2022 17th ACM/IEEE international conference on human-robot interaction (HRI)* (pp. 412–421).

Taylor, A., Tanjim, T., Cao, H., & Lee, H. R. (2024). Towards collaborative crash cart robots that support clinical teamwork. *Proceedings of the 2024 ACM/IEEE international conference on human-robot interaction* (pp. 715–724).

Tennent, H., Shen, S., & Jung, M. (2019). Micbot: A peripheral robotic object to shape conversational dynamics and team performance. In *2019 14th ACM/IEEE international conference on human-robot interaction (HRI)* (pp. 133–142).

van Den Broek, M. K., & Moeslund, T. B. (2024). What is proactive human-robot interaction? A review of a progressive field and its definitions. *ACM Transactions on Human-Robot Interaction*, *13*(4), 1–30.

Weber, A. (2023, August 17). *Collaborative robot do's and don'ts*. ASSEMBLY. https://www.assemblymag.com/articles/97969-collaborative-robot-dos-and-donts

Wilk-Jakubowski, G., Harabin, R., & Ivanov, S. (2022). Robotics in crisis management: A review. *Technology in Society*, *68*, 101935.

Williams, T., Matuszek, C., Mead, R., & Depalma, N. (2024). Scarecrows in oz: The use of large language models in HRI. *ACM Transactions on Human-Robot Interaction*, *13*(1), 1–11.

Zaccaro, S. J., Dubrow, S., Torres, E. M., & Campbell, L. N. (2020). Multiteam systems: An integrated review and comparison of different forms. *Annual Review of Organizational Psychology and Organizational Behavior*, *7*(1), 479–503.

Zhang, R., Li, A., & Gong, Y. (2021). Too much of a good thing: Examining the curvilinear relationship between team-level proactive personality and team performance. *Personnel Psychology*, *74*(2), 295–321.

Zhang, Y., Narayanan, V., Chakraborti, T., & Kambhampati, S. (2015). A human factors analysis of proactive support in human-robot teaming. *2015 IEEE/RSJ International conference on intelligent robots and systems (IROS)* (pp. 3586–3593).

Zhu, L., & Williams, T. (2020). Effects of proactive explanations by robots on human-robot trust. In *Social robotics: 12th international conference, ICSR 2020, Golden, CO, USA, November 14–18, 2020, Proceedings 12* (pp. 85–95).

CHAPTER 9

AI AND DESIGN COLLABORATION: NOT A FULL MEMBER (YET)

Mark A. Clark[a] and Daniel Graff[b]

[a]*Kogod School of Business, American University, USA*
[b]*College of Design and Innovation, Tongji University, China*

ABSTRACT

Design consultancies rely both on individual expertise and collaborative processes to achieve innovative performance for their clients. As artificial intelligence (AI) increases in utility, these firms and others using design thinking processes are faced with how to incorporate AI into their work and how to fashion a position for AI in their workforce. Is AI best seen as a tool? An expert? A full collaborator? A competitor for jobs? This chapter outlines issues faced by the design field as AI enters its domain, including AI capabilities, needed human collaboration skills, and the way in which AI may support and potentially replace tasks and people. Drawing on a focused set of interviews with designers and their managers, we outline a case of one company grappling with the introduction of AI into their design process and products. Their challenges include understanding how AI can support design collaboration, developing the skills to leverage AI capabilities, and planning how AI use will affect their workforce roles. These findings suggest that design firms seeking to benefit from AI must mindfully define collaborative success in terms of relatively short-term outcomes such as client deliverables as well as longer-term considerations such as employee skills training, retention, and succession planning.

Keywords: Design thinking; artificial intelligence; team; workforce; design collaboration process; qualitative methods

AI in Teams: Research on Managing Groups and Teams, Volume 21, 151–169

Published under exclusive licence by Emerald Publishing Limited
ISSN: 1534-0856/doi:10.1108/S1534-085620260000021022

> The next steps in AI will be more critical advancements than the discovery of fire and electricity. (Kent Walker, President, Google, presentation in February 2023)

AI ENTERS THE DESIGN FIELD

Design collaborations depend on the pairing of expertise, distributed among those who contribute to a project, and the methods and processes which shape the work. Introducing AI and its related systems, models, and tools into these dependent relationships carries potential for changing not only the way that collaborative design is produced but also the quality and nature of the product outcomes and the shape of the workforce itself. In this chapter, we explore the use of AI in design collaborations, describing its challenges and opportunities, building on the emerging literature on AI–human teaming (e.g., Demir et al., 2018). We draw from interviews with key informants who have practical design experience (e.g., designers, design managers) to build understanding of AI integration into design methodology (i.e., how designers work) and design cognition (i.e., how designers think) to illustrate issues involved in successful collaboration with AI in design.

As a broad field that includes a variety of forms and applications, design has historically welcomed novel processes and multiple disciplines into its collaborations. Yet, like most modern industries, design faces uncertainty about how AI can support its aims. AI can take the form of large and natural language models (LLMs), machine learning, deep learning, and generative AI, all of which may be relevant to design collaborations. For the remainder of this chapter, we will use the term "AI" as an umbrella term to include such related concepts. AI is variously seen as a tool, outside expert, teammate, or competitor (see, e.g., Anthony, 2021; Lyons et al., 2019; Rodgers & Huxor, 1998) that can automate or augment performance tasks (Raisch & Krakowski, 2021) rather than necessarily replace human team members.

Existing organizational research has revealed important questions to explore regarding the use of AI in design innovation. For instance, what is the most suitable work for AI in design? Should AI be used primarily as an informational resource, or as a way to produce configurations of existing information and integrate ideas of human team members? What human skills and competencies are needed to effectively leverage AI within a design collaboration? How can AI support design cognition and design methodology? Under what conditions are humans more or less dependable than AI, or more effective in producing innovative design work?

Next, we offer an overview of design work and then briefly discuss known aspects of collaborative work, following this with findings from a case example, ending with discussion.

Design

The broad field of design encompasses a wide range of tasks and intentions, spanning fields such as architecture, software, consumers products such as automobiles and toys, and much more. We build on prior definitions (e.g., Ralph & Wand, 2009) to describe design as the activities of a human or machine in creating or contributing to the creation of physical or conceptual things. This definition focuses on the outcome – whether concepts or physical artifacts – which does not limit designers (i.e., those who do the design work) to be persons, as long as the outcomes are produced. It focuses also on the physical or conceptual design outcome, rather than on the process of designing (i.e., creative problem-solving process). While the focus in this book chapter is on more traditional design outcomes, such as products (physical and software), it also provides guidelines to newer design disciplines, such as service designs (conceptual).

Design tasks may be highly creative or more mundane. Design may involve collaborators working closely together in space and time or dispersed more broadly across locations, persons, and organizations (Cross, 1982). Within design work, AI can take different roles. AI in design work can be seen simply as a tool to aid designers in their work, but it can also be seen as a team member collaborating with human designers (Graff et al., 2026). We will refer to the first as *AI as a design aid*. Here, AI is a tool supporting the designer throughout the design process to achieve the designer's goal. We will term the latter role as *AI as a designer*. In the AI as a designer view, AI takes the role of a team member in a design project contributing to the creation of physical or conceptual things.

Design Thinking

An important application of design principles is realized through "design thinking," which refers to a set of processes, often delineated as stages or phases, intended to support innovation in products and services (Brown, 2008; Elsbach & Stigliani, 2018; Liedtka, 2015). These processes and the perspective they represent grew from early work on the origins of design and its methodology as a distinct discipline during the 1960s (Cross, 1982). Starting in this era, researchers began to explore and catalog designers' methods (how designers work) as distinct from cognition (how designers think). An important purpose of this research was to provide designers with practical guidelines for design projects (Jones, 1970), in contrast to the intuitive and experimental work modes common before then (Cross, 2023).

This more organized perspective led design thinking to be conceptualized as involving specific activities related to identification of needs, idea generation, and testing (Micheli et al., 2019), often using multidisciplinary team collaboration (Seidel & Fixson, 2013). Several variations of design thinking have been developed, generally including divergent and convergent in relatively distinct stages or in more fluid phases. In the 1990s, IDEO, a design and management consultancy, and the Hasso Plattner Institute of Design at Stanford University (commonly referred to as the d.school) applied the academic research on design practice to enhance understanding of design value to audiences outside of traditional art and architectural design (Hargadon & Sutton, 1997). Their aim was to provide services and support to a broad range of industries, which proliferated in the 2000s as a collection of training models and related workshops. Many books about design thinking published in this era, such as *The Art of Innovation* by IDEO leader Tom Kelley (2001), *The Design of Business* by Roger Martin (2009), and *Change by Design* by Tim Brown (2009), helped popularize the concepts and use of design thinking outside of the design discipline.

In this chapter, we follow their lead in offering a simplified version of design thinking as a human-centered, problem-solving approach that consists of five stages: (1) research, empathize, and define; (2) ideation; (3) prototype; (4) test and feedback; and (5) implement and commercialize.

In the first stage, the designer gathers a deep understanding of a problem environment and the user perspective in order to define an issue and create a design brief. The user is a person, target audience, or constituent group who interacts with elements of their environment which may be improved through design innovation. The problem in this context typically relates to a product, service, or system. It may be apparent to the user, such as the design of a replacement bridge to connect neighborhoods, or less realized, as seen in areas of breakthrough technologies such as the shift from mobile telephones to multifunctional smartphones. Understanding the perspective of the user requires empathy (McDonagh-Philp & Lebbon, 2000), in terms of understanding these needs, values, feelings, and preferences, and this understanding may be accomplished through a variety of quantitative (e.g., surveys, archival data) and qualitative methods (e.g., observations, interviews). The resulting design definition briefly summarizes findings from research on empathy, clearly describing the problem and users involved.

The second stage, ideation, involves designers generating novel approaches to address user problems through creativity techniques such as brainstorming. In the next stage, potential solutions based on these ideas are further developed through prototyping, in which the ideas generally are advanced into physical artifacts. In the fourth stage, the physical prototypes are then tested with potential users to receive feedback and iterate toward more refined solutions. Finally, in the fifth stage, solutions are implemented and commercialized, often integrating with broader organizational systems such as logistics, operations, marketing, and human capital. We discuss these stages further in the Findings: How *Forward* Uses AI in Design Collaboration section of this chapter.

Design Collaboration

Collaboration in design may refer to any interaction of individuals within a spectrum of collective work, including relatively independent sequential or iterative instances, broad cooperation based on shared goals, and intensive interactions which combine disparate areas of expertise, among other configurations. Design collaboration occurs often within multidisciplinary teams, in which designers work with other functions to develop new products and services. Within the related literature, scholars have largely discussed task-related factors such as knowledge and work roles, as well as interpersonal factors including diversity, trust, and communication (Nguyen & Mougenot, 2022). We also expect that there is much to learn about the principles of human–AI collaborations which, although bolstered by recent interest, have a relatively lean set of research-based findings. Some intriguing insights are beginning to emerge. For instance, Zhang et al. (2021) found that particularly weak design teams benefit from AI, but strong design teams performed worse. Our motivation for engaging in this study includes increasing understanding of issues around the use of AI in design collaborations.

Collaborative Skills in Design

To explore the operation and effectiveness of human–AI collaborations, it is necessary to draw upon understanding of the skills, factors, and processes related to collective efforts. At perhaps the most basic level, the research literature demonstrates that there are sets of knowledge, skills, and abilities (KSAs) that are associated with cooperation among persons and task components, over a wide variety of tasks (Campion & Campion, 2023; Morgeson et al., 2005; Stevens & Campion, 1994) and contexts (Borman & Motowidlo, 1993). More recently, Bell et al. (2018) explicated related process interactions among collaborators that are important to contextual performance in categories of affect, behavior, and cognition.

Further research suggests that there are specific skills beneficial for design collaborations. Tavčar et al. (2007) find that design collaborations require rich and intensive communication, particularly in virtual settings which require a high level of trust. This operationalizes, for example, as proficiency in visual technology and independent work. This study also suggests, somewhat counterintuitively to the idea that good collaborators might prefer collectivism, that persons from individualistic cultures are more likely than those in collectivistic cultures to have an easier time collaborating in virtual design teams due to their ability to be independent and to trust others.

One interesting line of research suggests that the specific skills used in design collaborations vary according to the experience of the design team members (Kleinsmann et al., 2012). In samples of students and professional designers, novice designers working together used trial and error methods of problem solving, searching for simple solutions without necessarily seeing the broader picture. More experienced collaborators engaged in increased information sharing and better understanding of the situational and conceptual range of the tasks, while highly experienced designers (7–10 years) collaborated with less explicit discussion, holding common procedural knowledge on design processes.

This progression of skills with experience may be explained, at least in part, by the reliance of design collaboration on the development of shared understanding, which is a product of expertise communicated over time and tasks as the designers develop new products and services (Nguyen & Mougenot, 2022). Shared understanding is particularly important in the typically multidisciplinary design teams which benefit from rich forms of communication to integrate and apply their differential knowledge (Graff & Clark, 2019).

AI on the Team?

With this understanding of the purposes, process, roles, and skills associated with design thinking collaboration, we can begin to ask appropriate questions about how AI is deployed in organizational design processes and how it might be more effectively leveraged. We expect, for instance, that the use of AI will be influenced by the conceptualization of AI held by designers and managers, in terms of value to their work and fit with the way they process information tasks. We will also investigate how AI is used, perhaps differentially, across design thinking stages. Finally, given the importance of the user experience (UEX) in design thinking, we will ask about AI's effects on or interaction with end users.

METHOD

To explore these areas, we conducted five semi-structured research interviews drawn through a modified convenience sample technique within the case organization, building from existing connections of the authors with designers and managers. The interviews with this focal organization comprise a subset of our total sample which targeted multiple organizations in varied industries and were approved as protocol IRB-2024-114 by the American University Institutional Review Board and Office of Research Integrity in November 2023. To gain perspectives of the variety of organizational roles who are jointly responsible for design collaborations and outcomes, we targeted interviewees who specialized in or were heavy users of AI as well as those more marginally affected by AI use in their organization. This strategy resulted in a relatively small sample of two design managers, a design specialist for AI, and two additional front-line designers within our focal organization. For the purposes of understanding the company, its employees, and clients, we also reviewed company public documents and other online information. Interviews, which followed a prescribed set of questions, were recorded and transcribed for research purposes. We augment the findings from our specific sample with our own understanding of issues related to AI in design that have been gained through our work with design companies, design and business students, and our familiarity with the relevant academic and practitioner literatures.

Interview Protocol

The semi-structured interview protocol consisted of open-ended questions focusing on a set of related themes, based on our understanding of collaboration in design thinking, in the following four categories:

(1) the conceptualization and role of AI for the interviewee's organization and job;
(2) the influence of AI on design processes and production methods;
(3) the manner in which design staff think, including how they process information and ideas;
(4) how AI influences the customer experience.

Given the semi-structured nature of the interviews, interviewers were free to explore interesting themes in more detail and were not required to ask every question in the protocol.

Analysis

We engaged in a thematic analysis process to develop constructs and relationships that form the basis of our case examples. Following established qualitative analytic methods (Miles & Huberman, 1994; Strauss & Corbin, 1998), our literature review and research questions played a sensitizing role, suggesting *a priori* constructs. After each interview, the authors recorded their impressions into preliminary codebooks. We then compared each other's coding with the goal of attaining dialogical intersubjectivity (Kvale, 1994), a form of reliability via discussion. A graduate assistant supported the input and analysis of transcripts and themes in the NVivo software package.

CASE STUDY SAMPLE

The design firm *Forward* is a software company that designs and develops digital services and products, such as custom interfaces for large corporate information systems, with a mission to achieve progress through collaboration ("Forward" is a pseudonym for the company name; other identifying information is also disguised for confidentiality purposes). Based in Europe, *Forward* employs a staff of over 600 designers and other employees, operating offices and serving clients in large urban areas in several countries. It has won awards for its workplace culture.

Forward's client engagement model includes customer managers who spearhead projects, collaborating simultaneously with multiple resource teams and individual specialists. Their work tends to be on enterprise-level solutions for internal client projects, such as building interfaces for industrial software packages, tailored to specific company needs. Their clients span a variety of industries, including media, banking, automotive original equipment manufacturers, and public sector entities. *Forward*'s organization is project-based, and like many software firms has a legacy structure adapted from hardware companies. The *Forward* workforce structure is relatively flat, with project teams as the locus of work, and each individual designer afforded substantial autonomy within the framework of the engagement with the client. Generally, their approach follows Agile development methodologies and design thinking processes, including UEX for optimizing client outcomes. The company sees itself as being at the forefront of technological implementation, with a culture that embraces strategic change. As a fast-moving, growing company, it touts its value as caring and doing the right thing for clients, including going the extra mile on each project and becoming the best at integrating the latest software.

Forward considers AI and LLM models and tools as critical to emerging client expectations and project needs. Clients depend on *Forward* for solutions, one designer manager noted, because "we create real things" that require skills that the client does not have in-house. He emphasizes, though, that the benefits from AI use – and the limits on how it will be used – depend on how it fits *Forward*'s customer engagement approach. He elaborates,

> We have always tried to win with the way our people behave and how much we care about the cases. Because we are a very people-focused company. That has historically been a winning factor for us, that when we come to a project the customer thinks, feels that we care … then we go the extra mile to try to do the right thing.

FINDINGS: HOW *FORWARD* USES AI IN DESIGN COLLABORATION

According to our interviewees, as a company *Forward* was very aware of the need to engage with AI in their work, both in the way that it could augment their business, and to meet the expectations of their clients. On the level of designers and design managers, there was tactical recognition of specific utilities of AI tools, burgeoning awareness of their capabilities, and varying knowledge of how to leverage their features. There was also some skepticism in how well AI could be implemented in bespoke client projects, as well as a hint of cynicism as to how it would be deployed. Considering these multiple perspectives, we found that AI affected *Forward* in two main areas: the *design work* itself, including at specific stages of design thinking, and the *workforce*, including individual preparedness through training and development, as well as longer-term strategies in job roles, hiring, and other investments.

One key concept that cuts across the role of AI in design work and workforce needs is that of *prompt architecture*. A prompt is the verbal instruction given to guide AI to help it generate effective results. Crucially, writing prompts that effectively leverage AI software is itself an art and science that is becoming a specialized occupation both within organizations and with outside contract experts who provide prompt engineering services to the organization (McMillen et al., 2023). It should be taken as a given that all collaborative interactions of humans and AI in the design context are dependent on prompts, and any results, therefore, presuppose their use.

AI in the Design Process

> If AI can do a job, it can definitely do that [job] better than a human.… If not today, … in 5 years.

The work of a design firm such as *Forward* involves a heavy dose of client interaction, because many of their projects center on customizing software solutions for specific needs and data configurations. As the product manager above notes, AI may be a more reliable worker, but only if a given task is within its skillset. A typical project might consist of, for instance, creating a bespoke interface for an existing commercial application (e.g., Salesforce). In such a case, the client wants to have an easy-to-use portal which uses their own lingo and data, paralleling their distinctive work processes. This type of work has been done to some degree for decades, without AI assistance. Other projects might also include deeper-level functions sometimes employing AI, such as described by a project manager, "the client wanted to [create] a system for using AI to fetch insights from their own existing data."

Our interviewees described their understanding of AI capabilities, the readiness to use AI – by themselves and their colleagues, and the ways in which they have actually used it to date. They spoke of the extent of its general utility to projects and clients, as well as specific support of design processes, goals, and application at various design thinking stages. Their reviews ranged from very positive and accepting including being willing to learn how to best exploit its capabilities, while also exhibiting some wariness. One design leader noted,

> I noticed that understanding of what AI is and what it does can vary a lot, and it's very dangerous.... it's a black box with some sort of intelligence in it.

In the next section, we disclose how *Forward* design employees incorporate AI into their collaborative and individual work. Generally, the project teams depicted their deliverables as design innovation, although the level and type of creativity and novel solutions varied widely. We discuss these findings within each of the design thinking stages, noting the variance of usage across stages, the challenges and limitations, and the range of designer capabilities of exploiting AI as a resource, tool, or collaborator.

Stage 1: Research, Empathize, and Define

The first stage of a design thinking project includes building understanding of both the client and the technical topics at hand through empathetic research methods and often culminates in useful, operational definitions. This stage performs a critical role in the design process where the user is represented in how the product or service will be devised.

As noted by one of design managers, *Forward*'s success depends on good relationships with customers. From this manager's perspective, getting to know the client and their needs was the first key to a successful engagement. Once there was an initial agreement in place with the client, the project began with a "sprint" meeting of project team members that set goals, priorities, workplans, and resources for a relatively short period, such as 2–4 weeks. Importantly, this manager notes that *Forward* also included a heavy emphasis at this stage on assessing "...the capabilities of the client organizations, in terms of what data they have, what structures, what systems, what people they have, what kind of sentiments [and] attitudes do they have?"

Perhaps the most obvious use of AI at this stage was to assist in conducting organized background research on clients and the technical topics of the engagement. Designers reported that they use AI for these purposes,

> [...] it's a lot about this time, saving and handling large amount and quantity of data.... If you have large access sheets of data or large gathered data, using AI tools, I think, could be quite helpful in analyzing the key things and themes.

Another design manager believed that AI can produce variations of market data with relative ease, because they could "...ask the system to come up with 10 insights regarding companies' presence in the market from the point of view of the customers globally. Boom, then you have it."

One lead designer gave an example of using AI for a car manufacturer who wanted to understand "their customer experience in the early phase of ownership" but did not know where to start. The designer began by using AI to search for online customer reviews and then delved into the automotive company's customer service archives to determine how the company is "perceived from the user point of view." Another designer described a similar effort to analyze customer data, where the client wanted to both understand their end users and "how to make efficiencies internally in their organization."

A further example was given by another designer, who reported that "with generative AI, you can go through unstructured data like call center data" to make sense of it. This designer also expressed the need to be cautious with what AI offers as results, "But then there's the accuracy question that it's not so good. I don't know how accurate [AI results] are nowadays."

A design leader reported that *Forward* also used AI to help improve research within the organization, beyond client projects. *Forward* launched an "initiative to understand how to do the digital experience better, but also how to make efficiencies internally in their organization." One great advantage of AI considered for this initiative was its high speed in processing data, and the related ability to draw upon a prodigious breadth of information. Critically, AI also included the ability to undertake tasks for a workforce that were otherwise engaged. As one designer put it, "We've used GenAI to gather insights from client feedback, something designers used to do manually." In this case, rather than simply using AI to plough through a large set of text files, as previous software had done, "The AI did the first transcribing from voice to text." The designer believed this process to be different than human or earlier automated transcribers, perhaps superior in some ways such as capturing more specific data such as "identifying the different actors in the call which you might forget otherwise."

Stage 2: Ideation

The second stage of design thinking centers on the generation and selection ideas, offering a creative array of options to think through, in search of fitting a solution to client needs. Ideation may operate at the individual or collective levels. In client engagements requiring a high level of creativity or acceptance by multiple stakeholders, a collaborative process for ideation becomes especially important, as individuals sharing ideas benefit from bringing together disparate perspectives into a context where they can be used (Clark et al., 2000). AI is generally considered to have great potential for generating ideas quickly, when used with effective prompts (Medeiros et al., 2025). Our interviewees reported that AI was used for ideation, but perhaps, to a lesser extent, than they (or us) initially perceived its utility in this area.

The designers we spoke with gave credit to AI for "replacing big parts" of the design workload – "development work, thinking work, calculations, business analytics" and more, according to one design manager. But as one designer pointed out, "most projects have been focused on optimization," rather than more creative tasks. His colleague agreed, "it's about how to use AI to be more efficient. How can you, for example, reduce the time of research analysis or support ....It's currently figuring out which opportunities are the right ones because there are many." The manager above agreed that AI had not really yet changed how the designers work; "it doesn't replace a lot of the process that we do."

Stage 3: Prototype

The third stage of design thinking involves creating sample products that the client, internal or external, can compare, ideally leading to products and services that can be tested and used. These samples are typically reviewed quickly by clients, users, or the designers themselves, allowing ongoing iteration of prototypes that draw increasingly closer to an optimal design. At *Forward*, the practice of quick prototyping has been ingrained into the company culture. As one designer put it,

> We have these core values of transparency and iterative process. Always learn from your mistakes, and then iterate and approve. This kind of thinking and setup is very much incorporated in our ways of working and internal structures. It's a lot about internally sharing learning, sharing opportunities, collaborating and iteratively work on further developing offers or opportunities for our clients.

Producing a range of relatively simple prototypes had proven to be a useful application of AI technology for *Forward*. One manager spoke of using AI-generated prototypes to quickly offer multiple variations of a product for use in an early pitch to a client who was thinking through options. As he put it, "a lot of work like production level design work is already getting replaced with these [AI/LLM] tools and systems." The product commissioned was an interface for a commercial software program, customized for use such that it included the client organization's specific data categories. To generate viable options for the client, the design manager responsible for the account went through standard processes of research and ideation.

When it came to the prototype stage, however, rather than assigning two or three junior designers to sketch out or wireframe an interface design, the manager focused his own efforts on writing an effective prompt that would produce variations of an interface that met the client needs. Not only did this result in more fully developed prototypes – "you can ask the system to come up with 10 insights" – but was also much quicker and didn't require the work of the junior designers. As he stated, "you have a prototyping process that is shorter, because it can be more immediately customizable to what the user is looking for."

Beyond the speed and efficiency of the prototype, this manager believes that AI has been changing the type of product needed, and therefore, the type of prototype required.

> It not only changes the prototyping, but it kind of also removes the need for traditional interfaces in general. We don't even need the buttons anymore. If we're using natural language, you don't have to have buttons. I'm not communicating with buttons well, technically aired through this software, but it's kind of like it's changing so much that everyone is here still a little bit like blown away. I'm not sure what to do.

On a more immediate and practical level, one designer reported that AI supported both variety and cost savings in an area critical to the company's product design – expanding their stock of images to be used in prototyping. Essentially, the AI capabilities allowed designers to simply create prompts for the type of pictures that they needed for a given project. This saved them from having to create pictures in the more time- and resource-intensive manner that they employed in the past, such as creating graphics with traditional software, taking pictures of tangible objects, or purchasing pictures from outside sources.

One interesting and somewhat unexpected perspective from a design manager was that designers may have actually distanced themselves from their work when using AI. He commented, "You can say that the machine did it for me, so don't get mad at me."

This distancing also can inform the rationalization of managers in rationalizing their decisions about the use of AI, because they do not need to invest as much time or resources in design outcomes produced by AI as compared to employee work hours when not using AI. Thus, it may be less risky for managers to use AI, because they are not investing their resources at the same level as was needed when they had to spend many work hours of their designers to complete their tasks without AI. Put another way, managers do not risk as much of their budget, as one mentioned – "you don't have that time and money spent." According to this manager, using AI to prototype allowed the company "to do more, to learn more, with less risk."

Stage 4: Test and Feedback

The fourth stage of design thinking involves placing the product into context, where it interacts with the environment and users, creating opportunities for reactions, criticisms, and new directions. This testing stage overlaps conceptually with and is sometimes deemed to be an extension of the previous stage, because prototypes cycle iteratively in response to feedback from users and other factors in the environment. For example, one design manager discussed a major advantage of AI use in feedback as the cycle speed of determining product or prototype failure, "if you fail like, you can fail in 2 days. Back in the day it used to be hundreds of thousands of Euros and months to kind of come to the realization."

The designers and managers at *Forward* described their use of AI tools in testing and feedback as minimal, although they did relate some relevant instances. Generally, their focus was more on the prior stages with a bit of testing or feedback added, such as when using AI to assess their own organization. As one designer noted, some assessment of AI tools came through their use of AI in the research stage, "We've tried using AI on our own internal processes as a way to understand the technology better. Clients appreciate that, as it shows we're testing the tools ourselves."

It seems likely that, in general if not specifically at *Forward*, there is an opportunity for design companies to leverage the capability of AI tools in feedback and testing stages.

One designer expressed that he felt the urge to test himself against the AI tool in its organization and analysis of the workflow data, stating, "I actually read through a whole bunch of the summaries, though, to just see that." It was a little bit of a sanity check, you know. Is it like, "Wait are these summaries?"

Stage 5: Implement and Commercialize

The fifth stage of design thinking entails delivering a product or service into production and connecting to organizational systems, supply chains, and broader user bases. It may seem evident that the use of AI has significant potential for fully producing client products, as presaged in the software interface prototyping discussed earlier. Nonetheless, the design staff at *Forward* did not report using AI for commercialization and implementation tasks. Indeed, several acknowledged clearly that this stage was beyond their current interests or capabilities as an organization, in terms of understanding how AI could best be employed for these purposes. As one designer pointed out, "...the real potential for design is much larger. However, we're not quite there yet."

AI and the Workforce

The effect of AI use and AI potential on design collaboration not only influences design content but also has important ramifications for workflow and the configuration of the people who comprise and work within the organization's structure and the skills associated with leveraging AI collaboration. There are a number of ways that AI affects the workforce and its work, including the roles shared among employees and AI tools (e.g., through workforce planning, recruitment, and selection) and the readiness of the designers (e.g., through training and experience). These areas involve understanding the skills needed to undertake design work, to collaborate with or benefit from the support of AI, and how to both conceptualize and leverage the power of AI tools.

AI and Workforce Roles

An organization's workforce is traditionally considered to be composed of people who fill roles that are structured to complete tasks leading toward mission fulfilment. These people and roles are organized through reporting relationships, formal units including divisions, departments, and teams, shared tasks, and less formal networks of shared knowledge, personal relationships, and other characteristics (Espinosa & Clark, 2014). As discussed previously, the entry of AI into the workplace as a collaborator has potential for support, change, and perhaps disrupt workforce configurations as it takes a role in completing the organization's work.

At *Forward*, AI forays into the workforce have included a number of tasks that otherwise have been fulfilled by junior-level employees, such as the creation of multiple prototype designs to elicit a client's preferred options. While the advantages in time and resource efficiency were readily apparent, the implications for the workforce were also potentially game-changing. As one designer put it, "Are we afraid that it's taking our job as an interface designer? Sure." Examples abounded of specialty functions that might be replaced, along with the designers who performed the related tasks, such as in the use of AI to "generate images that visualize what is otherwise very hard to describe."

On the other hand, *Forward*'s staff expressed that there are areas that AI cannot replace employees, whether at this time or perhaps even in the future. This belief seemed to stem from perceptions that some critical tasks cannot be completed by AI. For instance, one design manager noted that "the marketing department cannot replace the brand designer with AI, just because there still needs to be someone commanding the systems." This quote seems to reflect the view that it is important for a human to have an overall perspective on how AI is deployed, perhaps particularly for those areas with closer connection to clients. Another designer questioned whether AI can be relied upon for producing novel insights and designs: "Innovation? Well, certain people can look very far. And certain people less. I was always thinking how [AI] is gonna affect my tools, or take my job."

We had interesting conversations with designers, design leaders, and managers about how such changes in tasks assigned to AI might affect the workforce as it cycles and builds, incorporating new employees and preparing them to take on increasingly complex job functions. For instance, one manager recounted that early in his career he was tasked with quickly creating multiple prototypes for a variety of clients and topics and that this helped him to develop understanding that served him well in later customer liaison and managerial roles. Naturally, the question arose as to how the next generation of junior designers could acquire similar or equivalent experience to support their career development. Relatedly, we wondered how *Forward* would plan its potentially changing roles, who it might hire with what qualifications, and for what specific tasks and roles. How would *Forward* retain the junior members of its workforce, and how would they be readied to fill future managerial and customer interface positions, when they would be less likely to gain the sort of experience that their predecessors enjoyed?

This manager responded that he believed that the nature of the lower level work would change, but that it would still provide valuable experience for junior employees. "The lower level work," he said, "is going to be the use of new [AI] tools that have these capabilities." However, this prediction may not follow well from his earlier discussion of his own creation of prompts to generate multiple prototype options for clients, rather than assigning the same task to junior designers as he had done in the past.

A design leader, whose responsibilities included special projects to explore potential applications of AI to client and internal work processes, believed that the key to developing designer capacity for leveraging AI, whether junior or more experienced, was to involve those designers in collaborations where they could compare approaches and insights – "creating opportunities for people to work on projects, have concrete discussions, and develop hands-on demos is essential." Another designer noted that the role of designers in collaborating with AI was more like a "curator" than a "creator."

AI and Workforce Readiness

It is clear that collaboration with AI demands knowledge of AI capabilities, a variety of skills and processes including interface proficiency (e.g., writing prompts) and understanding collaborative problem-solving processes. *Forward*'s designers and managers spoke to us of their own KSAs and deficits, as well as the organization's approach to building employee readiness to best leverage AI collaboration potential. This approach includes preparing designers through training and development, as well as strategic planning for job roles, recruitment, hiring, and related human capital investments.

One area of the organization that *Forward* believed to be a strength is the way it embraces technological solutions, including employee willingness to engage in the sometimes arduous work needed to hone their craft. This allowed them to stay a step ahead of their competitors and to serve their clients. As one design manager put it, "companies don't have skills in-house, so contract to [Forward] for solutions – we create real things."

One designer we spoke with was tasked with a special project to develop and pilot training programs for AI collaborations within *Forward*. He led a small team of six members, including strategic consultants, technicians, and designers. He reported that most of their time had been spent developing "demos" (demonstration programs) that simulate client projects, which are then used as training vehicles for designers. He emphasized that the active use of these demos is necessary, as "the topic is difficult to grasp unless you have a concrete project or playground" and also because the identification of needed skills and the development of successful processes must come from the designers themselves. "We map out a process with them to identify where AI could disrupt and improve efficiency… demonstrating potential through developing specific internal processes," he stated.

The focus of skill development to date relates to the design thinking stages where AI has so far been emphasized at *Forward*. To benefit from AI's capability for research and empathy in stage 1, designers must learn to fashion effective prompts which delve into the repository of data on a topic, incorporating benchmarks and other relevant examples, and also seek information about clients, their needs, and their users. As noted earlier, crafting prompts has become something of a specialty area, with numerous resources and training programs dedicated to this critical skill, which involves knowledge of the topic area as well as of the capabilities of the AI software (Graff et al., 2026). The special projects designer spoke of the value of solutions available with the use of a good prompt, but also the inherent risk of relying on AI too much, "this new technology may be like a hammer, overused for solving problems."

For the ideation stage, it is critical to consider designers' readiness to effectively utilize AI tools. First, designers must themselves be equipped with skills in ideation, particularly in structuring disparate information so that it addresses client and end user needs, matching it to the directions given by empathy research in the prior stage. Second, designers must gain skills in understanding and exploiting the capabilities of AI as it continues to advance. Significantly, this readiness may include learning to treat AI as a collaborator rather than, as one design manager termed it, simply "a highly special tool with all the fancy plugins."

Prototyping often relates strongly to the core competency of design firms. However, in the case of *Forward*, firms may increase their reliance on AI tools, rather than junior designers, to create prototypes and iterate them quickly with clients. Crafting prompts, which for prototyping involve a relatively high sophistication compared to research stage prompts, may become a core skill area (Medeiros et al., 2025). Not surprisingly, the designers report that their use of AI in prototyping was still closer to creating efficiencies (e.g., variations of a customer interface; low-cost graphics) rather than deep innovation. Generally, they acknowledged this as a skill deficit on the part of the designers, even as they speak confidently of their progress in future AI innovation.

The training programs take other forms as well. One designer described company-wide "half-day internal hackathons" at *Forward*, where ad hoc teams of various roles competed in time-intensive AI prompt engineering sessions designed to determine how AI could help to address a particular client issue. For this designer, the hackathon was "the first time really working with this [AI] tool other than just asking questions [for research stage design work]." Rather, the event was designed to determine how AI could help to address a particular client issue and to build relevant skills in the design team. *Forward* designers also reported learning AI insights from social media platforms, including as one designer mentioned, "... if you go to Instagram and you follow professional designers, you see a lot of videos.... People are very open about showing how they do things."

At times, the need to upgrade their skills and keep up with the evolving nature of AI may lead to a bit of learning fatigue. However, designers at *Forward* believed that as their skills with AI develop, so too would the efficiency and quality of their design work products.

DISCUSSION

> We're just at the optimization stage now, but the real potential for design is much larger. However, we're not quite there yet.

Our discussions with designers and design managers, considered within the context of existing research and the focal company, offer some intriguing insights. These add to our understanding of how AI is being used in design collaborations and suggest avenues for further research. First, as pointed out previously (including the quote from a Forward manager listed just above this paragraph), designers at *Forward* have been deploying AI for efficiencies in stages including research, ideation, and prototyping. However, the use of AI for innovation or quality improvements in client deliverables was not well-realized. Some opined that AI quickly reached its limits short of true innovation, instead relying only on recombination of existing works. Our interviewees attributed this limited use to the designers' incomplete understanding of AI capabilities and skills in leveraging them. In the future, designers hoping to benefit from this technology more fully must spend some effort in getting to know their AI collaborators.

Relatedly, AI is not currently considered to be a full collaborator or true teammate for the design teams at *Forward*, but the role of AI in design collaborations is likely to grow beyond its current use in relatively simple optimization tasks. Thus, both persons and AI must develop collaborative skills, including those recognized by teams scholars (e.g., affect, behavior, and cognition), and design researchers (e.g., visualizations). Additional implications include that it is likely that as AI increases its place on design teams, some positions filled currently by humans may change or be eliminated.

This new hybrid of AI and people in the workforce not only fulfilled tasks that are part of the organization's work but also had potential to "create market demand," according to one design manager. It is likely that organizations adopting AI will need to reassess their workforce needs in coming business cycles, determining the effective configuration of AI–workforce collaboration.

Some interesting questions arose from our discussions which we do not yet have sufficient data or insights to address. For example, we wonder about the effects of the mental models of the human design collaborators, formed through field of study, prior experience, and work style preferences. For instance, designers can come from a variety of disciplines, including engineering and the visual arts. How might these perspectives influence the way the designers interact with AI? Another question relates to the optimal method of sharing information among humans and AI collaborators. Companies following design thinking traditions typically will employ a variety of communication techniques, including narratives, analogies, and visualizations (Graff & Clark, 2019). Many AI programs already reduce the need for complex interfaces – "no buttons are needed" in the words of one design manager. What combination of natural language, graphics, or other communication channels will best serve human–AI collaborations?

Finally, how will AI transform design collaborations in their process and, as technology and user skills increase, in their outcomes? Will AI work for the benefit of their human collaborators and organizations, or will AI outgrow them? Can AI extend careers, allowing people to continue work that interests them while removing the relative drudgery of lower-level tasks? Will organizations continue to invest in people as well as in technology, including training people to drive effective collaborations with AI? Will organizations invest in and build their own customized AI to fuel their business direction? Future research can address all of these questions.

The path to successful collaboration for AI and human designers is not well-marked, and as yet collaborators are moving toward an uncertain future. As the special projects designer wisely noted, to reach success in AI design collaborations "I have to take all my stakeholders with me on that journey."

REFERENCES

Anthony, C. (2021). When knowledge work and analytical technologies collide: The practices and consequences of black boxing algorithmic technologies. *Administrative Science Quarterly*, 1–40. https://doi:10.1177/00018392211016755

Bell, S. T., Brown, S. G., Colaneri, A., & Outland, N. (2018). Team composition and the ABCs of teamwork. *American Psychologist, 73*(4), 349–362. https://doi.org/10.1037/amp0000305

Borman, W. C., & Motowidlo, S. J. (1993). Expanding the criterion domain to include elements of contextual performance. In N. Schmitt & W. C. Borman (Eds.), *Personnel selection in organizations* (pp. 71–98). Jossey-Bass.

Brown, T. (2008, June 1). Design thinking. *Harvard Business Review*, 1–10.

Brown, T. (2009). *Change by design: How design thinking transforms organizations and inspires innovation*. HarperBusiness.

Campion, M. A., & Campion, E. D. (2023). Machine learning applications to personnel selection: Current illustrations, lessons learned, and future research. *Personnel Psychology*, *76*(4), 993–1009. https://doi.org/10.1111/peps.12621

Clark, M. A., Anand, V., & Roberson, L. (2000). Resolving meaning: Interpretation in diverse decision-making groups. *Group Dynamics: Theory, Research, & Practice*, *4*, 211–221. https://doi.org/10.1037/1089-2699.4.3.211

Cross, N. (1982). Designerly ways of knowing. *Design Studies*, *3*(4), 7. https://doi.org/10.1016/0142-694X(82)90040-0

Cross, N. (2023). Design thinking: What just happened? *Design Studies*, *86*, 101–187. https://doi.org/10.1016/j.destud.2023.101187

Demir, M., Cooke, N. J., & Amazeen, P. G. (2018). A conceptual model of team dynamical behaviors and performance in human-autonomy teaming. *Cognitive Systems Research*, *52*, 497–507.

Elsbach, K. D., & Stigliani, I. (2018). Design thinking and organizational culture: A review and framework for future research. *Journal of Management*, *44*(6), 2274–2306. https://doi.org/10.1177/0149206317744252

Espinosa, J. A., & Clark, M. A. (2014). Team knowledge representation: A network perspective. *Human Factors: The Journal of Human Factors and Ergonomics Society*, *56*(2), 333–348. https://doi.org/10.1177/0018720813494093

Graff, D., & Clark, M. A. (2019). Communication modes in collaboration: An empirical assessment of metaphors, visualization, and narratives in multidisciplinary design student teams. *International Journal of Technology and Design Education*, *29*, 197–215. https://doi.org/10.1007/s10798-017-9437-9

Graff, D., Clark, M. A., Li, D., & Xia, L. (2026). *Design thinking with artificial intelligence: A practical guide for business innovation*. Palgrave MacMillan (SpringerNature). https://doi.org/10.1007/978-3-032-10543-1

Hargadon, A., & Sutton, R. I. (1997). Technology brokering and innovation in a product development firm. *Administrative Science Quarterly*, *42*(4), 716–749. https://doi.org/10.2307/2393655

Jones, J. C. (1970). *Design methods: Seeds of human futures*. Wiley-Interscience.

Kelley, T. (2001). *The art of innovation: Lessons in creativity by IDEO, America's leading design firm*. Currency.

Kleinsmann, M., Deken, F., Dong, A., & Lauche, K. (2012). Development of design collaboration skills. *Journal of Engineering Design*, *23*(7), 485–506. https://doi.org/10.1080/09544828.2011.619499

Kvale, S. (1994). Ten standard objections to qualitative research interviews. *Journal of Phenomenological Psychology*, *25*, 147–173. https://doi.org/10.1163/156916294X00016

Liedtka, J. (2015). Perspective: Linking design thinking with innovation outcomes through cognitive bias reduction: Design thinking. *Journal of Product Innovation Management*, *32*(6), 925–938. https://doi.org/10.1111/jpim.12163

Lyons, J. B., Wynne, K. T., Mahoney, S., & Roebke, M. A. (2019). Trust and human-machine teaming: A qualitative study. In W. Lawless, R. Mittu, D. Sofge, I. Moskowitz, & S. Russell (Eds.), *Artificial intelligence for the internet of everything* (pp. 101–116). Elsevier. https://doi.org/10.1016/b978-0-12-817636-8.00006-5

Martin, R. L. (2009). *The design of business: Why design thinking is the next competitive advantage*. Harvard Business Review Press.
Medeiros, K. E., Marrone, R. L., & Reiter-Palmon, R. (2025). A time-saving dishwasher: AI's role in team creative processes. In S. Paletz & S. S. Dubrow (Eds.), *Research on managing groups and teams: AI in teams* (pp. 79–96). Emerald Publishing.
McDonagh-Philp, D., & Lebbon, C. (2000). The emotional domain in product design. *The Design Journal*, *3*(1), 31–43. https://doi.org/10.2752/146069200789393562
McMillen, R., Henderson, B., & Rosenbush, S. (2023, October 5). The new jobs for humans in the AI era. *Wall Street Journal*.
Micheli, P., Wilner, S. J. S., Bhatti, S. H., Mura, M., & Beverland, M. B. (2019). Doing design thinking: Conceptual review, synthesis, and research agenda. *Journal of Product Innovation Management*, *36*(2), 124–148. https://doi.org/10.1111/jpim.12466
Miles, M. B., & Huberman, A. M. (1994). *Qualitative data analysis* (2nd ed.). Sage.
Morgeson, F. P., Reider, M. H., & Campion, M. A. (2005). Selecting individuals in team settings: The importance of social skills, personality characteristics, and teamwork knowledge. *Personnel Psychology*, *58*(3), 583–611. https://doi.org/10.1016/B978-0-12-817636-8.00006-5
Nguyen, M., & Mougenot, C. (2022). A systematic review of empirical studies on multidisciplinary design collaboration: Findings, methods, and challenges. *Design Studies*, *81*, 101–120. https://doi.org/10.1016/j.destud.2022.101120
Raisch, S., & Krakowski, S. (2021). Artificial intelligence and management: The automation-augmentation-paradox. *Academy of Management Review*, *46*(1), 192–210.
Ralph, P., & Wand, Y. (2009). A proposal for a formal definition of the design concept. In K. Lyytinen, P. Loucopoulos, J. Mylopoulos, & B. Robinson (Eds.), *Design requirements engineering: A ten-year perspective. Lecture notes in business information processing* (Vol. *14*). Springer. https://doi.org/10.1007/978-3-540-92966-6_6
Rodgers, P. A., & Huxor, A. P. (1998). The role of artificial intelligence as 'text' within design. *Design Studies*, *19*, 143–160.
Seidel, V. P., & Fixson, S. K. (2013). Adopting design thinking in novice multidisciplinary teams: The application and limits of design methods and reflexive practices. *Journal of Product Innovation Management*, *30*, 19–33. https://doi.org/10.1111/jpim.12061
Stevens, M. J., & Campion, M. A. (1994). The knowledge, skill, and ability requirements for teamwork: Implications for human resource management. *Journal of Management*, *20*(2), 503–530.
Strauss, A., & Corbin, J. (1998). *Basics of qualitative research: Techniques and procedures for developing grounded theory*. Sage Publications, Inc.
Tavčar, J., žavbi, R., Verlinden, J., & Duhovnik, J. (2007). Skills for effective communication and work in global product development teams. *Journal of Engineering Design*, 557–576. https://doi.org/10.1080/09544820500273797
Zhang, G., Raina, A., Cagan, J., & McComb, C. (2021). A cautionary tale about the impact of AI on human design teams. *Design Studies*, *72*, 100990. https://doi.org/10.1016/j.destud.2021.100990

CHAPTER 10

PARTICIPATORY AI: CHILDREN AND FAMILIES CO-DESIGNING AND COLLABORATING WITH AI SYSTEMS

Elizabeth Bonsignore[a], Dinesh Kumar Nanduri[a], Elana Blinder[a], Yi-Hsieh Lin[a], Utkarsh Dwivedi[a], Mona Leigh Guha[b], Medha Tare[b] and Hernisa Kacorri[a]

[a] *University of Maryland College of Information, USA*
[b] *Joan Ganz Cooney Center at Sesame Workshop, USA*

ABSTRACT

The case studies in this chapter explore how children and families envision using artificial intelligence (AI) systems in their everyday lives to support personal expression, creativity, language learning and cultural preservation. We present two case studies: the first describes the ways in which children experiment with emerging generative AI (gen AI) tools for creative expression, and the second shares how children team with their parents and grandparents, alongside a gen AI chat system, to help them brainstorm design ideas for supporting culturally responsive language learning. In the first case study, children work with AI tools primarily in dyads (AI and individual child). In the second case, we share how children and parents take on different roles and perspectives as they team with the AI chatbot to consider how AI can support their goals for preserving cultural and familial memories through language learning. All the cases in this

AI in Teams: Research on Managing Groups and Teams, Volume 21, 171–195

Published under exclusive licence by Emerald Publishing Limited
ISSN: 1534-0856/doi:10.1108/S1534-085620260000021025

chapter employ a participatory design (PD) approach that directly involves the children and families in voicing their personal perspectives, concerns, and desires as they encounter and engage AI-infused technologies in their everyday lives.

Keywords: Child–computer interaction; AI literacy; children; families; participatory design; language learning; creativity

AI systems have become integral, ubiquitous components of our everyday lives. For youth, in particular (7–17 years old), AI-infused technologies underpin the social media platforms they use, the increasingly procedurally generated[1] video games they play, chatbots that help them with homework, streaming services that recommend what they should watch next, and voice assistants they may encounter at home. Moreover, AI is baked into the future workplaces that today's youth will soon inhabit: several technology industry and research summaries reflect that AI is impacting almost every field, from healthcare to agriculture and gaming to education (Balakrishnan et al., 2020; Zhang et al., 2021).

Adult professionals are exploring the various strengths and weaknesses of using gen AI in design (Clark & Graff, this volume). As noted above, youth are also increasingly encountering, interacting, and collaborating with AI systems. Therefore, while most of the chapters in this volume focus on professional and/or adult use cases for human–agent teams (HATs), this chapter focuses on children working with AI systems, whether by teaming with each other or family members. The exploratory case studies described in this chapter aim to address current and emerging research efforts to pursue "AI4All" (AI for all) learning and literacy goals (Posner & Fei-Fei, 2020; Touretzky et al., 2019, 2022) while considering how children and families envision using AI systems in their everyday lives. We are particularly motivated by calls for more participatory approaches that promote community involvement in machine learning (ML) and AI, with the goal of developing more "equitable, robust, responsible, and trustworthy AI" (Birhane et al., 2022, p. 1). In response, all of the cases in this chapter employ PD techniques with users (Kulynych et al., 2020; Schuler & Namioka, 1993), with the goal of including and representing the perspectives, concerns, and desires of children and families as they encounter and engage AI-infused technologies in their everyday lives.

In addition to its focus on techniques that include users in more direct, participatory ways than typical methodological approaches (e.g., interviews, user-testing, indirect field observation), this chapter offers insights on how some of our youngest citizens/users conceptualize and collaborate with AI systems. All

[1]"Procedural content generation (PCG) in games refers to the creation of game content automatically using algorithms" (Togelius et al., 2011, p. 1), and are often considered a type of AI-supported system (Smith, 2021; Togelius et al., 2011).

the cases in this chapter focus on users who are younger than previous AI learning studies, many of which focused on youth at the high school or undergraduate levels. Overall, our work represents increasing efforts over the past 5–10 years to involve children as young as early primary school (7 years old) to middle school (13 years old).

This chapter explores patterns of collaboration that emerged in small teams of adults and children interacting with AI in different capacities (e.g., children testing each other's AI image classifiers, building upon each other's creative expressions with AI, or collaborating with parents and grandparents to preserve cultural stories and endangered languages). Despite the multigenerational co-design team approach used to frame the studies and to analyze children's interactions with AI systems, the human–AI teaming tasks and design prompts were mostly limited to human–AI dyads (vs human–AI "teams"). Thus, for this chapter, we take the approach that the HATs can be a dyad of one human and one AI, given that the dyad is interactive, contained, and is a (temporary) delineated unit with a shared goal (e.g., Carter-Browne et al., 2021; Demir et al., 2020; Muller, 2023). We also examine more traditional cases of HATs that include children, such as multiple children or teams of adults and children brainstorming together. The two exploratory studies described in this chapter include PD sessions in which (1) children experimented with various approaches to collaborate with AI systems to support their creative play and (2) children and adults in the United States and India brainstormed ways that gen AI systems might enhance language learning tailored to individual and cultural contexts. For the second case, children and adults in the USA first pilot tested a co-design process that was then implemented with children and parents/grandparents in India.

RESEARCH LANDSCAPE: YOUTH, AI LITERACIES, PD

In this section, we situate our case studies within the AI research landscape across the fields of technology design and informal learning for children. First, we discuss AI literacy and the AI4All learning framework, a set of learning outcomes and pedagogical principles that aim to promote children's understanding of, and proficiency with, the AI systems that are ubiquitous in their everyday lives. We then describe cooperative inquiry (CI) (Druin, 1999), a PD approach that assumes that children are active partners with adults in multigenerational design teams, contributing their perspectives, evaluations, and ideas for co-designing existing and emerging technologies for children. Finally, we summarize prior work with children exploring machine teaching and problem formulation that set the stage for our two case studies.

AI Literacies and AI4All Learning Framework

Given the proliferation of AI tools and systems in daily life, our approach to AI activities with children adheres to Druga et al.'s (2022) overarching definition: "AI literacies include the ability to read, work with, analyze and author with AI" (p. 1). This definition encompasses the acquisition of skills and competencies that enable youth to use AI across all the contexts of their lives (e.g., "as a tool online, at home, and in the workplace" (Long & Magerko, 2020, p. 598)). Perhaps most importantly, it also acknowledges the development of an empowering mindset for critiquing existing AI models and creating new ones (Druga et al., 2022).

Our efforts focus on empowering children as young as seven years old to be the teachers of machine learning classification models and to collaborate as co-designers of AI tools that support creative expression and language learning. This work is aligned with a growing number of studies (e.g., Druga et al., 2019, 2022; Hitron et al., 2018; Vartiainen et al., 2020, 2021) that pursue emerging AI4All curricular goals to teach AI concepts to children as early as the first few years of school (Touretzky et al., 2019). A guiding principle for AI learning and literacy activities is to be accessible to children with little or no programming experience. The cases presented in this chapter were conducted in an informal, out-of-school learning context, so we were not bound by more formal curricular and/or assessment criteria. Although exploratory in nature, each study sought to incorporate learning components from the AI4All framework (e.g., "machines learn from data").

Despite the ubiquity of AI technologies, most of the people who build AI systems are not representative of those who use them, which can only serve to reinforce existing inequities (Zhang et al., 2021). Moreover, many of the youth with whom we work come from non-dominant groups historically under-represented in Science, Technology, Engineering, and Mathematics (STEM), including girls and children of color (see Table 10.1). Broadly, our work addresses a fundamental research agenda for informal science learning, which is to uncover connections between co-design/creative construction experiences and youth engagement in broader STEM learning pathways (Kafai & Burke, 2013; Tissenbaum et al., 2019, 2021). Specifically, we aim to demystify and make visible current black-box machine learning/teaching models and to expose children to AI toolsets for creative expression and language learning (e.g., Kafai et al., 2012). In this way, we hope to increase AI explainability and children's overall AI literacy, comfort, and ease with which they work with and within AI systems.

Table 10.1. Case Study 1 Child Participants: Co-designing with AI for Creative Expression.

Child Pseudonym	Age	Gender	Race/Ethnicity
Ezra	12	Male	African American
Balthazar	11	Male	African American
Alan	11	Male	Asian
Miguel	11	Male	Latino
Ginger	13	Female	African American
Helena	10	Female	African American
Lothian	8	Male	Asian
Elias	8	Male	Asian
Natalie	8	Female	Caucasian
Neysa	8	Female	Caucasian
Ophelia	8	Female	Asian

CI: A Multi-generational Team Approach to Co-designing with Children

A promising approach to ground these AI4All efforts is to integrate PD techniques within AI learning activities, which encourage children to become "active, playful director(s)" (Karmann, 2017, p. 1) of AI-infused technologies. PD includes best practices and research methods with the core philosophy of including end-users as active participants in the technology design process (Muller, 2008; Schuler & Namioka, 1993). As a design philosophy, PD grew out of the Scandinavian trade union movement of the 1970s, which focused on giving union workers an active voice in the design of computers they were required to use (Bødker et al., 2000). PD is often used synonymously with the term, "co-design" ("cooperative" or "collaborative design"), which typically emphasizes an equal partnership between designer and end-user and enlists user participation as early in the design process as possible (Bødker et al., 2000; Walsh et al., 2013).

Similarly, participatory ML methods position end-users as experts in their everyday experiences (Birhane et al., 2022). Participatory ML methods aim to reduce bias and promote people's comfort level with AI-based interactions by empowering them to formulate problems for AI-systems to solve, such as blind and/or visually impaired users developing their own image classifiers (Kacorri, 2017; Kacorri et al., 2017) or users training a portable object/gesture recognition system to complete simple everyday tasks such as opening and closing a book to turn off a light (Karmann, 2017). The studies in this chapter involve PD-based approaches to AI learning and literacy, with one case (Case 2) involving families of one or more "teams" of parents/grandparents and children brainstorming features of an AI-based language learning system. While many studies exist that examine teamwork and collaboration between parents and educational professionals (e.g., Bacon & Causton-Theoharis, 2013; Halimah et al., 2023), and families learning and designing together (Roque, 2016, 2020; Stefanidi et al., 2024), this chapter focuses on the field of child–computer interaction[2] and the roles that children and parents take up (e.g., Cho et al., 2019; Roque et al., 2016; Yip et al., 2016) as they brainstorm ways that gen AI might support language learning and cultural preservation.

While Case 2 also included sessions where family members co-design together, all the case studies presented in this chapter involve a multigenerational co-design team known as KidsTeam (Druin, 1999, 2002, 2005; Fails et al., 2012; Guha et al., 2013; Walsh et al., 2013). KidsTeam is comprised of children, typically 7–12 years old, and adult designers/researchers who work as design partners to create technologies *with* and *for* children (Druin, 1999). The group follows a PD-based approach known as CI (Druin, 2002; Fails et al., 2012; Guha et al., 2013). Although children have played a variety of roles in the design process over

[2]See the *International Journal of Child-Computer Interaction (IJCCI)* and the ACM Conference on Interaction Design and Children for more: https://www.sciencedirect.com/journal/international-journal-of-child-computer-interaction and https://www.interaction-design.org/literature/conference_series/idc.

the past two decades of PD research (e.g., users, testers, informants), CI emphasizes an equal partnership between children and adults in multigenerational design teams (Bonsignore et al., 2013). The goal of CI is to highlight children's perspectives and preferences throughout the design process, rather than obtaining their feedback at the **end** of the design cycle or simply observing their use of a finished product or system. CI emphasizes equal partnership as much as possible, focusing on the concept of *idea elaboration*, where children and adults share and build upon each other's ideas (elaborate) as they explore, design, and evaluate new technologies. Due to the emphasis on equal partnerships between children and adults, we often refer to the process as co-design.

CI offers a variety of techniques that can be used by intergenerational teams throughout the design process (Fails et al., 2012; Walsh et al., 2013). Several of the following co-design techniques were used in the exploratory studies:

- Bags of Stuff, which involves the use of low-fidelity, paper-based materials for prototyping and brainstorming;
- Big Paper, which enables brainstorming and ideation through storyboarding and speculative scenario-building;
- Sticky Noting, which uses post-it notes and annotations to evaluate different features and characteristics of emerging systems or prototypes; and
- Layered Elaboration, which employs layers of annotations to highlight, evaluate, or re-design various features of system prototypes/products, for example, annotating wireframes for a mobile app (Fails et al., 2012, 2022; Walsh et al., 2013).

Exploring Machine Teaching and Problem Formulation with Children

The two case studies described in this chapter are part of a larger body of work in which we implemented CI/co-design sessions with children to explore their conceptualizations of AI systems and to gain insights into the design of AI literacy activities for children and families (Dwivedi, 2021; Dwivedi et al., 2021, 2024, 2025). The details of our prior work can be found in Dwivedi et al. (2021, 2024). Here, we briefly summarize what we observed in these early co-design sessions regarding HAT interactions.

Our prior work included a series of participatory machine-learning studies in which children assumed the role of teachers and testers of machine teaching models and also imagined and specified the types of everyday problems that they wanted AI systems to tackle. The first two of these studies highlighted how ML activities can be designed so that pairs of children can exchange each other's models to promote reflection, discussion, pattern recognition (Dwivedi et al., 2021), while the third study afforded children opportunities to structure their problem formulation process and then share their findings with peers and adult team members (Dwivedi et al., 2024).

In the first two ML studies, children (7–13 years old) and adult co-designers collaborated to train image classifiers and test each other's models for robustness. As noted in the introduction, the children started out as human–AI dyads, with each child training their AI image classifiers individually. Each child then swapped their classifier with another child and to test their ML models against each other. During swapping/testing, the children moved from child–AI dyads to small HATs of 2 children and 1–2 adults who tested each child's classifier. When children swapped classifiers, they compared their training sets and reasoned together about possible patterns for improving them. For example, when children swapped and tested each other's models, they became more aware of the effects of noise in their training data – whether in image backgrounds or lower confidence due to confusion in recognizing different faces. In some instances, children would devise new training examples to see how they could confuse their partner's image classifier, which highlighted the playfully competitive nature of children working in small teams to train an AI (e.g., trick your partner's image classifier with photo bombing!). Meanwhile, adults in the team took on the more coach-like role of sounding board, or provided scaffolding questions (e.g., "if you think the color in the background messes with the confidence, how do you think we can improve it?").

In our third co-design session from prior work, children engaged in co-design to facilitate problem formulation, which is also explored in Clark and Graff's work on design thinking with adult designers (this volume). In this design session, we explored how co-design involving teachable machines facilitates problem formulation to support AI literacy. We included problem reduction heuristics into a structured storyboard and invited 10 KidsTeam child designers (ages 8–13) and 9 adults to co-design a teachable machine. Our initial "team" configuration focused on individual child–AI dyads, though adults served as facilitators and sounding boards. We observed that children drew from personal experiences when formulating AI problems; they assumed voice and video capabilities, explored diverse machine-learning approaches, and planned for error handling. While this co-design session did not explore how teams of children might design a single teachable machine, we found that the children enjoyed comparing and discussing each other's designs and comparing options for error-checking. Interestingly, the design metaphors that children used in their AI problem formulation for everyday contexts stood in contrast to co-design sessions in which children storyboarded options for supporting creative expression and social play. We noted that when children experienced machine teaching activities and then designed their own teachable machine to solve a problem of their choice, they mostly did not anthropomorphize their machines beyond naming them. Instead, children's designs reflected supertools, telebots, and active appliances rather than designing for teammates, intelligent agents, and social robots (Dwivedi et al., 2024). In the Discussion section, we compare these design metaphors from prior work to those we observed when children engage with AI to support creative expression (Case Study 1).

Both of the case studies presented in this chapter grew out of our efforts to explore children's engagement with AI concepts and their interest in using AI systems to support their own creativity and learning. With the exception of human–computer interaction workshops (e.g., Nanduri & Bonsignore, 2023), this chapter represents the first published findings of our two case studies.

EXPLORATORY CASE STUDIES

Case 1: Collaborative/Creative Storytelling/Dialog/Artwork Creation

For the first case, we posed the following questions: How might children imagine a machine that could promote their creativity or boost them out of boredom? Would children interact with a gen AI as a creative collaborator or an entertainment platform, or something in-between? Would it be an either–or or a both–and?

Case 1 touches on the results of a co-design partnership that explores how children conceive of collaborating with an interactive AI system to support their creative play. For this partnership, KidsTeam worked with the Joan Ganz Cooney Center at Sesame Workshop[3] and a small technology start-up to help explore an AI-based creative collaboration platform for children. We held two 90-minute co-design sessions with 11 children and 10 adults in November/December 2022, during the same week that the gen AI toolset, OpenAI, was released to the public (OpenAI, 2022). Developers from the technology start-up introduced the children to a suite of independently developed OpenAI tools known collectively as *Story Jam*. The toolset included (1) a *Playground* text generator modified slightly from the ChatGPT large language model (LLM), which could produce short paragraphs, essays, or stories based on children's prompts and questions; (2) a *Character* Jam voice-enabled chatbot with which the children could hold free-form conversations; and (3) *Image Jam*, an AI art creation interface employing DALL-E-2 (Radford et al., 2019; Schulman et al., 2022).

The goal of our first session was to familiarize children with the tools in a free-form manner, with as few direct prompts and/or direction as possible, other than asking the children to collaborate creatively with the various AI tools that were being integrated with the *Story Jam* prototype. Goals for our second session were shaped by insights drawn from the first session, with a focus on **social play**: we invited the children to brainstorm ways to use the various AI tools (separately or in combination) to play with friends. For each session, children and adults worked in small teams of 2–3 children with 2 adults, rotating through "stations" where the team would focus on a specific *Story Jam* creativity tool, such as the *Character Jam* chatbot. While each team discussed and shared different ideas for interacting with the specific AI tool at their respective station, each child tended to focus on an individual creation with the help of the adults, rather than coordinating their human–AI interactions as a team. The children's preference for individual creation may have been a function of technology distribution: even while they discussed their ideas and questions as a group, each child interacted with an individual iPad loaded with the *Story Jam* prototype. This often resulted in individual "heads-down" interactions while each child created prompts, engaged verbally with a chatbot, or searched for/created images. However, after a few minutes

---

[3]The Joan Ganz Cooney Center is a non-profit research lab within Sesame Workshop. It is named for the co-founder of the educational television show, Sesame Street. Its mission is to "advance positive futures for kids in the digital world" (https://joanganzcooneycenter.org/).

Table 10.2. The "takeaways" from the December 2022 Beta Release Version of the OpenAI ChatGPT Tool, Which Analyzed Children's Story Prompts and Human–AI Story Ideas as Training Data.

ChatGPT started its analysis with the statement: *"Some patterns that I notice in the prompts are:"*	**One adult co-design team member prompted ChatGPT with the following question:** *"These were all written by children. Why do you think they interacted with the AI in this way?"*
– Many of the prompts relate to writing stories, songs, or poems – Some of the prompts involve fantasy or supernatural elements, such as mermaids, witches, ghosts, and aliens – Some of the prompts involve historical or famous figures, such as Mike Tyson, Mohammed Ali, and Pinocchio – Some of the prompts involve animals, such as dogs, elephants, mushrooms, and cats *[author's note: unsure why mushrooms are listed as animal]* – Some of the prompts involve themes of fear or horror, such as scary stories, blood, and the black plague – Some of the prompts involve the prompt giver requesting a specific length or word count for the written piece	**ChatGPT:** "It is difficult for me to say for certain why the children interacted with the AI in this way, as I do not have access to any information outside of my training data. However, some possible reasons for their behavior could be that that they were curious about what the AI could do, they wanted to see if the AI could understand and respond to their prompts, or they were using the AI as a tool to help them generate ideas for their own writing. Additionally, children may be more likely to use their imagination and creativity when interacting with AI, which could explain the fantastical and imaginative nature of many of the prompts."

of individual human–AI interaction, all the children enjoyed sharing their creations and providing feedback to each other about what they liked, what they had trouble with or disliked, and ideas they had for building upon the tools.

During a debrief after our first session, adult team members prompted ChatGPT to identify patterns in the stories and conversations that the children had created to explore how the system's analysis compared with the adult discussion (see Table 10.2 for several of the themes summarized by the gen AI tool). We found that the system contributed a straight-forward initial thematic analysis of the children's creations (cf., Stokel-Walker, 2023). One of the AI's responses aligned with a salient theme that adults observed, specifically: "the children were curious about what the AI could do" and would pose sometimes extreme, silly questions and story situations to see how and "if the AI could understand and respond." The following sub-sections detail specific design themes and exploratory findings that we uncovered from the children's interactions during our two co-design sessions.

Entertainment Platform Versus Creative Collaborator

An overarching theme regarding the children's interaction with each of the tools was their desire to have the *Story Jam* prototype entertain them, rather than viewing it as a creative collaborator. One adult used the phrase "AI as court-jester," which is an apt summary of the ways in which the children interacted with the AI-tools (e.g., testing the tools' boundaries with stories about murder, dismemberment, violence, and "poop sandwiches"). In retrospect, the children could have been prompted by our invitation to "play around" with each AI-based tool, rather than explicitly to "do something creative with the AI." We did not explicitly ask the children to "create something together with the AI." We could have tied the question more closely with one of our session's warm-up questions: "What was the last thing that you did that was creative?" KidsTeam child designers are also used to "playing around" with and testing prototypes, so they may have been primed to explore and evaluate the features of the tools rather than co-create with them.

Of note, children's responses to the warm-up also raised interesting insights into the types of activities they consider to be "creative." Beyond sharing that writing a story or performing a song were examples of being creative, several of the children explicitly justified seemingly mundane everyday actions as creative acts. For example, one boy mentioned that finding a way to do a homework problem could be creative, while a girl mentioned that one of her creative acts was to make a good play during a soccer game. The children's responses to the warm-up question highlight how they notice potential creativity in everything that they do. This insight hints at a possible reason that the children viewed Story Jam components as **tools**, rather than more fully collaborative team members. That is, the children may have wondered at the specific, separated functions of the *Story Jam* suite of gen AI tools (e.g., *Character Jam*; DALL-E for art). They may have viewed the distinct function served by each component as a tool specialized for a distinct task, not as a collaborative, holistic team member that could also be creative in almost everything it could do. Indeed, the OpenAI organization refers to its various LLM components as a "toolset," not necessarily a supportive collaborator with multiple, integrated talents.

"Magic Button" When I'm Stuck, Need a Generative Boost, or a Random Surprise

During our first session's whole group discussion, as we summarized ideas across the *Story Jam* tools, one child noted that they wished the *Playground* interface could sometimes continue with more than one paragraph or series of sentences, that is, to help them be more generative with their story ideas. This prompted a discussion about having a "magic word" or "magic button" feature that would help a child user "get unstuck," like story starters and prompts that are often used in primary school writing (Kucirkova & Kamola, 2022; Kuo et al., 2024). Some of the children asked for their own code-word that would alert the AI that they needed help; others thought that an interactive feature, like a button, would work. Whether it was a magic button or a code word, the children's desire for an interactive help feature revealed that they desired control and agency over when they received help from the system. Similar to their efforts to spark random and extreme responses from the AI, we observed that random responses enhanced the children's playful interactions with the system, reinforcing the notion that it could serve as a "court jester" of entertainment. During the adult debrief, we also discussed options for adding a variety of "magic" actions to the button, such as providing random surprises (unexpected story twists or characters).

Children Compete with, Are Challenged by, or Collaborate with AI Characters/Game Mechanics

During our second session, children and adults worked together in small teams to brainstorm ways that they could creatively interact with the *Story Jam* toolset when they were **with friends**. While each team developed a different social scenario, that used the existing *Story Jam* toolset or incorporated new design features, all teams generated a list of specific AI characters with whom they wanted to interact. Characters included antagonists that children felt could challenge themselves and their friends, and collaborators that might provide rewards or opportunities for co-creation.

For one AI antagonist, a team of three children developed an "evil" AI that could generate a variety of Escape Rooms that groups of friends would need to conquer. Another team created a boss monster to "beat" in a game-based competition, such as a mutant T-Rex that children could fight (individually or with friends). Regarding an AI collaborator, another group designed an AI that would help them co-create a multi-level parkour obstacle course for friends, depending on their friends' respective skill levels. In this case, the AI would work with one or more children to imagine and co-create the parkour space. Similarly, the Escape Room team's social scenario was not only antagonistic. It also included an "Inventory AI" who would grant rewards for beating Escape Room levels (or whom you and your friends could pay for rewards, using in-game currency).

In addition to designer-crafted AI characters with whom to collaborate or fight, children wanted to create their own AI partners and/or antagonists, using Image Jam or other visual and audio tools. The desire to have a wide variety of AI-based "non-player characters" with whom to compete against or collaborate with was a recurring theme. Interestingly, when children considered how they would interact with the AI when playing with their friends, most saw themselves working **against** or competing with the AI. That is, even if the children worked with an AI to design a scenario (e.g., the parkour course or an Escape Room), the AI often became the antagonist when children imagined playing with friends. Essentially, once a team of children were situated in a scenario, they seemed to opt for an "us against the machine" stance.

Blended, Embodied Creations: Combining "Real World" Physical Proxies and Digital Stories

In both sessions, younger children expressed a desire for more tangible creations. This finding seems to be related to AI studies that have revealed how many novices have a techno-optimist expectation that AI systems can build anything you describe and rarely, if ever, make mistakes (Dwivedi et al., 2021). During the first session, the two youngest boys asked the AI to "make" physical things (a calculator, a video game) or assumed that one word (car) would result in an exact image that they imagined in their mind's eye. They also emphasized non-digital creations when they tested the boundaries of the AI's expression. For example, one boy asked if the Character Jam chatbot would "actually talk about making 'poop sandwiches' with me?"

During the second co-design session, one group expanded on this desire to incorporate material, "real world" objects by describing ways that the AI could capture photos of physical objects that children created, like a pipe-cleaner horse, and somehow "mash" them into their story worlds with Image Jam. Two children expressed a desire to create "mash-ups," such as selfies augmented with fantastical characteristics, like "snakes coming out of your face." These suggestions also came from children who had previously worked with Meta Demo Lab's animated drawing tool (*Sketch Meta Demo Lab: Vision AI*, 2025), with which users can upload and animate sketches (like Google's PoseNet/TensorFlow toolset).

Across both sessions, children described a desire to upload selfies or to create self-portraits that could then be integrated into story worlds and stories that they co-created with the AI. They also asked if they could upload images of favorite toys or pets and transfer them into a virtual space. Children either wanted some mixed reality version of themselves or the ability to mix and match various types of images and image genres. Their descriptions were reminiscent of card games that preschool and primary school age children play to focus on and learn descriptive language, such as Mix and Match Monster Cards or Mix and Match books.

Session Synthesis: From Individual Tools to Holistic Creative Collaborator

Most of the children preferred the more naturalistic, conversational interactions that they could have when using the chat-specific, turn-taking component of *Character Jam*, and all asked for the tools to be presented as an integrated platform ("I want to see the AI [when I talk to it]," referring to *Character Jam*). Many of the children also requested more explicit onboarding and/or scaffolding to help them co-create more effectively with the AI tools as an overall system. Ultimately, the children in our group wanted to both collaborate and compete with the AI toolset, implying a fluidity and range of interaction that is more aligned with a team mate rather than a toolset. They wanted to "trash talk AIs to defeat them;" they imagined an evil Boss AI that must be beaten and a benevolent Inventory AI who gave them rewards; they aspired to host an AI party with friends; and asked the AI to integrate real objects from their everyday lives (e.g., a pet or favorite toy) into personal stories.

Case 2: Children and Families Co-design Language Learning/Preservation Tools Using AI Systems

For the second case, we focused on the following questions: What are children's design preferences when interacting with AI-driven story creation tools in a language-learning context? How do they perceive the cultural relevance of gen AI imagery in their co-created stories? How does collaboration between children and adult family members shape the cultural depth and authenticity of stories to support language learning?

In response to the United Nations Educational, Scientific and Cultural Organization (UNESCO)'s warnings about the rapid loss of linguistic diversity under the dominance of global languages (*UNESCO Project: Atlas of the World's Languages in Danger – UNESCO Digital Library*, n.d.; UNESCO, 2025), our second case study explored how gen AI might support language revitalization through culturally grounded storytelling. The study's overarching goal was to investigate ways for integrating gen AI into language learning pedagogy through PD sessions with young Telugu-speaking learners and their families. The PD sessions helped to uncover children's design preferences for culturally responsive AI tools; examined how AI can foster intergenerational collaboration and cultural transmission; and highlighted storytelling as a potentially rich mechanism for language acquisition, facilitated by gen AI's ability to personalize learning experiences. The case study also touched on ethical considerations for designing gen AI tools, promoting inclusivity, bias mitigation, and protection of cultural integrity.

The co-design sessions for this case were implemented using the CI approach followed by KidsTeam, which were implemented with Telugu-speaking families in India (Nanduri, 2024; Nanduri & Bonsignore, 2023). The session plans were first pilot-tested with KidsTeam children to ensure the feasibility and format for conducting a subsequent co-design session with Telugu-speaking families in India. The KidsTeam pilot session engaged eight children (7–12 years), all English speakers, most of whose families are from non-Western backgrounds, including children of Chinese, Korean, and Nigerian descent (US-born children of immigrant parents and/or grandparents). All children were familiar with AI-based systems such as OpenAI's gen AI chatbot, ChatGPT and their digital image generator, DALL-E. The goal for the KidsTeam pilot session was to explore how well children might interact with gen AI and to solidify the types of activities that the children and families in India might engage in for co-designing a language learning system with an AI-based chatbot helper. Two subsequent sessions were developed from this pilot session which involved children and families in India (see Table 10.3 for participant details). Three of the families participated remotely via Zoom. For the rest of the sessions, the second co-author of this chapter, an experienced KidsTeam adult co-designer, visited the families in their homes in person. In this chapter, we focus on the two co-design sessions that were conducted with Telugu-speaking Indian families (Nanduri, 2024).

Co-design Session 1: Child–AI Co-design Through Storytelling

In the first session in India, 13 children were invited to bring a meaningful cultural artifact from their home – such as a traditional object, family heirloom, or festival item – and share a personal story connected to it. These stories served as the foundation for co-designing with AI. This co-design technique is known as the "Talisman" approach (https://www.talismantoolkit.com/). Talisman promotes inclusion and engagement among co-design partners by privileging objects that

Table 10.3. Case Study 2 Family Participants: Co-designing AI Systems to Support Language Learning and Language Preservation.

	Child Participants	Parent/Grandparent Participants				Session Format
	P1, P2	Mother	Father			In-person
	P3	Mother	Father	Grandmother	Grandfather	In-person
	P4, P5	Mother	Father			Remote (Zoom)
	P6	Mother	Father			Remote (Zoom)
	P7	Mother				In-person
	P8, P9	Father				Remote (Zoom)
	P10, P11	Mother	Father	Grandmother		In-person
	P12, P13	Mother		Grandmother	Grandfather	In-person
Total	13 children	7 Mothers	6 Fathers	3 Grandmothers	2 Grandfathers	

Notes: Eight families participated (13 children, 7 mothers, 6 fathers, and 5 grandparents). The breakdown of family members is listed in Table 10.3. All participants speak Telugu; all live in India.

are personally selected by co-design partners, rather than the typical approach of using designer-provided materials (Elsayed-Ali et al., 2023).

Children began by narrating their story in their own words and then collaborated with ChatGPT to expand, rewrite, or reimagine their stories. All the children demonstrated a preference for posing prompts and questions to the chatbot using voice commands while receiving responses in writing. Specifically, participating children in India noted that they felt that seeing words in the chatbot's text responses might also help them learn languages better. The bilingual Indian children also expressed an interest in interacting with the chatbots in both English and Telugu, noting that "if we keep speaking and writing in Telugu then we can save the language." Indeed, the children regularly asked the chatbot language and grammar-related questions (e.g., "How do we say 'events' in Telugu?"). As they interacted with the AI, children experimented with images and tried different prompts, sometimes challenging the AI to "think" more like them. Children also emphasized a desire for an art creation system that could seamlessly accept children's physical drawings and sketches, then enhance and customize them in response to the children's verbal commands (e.g., telling the chatbot, "you know how to wear pancha," a specific type of clothing also known as the "dhoti").

Co-design Session 2: Intergenerational Reflections and Dialogs

During the second phase of the session, participants shifted from solo storytelling to family-based reflection. Children shared their AI-generated stories with parents and grandparents, prompting conversations about the role of AI in everyday learning. In contrast to most children who participate in KidsTeam, the families were not familiar with CI-based co-design techniques. However, these sessions adhered to the same open-ended dialogue and idea-elaboration that is central to CI and child co-design practices (Bonsignore et al., 2013; DiSalvo, 2016). Throughout this part of the sessions, the lead co-designer in India (and second co-author to this chapter) encouraged families to collaboratively reflect on how AI might be adapted into their home environments for language learning.

Through these conversations, family members discussed the cultural appropriateness of AI-generated narratives, the importance of language accuracy, and their aspirations for AI tools that could support shared learning across generations. The sessions created space for differing views to surface and for family members to co-imagine AI as a bridge – not just between language and learning, but between the past, present, and future of their cultural identity.

Together, the two phases of co-design laid the groundwork for understanding how human–AI teams – especially within families – form, collaborate, and negotiate meaning in the context of language preservation. Our observations and analysis of the children's interactions with the ChatGPT gen AI system and their subsequent co-design discussions with parents and grandparents are summarized below.

Human–AI Team Structures and Collaboration Dynamics Initially, children engaged individually with ChatGPT to expand on stories inspired by cultural artifacts they brought from home through the Talisman co-design technique. With each interaction, they explored what it meant to co-create with AI. For the most part, children seemed curious, playful, and unafraid to test the tool's creative limits (as was the case with the US-based KidsTeam children in Case Study 1). Children did not follow a fixed script; rather, they preferred to experiment, adjusting prompts on the fly, challenging AI outputs, and reshaping stories until they felt personally and culturally meaningful.

Similar to Case Study 1, we observed that children perceived ChatGPT as a co-author, an idea-generator, and a sounding board. Excited by the stories they had crafted, children prompted ChatGPT to embellish their creations. For example, they asked, "Can you make my story into comics?," "Can you color my sketch?," and "What do you call Veena in Telugu?" They often pushed the AI beyond text, into a world of visual imagination. These requests highlighted how children viewed AI not as a passive assistant, but as a teammate in multimodal creativity.

In the second co-design session, children shared and refined their AI-co-created stories with their parents and grandparents. The first session's story repository became entry points for deeper conversations with their families, which transformed solitary storytelling into a collaborative, intergenerational exploration of culture, language, and values. These reflective sessions reshaped the child–AI dyad into a dynamic family team, where AI served not only as a creative tool but as a catalyst for dialog across generations.

Children proudly shared their design choices, while parents and grandparents responded mostly with curiosity. Most of the adults affirmed their children's creativity yet raised thoughtful concerns about language fidelity and the role of AI in shaping learning habits. Specifically, the children's comments also reveal how culturally limited tools may fall short of effectively enabling the preservation of heritage languages. This finding underscores the importance of the human ability to notice nuance and to use it to train and refine systems that promote language learning. One parent reflected on a design session where their child explored the topic of rice: "She started with our kind of rice, but then asked the AI about brown rice, harvesting, and why different countries eat it differently." The parent noted that this curiosity, sparked by AI, expanded the child's understanding of culture beyond the familiar, prompting new interest in global traditions and languages. We observed that these moments reminded families that cultural storytelling was not only about imagination but also about discovery.

While grandparents were often less vocal about the technical aspects, we observed that their presence added emotional depth and historical memory. Some families envisioned AI as a tool to preserve intergenerational stories. "Maybe if AI lets them record the stories we want to say – for future generations – that can make us excited," one parent suggested, imagining AI as a means of capturing ancestral voices rather than replacing them. Interestingly, no adults were concerned that an AI system might also destroy or overwrite the stories that their children had created and the ones they built upon with their children. They primarily viewed the stories as a preservation tool that might constantly be built upon.

Together, these conversations revealed a nuanced collaboration where children led with curiosity, adults guided with care, and AI played a flexible supporting role. The outcome was not only richer stories, but a model for family-centered, culturally grounded human–AI partnerships. This finding builds upon PD methods used with families to promote STEM learning and identity (Roque, 2016, 2020; Roque et al., 2016).

Patterns of Communication and Team Design Thinking The Telugu-speaking Indian family teams exhibited diverse communication patterns, ranging from authoritative (parent-led) to collaborative (joint exploration). For example, we observed a distinct interplay between structured guidance from adults and exploratory, child-driven creativity. Parents actively supported their children's creative expression, frequently acknowledging and validating their contributions while gently steering discussions toward culturally significant aspects of storytelling. The roles that parents and grandparents assumed while sharing responses to their children's interactions with gen AI align with the complementary roles adults can play in the co-design process (Yip et al., 2016, 2017). These roles focus on the relationship-building, facilitation, and elaboration actions that trusted adults like parents and grandparents may enact during co-design sessions (Yip et al., 2017).

The "team design thinking" approach observed during the sessions was both iterative and reflective, evolving naturally through the diverse dynamics of each family. Children led with imaginative spontaneity – frequently proposing whimsical characters, fantastical plot twists, or playful AI features such as voice-driven interactions and animated storybooks. Parents, in turn, engaged with these ideas through a more evaluative and cultural lens, offering gentle guidance to align the stories with traditional values, linguistic accuracy, or moral undertones.

The "team design thinking" approach we observed in this case study was also rooted in co-creation across generations – children led with imagination, while parents and grandparents offered cultural and emotional scaffolding. One family's interactions highlight this theme: one of the children, inspired by his favorite festival memory, created a story with ChatGPT about his memories of buying new clothes for every holiday. Delighted, the child proudly shared the story with his adult co-designers. The parent responded with appreciation and then gently pointed out, "In our tradition, you know why we buy clothes? Because it's a sign of gratitude and renewal." This feedback reframed the story's message without diminishing the child's vision. Meanwhile, the grandparent added, "Wearing new clothes is a symbol of cleanliness/hygiene and a way of saying we're now refreshed and ready for the new season."

The various roles that adults and children played as they elaborated upon each other's ideas revealed how a story co-designed with AI could become a shared canvas for intergenerational dialogue. Children brought creativity; parents shaped narratives with cultural accuracy; grandparents anchored them with memory and meaning. Together, they practiced iterative co-design – refining outputs through empathy, cultural reflection, and shared storytelling.

Navigating Conflicts and Power Dynamics Children approached AI with curiosity and bold imagination – but friction surfaced when the tool failed to grasp the subtleties of their culture. One child, eager to illustrate a traditional scene, was puzzled when the AI generated an image of a Telugu priest eating lunch that didn't match their lived reality. These mismatches didn't discourage them – instead, they became sparks for inquiry. Children reworded prompts, critiqued inaccuracies, and insisted on representations that "felt right." For them, AI was not an all-knowing oracle, but a responsive collaborator: one they could question, reshape, and occasionally override.

When the children shared the stories they had co-created with an AI chatbot with adult family members, a new dynamic unfolded. The creative freedom children embraced often met cautious scrutiny from parents and grandparents. Concerns ranged from educational depth to cultural authenticity. "The AI gave Telugu translations, but they don't always follow grammar or make sense. It's important children learn correct language, or they'll get confused," warned one parent, worried about linguistic distortion. Others were uneasy about over-reliance: "If AI fixes their spelling right away, how will they learn what they did wrong?" and "writing by hand creates a visual and auditory imprint – if AI skips that, they lose something vital."

Despite these tensions, the design sessions fostered productive dialog. Children and adults negotiated meaning and purpose, refining design ideas in ways that balanced creativity with cultural integrity. With facilitation support, families reached shared understandings of how AI could serve both educational and heritage-preserving goals. Rather than stalling the process, these intergenerational conflicts enriched the collaboration and highlighted the importance of ethical guardrails and cultural sensitivity in designing AI for family learning contexts.

Families commonly envisioned their "dream AI" as a culturally sensitive, conversational companion capable of adapting to individual learning styles and reflecting their heritage. For many, the ideal AI would support bilingual dialogue, offer personalized story generation based on local traditions, and serve as a bridge between generations – helping elders pass down language and stories in a format children found engaging.

Sample AI-supported Language Learning Ideas from Family-oriented HATs The intergenerational exchanges between children and their adult caregivers (parents and grandparents) resulted in a suite of conceptual design recommendations that can invite future prototyping work for culturally responsive AI systems to support language learning and preservation.

An Interactive AI Storybook idea, for example, responded directly to concerns about AI bypassing natural learning rhythms. With features like voice-text hybrid interaction, reading assistance, and pronunciation practice, parents commented that this type of AI-support could help children grow confident in Telugu while satisfying parental hopes for language integrity.

A Cultural Creativity Kit struck another balance – blending hands-on crafts with digital storytelling. Children could create, write, and illustrate with the help of an AI companion, while parents saw it as a way to reinforce traditional skills like handwriting and script learning through modern engagement.

To support immersive, collaborative family learning, two extended reality prototypes emerged during the co-design sessions. First, a Learning Wall Projector turned home spaces into playful classrooms, encouraging collaborative exploration of Telugu stories, history, and vocabulary. In addition, an Ancestral Story Garden with AR use could let families walk through tales together – bringing generations into a shared, embodied narrative space.

Other ideas, like transforming cultural speeches into tactile AI-enhanced storybooks, addressed parents' concerns that children find traditional teachings dull. We observed that both children and parents felt that interactive books could make ancient wisdom touchable, audible, and alive – bridging old values with new formats. Relatedly, projects like an Audio/Visual Interactive Museum and Intergenerational Knowledge Transmission Platform offered communal spaces and tools where elders and youth could co-create, preserve, and pass down language and stories. This highlighted both adults and children's desire to have gen AI serve as a responsive bridge between generations. This case study illuminated how the future of human–AI collaboration in family learning may explore long-term engagement across diverse linguistic communities, to develop tools that adapt to family values and cultural norms.

DISCUSSION

Each case in this chapter aimed to support AI learning and literacy goals for children with little or no programming experience, such as promoting the understanding that computer systems use sensors (e.g., cameras) to perceive the world and learn from data (Touretzky et al., 2019). Each case engaged children through participatory machine learning/teaching and PD. Although the co-design sessions were conducted with children and adults working in small groups of 3–4 design partners (e.g., two children with one or two adults), most of the interactions within these groups focused on individual child–AI interactions. For example, each child in Case Study 1 explored the *Story* Jam toolset on an individual iPad (one-child to one-tablet). Similarly, in Case Study 2, each child started out interacting individually with ChatGPT to create their stories. However, throughout the sessions, we observed that each child would also share their reactions within their small group (Case Study 1), or we observed parents and grandparents prompting child co-designers to probe a gen AI chatbot with more culturally relevant storytelling perspectives. Thus, human–AI teaming surfaced in two main ways:

- teams of children and adults brainstorming playful social scenarios where friends collaborated or competed with an AI prototype designed to support creative expression (Case 1); and
- family members collaborating to co-design an AI-focused family storytelling and language learning system (Case 2).

Common Themes

Despite the different co-design goals for each case, several overarching themes emerged.

Testing the Boundaries of Limits of AI Systems: Can We Prank the AI?

First, whether individually or in teams, children playfully tried to push the boundaries of what they understood to be an AI system's robustness or capabilities. This aligns with findings from Druga et al. (2022), which engaged parents and children in AI literacy tasks to see how they can train it to do silly tasks. Relatedly, we found that, even as AI technologies become more embedded in children's everyday lives, when children gain more opportunities to tackle overhyped claims about the infallibility of AI through creativity tools such as *Story Jam* (Case Study 1), or in conversation with their families (Case Study 2), they began to reflect more critically on the utility and limits of AI.

Similarly, in prior PD and participatory machine-learning work that we conducted (Dwivedi et al., 2021, 2024), when children are empowered to build their own teachable machine, they are no longer mere users of AI. In combination with recent work by Vartiainen et al. (2021) and Hitron et al. (2018), our PD collaboration with children reinforces techniques that researchers and practitioners may use to encourage children to reflect critically on how AI may be used in their everyday lives. Children gained a healthy critical view of the limitations and constraints of their designs as they playfully pushed the limits of creativity tools (Case Study 1) or trained and tested existing machine learning models (Druga & Ko, 2021; Dwivedi et al., 2021).

Different Contexts Promote Different AI Roles and Design Metaphors
Interestingly, prior work on the ways in which children used in AI problem formulation for everyday contexts (Dwivedi et al., 2024) stood in contrast to co-design sessions in which children storyboarded options for supporting creative expression and social play (Case Study 1). Problem formulation is a type of problem definition, finding, and restructuring, which Medeiros and colleagues (this volume) suggest can be benefitted by using gen AI so as to draw on a larger set of information.

When children have experienced machine teaching with existing tools (e.g., Google Teachable Machine) and are then asked to build their own teachable machine, we found that for the most part, they did not anthropomorphize their machines beyond naming them or giving them pronouns (Dwivedi et al., 2024). Instead, children's designs tend to align with proposed changes in design metaphors for AI (Chan et al., 2021; Shneiderman, 2020, 2022); they moved away from *intelligent agents, teammates, assured autonomy, and social robots*. The most prevalent design metaphors reflected in children's ideas were *supertools, tele-bots, control centers, and active appliances*. Shneiderman (2022) suggests that "successful designers avoid mimicking human models and pursue supertools, tele-bots, active appliances, and control centers that support human control over technology while ensuring high levels of automation" (p. 97).

This approach is in direct contrast to the persona-driven AI characters that children devised for supporting their creative expression and social play, such as the evil AI that would generate increasingly difficult Escape Rooms for friends to tackle together in an effort to triumph over tough challenges (Case Study 1). When designing for creative expression, children's AI systems and counterparts took on character roles and human persona attributes, whereas in problem formulation contexts (Dwivedi et al., 2024), children tended to design and consider AI systems as helpers or tools, with little anthropomorphization.

It may seem unsurprising that the design metaphors that children applied to their AI designs were grounded in their contexts of use. That is, when considering teachable machines to support their everyday tasks and activities, children tend to frame their systems as tools (Dwivedi et al., 2024), while these systems morphed into playmates, frenemies, or nemeses when used in more creative, playful contexts. However, it was interesting to observe how children had a nuanced sense of the range of design metaphors they wanted, based on different contexts of use.

Overall, the final Case Study in this chapter revealed that designing **with** families offers interesting design options for AI in language learning. Children approached AI as playful co-authors, pushing boundaries and seeking personalization, while parents and grandparents acted as cultural stewards, anchoring the experience in tradition, ethics, and educational depth. Though tensions surfaced around translation fidelity, handwriting, or AI's overreach, these conflicts became sites of co-learning. When thoughtfully guided, AI became not just a tool, but a mediator for intergenerational dialogue, storytelling, and mutual understanding.

The future of human–AI collaboration in family learning lies not in replacing tradition, but in augmenting it with sensitivity, adaptability, and imagination.

Future work should explore long-term engagement across diverse linguistic communities, develop tools that adapt to family values and cultural norms, and deepen the emotional intelligence of AI to foster trust and relevance. As this study shows, when children's creativity and elders' wisdom converge – with AI as a respectful companion – the result is more than just improved literacy. It's a living, evolving relationship between generations, language, and technology – a collaborative model where culture is not just preserved, but actively reimagined together. As with other kinds of teams, the communication, collaboration, and resulting convergence between different perspectives from different teammates, particularly when using PD methods with children, generated creative and culturally insightful design themes and implications.

CONCLUSION/FUTURE WORK

In this chapter, we presented exploratory studies of children and families co-designing with AI-infused systems. The two cases demonstrate how children have collaborated with AI systems:

- individually and in small groups to explore how AI tools might support their creative expression; and
- with family members to explore how they might capture family memories and culturally relevant stories while learning and preserving heritage languages.

Our cases touched on the ways in which children might take on different roles, whether responding to each other's creative storytelling prototypes or brainstorming with their parents and grandparents about how they might use gen AI to help preserve their cultural heritage and language. However, there remains scant work that explores human–AI team collaboration with children across contexts and with more than dyads (single child interacting with a gen AI) or beyond a single-family setting. The findings in this chapter serve as a call to action for future researchers, designers, and practitioners to consider more expansive configurations of children–AI teams. For example, would children in larger teams or in teams with assigned specific roles position themselves as antagonists, as we found through the "*us vs the machine*" theme from Case Study 1?

Our goals have been to offer initial lessons learned and to inspire related work where younger children with little to no programming/coding experience can acquire and practice AI literacies while teaming with AI and each other. Like similar AI4All studies with younger children (7–13 years old), we found that children gain a more nuanced, skeptical appreciation for the limitations of AI systems such as the need for robust training data, fulfilling an AI literacies/AI4All learning framework goal for children. Once young non-experts have been exposed to a variety of machine learning/teaching models and how they work, these systems are no longer black boxes. Instead, they gain a foothold on explainability, and AI literacy empowers them to critique and create new models to their everyday lives and design creative responses to emerging challenges. Perhaps most importantly, when given opportunities to engage in creative ideation and cultural preservation, children were eager to push the boundaries of what adults have considered with AI. In both cases, children were not only acquiring and practicing AI literacies such as collecting training data and experimenting with prompts and interactions with chatbots; they were also empowered through co-design to imagine new AI tools and systems to support their daily activities and goals.

We look forward to expanding our efforts to support children's collaboration with AI systems from a single child training simple image classifiers or working with smart chatbots to larger, multi-generational teams of children and their trusted adults who can take on many different roles and actions to support their everyday needs. Overall, whether children collaborate in individual human–AI dyads, or more traditional HATs, our studies have found that multigenerational PD approaches not only support improved AI literacy and critical reflection on the advantages and limitations of AI-systems in the multi-faceted contexts of children's lives, they also hold potential to promote stronger relationships between generations, language, and technology – a collaborative model where culture is not only preserved, but reimagined.

ACKNOWLEDGMENTS

We thank the children of KidsTeam who participated in both case studies, along with their parents. We also thank the children and families in India who participated in Case Study 2. Finally, we acknowledge and are grateful to Manny Fassihi and Josh Benjamin, the wonderful designer/entrepreneurs who crafted the *Story Jam* prototype and worked closely with KidsTeam and the Joan Ganz Cooney Center throughout October 2022–June 2023.

REFERENCES

Bacon, J. K., & Causton-Theoharis, J. (2013). 'It should be teamwork': A critical investigation of school practices and parent advocacy in special education. *International Journal of Inclusive Education*, *17*(7), 682–699. https://doi.org/10.1080/13603116.2012.708060

Balakrishnan, T., Chui, M., Hall, B., & Henke, N. (2020). *The state of AI in 2020*. McKinsey and Company. https://www.mckinsey.com/business-functions/mckinsey-analytics/our-insights/global-survey-the-state-of-ai-in-2020#

Birhane, A., Isaac, W., Prabhakaran, V., Diaz, M., Elish, M. C., Gabriel, I., & Mohamed, S. (2022). Power to the people? Opportunities and challenges for participatory AI. *Equity and access in algorithms, mechanisms, and optimization* (pp. 1–8). https://doi.org/10.1145/3551624.3555290

Bødker, S., Sjögren, D., Ehn, P., & Sundblad, Y. (2000). Co-operative design – Perspectives on 20 years with "the Scandinavian IT Design Model." *Proceedings of NordiCHI 2000* (pp. 1–9).

Bonsignore, E., Ahn, J., Clegg, T., Guha, M. L., Yip, J. C., & Druin, A. (2013). Embedding participatory design into designs for learning: An untapped interdisciplinary resource? *To See the World and a Grain of Sand: Learning across Levels of Space, Time, and Scale: CSCL 2013 Conference Proceedings Volume 1 – Full Papers & Symposia*, *1*, 549–556. https://www.isls.org/cscl/2013/Volume%201%20Final%20CSCL%202013%20Proceedings.pdf

Carter-Browne, B. M., Paletz, S. B. F., Campbell, S., Carraway, M., Vahlkamp, S. H., Schwartz, J., & O'Rourke, P. (2021). *There is no "AI" in teams: A multidisciplinary framework for AIs to work in human teams* (pp. 1–94). Applied Research Laboratory for Intelligence and Security (ARLIS). https://www.arlis.umd.edu/sites/default/files/2022-03/No_AI_In_Teams_FinalReport%20(1).pdf

Chan, J., Daumé III, H., Dickerson, J. P., Kacorri, H., & Shneiderman, B. (2021). Supporting human flourishing by ensuring human involvement in AI-infused systems. *Human centered AI workshop* (pp. 1–5). https://drive.google.com/file/d/1o2Rk8qrciy2_vfuropEoiyVwvK6LK9Cf/view

Cho, A., Herrera, R. G., Chaidez, L., & Uriostegui, A. (2019). The "Comadre" Project: An asset-based design approach to connecting low-income Latinx families to out-of-school learning opportunities. *Proceedings of the 2019 CHI conference on human factors in computing systems* (pp. 1–14). https://doi.org/10.1145/3290605.3300837

Demir, M., McNeese, N. J., & Cooke, N. J. (2020). Understanding human-robot teams in light of all-human teams: Aspects of team interaction and shared cognition. *International Journal of Human-Computer Studies*, *140*, 102436. https://doi.org/10.1016/j.ijhcs.2020.102436

DiSalvo, B. (2016). Participatory design through a learning science lens. *Proceedings of the 2016 CHI conference on human factors in computing systems* (pp. 4459–4463).

Druga, S., & Ko, A. J. (2021). How do children's perceptions of machine intelligence change when training and coding smart programs? *Interaction design and children* (pp. 49–61). https://doi.org/10.1145/3459990.3460712

Druga, S., Christoph, F. L., & Ko, A. J. (2022). Family as a third space for AI literacies: How do children and parents learn about AI together? *CHI conference on human factors in computing systems* (pp. 1–17). https://doi.org/10.1145/3491102.3502031

Druga, S., Vu, S. T., Likhith, E., & Qiu, T. (2019). Inclusive AI literacy for kids around the world. *Proceedings of FabLearn 2019* (pp. 104–111). https://doi.org/10.1145/3311890.3311904

Druin, A. (1999). Cooperative inquiry: Developing new technologies for children with children. *Proceedings of the SIGCHI conference on human factors in computing systems (CHI '99)* (pp. 592–599). https://doi.org/10.1145/302979.303166

Druin, A. (2002). The role of children in the design of new technology. *Behaviour & Information Technology*, *21*(1), 1–25. https://doi.org/doi:%252010.1080/01449290110108659

Druin, A. (2005). What children can teach us: Developing digital libraries for children with children. *The Library Quarterly*, *75*(1), 20–41. https://doi.org/10.1086/428691

Dwivedi, U. (2021). Introducing children to machine learning through machine teaching. *Interaction design and children* (pp. 641–643). https://doi.org/10.1145/3459990.3463394

Dwivedi, U., Elsayed-Ali, S., Bonsignore, E., & Kacorri, H. (2024). Exploring AI problem formulation with children via teachable machines. *Proceedings of the CHI conference on human factors in computing systems* (pp. 1–18). https://doi.org/10.1145/3613904.3642692

Dwivedi, U., Gandhi, J., Parikh, R., Coenraad, M., Bonsignore, E., & Kacorri, H. (2021). Exploring machine teaching with children. *IEEE symposium on visual languages and human-centric computing 2021*. https://doi.org/arXiv:2109.11434v2

Dwivedi, U., Qiao, Y., Hong, J., Bonsignore, E., & Kacorri, H. (2025). *IAMGroot: Exposing children to machine teaching with augmented reality art* [Manuscript submitted for publication].

Elsayed-Ali, S., Bonsignore, E., & Chan, J. (2023). Personal objects as design materials: A Case Study of co-designing safe spaces with young adults. *Computer supported cooperative work and social computing* (pp. 235–240). https://doi.org/10.1145/3584931.3606991

Fails, J. A., Guha, M. L., & Druin, A. (2012). Methods and techniques for involving children in the design of new technology for children. *Foundations and Trends® in Human–Computer Interaction*, *6*(2), 85–166. https://doi.org/10.1561/1100000018

Fails, J. A., Ratakonda, D. K., Koren, N., Elsayed-Ali, S., Bonsignore, E., & Yip, J. (2022). Pushing boundaries of co-design by going online: Lessons learned and reflections from three perspectives. *International Journal of Child-Computer Interaction*, *33*, 100476. https://doi.org/10.1016/j.ijcci.2022.100476

Guha, M. L., Druin, A., & Fails, J. A. (2013). Cooperative Inquiry revisited: Reflections of the past and guidelines for the future of intergenerational co-design. *International Journal of Child-Computer Interaction*, *1*(1), 14–23. https://doi.org/10.1016/j.ijcci.2012.08.003

Halimah, L., Yuliariatiningsih, M. S., & Mirawati. (2023). Strategies for optimizing partnership: Workshop on teamwork for teachers and parents in early childhood education. *International Journal of Early Years Education*, 1–18.

Hitron, T., Wald, I., Erel, H., & Zuckerman, O. (2018). Introducing children to machine learning concepts through hands-on experience. *Proceedings of the 17th ACM conference on interaction design and children* (pp. 563–568). https://doi.org/10.1145/3202185.3210776

Kacorri, H. (2017). Teachable machines for accessibility. *ACM SIGACCESS Accessibility and Computing*, *119*, 10–18. https://doi.org/10.1145/3167902.3167904

Kacorri, H., Kitani, K. M., Bigham, J. P., & Asakawa, C. (2017). People with visual impairment training personal object recognizers: Feasibility and challenges. *Proceedings of the 2017 CHI conference on human factors in computing systems* (pp. 5839–5849). https://doi.org/10.1145/3025453.3025899

Kafai, Y. B., & Burke, Q. (2013). The social turn in K-12 programming: Moving from computational thinking to computational participation. *Proceeding of the 44th ACM technical symposium on computer science education* (pp. 603–608).

Kafai, Y. B., Fields, D. A., & Searle, K. (2012). Making technology visible: Connecting the learning of crafts, circuitry and coding in youth e-textile designs. In J. van Aalst, K. Thompson, M. J. Jacobson, & P. Reimann (Eds.), *The future of learning: Proceedings of the 10th international conference of the learning sciences (ICLS 2012)* (Vol. *1*, pp. 188–195). International Society of the Learning Sciences.

Karmann, B. (2017, May). *Objectifier Spatial Programming by Bjø rn Karmann\textbar Experiments with Google*. https://experiments.withgoogle.com/objectifier-spatial-programming

Kucirkova, N., & Kamola, M. (2022). Children's stories and multisensory engagement: Insights from a cultural probes study. *International Journal of Educational Research*, *114*, 101995. https://doi.org/10.1016/j.ijer.2022.101995

Kulynych, B., Madras, D., Milli, S., Raji, I. D., Zhou, A., & Zemel, R. (2020, July). *Participatory approaches to machine learning*.

Kuo, H.-C., Chang, C.-Y., Wang, J.-P., Wu, E. L., & Li, P.-L. (2024). Creating my own story: Improving children's creative thinking and composition creativity through a three-staged individual-group-individual story writing framework. *Cognitive Development*, *72*, 101513. https://doi.org/10.1016/j.cogdev.2024.101513

Long, D., & Magerko, B. (2020). What is AI literacy? Competencies and design considerations. *Proceedings of the 2020 CHI conference on human factors in computing systems* (pp. 1–16). https://doi.org/10.1145/3313831.3376727

Muller, M. (2008). Participatory design: The third space in HCI. In A. Sears & J. Jacko (Eds.), *The human-computer interaction handbook: Fundamentals, evolving technologies, and emerging applications* (2nd edn., pp. 1061–1082). Taylor & Francis.

Muller, M. (2023, August). *Exploring human-AI co-creativity under human control: Framing, reframing, brainstorming, and future challenges (workshop keynote)* [Keynote Address]. EthAIcs Workshop IJCAI, Macao.

Nanduri, D. K. (2024). *Exploring the role of generative artificial intelligence in culturally relevant storytelling for native language learning among children* [University of Maryland, College Park].

Nanduri, D. K., & Bonsignore, E. M. (2023). *Revitalizing endangered languages: AI-powered language learning as a catalyst for language appreciation*. https://doi.org/10.48550/ARXIV.2304.09394

OpenAI. (2022, November 30). Introducing ChatGPT [Technology]. *Product*. https://openai.com/index/chatgpt/

Posner, T., & Fei-Fei, L. (2020). AI will change the world, so it's time to change AI. *Nature*, *588*(7837), S118–S118. https://doi.org/10.1038/d41586-020-03412-z

Roque, R. (2016). Family creative learning. In *Makeology* (pp. 47–63). Routledge.

Roque, R. (2020). *Building relationships and building projects: Designing for family learning. Designing constructionist futures: The art, theory, and practice of learning designs* (pp. 195–203). MIT Press.

Roque, R., Lin, K., & Liuzzi, R. (2016). "I'm Not Just a Mom": Parents developing multiple roles in creative computing. *Transforming learning, empowering learners: The international conference of the learning sciences (ICLS) 2016* (p. *1*). https://doi.org/10.22318/icls2016.86

Schuler, D., & Namioka, A. (1993). *Participatory design: Principles and practices.* L. Erlbaum Associates.

Shneiderman, B. (2020). Human-centered artificial intelligence: Reliable, safe & trustworthy. *International Journal of Human–Computer Interaction, 36*(6), 495–504. https://doi.org/10.1080/10447318.2020.1741118

Shneiderman, B. (2022). *Human-centered AI.* Oxford University Press. https://doi.org/10.1093/oso/9780192845290.001.0001

Sketch Meta Demo Lab: Vision AI. (2025). *Computer software.* Meta. https://sketch.metademolab.com/

Smith, G. (2021). The future of procedural content generation in games. *Proceedings of the AAAI Conference on Artificial Intelligence and Interactive Digital Entertainment, 10*(3), 53–57. https://doi.org/10.1609/aiide.v10i3.12748

Stefanidi, E., Wassmann, J. L. B., Woźniak, P. W., Spellmeyer, G., Rogers, Y., & Niess, J. (2024). MoodGems: Designing for the well-being of children with ADHD and their families at home. *Proceedings of the 23rd annual ACM interaction design and children conference* (pp. 480–494). https://doi.org/10.1145/3628516.3655795

Stokel-Walker, C. (2023). ChatGPT listed as author on research papers: Many scientists disapprove. *Nature, 613*(7945), 620–621. https://doi.org/10.1038/d41586-023-00107-z

Tissenbaum, M., Sheldon, J., & Abelson, H. (2019). From computational thinking to computational action. *Communications of the ACM, 62*(3), 34–36. https://doi.org/10.1145/3265747

Tissenbaum, M., Weintrop, D., Holbert, N., & Clegg, T. (2021). The case for alternative endpoints in computing education. *British Journal of Educational Technology, 52*(3), 1164–1177. https://doi.org/10.1111/bjet.13072

Togelius, J., Kastbjerg, E., Schedl, D., & Yannakakis, G. N. (2011). What is procedural content generation?: Mario on the borderline. *Proceedings of the 2nd international workshop on procedural content generation in games* (pp. 1–6).

Touretzky, D., Gardner-McCune, C., Martin, F., & Seehorn, D. (2019). Envisioning AI for K-12: What should every child know about AI? *Proceedings of the AAAI Conference on Artificial Intelligence, 33*(01), 9795–9799. https://doi.org/10.1609/aaai.v33i01.33019795

Touretzky, D., Gardner-McCune, C., & Seehorn, D. (2022). Machine learning and the five big ideas in AI. *International Journal of Artificial Intelligence in Education.* https://doi.org/10.1007/s40593-022-00314-1

UNESCO Project: Atlas of the World's Languages in Danger – UNESCO Digital Library. (2025). Retrieved March 28, 2024, from https://unesdoc.unesco.org/ark:/48223/pf0000192416

United Nations Educational, Scientific and Cultural Organization (UNESCO). (2025). *Languages matter: Global guidance on multilingual education.* UNESCO. https://doi.org/10.54675/MLIO7101

Vartiainen, H., Tedre, M., & Valtonen, T. (2020). Learning machine learning with very young children: Who is teaching whom? *International Journal of Child-Computer Interaction, 25*, 100182. https://doi.org/10.1016/j.ijcci.2020.100182

Vartiainen, H., Toivonen, T., Jormanainen, I., Kahila, J., Tedre, M., & Valtonen, T. (2021). Machine learning for middle schoolers: Learning through data-driven design. *International Journal of Child-Computer Interaction, 29*, 100281. https://doi.org/10.1016/j.ijcci.2021.100281

Walsh, G., Foss, E., Yip, J., & Druin, A. (2013). FACIT PD: A framework for analysis and creation of intergenerational techniques for participatory design. *Proceedings of the SIGCHI conference on human factors in computing systems* (pp. 2893–2902).

Yip, J. C., Clegg, T., Ahn, J., Uchidiuno, J. O., Bonsignore, E., Beck, A., Pauw, D., & Mills, K. (2016). The evolution of engagements and social bonds during child-parent co-design. *Proceedings of the 2016 CHI conference on human factors in computing systems* (pp. 3607–3619).

Yip, J. C., Sobel, K., Pitt, C., Lee, K. J., Chen, S., Nasu, K., & Pina, L. R. (2017). Examining adult-child interactions in intergenerational participatory design. *Proceedings of the SIGCHI conference on human factors in computing systems* (pp. 5742–5754). https://doi.org/10.1145/3025453.3025787

Zhang, D., Mishra, S., Brynjolffson, E., Etchemendy, J., Ganguli, D., Grosz, B., Lyons, T., Manyika, J., Niebles, J. C., Selitto, M., Shoham, Y., Clark, J., & Perrault, R. (2021). *The AI index 2021 annual report.* AI Index Steering Committee, Human Centered AI Institute. https://aiindex.stanford.edu/wp-content/uploads/2021/03/2021-AI-Index-Report_Master.pdf

CHAPTER 11

"IT'S YOUR TURN TO CARRY THE AI, SOLDIER!" ARTIFICIAL INTELLIGENCE AND THE CHALLENGES OF INTRODUCING NEW TECHNOLOGIES TO TACTICAL MILITARY TEAMS

Samuel Canter

George Mason University, USA

ABSTRACT

Recent scholarship on the utilization of artificial intelligence (AI) tools by military teams has focused predominantly on the potential for cognitive and cultural disruptions to existing team dynamics. Less explored but equally critical to the future of military teams are the practical challenges inherent to the incorporation of a new technology at the tactical, small-unit, or end-user level. Employing historical evidence derived from cases featuring the introduction of novel technologies into the tactical environment can help identify the potential practical impacts of AI tools on military teams, including insufficient individual technical training, poor hardware design and survivability, cumbersome physical weight, equipment prioritization and displacement, operations and maintenance costs, and increased scrutiny from higher elements. The findings suggest that while the potential uses for AI as a discrete tool may indeed prove

AI in Teams: Research on Managing Groups and Teams, Volume 21, 197–212

Published under exclusive licence by Emerald Publishing Limited
ISSN: 1534-0856/doi:10.1108/S1534-085620260000021027

groundbreaking, its impact on the human dynamics of military teams is likely to follow familiar trends.

Keywords: Tactical teams; artificial intelligence; military technology; military teams; military culture; tactical technology; tactical culture; military equipment; team dynamics

INTRODUCTION

A future military battlefield featuring tactical AI tools will constitute a multifaceted and multi-domain phenomenon. Autonomous drone swarms will provide advance reconnaissance and strike targets of opportunity, providing a return on investment many times over their cheap production costs. Intelligent optical and audio sensors will recognize patterns in enemy disposition and maneuver and relay that information as finished intelligence analysis to soldiers on the ground. Advanced fire support computers will independently identify targets far in advance of human eyes, and they will execute indirect fire missions with a rapid precision unfathomable to previous generations of artillerymen. As ground troops advance, unmanned vehicles will trail behind infantry soldiers, carrying vital supplies, providing mounted fire support, and conducting medical evacuation.

This vision of an AI-dominated battlefield requires no great leaps of imagination to reify. As of 2025, the aforementioned AI tools are already a reality in some early form, even as their widespread proliferation and fielding are still years away (Feickert, 2025; Phillips-Levine & Mills, 2024). Though the ultimate promise of AI in the military sphere belongs to the future, first that promise will have to contend with more familiar dynamics rooted in the past – namely, the standard operating procedures, interpersonal dynamics, and unique cultures of small-unit military teams. The collision of new technologies and existing team dynamics yields an important question. How will AI tools impact human team dynamics and military teams at the tactical level?

This chapter contends that, notwithstanding the disruptive potential or unprecedented capabilities of AI tools themselves, AI impacts to human team member dynamics will be initially characterized by the same mundane effects that are inherent to the incorporation of any new technology, whether intelligent or not. By coupling insights derived from three historical case studies featuring the introduction of new military technologies – tanks, radios, and blue force trackers (BFTs) – with more granular insights related to contemporary tactical realities, this chapter reveals an array of immediate challenges and opportunities that will define the impact of AI on tactical teams long before the futuristic visions of fully automated warfare come to fruition. Moreover, many of the impacts of AI on human team member dynamics will take place far from the public eye, in training centers, maintenance depots, and military garrisons rather than on the battlefield or in combat. Insufficient individual technical training, poor hardware design and survivability, cumbersome physical weight, equipment prioritization and displacement, operations and maintenance costs, and increased scrutiny from a supervisory headquarters will all continue to effect tactical team dynamics as they have previously, irrespective of the revolutionary nature of the technology in question.

ANALYTICAL SCOPE

Many ideas regarding military AI tools carry implicit assumptions that imply sleek, lightweight, or even non-corporeal tools, all of which are natural extensions of mental models – both popular and scholarly – that treat AI technologies as inherently futuristic (Ortmor Agency, 2024). Conversely, this chapter rejects such images and explicitly proceeds from the standpoint that many tools employed at the tactical level will constitute moderately sized physical objects or cumbersome pieces of hardware. There are four substantive reasons to make an assessment that military AI tools will be characterized by physical bulk and size.

First, previous military-technical trends consistently exhibited an arc toward modularity, and senior defense leadership relentlessly focused on getting the capabilities into the hands of the end-users. Radios, computers, and unmanned aerial vehicles each began their military careers as large pieces of equipment located or controlled at the strategic headquarters level, before gradual miniaturization enabled their proliferation to the operational and tactical levels as well (Thompson, 2023). AI tools appear on course to follow the same trend but still reside in the early stages. Second, current operational concepts across the Department of Defense (DoD) assess that in the event of Large-Scale Combat Operations, tactical units will likely operate in a digitally disconnected or physically isolated environment, cut off from higher headquarters communications (Foltermann, 2021). In such scenarios, critical tactical capabilities and enablers must continue to operate for small units. Therefore, AI tools located in a distant server-farm or cloud environment that convey information via vulnerable telecommunications or text channels will be of limited value to tactical users. AI tools must, therefore, remain completely self-contained at the tactical level, a strength necessarily correlated with physical size.

Third, any hardware employed at the tactical level amidst harsh conditions requires a degree of physical resiliency that is commonly afforded by increased size, larger batteries, and layered protection, all of which add weight. Finally, recent attempts by DoD entities to miniaturize equipment such as batteries, headsets, and rifles demonstrate the profound and enduring challenges in creating small and lightweight products for users at the tactical level (Luckenbaugh, 2024; Tegler, 2023). Indeed, more than eight decades after the introduction of man-portable radios to U.S. infantry formations, several configurations still in use – along with the necessary batteries and equipment to sustain a three-day mission – can weigh dozens of pounds and take up an inordinate amount of space in the typical dismounted infantry soldier's kit.

While the insights in this chapter may have cross-national applicability to military teams writ large, they are explicitly informed by case studies and insights derived from the U.S. military and its unique organizational and cultural milieu. Finally, at the tactical level, it is ground combat teams in particular – such as a typical Army or Marine Corps rifle squad – that will bear much of the impact of new AI military tools. In that sense, this chapter belongs very much to the vein of military analysis and philosophy which holds that even amidst a proliferation in groundbreaking military technologies, "putting your young men in the mud," is still the ultimate guarantor of holding and defending ground (Fehrenbach, 2001, p. 250). While insights are also generally applicable to the Navy and Air Force, those two services – fundamentally oriented on ships and planes – possess cultures more comfortable relying upon advanced technologies and tools to achieve missions compared to the Army.

The analysis in this chapter also focuses exclusively and deliberately on the tactical level of warfare. For almost a century, Western military doctrine has conceptualized three levels of warfare: the tactical, operational, and strategic. All three levels are comprised of various teams and multiteam systems. Whereas human teams at the strategic and operational levels are composed primarily of staff officers or bureaucrats collaborating in an office or rear-echelon setting, the tactical level of warfare features human teams that execute direct or kinetic military actions across a number of hostile and austere environments. The impact of AI tools on team dynamics at the strategic and operational levels is already ably captured within existing analyses that focus on cognitive and cultural elements, especially for planning, intelligence, and the cohesiveness of the staff organizations. However, at lower echelons where more mundane variables come into play, a large gap in analysis persists.

EXTANT LITERATURE

At a fundamental level, tactical teams comprised of humans will inevitably maintain, program, operate, and partner with AI tools in the military environment. Recognizing this reality, both military professionals and scholars have presented an array of analyses targeting the nexus between new AI technologies and traditional human teams. These analyses focus on what new impacts the AI tools will have on tactical teams, whether cognitively, culturally, or tactically. However, due to both the relative nascence of the topic and the inherent "futuristic bent" of AI studies, extant literature is at risk of disregarding more banal, but no less significant, physical effects taking place at the tactical team level, and in this context, human team dynamics represents an especially significant missing piece.

AI research and analysis conducted by social scientists, rather than exclusively by engineers and computer scientists, has proliferated exponentially in the first quarter of the 21st century. An important subfield of this literature pertains directly to the use of AI tools in a military environment, where works are often authored by serving military officers and defense officials, professionally knowledgeable and invested in the topic (Coombs, 2024; Glonek, 2024). However, despite military authors ostensibly residing closer to the "ground truth" of military team dynamics, analyses published in both academic and professional journals largely tend to focus on unprecedented or novel technological dynamics, and multiple authors omit the potential impacts of tactical AI on human team dynamics (Coombs, 2024; Mabes, 2024; Mancillas, 2020; Ryseff, 2024).

The gap is a natural result of four analytical dynamics. First, analyses by serving military officers tend to appear in professional military journals, which often encourage authors to focus on the future of warfare and anticipate potential disruptions, even more so because writing about the unknowable future is generally safer ground for serving military officers as opposed to critiquing present operations. Second, authors lack a robust record of usable data and case studies pertaining to the use of AI in military teams, though this factor will surely diminish in significance as technologies mature. Nonetheless, so long as most AI technologies with military applications reside in developmental stages and lack a large body of use cases, the bulk of literature will naturally default to a futuristic bent. Third, where usable insights into the practical impacts of AI tools in tactical settings do exist, they are more likely to be explored internal to bureaucratic and organizational contexts rather than public-facing scholarship, due to the closely guarded nature of military information, which is often classified. Finally, much of the extant literature is also geared toward strategic and operational applications, either explicitly or implicitly (Thibert, 2024). For example, a prominent category of literature deals with the effect of AI tools on intelligence operations, where use scenarios for the role of AI in collection, targeting, or analysis are more readily evident than incorporation of AI into tactical teams (Cooper, 2024).

At the confluence of the four dynamics that shape the existing literature, a significant and emerging gap is taking shape, primarily concerning the practicalities of how AI tools employed at the tactical level will impact human team dynamics and existing team mental models. Previous authors have studied the issue of trust between human actors and AI tools like Large Language Models, exploring "why the military can't trust AI" (Lamparth & Schneider, 2024). Research is also needed to explore the impacts of AI on human teammates' trust in each other. For example, Army officers Benjamin Scott and Andre Michell (2022) posit a spectrum of tasks to create an AI-enabled tactical headquarters, in which widespread data literacy and data storage capacity are necessary before AI tools are full integrated, but do not heavily explore the role of interpersonal dynamics in enabling this spectrum. As another example, discussions of training often focus on using AI as a tool or medium for tactical training, instead of training to use AI tools for military applications (Kramer, 2024).

Given the epistemological constraints and the resultant lacuna emerging across literature, there is a need to more deeply explore the physical and human impacts that AI technologies will have at the tactical level. In the absence of a robust array of contemporary use cases, turning to history can offer the possibility of analogous episodes that offer a richer context for inquiry, made possible by the passage of time, a mature historiography, and a robust and accessible documentary record. While a case study approach may fall short in edifying the novel nature of AI technology, it offers additional value for framing the constant variable of human team dynamics at the tactical level, regardless of the nature of the technology in question.

HISTORICAL CASE STUDIES

While AI technologies may be rightly classified as groundbreaking or unprecedented, the dynamics that result from introducing a new technology into a tactical military team are not necessarily so. Proceeding from the historian's standpoint that analogies are, in the words of David Hackett Fisher, "devices for discovering explanations" and possible even "very useful explanatory tools" in of themselves, this chapter recognizes value in identifying historical case studies to help frame the contemporary impacts of AI on tactical teams (Fisher, 1970, p. 243). In employing historical case studies, it is evident that comparisons between the technologies themselves across time are highly imperfect. AI, for example, can be categorized as either a "general-purpose technology" or as an umbrella term for multiple functions, in contrast to a rifle or radio which are designed and used for specific functions (Glonek, 2024, p. 93). This broad categorization of AI tools renders direct technical comparisons with previous technologies of little use. It is the dynamics of the human team, rather than the technology in question, that constitutes the more enduring variable for analysis across time.

The four core functions of tactical military teams are to shoot, move, communicate, and survive (U.S. Army, Field Manual 7-0, 2021a, p. 2-1). Contemporary AI tools are designed to support or complement these functions, not to replace them. It is, therefore, instructive to look at previous technologies that significantly impacted the shoot, move, communicate, and survive paradigm for tactical teams. Three technological tools in particular – the tank, the radio, and the BFT – yield valuable insights into technological impacts on team dynamics across the historical literature.

The Tank

Of the three, the tank constituted the most viscerally obvious technological change. From its introduction to the battlefield in 1917 to the present day, the effects of the tank on tactical team and interpersonal dynamics were numerous. The need to crew tanks created a new type of team dynamic – smaller than the traditional infantry squad, exceedingly intimate by virtue of the physically cramped conditions within the vehicle, and highly dependent on operating in seamless unity as the vehicle commander, driver, loader, and gunner worked together. For personnel assigned to tanks or similar armored vehicles, mechanical knowledge and time spent conducting maintenance constituted core elements of their duties to a far greater extent than other combat-focused occupations, including the traditionally technical Field Artillery. In a garrison environment, maintenance of armored vehicles subsumed an inordinate amount of time for personnel relative to their fellow soldiers in infantry occupations, who in contrast usually bore responsibility for simply maintaining their rifles and their physical health.

Tank crews also subverted traditional hierarchies, though the tank commander in each vehicle was unmistakably in charge. However, the tank driver, who was still a junior member of the crew, exerted an immediate agency over events through speed, direction, and steering of the vehicle that had no parallel in a traditional infantry squad (Mudd, 1999). Moreover, for U.S. military tanks, the ability to shoot relied in large part on the most junior member, the loader. In addition, while tanks were initially deployed in WWI to support infantry advances by WWII this situation had largely reversed, as tanks spearheaded advances and dismounted infantry soldiers provided close support and protection from enemy anti-tank crews, preventing mobility kills or enemy sabotage to vulnerable tank tracks.

Finally, developing and internalizing effective concepts for use of this new technology "required men to accommodate these machines into their experiences and perspectives," including presenting an image of tanks that the public could appreciate and support, a vital undertaking for any war effort (Bartels, 2018, p. i). This in turn led tactical team members to develop clear and simple characterizations of the new technology – including christening their tanks with pet names – in addition to feeding a unique cultural pride around the Armored profession.

The Radio

The widespread use of the radio by tactical teams came more than two decades after the tank, but arguably exerted an even greater – if less visceral – influence on team dynamics. By the end of WWII, when tactical radio use began to expand beyond headquarters and to tactical teams dispersed in the field, combined arms warfare – the synchronization and phasing of infantry, air, armor, and artillery – dominated military operations, and created significantly more complex communication requirements (Thompson, 2022). Tactical leaders were contending with new reporting requirements to higher elements and had to balance the ability to see and convey a wider picture to their leadership while leading their team members on the battlefield. Conversely, a higher-level headquarters no longer needed to rely upon the use of runners, continuously run telephone wires, or archaic signaling devices such as flags and carrier pigeons to gather information from tactical teams (Lobdell, 2021).

The radio enabled higher level leaders to reach down directly and request information, but in doing so created a countless array of minor dilemmas for small unit leaders, especially if the higher headquarters grew greedy for information. Should attention be focused on leading subordinate troops, or reporting to a superior officer? The best tactical leaders found a way to balance the two, but radio communication created a new set of human team dynamics for tactical units to reckon with. After initially being the purview of a specialized signal corps, the radio saw incorporation into conventional infantry units as well (Lobdell, 2021). The tactical democratization of the radio thus necessitated the training of select non-specialist personnel to become radio and telephone operators. Early radio operators required a higher-than-average level of technical expertise and communication ability and were ideally selected from among the team for intelligence and reliability (Hedberg, 2010). However, if dismounted, they also required the requisite physical strength to carry heavy radio equipment while keeping pace with the tactical leader they shadowed. Though usually a junior team member, the radio telephone operator became distinctly separate in many respects from his teammates, with a role to often shadow the leader throughout a mission or duty day. Though not all tactical teams had the luxury of specially assigning personnel to undertake radio duties, all tactical teams were increasingly expected to provide a steady flow of data and answers to higher headquarters, as radio communications imbued many military commanders with an increasingly vociferous appetite for information. Finally, unlike with the tank, use of the radio became more widespread over time, moving from a specialty piece of equipment to something more accessible to the general soldier. Yet even after eight decades, the radio is not yet standard equipment for every tactical team member.

The Blue Force Tracker

Though more similar to the radio in size and function, the BFT both exacerbated existing dynamics and created new ones, with significant implications for leadership hierarchies. Heightened situational awareness enabled by technology was exemplified by the BFT, an umbrella term for specific systems, sensors, computers, and trackers that aimed to provide commanders and headquarters with a near real-time common operating picture. As digital displays, Global Positioning System (GPS) trackers, and a multitude of new sensors proliferated throughout military formations in the late 1970s and beyond, tactical leaders gained unprecedented access to real-time information on the disposition and action of friendly troops. The increase in battlefield awareness, however imperfect, resulted in fundamental changes to team dynamics, especially for those in leadership positions. More than ever, military leaders needed to distinguish "the essence of command from its implementing systems" lest they fall into traps of technological overreliance or mistakenly view military leadership as an exercise in systems employment rather than a more intuitive art (Madigan & Dodge, 1994, p. 30). Nonetheless, the perception that the BFT enabled commanders to micromanage subordinate units also emerged (Tiron, 2003). Moreover, a 1997 study of BFT employment in field training warned that tactical leaders "could grow too dependent on 'perfect' information and hesitate to seize initiative in the absence of a complete picture" (Hanna, 1997, p. 4). Finally, a basic disparity emerged insofar as BFT technologies inordinately aided the tactical leader occupying an appropriately furnished headquarters but failed to provide the same situational awareness to individual team members occupying forward positions due in large part to physical constraints. For example, the same 1997 study found that furnishing individual infantry soldiers with BFT headsets required them to carry "70 lbs. of batteries for 24 hours of operations" (Hanna, 1997, p. 3).

Generalizable Trends Across the Three Cases

Several potentially generalizable trends emerge from the three case studies regarding incorporating new technologies into tactical teams and the human factors attendant to such a phenomenon. First, the incorporation of new technologies can subvert traditional team hierarchies, primarily through granting the technology end-user – traditionally a junior team member – an outsized degree of importance to achieving the mission, or imbuing them with a special esteem that their non-technologically specialized peers lack. Conversely, technology can also further stratify existing hierarchies, providing leaders with the tools of micromanagement, and thereby robbing subordinates of opportunities to take independent initiative. Second, interpersonal dynamics among junior team members may also shift, with technically empowered or knowledgeable junior members assuming a different role than their peers. Third, training also emerges as an important factor, with the dynamics of training dependent in large part on the manner of employment for the tool. If a tool or technology is intended for use by a small subset of the population, then lengthy and detailed training is feasible. However, if a technology is intended for widespread use by all members of the force, the training is far more likely to be rudimentary, genericized, and in the contemporary era poorly delivered via an online medium vice in-person instruction.

If tactical teams do not continuously invest in the appropriate level of technical training for assigned personnel, the skills to employ technical tools can easily atrophy. Fourth, the physical weight and size of the object constitutes an inescapable element for soldiers, while the need for extensive battery power in a hostile environment consumes logistical planning and takes up physical space in a soldier's pack. Ultimately, the incorporation of a new technology – especially one with a visceral impact like the tank – may in certain cases impact the culture of human teammates, shaping or changing the way human teammates view each other, and themselves. Finally, the potential for an increased scrutiny from higher headquarters – aided and abetted by various technologies – emerges as a potential concern that challenges the "mission command," which is the culture of empowerment and delegation that the U.S. military attempts to foster (U.S. Army, ADRP 6-0, 2022).

THE IMPACT OF AI TOOLS ON TACTICAL MILITARY TEAMS

Given both the historical case studies and the gaps in current literature, it is clear that analyses which focus predominantly on how AI will affect human–agent tactical teams are at risk of disregarding the more basic and temporally immediate dynamics of how those same technologies will affect human tactical teams. Informed by the three case studies and the realities of current military team dynamics, the following sections posit several significant effects that new AI tools will have on the dynamics of tactical teams: insufficient individual technical training, poor hardware design and survivability, cumbersome physical weight, equipment prioritization and displacement, operations and maintenance costs, and increased scrutiny from higher headquarters. While none are insurmountable or preordained, on balance they will present a broad array of practical challenges for human team cohesion, relationships, and effectiveness.

Physical Size and Makeup

The first factor for consideration is arguably the most banal but also the least studied in the contemporary publicly accessible literature on AI and tactical teams: the physical makeup of the AI tool, specifically weight, size, and resilience.

As noted previously, there is ample reason to suggest that AI tools will take the form of sometimes sizable physical objects, due to current military doctrine, the proven challenges of equipment miniaturization, the requirement for long-lasting batteries, and the need for physical equipment resilience in harsh conditions. Therefore, a basic element that any tactical team will have to deal with is the physical weight of the object.

There are obvious practical difficulties attendant on physically carrying new technologies, whether on a vehicle or dismounted. Every item added to a mission packing list requires a trade-off, and it is possible that command pressure to bring along initially untested AI tools for the wrong reasons will require not taking something more useful, or at the very least something more supportive of soldier morale. Correctly or incorrectly, the individual soldier may then grow to resent the presence of a tool directed by leadership that provides them questionable or unappreciated value in lieu of something more viscerally impactful, such as food, ammunition, or extra clothing. The survivability and physical resilience of the equipment also matters for team dynamics. In training environments, team members will encounter pressure to carefully preserve and protect delicate or non-resilient equipment amidst harsh weather or field conditions, and they will risk personal liability if the equipment is damaged. Fear of equipment loss and associated leadership pressures may result in the deliberate underutilization of the tool, impacting training value and individual proficiency, and allowing skills to atrophy from non-use.

Training, Teaching, Specialization, and Impacts on Team Dynamics

As AI tools become increasingly incorporated into tactical teams, military leaders and strategic planners will have to wrestle with a broader debate framed in the AI context: the appropriate level of technical training for their personnel. Will AI technologies be so ubiquitous as to demand that every individual servicemember achieve baseline proficiency? Or will competing job demands and scarce training resources, coupled with varying levels of technical aptitude among potential trainees, necessitate only a small number of team members become specially educated? The historic case studies suggest that initially the latter dynamic will dominate, and only a select few tactical team members will undergo the full spectrum of training required to effectively employ AI tools, meaning that AI tools will initially reside in the realm of niche specialization. The prevalence of niche specialization is a function of three enduring military realities: varying levels of technical aptitude among teammates, scarce training resources, and a plethora of competing job demands.

The consequences of this niche specialization for team dynamics are numerous. As an example of scalability, when only one or two members of a nine-member infantry squad are trained to employ an advanced technology, other team members may inordinately lean on or pressure the specially trained personnel to provide aid or technical guidance, placing added job stress on the individuals in question. Simultaneously, in an environment of constantly competing demands, personnel may be selected for training based merely upon calendar availability rather than any specially selected technical aptitude. In extreme cases, personnel may even be sent to training to temporarily remove them from the rest of the team.

Another challenge when integrating AI in human teams is in the training realm. Selected personnel will not only require technical skills, but also teaching skills, as they will be expected to return to their team and effectively share their specialty knowledge, sometimes referred to as "training the trainer" (Lohr, 2023). Absent the aptitude, time, or motivation to teach others, the necessary knowledge will not proliferate throughout the team. Technical training will inevitably take team members away from other duties, a dynamic which may potentially breed resentment, especially if the technical training offers members a respite from more undesirable activities or harsher working conditions that their peers must endure. Moreover, team members may prove reluctant recruits to technical training if, for example, they view it as a deviation from their traditional job aptitudes. This dynamic may prove especially acute in combat-arms professions like Infantry and Armor, where the team culture places a premium value on performing the often difficult and unglamourous duties that a combat-arms job requires. Finally, training only select individuals may create a single point of failure for employing an AI capability, with significant consequences for the team should the trained individuals become incapacitated. The need to increase resiliency may further encourage militaries to incorporate AI tools into basic training.

Inventory, Supply, and Maintenance

Another practical reality to consider is that each piece of military equipment must be documented and signed for in an official inventory document often referred to as a "property book." The property book signatory – or "hand receipt" holder – assumes responsibility for all equipment, including potential financial or criminal liability for all broken, damaged, or missing equipment (U.S. Army Quartermaster School, 2021b). Given that AI tools will likely begin as inordinately expensive items relative to other pieces of tactical inventory, widespread team cultures of risk avoidance may therefore incentivize equipment non-use, as keeping AI tools securely under "lock and key" will constitute a prudent strategy for avoiding potential financial liability. Moreover, the hand-receipt holder may often pass responsibility for equipment down to a designated "sub-hand receipt holder" of lower rank. Passing responsibility for sensitive equipment down to the lowest level, especially when that junior team member may not even have access to the secure storage facilities in which it is kept, may contribute to feelings of resentment among military teams.

Maintenance issues, which constitute a broad reality across all types of military equipment, will undoubtedly exert a large impact on team dynamics. For example, in the case of autonomous vehicles in the United States Army, the existing centralized maintenance system "creates a bottleneck within large formations and lacks dynamic self-repair and diagnostic troubleshooting needed to maintain operational tempo" (Nimmons & Oathout, 2022, p. 10). Given the type of high-tempo warfare the Army expects to encounter in a future scenario, correcting this issue would require the proliferation and integration of trained maintenance personnel across tactical teams, and resulting in a higher "tooth-to-tail ratio" (McGrath, 2007). Mundane but frequent manifestations of this dynamic in tactical teams can include something as simple as formulating a travel manifest. Who gets the last seat in the truck or the helicopter, the technically specialized maintainer who is vital to upkeeping the autonomous vehicle, or the regular rifleman or machine gunner?

Team Roles, Responsibilities, and Culture

The incorporation of AI technologies may generally alter the way human teammates view each other and themselves, including roles and responsibilities. Two sub-dynamics can drive this shift. First, AI technology may eventually assume a lead role in military operations rather than a supporting one. Second, the visceral nature of the technology may be a factor, as an AI tool embedded in a wristwatch exerts far less of a visceral impact than a multi-ton autonomous vehicle able to provide supporting fire from a mounted machine gun. For large and autonomous AI tools, the best analogy from the case studies is the armored tank, which assumed a leading and visceral role in military operations that the radio or BFT did not. A potential shift in a human-centric cultural outlook wrought by AI tools may prove especially acute among more elite soldiers, selected for their above average human traits of physical and mental resilience. A team culture such as among Army Special Forces that embraces the notion that "humans are more important than hardware" may prove more susceptible to tension as AI tools assume a more impactful role in tactical operations (Claudio, 2020).

Command Scrutiny and Information Sharing

Perhaps the most negative and enduring impact of AI tools on military teams will come because of the increased scrutiny and administrative mandates emanating from higher-level headquarters. The fielding of new technology is usually accompanied by a series of new metrics or reporting criteria imposed on users in order to enable high-level evaluations of efficacy and measures of effectiveness. Such directives are undoubtedly desirable from a resourcing and evaluation standpoint, and to ensure warfighting technologies are continuously improved. Yet notwithstanding these broader benefits, the increased reporting criteria can create new pressures on tactical teams: altering human team dynamics, creating environments of stressful tension and pressure, and, in some cases, even perversely encouraging reduced use of the technology in question. Furthermore, the long and ignoble history of false metrics reporting throughout the U.S. military suggests that directives for tactical teams to provide more metrics and data can easily lead to a misleading or incomplete picture that ultimately harms the very efforts an organization is attempting to improve and optimize (Gartner & Myers, 1995: Vego, 2011).

Senior U.S. DoD leadership devotes an inordinate amount of their public remarks to AI technologies vice other technologies employable at the tactical level, and several AI programs are managed directly by department senior leaders

(Clark, 2024). With increased attention often comes increased scrutiny, which can extend down the chain of command and manifest at the lowest echelons of tactical teams in curious ways. The pressure of having superior officers and units "breathing down your neck" can inject tension among team members, and on occasion foster perceptions among teammates that a tactical leader is devoting more time and energy to placating superiors than taking care of subordinates. Moreover, Wong and Gerras (2015) found that unrealistic data demand from a higher echelon contributes to creating a culture of casual dishonesty, undermining the core value of trust on which military teams are built. Given that several AI tools employed at higher headquarters will focus on predictive analytics for maintenance and repair, the demand signals for tactical units to provide ever more data will likely grow. In addition, metrics on the efficacy and efficiency of the AI tools themselves will in turn shape funding and fielding decisions at higher strategic levels.

A significant divide may also emerge between tactical teams and their higher headquarters as the lofty perceptions of what AI tools can achieve encounter the fundamental realities of existing capabilities. The difference in outlook will emerge as a natural result of different milieus: the tactical end-user, schooled in niche technical training, will be the ultimate subject matter expert on the capabilities of a given AI tool, including how capabilities that functioned under ideal test or garrison conditions entropy amidst operational friction and environmental challenges. Conversely, the senior officer at a higher headquarters, lacking such training, will possess potentially superficial perceptions of AI capabilities, including those shaped by popular perceptions, and may, therefore, fail to understand why the tools do not perform as advertised. In such scenarios, blame cast on the tactical teams for failing to employ AI technology correctly may ensue.

CONCLUSIONS

Regardless of the novel or revolutionary nature of AI technologies in the military context, its impact on human team dynamics at the tactical level will likely follow familiar trends, at least in the near-term. Many of these trends will prove disruptive in nature, as they have in the past. The historical record of previous tactical technology implementations – the tank, the radio, and the BFT – suggest that to a degree, negative and disruptive impacts are simply inherent to the introduction of any new technology in tactical settings. However, tactical teams and their respective organizational leaders can take certain measures to mitigate negative impacts while simultaneously maximizing the utilization of AI technology through early growing pains. At the very least, an increased awareness of potentially negative impacts will help to reduce potential organizational surprise. In the meantime, what can be done to mitigate harmful effects to human team dynamics?

First, mitigative measures should start at the top, specifically with higher headquarters elements and military commanders that exercise control over tactical teams. Military leaders should continue to embrace the ethos of U.S. military doctrine and culture that empower subordinates to take independent action, resisting the urge to micromanage even as access to increasingly sophisticated AI tools may tempt them to do so. Resisting micromanagement is even more important considering the context of the global military environment, with future operations very likely involving isolated tactical teams, cut off from guidance and operating independently.

Furthermore, military leaders should take a more permissive view of AI tools utilization at the tactical level. As AI tools are fielded to tactical teams, they will break, they will become damaged, they will get lost, and they will go through many trials and errors before reaching optimal employment. Despite best efforts, measures of effectiveness may not be neatly captured by directed reporting requirements or mandated data collection. In understanding that these dynamics are inherent to any new technology fielding at the tactical level, military leaders can reduce the negative pressures and stresses on tactical teams that often accompany such efforts and prevent the emergence of a general risk aversion that hampers technology optimization and lesson learning.

At lower echelons, and down to the end-user, avoiding familiar human team pitfalls may depend ultimately on individual aptitudes. In that regard, selection and training of personnel who will operate AI tools is a vital factor. Military organizations should also carefully compare alternative models for integration. For example, rather than adopt the model of a radio telephone operator – one team member who is specially trained and assigned – units can adopt the model of medic or artillery observer support. In those instances, specialist personnel split their time between being embedded with the tactical team they support versus returning to a medical or artillery unit so that they can train with fellow specialists and conduct administrative activities. This model has its own pitfalls. For instance, medics or artillery observers can feel socially isolated from the rest of the tactical team while acting as embedded support. On balance, however, this arrangement does allow for more specialized training and professional concentration while still enjoying linkage to a designated tactical team. The embedded specialist role thereby potentially reduces the impacts to human team dynamics described in the pages above.

Finally, other problems will inevitably be solved or mitigated by technological progress and capability maturation, though neither of these factors is preordained. For example, a modular or self-sustaining power source for the tactical level may constitute a true paradigm shift for many of the dynamics surrounding weight and battery life. While various power sources have been suggested, including small modular nuclear reactors, these technologies are still in the earliest stages of discussion and conceptualization (Department of Defense, 2024). Nonetheless, even in the absence of modular battery solutions, the physical size of tactical AI tools can be expected to shrink over time. Likewise, akin to the tank and radio, the use of AI tools will eventually become culturally normalized across large portions of the force. Yet the fact that 80 years after its incorporation, most soldiers in the United States still do not have regular access to a tactical radio is indicative of the long arc that tactical technologies must transit before they achieve their ultimate promise. In the lengthy interim, both professionals and scholars must remain mindful of the often immutable and challenging human dynamics that still characterize tactical teams; dynamics that continue to stubbornly stand firm amidst the technological advancements that beset them.

REFERENCES

Bartels, K. (2018). *Not quite mechanical: Tanks and men on the western front* [Unpublished master's thesis]. Arizona State University. https://www.proquest.com/openview/1105437de26be72fdffd02bad2fc1b77/1?pq-origsite=gscholar&cbl=18750&diss=y

Clark, J. (2024, January 26). Defense innovation official says replicator initiative remains on track. *DOD News*. https://www.defense.gov/News/News-Stories/Article/Article/3657609/defense-innovation-official-says-replicator-initiative-remains-on-track/

Claudio, B. (2020, November). Humans are more important than hardware: Start acting like it. *Marine Corps Gazette* (pp. 14–19). https://www.mca-marines.org/wp-content/uploads/Humans-Are-More-Important-Than-Hardware.pdf

Coombs, R. A. (2024, May). AI integration for scenario development. *Military Review*. US ISSN 0026-4148.

Cooper, N. B. (2024, October 10). AI and intelligence analysis: Panacea or peril? *War on the Rocks*. https://warontherocks.com/2024/10/ai-and-intelligence-analysis-panacea-or-peril/

Department of the Army. (2021a). *Field manual 7-0: Training the force*. U.S. Army.

Department of the Army. (2021b). *Property book operations handbook*. U.S. Army Quartermaster School.

Department of the Army. (2022). *Army doctrine reference publication (ADRP) 6-0: Mission command*. U.S. Army.

Department of Defense. (2024, September 24). *DoD breaks ground on project pele: A mobile nuclear reactor for energy resiliency*. https://www.defense.gov/News/Releases/Release/Article/3915633/dod-breaks-ground-on-project-pele-a-mobile-nuclear-reactor-for-energy-resiliency/

Fehrenbach, T. R. (2001). *This kind of war*. Potomac Books. (Original work published 1963).

Feickert, A. (2025, January 23). The army's XM-30 mechanized infantry combat vehicle. *Congressional Research Service*. https://www.congress.gov/crs-product/IF12094

Fisher, D. H. (1970). *Historians' fallacies: Toward a logic of historical thought*. Harper.

Foltermann, A. Y. (2021, August). Adapting together: A unified view of distributed operations. *Proceedings*, *147*(8). https://www.usni.org/magazines/proceedings/2021/august/adapting-together-unified-view-distributed-operations

Gartner, S. S., & Myers, M. E. (1995). Body counts and 'success' in the Vietnam and Korean wars. *The Journal of Interdisciplinary History*, *25*(3), 377–395. https://doi.org/10.2307/205692

Glonek, J. (2024, May). The coming military AI revolution. *Military Review*, 88–89. https://www.armyupress.army.mil/Journals/Military-Review/English-Edition-Archives/May-June-2024/MJ-24-Glonek/

Hanna, M. (1997, July). Task force XXI: The army's digital experiment. *Institute for National Strategic Studies*, *119*. https://apps.dtic.mil/sti/tr/pdf/ADA394389.pdf

Hedberg, S. B. (2010). *The army amateur radio system: 1925–1941*. U.S. Army School of Advanced Military Studies

Kramer, K. (2024, June 20). *Training transformed: AI and the future soldier*. U.S. Army TRADOC Mad Scientist Laboratory. https://madsciblog.tradoc.army.mil/495-training-transformed-ai-and-the-future-soldier/

Lamparth, M., & Schneider, J. (2024, April 29). Why the military can't trust AI. *Foreign Affairs*. https://www.foreignaffairs.com/united-states/why-military-cant-trust-ai

Lobdell, L. F. (2021). *The radio: A study in information technology implementation*. U.S. Army School of Advanced Military Studies. https://apps.dtic.mil/sti/html/trecms/AD1161156/index.html

Lohr, A. (2023, August 17). Army finds a new way to 'train the trainers' in technical fields. *Federal News Network*. https://federalnewsnetwork.com/army/2023/08/army-finds-new-ways-to-train-the-trainers-in-technical-fields/

Luckenbaugh, J. (2024, April 2). Army hopeful troubled headset program is finally looking up. *National Defense*. https://www.nationaldefensemagazine.org/articles/2024/4/2/army-hopeful-troubled-headset-program-is-finally-looking-up

Mabes, J. W. (2024, April 4). *Rise of artificial intelligence: Implications to the fielded force*. U.S. Army TRADOC Mad Scientist Laboratory. https://madsciblog.tradoc.army.mil/485-rise-of-artificial-intelligence-implications-to-the-fielded-force/

Madigan, J. C., & Dodge, G. E. (1994, November). Battle command: A force XXI imperative. *Military Review*. https://www.armyupress.army.mil/Portals/7/military-review/Archives/English/100-Landing/Topics-Interest/Command-and-Control/Nov-1994-Madigan-scan.pdf

Mancillas, J. (2020, November 23). *Artificial intelligence: An emerging game-changer*. U.S. Army TRADOC Mad Scientist Laboratory. https://madsciblog.tradoc.army.mil/287-artificial-intelligence-an-emerging-game-changer/

McGrath, J. J. (2007). *The other end of the spear: The tooth-to-tail ratio (T3R) in modern military operations*. Combat Studies Institute Press. https://www.armyupress.army.mil/portals/7/combat-studies-institute/csi-books/mcgrath_op23.pdf

Mudd, J. L. (1999, Fall). Development of the American tank-infantry team during World War II in Africa and Europe. *Armor Magazine*. https://www.benning.army.mil/armor/eARMOR/content/issues/1999/SEP_OCT/ArmorSeptemberOctober1999web.pdf

Nimmons, J., & Oathout, P. (2022, Winter). Robots on tracks: What armor needs to make robotic combat vehicles work. *Armor Magazine*. https://www.benning.army.mil/Armor/eARMOR/content/issues/2022/Winter/1Nimmons-Oathout22.pdf

Ortmor Agency. (2024). *The future of military technology: Microsoft's night vision AR goggles for the U.S. Army*. https://www.ortmoragency.com/blog/night-vision-ar-goggles

Phillips-Levine, T., & Mills, W. D. (2024, March 6). Outgunned in the drone fight: The U.S. military is failing to adopt the next machine gun. *War on the Rocks*. https://warontherocks.com/2024/03/outgunned-in-the-drone-fight-the-u-s-military-is-failing-to-adopt-the-next-machine-gun/

Ryseff, J. (2024, November 8). Mastering human-machine warfighting teams. *War on the Rocks*. https://warontherocks.com/2024/11/mastering-human-machine-warfighting-teams/

Scott, B., & Michell, A. (2022, November–December). Enhancing situational understanding through integration of artificial intelligence in tactical headquarters. *Military Review*, 74–83. https://www.armyupress.army.mil/Journals/Military-Review/English-Edition-Archives/November-December-2022/Scott/

Tegler, E. (2023, September 25). Firing the army's new rifle and machine gun is a weighty experience. *Forbes*. https://www.forbes.com/sites/erictegler/2023/09/22/firing-the-armys-new-rifle-machine-gun-is-a-weighty-experience/

Thibert, J. (2024). Unveiling the future: The convergence of AI and strategic intelligence operations. *Global Security Review*. https://globalsecurityreview.com/unveiling-the-future-the-convergence-of-ai-and-strategic-intelligence-operations/

Thompson, S. (2022, April 22). *Walkie-talkies and 'operation gold rush.'* U.S. Army Communications-Electronics Command. https://www.army.mil/article/255952/walkie_talkies_and_operation_gold_rush

Thompson, S. (2023, August 30). *Miniaturization of communications equipment for the U.S. Army*. U.S. Army Communications-Electronics Command. https://www.army.mil/article/269529/miniaturization_of_communications_equipment_for_the_u_s_army

Tiron, R. (2003, December 1). Army's blue-force tracking technology was a tough sell. *National Defense Magazine*. https://www.nationaldefensemagazine.org/articles/2003/11/30/2003december-armys-blueforce-tracking-technology-was-a-tough-sell

Vego, M. (2011, October). The false promise of metrics. *Proceedings*, *137*(10). https://www.usni.org/magazines/proceedings/2011/october/false-promise-metrics

Wong, L., & Gerras, S. (2015). *Lying to ourselves: Dishonesty in the army profession*. Army War College Press.

PART 5

REFLECTIONS ON AI IN TEAMS

CHAPTER 12

HUMAN–ANIMAL TEAM MODELING FOR MORE EFFECTIVE HUMAN–AGENT TEAMING DESIGN

Heather C. Lum, Selena Evans, Rajeswari Jayakumar, Laura H. Inderberg and Sreya Suresh

Arizona State University, USA

ABSTRACT

Human–animal teaming (HanT) has long exemplified successful interspecies collaboration built on trust, communication, and mutual adaptation. As artificial intelligence (AI) systems become increasingly integrated into human teams, examining the dynamics of human–animal partnerships offers valuable insights into trust calibration, role negotiation, situational awareness, and ethical responsibility. This chapter explores how principles from human–animal collaboration can inform the design and deployment of human–agent teams, addressing challenges of transparency, autonomy, and human-centered interaction.

Keywords: Human–animal teams/teaming; human–agent teams/teaming; animal–agent modelling; heterogeneous teams; team cognition; teamwork

AI in Teams: Research on Managing Groups and Teams, Volume 21, 215–234

Published under exclusive licence by Emerald Publishing Limited
ISSN: 1534-0856/doi:10.1108/S1534-085620260000021030

INTRODUCTION

The ability of humans to form and function in teams is one of the cornerstones of modern civilization. From early hunter-gatherer groups to contemporary corporate and interdisciplinary scientific teams, human teaming has driven innovation, survival, and progress. Teams exhibit unique characteristics including shared goals, interdependence, role differentiation, and mutual accountability – that distinguish them from mere groupings of individuals (Salas et al., 2005). Understanding and optimizing these dynamics are essential to improving team effectiveness, especially in complex and high-stakes environments. Traditional team research has, for the most part, dealt with human–human teams, giving rise to model-building such as McGrath's Input–Process–Output model (1964), in which team effectiveness is explained by the conversion of inputs (such as skills and tools) to outcomes via team processes (Salas et al., 2005). Teaming takes many forms, including co-located workgroups, virtual teams, cross-functional teams, and high-reliability teams (e.g., in aviation or surgery). Each context presents distinct challenges. Virtual teams, for instance, often struggle with establishing trust and maintaining effective communication due to geographic and cultural dispersion (Gilson et al., 2015). In simple terms, a team comprises two or more individuals who communicate interdependently, share goals, and possess specific functions or roles to perform (Salas et al., 1992).

The definition of what a "team" is continuing to evolve due to the inclusion of non-human members such as AI, robots, and trained animals, expanding the way we think about teams to human–agent, human–animal, and even hybrid human–agent–animal teams. For example, AI is already helping doctors make diagnoses, and in search-and-rescue missions, dogs are working alongside their human counterparts to find lost people. In either instance, the non-human teammate is not merely a tool; it is actively assisting with team objectives – capable of sensing things, responding, and even learning in dynamic environments (Phillips et al., 2017; Berreta et al., as cited in Kaelin et al., 2024).

Lessons from human-only teams – such as the importance of shared goals and clear communication protocols – are critical for designing mixed teams (Chen et al., 2018). While, other characteristics may be unique to human–nonhuman teams. The increasing integration of artificial agents and decision-support systems into human teams introduces new dynamics. Human–AI (agent) teaming, for example, requires redefining trust, transparency, and delegation boundaries. Each of these non-traditional teams also possesses its respective characteristics and coordination issues. Human–agent teams (HATs), for example, depend largely on system transparency, algorithmic predictability, and human trust in autonomous decision-making. In contrast, HanTs are rooted in emotional connections, non-verbal communication, and species-specific training procedures (Phillips & Jentsch, 2016). Hybrid teams composed of humans, animals, and agents take this even further with multi-modal interaction systems, ethical issues, and requirements for adaptive team designs to fit various cognitive and behavioral abilities (Prada et al., 2024).

Why do we need to study these different kinds of teams more deeply? First, each type of team has specific strengths lacking in traditional human–human teams. Many animals have sensory and emotional capabilities that surpass human capacities, including the domestic dog that can detect seizures and locate victims of disasters. Similarly, AI agents can rapidly search for vast amounts of data and perform repetitive or dangerous tasks without fatigue. The study of these distinctions can unveil how various types of intelligence – biological, artificial, and hybrid – can be complementary to one another toward mutual objectives. Second, most academic models of human-only teamwork do not fully explain these distinctions. Most models of teamwork rely on assumptions of human cognition and behavior and might not stand when extended to multi-species or mixed-intelligence teams. For example, the concept of team cohesion or shared mental models must be re-examined if one of the members of the team is a robot or a dog. To better understand these challenges and opportunities, this chapter first examines HanTs and then HATs drawing from key research and real-world examples. Finally, it describes what the two have in common and what HanT can teach us about designing better HATs in the future.

HUMAN–ANIMAL TEAMING

The concept of HanT transcends traditional roles of animal domestication, positioning animals not merely as tools or companions but as active collaborators in joint human–animal enterprises. Rooted in centuries of cooperation, this practice is now increasingly informed by developments in ethology, cognitive science, and applied animal behavior. Humans have coevolved with animals throughout the history of our species (Stiner, 2002). Over the centuries, humans have used animals to harness their abilities and to manage workload in a more efficient way. Animal partners are assigned their roles in human–animal partnerships based on the physical and cognitive characteristics that make them able to replace or augment human skills (Billings et al., 2012). Contemporary HAnT are deployed in a wide array of settings, necessitating a reexamination of both their operational value and the ethical frameworks that govern their use.

In a comprehensive examination of HanTs, Phillips et al. (2016) described three main categories of human–animal relationships, based on the benefits they provide to humans. The first category comprises HAnT in which the animal(s) replace, multiply, or augment physical capabilities of humans. This category includes animals used as mount or pack transporters, such as horses, camels, elephants, or mules (replace human physical capabilities), oxen used to plow fields or pull heavy equipment (multiply human physical capabilities), and service animals that allow independence for owners with disabilities (augment human physical capabilities). The second category consists of HAnT in which the animal(s) provide comfort, inform, or augment emotional capabilities of humans. This second category includes pets (comfort), animals used in the treatment of anxiety or dyslexia (inform), and horses used in hippotherapy to improve social functioning and directed attention in children and adults on the autism spectrum (augment). The third category refers to HAnT in which the animal(s) multiply and augment human cognitive capabilities. Examples include the canaries used in coal mines to sense the presence of poisonous gases (multiply/replace human cognitive abilities), and canines used in law enforcement, military operations, sheepdogs, sled dogs, and search and rescue operators (augmenting human cognitive abilities).

The type of relationship necessary to work with an animal partner, just like the one required to work with fellow humans, requires effective communication, coordination, and trust. Nevertheless, successful dynamics in a HAnT require different mechanisms to build rapport, because of the species' differences in cognitive patterns (humans can think abstractly and self-regulate, while animals rely more on instinct) and because of the obvious communication barriers (humans and animals don't speak the same language).

Characteristics of HanTs

As Phillips et al. (2016) notice, the nature and depth of human–animal communication also depend on the cognitive abilities of animals. To effectively communicate with an animal team member, humans need to adjust their communication patterns in ways that facilitate comprehension for the other species, such as conveying messages primarily through body language, tone of voice, gestures, and emotive displays. Effective teamwork with animal team members is often achieved via extensive training, in which animals are trained/conditioned to pursue the goal shared with humans, and the humans learn how to best tailor verbal and nonverbal communication cues to their animals. Both types of team members need to learn how to "read" their partners before they can work together successfully.

Human–animal communication is bi-directional and dynamic, in that both the human and the animal team members learn from one another and influence one another. Human–animal communication encompasses both verbal and nonverbal patterns and can convey a vast array of messages and emotions (Phillips, 2016). Through effective communication, even though the relationship remains hierarchically skewed toward the human, animal partners learn to spontaneously support and even anticipate their humans' intents, working as coordinated team members.

Human–animal partnerships foster familiarity between team members of different species, and their interdependence is based on mutual trust. Human–animal collaboration and partnership often lead to emotional attachment and strong bonds between humans and animals. Armstrong Oma (2010) proposes that humans and animals engage in mutually beneficial social contracts based on trust and reciprocity. As Armstrong Oma explains:

> Humans trust animals to be docile and cooperative, while animals trust humans to protect them, feed them and care for them. [...] Fundamental trust forms the basis for animals to give up their autonomy, and for humans to claim responsibility. Even small domesticates like sheep and goats are potentially dangerous animals, but in the presence of trust, harmful situations (both for humans and animals) are avoided. (Armstrong Oma, 2010, p. 177)

In these relationships, both humans and animals forfeit the possibility of exercising aggression against the other species, so that they both survive and reap the benefits of the partnership. In a similar vein, Phillips et al. (2016) discuss the mutually beneficial nature of human–animal trust, in that "humans rely on animals for their judgment, skills, and obedience, while animals rely on humans for guidance and care" (p. 110). A fundamental element in the development of trust between human and animal team members is repeated exposure to each other, since consistent interaction allows the team members to be able to predict each other's behavior and to act accordingly (Phillips et al., 2016). In a nutshell, as summarized by Adams (2018), "Human-animal relations are complex, precarious, and fraught with paradox" (p. 1).

The way humans relate to animals is also heavily influenced by the type of cultural environment in which the relationship takes place. Descola (2018) examines four different types of human–animal modes of identification – animism, totemism, analogism, and naturalism. In animism, humanity is not ascribed to humans only, but also to animals, since "animals and spirits are said to possess social characteristics: they live in villages, abide by kinship rules and ethical codes, engage in ritual activity and barter goods" (p. 5). In totemism, groups of humans (tribes or families) feel a deep connection with a specific animal – a totem, with which they share characteristics. In Descola's words, "The main totem of a group of humans, most often an animal or a plant, and all the human and non-human beings that are affiliated to it, are said to share certain general attributes of physical conformation, substance, temperament and behaviour by virtue of a common origin emplaced in the land" (Descola, 2006, p. 10). Analogism, which was the main Western philosophy during the Middle Ages and Renaissance, human and animal species are conceived as different species on a continuum along their similarities and differences. Descola (2018) explains that: "analogism is predicated on the idea that all the entities in the world are fragmented into a multiplicity of essences, forms and substances separated by minute intervals, often ordered along a graded scale" (p. 12). Finally, according to naturalism, the predominant conception of human–animal relationships in modernity, we tend to ascribe certain characteristics (such as self-consciousness) exclusively to humans, and we use it to distinguish between human and non-human animals. As Descola (2018) explains: "what, for us, distinguishes humans from non-humans is the mind, the soul, subjectivity, a moral conscience, language and so forth" (p. 13).

A challenge to the notion of human exceptionalism is brought forward by Carter and Charles (2018). The authors encourage a reconceptualization of human–animal relations in which we consider "non-human animals as involuntarily embedded in social relationships" (p. 79). On the same note, Cudworth (2015) examines the violence that pervasively defines a lot of human–animal relationships in practices such as industrial livestock production and raises questions about "the embedding of violence in everyday practices" (p. 79).

Research on HanT

As summarized in Melson (2002), "since the late nineteenth century, two trends spurred by the Darwinian revolution have underscored human-animal commonalities rather than differences" (p. 248).

Research on the topic of human–animal relationships has aligned along two main theoretical traditions – the "human as animal" and the "animal as human" doctrines.

The "human as animal" trend stems from a behaviorist approach, which sees humans as simply yet another animal species, subject to the same principles and dynamics governing the behavior and cognition of other animals. Drawing upon evolutionary theory, this approach sees humans as simply more evolved animals, obeying the same developmental principles as other mammalians (Melson, 2002). On the other side, the "animal as human" trend of research examines the abilities of animals to engage in behaviors and cognitive processes deemed quintessentially humans, such as logical reasoning, multiple classification, or the display of emotions such as empathy, altruism, guilt, and pride (Melson, 2002).

A more recent (and still limited) third research approach to HanTs examines the relationship of humans and animals as interdependent systems and their dynamic interactions, analyzing how humans and animals influence each other's behavior and cognitive/emotional processes (Melson, 2002). The bulk of research on human–animal relations has focused (so far) almost exclusively on the human side of it, analyzing the attitude and perception of animals held by humans. Animals are rarely studied as contributing and mutually influencing agents (Adams, 2018).

In research about human–animal partnerships, the most studied species are dogs, horses, and even wild birds, due to the popularity of birdwatching. The relationship of humans and dogs constitutes one of the main areas of research due to dogs' common and emotionally intense bond with humans. As explained in Gee et al. (2021), "through the processes of domestication and natural selection, dogs have become adept at socializing with humans" (p. 1). Dogs' loyalty and affection toward their humans is proverbial, and Albuquerque et al. (2016) show that they can recognize human emotions. Horses may also be suitable for scientific inquiry about HanT because, as a species, horses have close connections with humans (e.g., in transportation, farming, leisurely riding) and can be taught to develop reciprocal relationships with humans (Menna et al., 2019). Horseback riding is frequently employed in animal-assisted therapies (AATs) and it has shown a beneficial effect on a plethora of physical and mental conditions, such as brain and spinal cord injuries, strokes, autism, and cognitive, behavioral, and emotional problems (Lessick et al., 2004). Adults with disability who undergo horseback riding show improvements in postural control, muscular control, balance, as well as emotional control and self-discipline, improved risk-taking abilities, increased self-esteem and sense of control (Lessick et al., 2004).

Furthermore, despite the lack of a bond per se between wild birds and birdwatchers, interactions with wild birds in their natural habitat have been shown to induce beneficial effects on humans. Galbraith et al. (2014) analyzed the practice of humans feeding wild birds and found that it was motivated by pleasure and strongly correlated with dog ownership. Likewise, Cox and Gaston (2016) found that bird feeding brought about a sense of relaxation and connection to nature. When inquiring about the motivations for bird feeding, the authors found that "the feelings of being relaxed and connected to nature were the strongest drivers" (p. 1).

Ultimately, the choice of the animal with which to work depends vastly on the animal's relational capabilities, which may derive from its history of coevolution with humans (Menna et al., 2019). Dogs are known to be the first species humans were able to domesticate (Freedman et al., 2014) and the co-evolution of dogs and humans has shaped dogs' ability to read the non-verbal language of humans more accurately than other species (Menna et al., 2019), making them particularly well-suited for human–animal teamwork. As expressed in Wang et al. (2016): "due to their cognitive and behavioral abilities, domestic dogs have been selected to fulfill a wide variety of tasks including hunting, herding and companionship" (p. 21).

Examples of HanT

HanTs have been successfully deployed in the treatment of psychological and psychosocial conditions. Given the limitations of solely pharmacological therapies, a more integrated approach to medicine seeks to consider all biological and psychological aspects of the patient (Menna et al., 2019). AAT leverages the benefits of the human–animal bond in therapeutic sessions with the goal of treating or managing chronic pain and behavioral disorders, such as anxiety, depression, and autism spectrum disorder by promoting a sense of relief from stress and the promotion of trust, motivation, and concentration (Menna et al., 2019). Particularly for children with emotional disorders or victims of neglect, the inclusion of dogs in the therapeutic process has shown to produce positive outcomes in terms of social skills (positive tone of voice, appropriate eye contact, diminished aggressiveness), verbalization, attention management, and sense of personal control (diminished learned helplessness; Kogan et al., 1999). Reichert (1998) has found that the inclusion of an animal in therapy sessions for children who were sexually victimized, "can help the sexually abused child disclose abuse and express feelings" (p. 177).

Besides AAT, pet ownership has also proved to be beneficial. Van Houtte and Jarvis (1995) found that pet ownership provides significant benefits to preadolescents in terms of increased autonomy and self-esteem. Likewise, Poresky and Hendrix (1989) examined pet ownership in relation to preschoolers and found that a child's social and intellectual development benefited greatly when the child had a strong bond with a pet. Research on human–animal teamwork has repeatedly shown the emotional benefits of such partnership for adults as well. As stated in Lum and Phillips (2024): "[...] animals [...] reduce stress by allowing individuals to retain a greater degree of self-determination and dynamic adaptation to immediate and prospective environments. Service animals, therefore, provide a means for individuals to live more independently" (p. 558).

Canines have long been employed in defense and security settings, from explosive detection and narcotics interdiction to search and rescue missions (Moyer, 2024). The integration of working animals into military and police operations exemplifies high-stakes HanT, where reliability and communication under duress are paramount. Detection dogs and trained rodents are increasingly used in ecological monitoring and public health. Canines assist in locating endangered species or invasive plants, while rats have been utilized to detect landmines (Poling et al., 2011) or diagnose tuberculosis (TB) through olfactory cues (Kanaan et al., 2021). In a study coming out of Mozambique, giant African pouched rats were trained to detect landmines (residual of the civil war that ended in 1992) via the smell of TNT, the main component of landmines. Giant African pouched rats were chosen because of their excellent sense of smell, their light weight (which would not be sufficient to detonate landmines), and their resistance to local parasites and diseases (Poling et al., 2011). After training based on principles of operant behavior, the rats were able to detect 100% of the landmines hidden in the area searched, with the added benefit of also finding additional other explosive devices containing TNT. The rate of false alarms was also well below the international standards for accreditation of mine-detection animals (Poling et al., 2011). The same rat species, the giant African pouched rat, can also be trained to smell TB. As reported in Kanaan et al. (2021), after a systematic review and meta-analysis of seven studies that had the rats identify TB from human sputum samples, it was found that "trained giant African pouched rats can use scent to discriminate sputum of TB individuals from that of healthy subjects at a high accuracy" (p. 4). Applications of HanT such as sniffer dogs or biosensor rats highlight the potential for animal partners to improve human life through safety and access to healthcare, in cost-effective and efficacious ways (Fiebig et al., 2020).

Team cognition in HAnTs can be considered an emergent process of dynamically negotiated cognition, co-produced both by humans and animals. An example of this bi-directional cognitive process is described by Troisi et al. (2019) in their study of scent detection dog-handler teams. In their review of factors that affect the performance of scent detection dogs, Troisi et al. (2019) argue that the handler can help mitigate the stress of scent detection work, since the handler's behavior can affect the persistence, arousal, and performance of the dog. They describe the influence of handlers on the dogs' behavior and that of dogs on the handlers. Dogs need to be responsive to their human partners' cues, and "handlers also need to be trained appropriately to recognize their dog's alert signals" (Troisi et al., 2019, p. 63). Only the shared cognitive processes of both handler and dog make scent detection successful.

Another example of interspecies distributed cognition is the case of human handlers and sheepdogs. Keil (2015) proposes that handlers and sheepdogs form an "interspecies cognitive system" (p. 508) in which the human scaffolds the sheepdog's cognitive limitations in handling the task alone, while at the same time recognizing and exploiting the sheepdog's species-specific skills. Keil (2015) likens this dynamic team cognition process to the parent–child relationship, in which the parent offers support to remediate the child's inabilities, while at the same time fostering the child's independence and development.

Emerging Directions for HanT

In general, the study of human–animal relationships and teamwork continues to be mostly regarded as a niche interest of branches of psychology that remain anchored around a human-centric framework, such as social psychology and critical psychology, and only see animals as useful pieces of the evolutionary puzzle to explain human behavior (Adams, 2018). Echoing Adam's (2018) lament, and after a comprehensive review of the available research, Amiot and Bastian

(2015) propose that the study of human–animal relationships should emerge as its own distinct discipline "that merits theoretical and empirical attention from psychology" (p. 6). As of now, the consensus seems to be that human–animal studies is the interdisciplinary study of human–animal relationships, drawing on elements of psychology, sociology, and zoology, but not limited to a primary method (Shapiro, 2020).

A notable exception to the general dismissal of human–animal relationships is offered by conservation psychology, which contends that interaction with animals improves physical and emotional well-being in humans, as well as facilitating a deeper connection to the natural world and more sustainable behaviors (Adams, 2018). The increased reliance on animals in specialized roles necessitates robust ethical standards. Animals engaged in teaming must be provided with appropriate care, rest, and enrichment. The use of positive reinforcement training, clear guidelines for workload limitations, and provisions for retirement or rehoming are essential to ensuring that animals are not exploited under the guise of utility. Furthermore, ethical review boards and animal welfare oversight should be integrated into institutional protocols involving animal teammates.

Despite promising results and the increasing interest toward AAT, further scientific examination into the interspecific relationships of humans and animals and the factors influencing them is needed to standardize animal education training and to refine the choice of suitable animals for and the pairing of individual humans and animals (Menna et al., 2019). Inspired by the successful cooperation of humans and animals, the design of synthetic agents such as robots and AIs has recently adopted a biomimetic approach to the design of synthetic agents, aiming to replicate bi-directional communication, interdependency, and trust characteristics of HanTs (Phillips et al., 2016).

HanT exemplifies a unique intersection of biology, behavior, and social cooperation. Far from being a relic of the past, it continues to offer innovative solutions across sectors. As the scientific understanding of animal minds deepens, so too must our commitment to fostering respectful and humane partnerships. The continued evolution of HanT will reflect not only our technical ingenuity but also our moral responsibility toward the animals with whom we share these endeavors. As AI and robotic technologies progress, comparisons are frequently drawn between machine and animal teammates. However, animals offer irreplaceable traits – empathy, adaptability, and sensory capabilities – that continue to make them invaluable in specific contexts. The future of HanT will depend on interdisciplinary collaboration among veterinarians, trainers, ethicists, and behavioral scientists to expand its scope while upholding high ethical standards. Moving forward, lessons from animal teams can help shape our approach to agent teams as human–agent collaboration becomes increasingly common in this digital age.

HUMAN–AGENT TEAMING

The integration of AI into collaborative settings has transformed traditional human–machine interactions into dynamic partnerships known as HAT. Unlike conventional automation, HAT envisions agents as proactive teammates capable of shared decision-making, learning, and adaptation. This shift necessitates a multidisciplinary approach encompassing human–computer interaction, cognitive science, and systems engineering. HAT brings together different types of capabilities: humans contribute intuition, ethics, and creativity, while agents offer speed, consistency, and computational power. From disaster response and healthcare to research and design, these teams are reshaping how we work.

HATs build upon principles from human–human teaming, adapting concepts such as shared mental models, situational awareness, and mutual trust to human–agent contexts. The T4 framework – Team Formation, Task and Role Development, Team Development, and Team Improvement – offers a process-oriented perspective for analyzing HAT dynamics. Specifically, Team Formation addresses how agents and humans come together, align on goals, and establish norms; Task and Role Development clarify each member's responsibilities and builds competence; Team Development focuses on nurturing coordination, shared understanding, and trust; and Team Improvement involves iterative learning, adaptation, and long-term viability. This framework enables a structured examination of both task-related cycles and developmental team processes (LLM Watch, 2023). Additionally, reinforcement learning frameworks have been proposed to model and evaluate teaming strategies, emphasizing the importance of belief-state reasoning and social considerations as agents and humans co-adapt over time. Additionally, reinforcement learning frameworks have been proposed to model and evaluate teaming strategies, emphasizing the importance of belief states and social considerations. In the context of AI, reinforcement learning refers to a machine learning approach where an agent learns to make decisions by receiving feedback from its environment in the form of rewards or penalties. This allows agents to adapt their strategies over time, making them better suited for dynamic team environments where conditions and human behaviors may change unexpectedly.

Characteristics of HATs

HATs are marked by distinct strengths and weaknesses on each side. Agents excel at fast computation, pattern recognition, and repetitive tasks. However, they lack human-like adaptability, empathy, and contextual judgment. Humans, on the other hand, are good at interpreting social cues and making value-based decisions but are prone to fatigue. Both agents and humans are prone to different types of processing and cognitive biases that may affect the outcome of the task. For example, an AI system can scan thousands of building layouts in a search-and-rescue scenario, but it won't intuitively recognize when a child's voice behind debris indicates higher urgency. The human responder is needed for that level of judgment. This asymmetry means task roles must be assigned thoughtfully. Agents should handle structured, logic-based functions, while humans take on complex, ethical, or interpersonal aspects. This division is essential to avoid overloading the agent with decisions it cannot make, or the human with tasks that are better automated (Abuhaimed & Sen, 2024).

Unlike human teams who communicate through body language, shared culture, or unspoken norms, agents require clearly defined instructions. Their communication is often limited to interface outputs or verbal commands, which can lead to misunderstandings or delays if the team isn't properly aligned. A core challenge is that agents lack a theory of mind, the cognitive ability to understand that others have their own beliefs, intentions, and perspectives (Premack & Woodruff, 1978; Baker et al., 2017). Without this ability, agents can't reliably predict human behavior in complex social contexts. This is where the concept and development of shared mental models (SMMs) become essential. SMMs refer to a common understanding between team members about the task, each other's roles, and how to respond to changing conditions (Cannon-Bowers et al., 1993). In HATs, developing these models requires deliberate interface design and real-time communication strategies. This matters because teams without shared models are more likely to experience errors, hesitation, or redundant work, especially in high-pressure settings such as emergency response or surgery (Iftikhar & Khan, 2021; Scheutz et al., 2017).

In HATs, trust must be continuously calibrated. That is, the human must trust the agent only to the extent that the agent is reliable and no more. Under-trusting the agent leads to inefficiency; while over-trusting it may cause harmful decisions. For instance, if an AI recommends evacuating a building based on sensor data, a human team member needs to understand how the AI arrived at that conclusion. Without an explanation, the human may either dismiss the advice due to lack of understanding or follow it blindly, potentially resulting in harmful consequences. Transparency supports trust calibration by allowing humans to make informed judgments about when to rely on or override agent recommendations. Transparent systems share their reasoning, data sources, and limitations with the human teammates. Doing so helps build confidence and enables the human to make informed judgments about when to accept or override the agent's suggestions (Drnec et al., 2016; Baber, 2020). This is why transparency matters.

Human teams adapt naturally by adjusting roles and strategies in response to unfolding events. Agents, however, require explicit programming or algorithms to achieve this kind of flexibility. Dynamic adaptation refers to the agent's ability to modify its level of autonomy and behavior in real time, depending on the context. What does this look like in practice? Imagine a surgical robot that normally waits for instructions from a doctor. But if the patient's vitals suddenly drop, it switches to a proactive mode by monitoring vitals, alerting the team, and preparing tools autonomously. This example is adaptive autonomy in action, and it is critical in time-sensitive scenarios where waiting for human input may cost lives (Martin & Barber, 1996; O'Neill et al., 2022). Interestingly, some of these dynamics echo what we observe in HAnTs. Like agents, animals require clear signals and task-specific training. However, trust in HAnTs is built through embodied interaction and emotional bonding, something artificial agents must simulate through consistent behavior and responsiveness. Where animals may sense distress or adapt to a handler's body language, agents require coded indicators and interface feedback to approximate the same level of attunement. Thus, while both teams require alignment, the mechanisms and affordances of trust, adaptability, and communication differ fundamentally and understanding these differences is essential when designing effective human–agent systems.

Research on HAT

Studies have shown that agents are excellent at assigning tasks efficiently because they operate without personal bias. However, when agents take over task delegation, human team members sometimes feel excluded or dissatisfied. This highlights a tension between maximizing efficiency and maintaining human agency in the team dynamic (Abuhaimed & Sen, 2024). When agents make mistakes, as they inevitably will, the way they recover matters. Research shows that if an agent explains what went wrong and expresses regret, humans are more likely to rebuild trust. Especially in high-risk environments, these social repair mechanisms are vital to sustained collaboration (Baber, 2020; Drnec et al., 2016).

Frameworks like T4 (Team Formation, Task Assignment, Team Development, Team Improvement) emphasize the importance of agents growing with their teams. Adaptive autonomy allows the agent to become more independent as it learns the team's norms and is less autonomous when human oversight is needed. This balance improves team resilience and adaptability over time (O'Neill et al., 2022; Jafari Meimandi et al., 2024). A human's previous exposure to agents plays a major role in the success of the team. People who have worked with AI before are more likely to trust it, understand its capabilities, and coordinate more effectively.

Examples of HATs

In disaster zones, HATs use robots and drones to locate survivors, assess structural damage, and deliver aid. While agents handle exploration and data gathering, human responders make final decisions. Systems like CSCATTT (Command, Safety, Communication, Assessment, Treatment, Triage, and Transport) have been adapted to include agents, leading to faster decision-making and better coordination (Jafari Meimandi et al., 2024). During public health emergencies or mass casualty incidents, AI-powered agents assist with triage, logistics, and treatment planning. Studies show that healthcare professionals working with agents have improved task distribution, communication, and decision-making under pressure. Regular training with these systems also increases human confidence in handling high-stakes situations (Sultan et al., 2021).

In research environments, AI agents act not just as tools, but as supportive collaborators. A data scientist might use one AI tool for literature review, another for data analysis, and a third for drafting technical summaries. This allows the human researcher to focus on creative problem-solving and hypothesis generation, while the agents handle time-consuming background tasks (Spataro, 2025). In software engineering, AI coding assistants suggest functions, detect bugs, and auto-generate documentation. These activities enable developers to focus on complex architectural planning. Similarly, in creative industries, agents help with idea generation or concept sketching, enhancing team creativity while preserving human judgment and originality (Ross et al., 2023; Singh et al., 2023).

Emerging Directions for HAT

With the rise of AI agents, technology is not just a passive tool controlled by humans. Instead, it's becoming an active teammate that can collaborate with people. AI capabilities have been advancing rapidly, doubling about every seven months since 2019 (Kwa et al., 2025 as cited in Lou et al., 2025). Modern AI systems can now "learn and act" on their own, showing potential to mimic human thinking, behavior, and decision-making (Dennis et al., 2023; Durante et al., 2024 as cited in Lou et al., 2025). These advances make AI useful in various areas like writing, research, design, and customer service.

As Lou et al. (2025) note, this technological shift signals a turning point in team science, where the lines between tool and teammate are becoming increasingly blurred. This ambiguity raises the question: Should AI merely simulate agency or actually possess it? While full human-like agency may not be necessary or even desirable, for effective teaming, research suggests that AI systems which exhibit goal-directed behavior, contextual awareness, and adaptive communication often foster better human collaboration (Rahwan et al., 2019). The appearance of agency, when paired with transparency and control, can enhance usability and trust without overstepping ethical boundaries.

Even as AI grows more capable, humans still provide essential skills, like emotional intelligence, tacit knowledge, and intrinsic expertise (Ibrahim & Abdulazeez, 2021). These human strengths are vital in situations that can be seen as more complex or under high pressure. When teams integrate AI effectively, human–AI collaboration capitalizes on human intuition and empathy, paired with AI's capacity for rapid synthesis of structured and unstructured information. This synergy is supported by empirical findings: Feuerriegel et al. (2022) demonstrate improved decision-making outcomes when human intuition is augmented by AI insights, and Hannebauer (1999) shows how AI agents function more effectively when treated and modeled as teammates in knowledge workflows.

For these teams to work well, humans need to understand how AI makes decisions. Studies show that when people see how AI arrives at its suggestions, like through risk scores or clear explanations, they are more likely to engage with the system and make better decisions (Fogliato et al., 2022; Jussupow et al., 2021). Without that understanding, people may rely too much on AI or reject its help entirely. Looking ahead, it is important to focus on building trust, setting clear responsibilities, and creating transparent ways for humans and AI to interact. Ethical guidelines and human-centered design will help ensure that AI supports human strengths rather than creating new risks. Like HanTs, successful human–AI collaboration will require input from specialists such as engineers, psychologists, and other experts to move forward thoughtfully and responsibly.

HUMAN–ANIMAL & HAT

To better understand the nature of human–agent collaboration, this section draws comparisons with the well-established practice of HanT. We begin by examining the foundational traits that make HanTs effective, such as asymmetry, trust, co-adaptation, and non-verbal communication, and then explore how these characteristics can inform the design and understanding of HATs. By using this analog, we highlight both shared opportunities and unique challenges that arise when teaming with non-human entities, whether biological or artificial. The increasing deployment of artificial agents in domains such as defense, healthcare, and logistics has prompted researchers to explore new frameworks for effective collaboration. HAT shifts the focus from tool use to cooperative engagement, where agents act as teammates rather than mere instruments (Chen et al., 2018). A compelling analog exists in the long-standing tradition of HanT, where humans and animals co-adapt to complete complex, often high-stakes tasks. This interspecies relationship offers a biologically grounded model of teamwork built on asymmetry, learning, and interdependence – qualities similarly present in human–agent relationships.

Shared Foundations of Human–Animal and HATs

Trust is foundational in both HAnT and HAT. In HAnTs, such as human partnerships with guide dogs or military working dogs, trust is earned over time through training, predictability, and shared experience (Serpell et al., 2017). Similarly, in HATs, agents must communicate with intent, explain reasoning, and behave reliably to foster appropriate trust and avoid over-reliance (Chen et al., 2018). Misaligned trust can lead to disuse or misuse, impacting team effectiveness. In both settings, communication is nonverbal, asynchronous, and often context sensitive. HanTs rely heavily on gestures, tone, and conditioning to achieve behavioral coordination (Grandin, 2009). Likewise, agents may use multimodal interfaces – such as visual cues, haptic feedback, or natural language processing – to facilitate understanding with human partners (Hancock et al., 2011). Designing communication systems that reflect the intuitive, redundant signaling found in HAnT could enhance robustness in HAT.

Training in HAnT is a bidirectional process; animals learn task rules while humans adjust expectations and behaviors accordingly. This model mirrors the co-adaptive design principle in HAT, where agents learn from human input and modify behavior over time (Zhang et al., 2024). Embedding mutual learning into HAT architectures – for example, via reinforcement learning with human-in-the-loop supervision – can help replicate the dynamic responsiveness seen in animal teams.

Successful HAnTs have clear role delineation, with each partner contributing according to their strengths. Detection dogs, for instance, excel in olfactory search, while handlers interpret findings and make mission-critical decisions. This division of labor offers a model for role allocation in HAT, especially in domains where AI outperforms humans in computation but lags in judgment, context-awareness, or empathy (Clancey, 2006). Designing agent teammates to complement rather than replicate human roles enhances team synergy.

HanT has long required ethical oversight, with standards for humane training, working conditions, and post-service care (Serpell et al., 2017). While artificial agents are not sentient, similar concerns arise around accountability, control, and the social implications of agent autonomy. Drawing ethical guidance from HAnT can help frame debates around human dignity, agency design, and acceptable delegation in HAT contexts (Gunkel, 2018).

Implications of HanTs for HAT Design

HAnT insights offer a valuable lens for improving HAT design by emphasizing the relational, adaptive, and ethical dynamics that make teams effective. HAnT reveals that successful collaboration relies on more than functionality; it requires mutual understanding, trust, and shared context.

Translating principles of effective HanTs to artificial agents in HATs, HAT systems should be:

- *Trust-aware*: Just as animals build trust through consistent cues and behavior, artificial agents should use transparent decision-making processes, explainable outputs, and reliable interactions to foster calibrated trust in their human partners. For example, an AI agent in the medical field should communicate the reasoning behind its diagnosis or recommendation, giving humans a chance to assess whether they should rely on the AI. Some guidelines associated with responsible and trustworthy AI have been described by the National Institute of Standards and Technology (2025).
- *Co-adaptive*: Animals in working relationships, like guide dogs or search-and-rescue dogs, learn and adjust to human commands and behaviors over time. Similarly, AI agents should adapt to human preferences, routines, and feedback. A co-adaptive AI in a collaborative writing tool might adjust the tone or modify its editing suggestions based on a user's existing content.
- *Context-sensitive non-human team members*: Animals, especially working animals, are responsive to emotional, social, and environmental cues from their human team members. For agents, it will be equally important to be able to process the cues given by human team members. Some of this has been studied by programs such as DARPA ASIST: Artificial Social Intelligence for Successful Teams (DARPA, n.d.), as well as others.
- *Context-sensitive human team members*: Part of the responsibility of the human handler is to try and ensure the safety of the working animal by having good situational awareness. Similarly, humans should have a base understanding of how the agent operates in order to work effectively with it.
- *Ethically grounded*: In HAnT, animals are often the most vulnerable team members. If animals are no longer seen as useful to human teammates, animals may be rehomed or even mistreated. In contrast, in HATs, humans may be more vulnerable than AI agents, facing ethical concerns, risks of information leaks, algorithmic bias, and potential job displacement.
- *Ascribe to accepted design mental models*: Designs that tap into human mental models of animal partners may help in the general acceptance of robot capabilities and limitations. Physical and behavioral likenesses to animals may be a means to accomplish this task.

- *Properly designed interaction models*: Designs that foster robot and human learning through interactions that resemble well established human–animal training relationships may be a means by which trust in robotic teammates can be established.
- *Understanding the roles and responsibilities of each team member*: Existing HanTs vary in the degree to which they resemble tool or teammate-like relationships that range in the complexity with which they interact and communicate with one another to accomplish work. If the goal is to foster human–robot relationships that resemble human–human teammates, modeling HanTs may be a logical intermediate step.

By adopting these principles, developers and policymakers can create artificial teammates that perform efficiently and integrate more naturally and ethically into human-centered ecosystems.

CONCLUSION

HanTs exemplify how effective collaboration can emerge despite vast differences in cognition, communication, and biology. These collaborations show that teamwork does not require shared language or logic but depends on mutual adaptation, trust-building, and complementary strengths. As we build artificial agents that are increasingly autonomous and socially embedded, the lessons from HanT – particularly in trust, co-adaptation, and role complementarity – provide a valuable framework. By drawing on this model, the future of HAT can be both technically robust and socially responsible.

Teaming is a multifaceted construction that lies at the intersection of psychology, communication, technology, and systems design. By building empirical research and real-world insights, organizations can foster teams that are not only effective but also inclusive, resilient, and ethically sound. As teamwork continues to evolve alongside emerging technologies, human-centric design and ongoing learning will remain foundational to success.

HATs are not just a technological innovation, but they are a transformation of how we work, make decisions, and solve problems. These collaborations already enhance performance across industries, but they demand thoughtful design, adaptive systems, and ethical oversight. For example, in sectors like healthcare, agents assist in diagnostic decision-making; in aviation, they help monitor systems and suggest corrective actions; and in education, they act as tutors. These transformations shift traditional roles, requiring humans to use tools and collaborate with agents that provide feedback, learn from behavior, and even suggest strategic decisions. The future of teamwork lies in building agents that are not just tools but trusted partners, who are capable of learning, adapting, and communicating alongside humans in complex, real-world tasks. As this field evolves, investing in human-centered design, trust calibration, and developing and maintaining accurate, SMMs and considering using animal models for AI team members will be key to unlocking AI's full potential.

REFERENCES

Abuhaimed, S., & Sen, S. (2024). Team performance and user satisfaction in mixed human-agent teams. *Proceedings of the 23rd international conference on autonomous agents and multiagent systems (AAMAS)* (pp. 1–9). International Foundation for Autonomous Agents and Multiagent Systems. https://www.ifaamas.org/Proceedings/aamas2024/pdfs/p4.pdf

Adams, M. (2018). Towards a critical psychology of human–animal relations. *Social and Personality Psychology Compass, 12*(4), e12375. https://doi.org/10.1111/spc3.12375

Albuquerque, N., Guo, K., Wilkinson, A., Savalli, C., Otta, E., & Mills, D. (2016). Dogs recognize dog and human emotions. *Biology Letters, 12*(1), 20150883. https://doi.org/10.1098/rsbl.2015.0883

Amiot, C. E., & Bastian, B. (2015). Toward a psychology of human–animal relations. *Psychological Bulletin, 141*(1), 6. https://doi.org/10.1037/a0038147

Armstrong Oma, K. (2010). Between trust and domination: Social contracts between humans and animals. *World Archaeology, 42*(2), 175–187.

Baber, C. (2020). Human-agents interactions in multi-agent systems: A case study of human-UAVs team for forest fire lookouts. *Proceedings of the 12th international conference on agents and artificial intelligence (ICAART 2020)* (pp. 347–354). SciTePress. https://doi.org/10.5220/0009369203470354

Baker, B., Gupta, O., Raskar, R., & Naik, N. (2017). *Accelerating neural architecture search using performance prediction*. arXiv preprint arXiv:1705.10823.

Berretta, V., Prada, R., & Paiva, A. (2024). *Developing teamwork: Transitioning between stages in human-agent teams. Frontiers in Computer Science, 6*, 1455903.

Billings, D. R., Schaefer, K. E., Chen, J. Y., Kocsis, V., Barrera, M., Cook, J., & Hancock, P. A. (2012). *Human-animal trust as an analog for human-robot trust: A review of current evidence* (Tech. Rep. No. ARL-TR-5949). U.S. Army Research Laboratory.

Cannon-Bowers, J. A., Salas, E., & Converse, S. A. (1993). Shared mental models in expert team decision making. In N. J. Castellan, Jr. (Ed.), *Individual and group decision making: Current issues* (pp. 221–246). Lawrence Erlbaum Associates.

Carter, B., & Charles, N. (2018). The animal challenge to sociology. *European Journal of Social Theory, 21*(1), 79–97. https://doi.org/10.1177/1368431016681305

Chen, J. Y. C., Lakhmani, S. G., Stowers, K., Selkowitz, A. R., Wright, J. L., & Barnes, M. (2018). Situation awareness-based agent transparency and human-autonomy teaming effectiveness. *Theoretical Issues in Ergonomics Science, 19*(3), 259–282. https://doi.org/10.1080/1463922X.2017.1315750

Clancey, W. J. (2006). Roles for agent assistants in field science: Understanding personal projects and collaboration. *IEEE Transactions on Systems, Man, and Cybernetics – Part C, 36*(2), 125–137. https://doi.org/10.1109/TSMCC.2006.871599

Cox, D. T. C., & Gaston, K. J. (2016). Urban bird feeding: Connecting people with nature. *PLoS One, 11*(7), e0158717. https://doi.org/10.1371/journal.pone.0158717

Cudworth, E. (2015). Killing animals: Sociology, species relations and institutionalized violence. *The Sociological Review, 63*(1), 1–18. https://doi.org/10.1111/1467-954X.1222

DARPA. (n.d.) *ASIST: Artificial social intelligence for successful teams*. https://www.darpa.mil/research/programs/artificial-social-intelligence-for-successful-teams

Descola, P. (2006). *Beyond nature and culture*. University of Chicago Press.

Descola, P. (2014). Modes of being and forms of predication. *Hau: Journal of Ethnographic Theory, 4*(1), 271–280.

Drnec, K., Marathe, A. R., Lukos, J. R., & Metcalfe, J. S. (2016). From trust in automation to decision neuroscience: Applying cognitive neuroscience methods to understand human-agent systems. *IEEE Transactions on Human-Machine Systems, 46*(3), 327–336. https://doi.org/10.3389/fnhum.2016.00290

Feuerriegel, S., Shrestha, Y. R., von Krogh, G., & Zhang, C. (2022). Bringing artificial intelligence to business management. *Nature Machine Intelligence, 4*(7), 611–613.

Fiebig, L., Beyene, N., Burny, R., Fast, C. D., Cox, C., & Mgode, G. F. (2020). From pests to tests: Training rats to diagnose tuberculosis. *European Respiratory Journal, 55*(3). https://doi.org/10.1183/13993003.02243-2019

Fogliato, R., Chappidi, S., Lungren, M., Fisher, P., Wilson, D., Fitzke, M., Parkinson, M., Horvitz, E., Inkpen, K., & Nushi, B. (2022). Who goes first? Influences of human-AI workflow on decision making in clinical imaging. *Proceedings of the 2022 ACM conference on fairness, accountability, and transparency (FAccT '22)* (pp. 1362–1374). ACM. https://doi.org/10.1145/3531146.3533193

Freedman, A. H., Gronau, I., Schweizer, R. M., Ortega-Del Vecchyo, D., Han, E., Silva, P. M., Galaverni, M., Fan, Z., Marx, P., Lorente-Galdos, B., Beale, H., Ramirez, O., Hormozdiari, F., Alkan, C., Vilà, C., Squire, K., Geffen, E., Kusak, J., Boyko, A. R., … Novembre, J. (2014). Genome sequencing highlights the dynamic early history of dogs. *PLoS Genetics*, *10*(1), e1004016. https://doi.org/10.1371/journal.pgen.1004016

Galbraith, J. A., Beggs, J. R., Jones, D. N., McNaughton, E. J., Krull, C. R., & Stanley, M. C. (2014). Risks and drivers of wild bird feeding in urban areas of New Zealand. *Biological Conservation*, *180*, 64–74. https://doi.org/10.1016/j.biocon.2014.09.038

Gee, N. R., Rodriguez, K. E., Fine, A. H., & Trammell, J. P. (2021). Dogs supporting human health and well-being: A biopsychosocial approach. *Frontiers in Veterinary Science*, *8*, 630465. https://doi.org/10.3389/fvets.2021.630465

Gilson, L. L., Maynard, M. T., Jones Young, N. C., Vartiainen, M., & Hakonen, M. (2015). Virtual teams research: 10 years, 10 themes, and 10 opportunities. *Journal of Management*, *41*(5), 1313–1337. https://doi.org/10.1177/0149206314559946

Grandin, T. (2009). *Animals make us human: Creating the best life for animals*. Houghton Mifflin Harcourt.

Gunkel, D. J. (2018). *Robot rights*. MIT Press.

Hancock, P. A., Billings, D. R., Schaefer, K. E., Chen, J. Y., De Visser, E. J., & Parasuraman, R. (2011). A meta-analysis of factors affecting trust in human-robot interaction. *Human Factors*, *53*(5), 517–527. https://doi.org/10.1177/0018720811417254

Hannebauer, M. (1999). From formal workflow models to intelligent agents. *Proceedings of the AAAI-99 workshop on agent based systems in the business context* (pp. 19–24). AAAI Press.

Ibrahim, I., & Abdulazeez, A. (2021). The role of machine learning algorithms for diagnosing diseases. *Journal of Applied Science and Technology Trends*, *2*(01), 10–19.

Iftikhar, R., & Khan, M. K. (2021). Human-agent team dynamics: A review and future research opportunities. *Proceedings of the 29th European conference on information systems (ECIS)*. https://doras.dcu.ie/29262/1/AAM_Iftikhar_Rehan.pdf

Jafari Meimandi, K., Bolton, M., & Beling, P. (2024). RL-HAT: A new framework for understanding human-agent teaming. *Proceedings of the AAAI Symposium Series*, *1*(1), 1–8. https://ojs.aaai.org/index.php/AAAI-SS/article/view/27480

Jussupow, E., Spohrer, K., Heinzl, A., & Gawlitza, J. (2021). Augmenting medical diagnosis decisions? An investigation into physicians' decision-making process with artificial intelligence. *Information Systems Research*, *32*(3), 713–735.

Kaelin, V. C., Tewari, M., Benouar, S., & Lindgren, H. (2024). Developing teamwork: Transitioning between stages in human-agent collaboration. *Frontiers in Computer Science, 6,* 1455903

Kanaan, R., Farkas, N., Hegyi, P., Soós, A., Hegyi, D., Németh, K., Horváth, O., Tenk, J., Mikó, A., Szentesi, A., Balaskó, M., Szakács, Z., Vasas, A., Csupor, D., & Gyöngyi, Z. (2021). Rats sniff out pulmonary tuberculosis from sputum: A diagnostic accuracy meta-analysis. *Scientific Reports*, *11*(1), 1877. https://doi.org/10.1038/s41598-021-81086-x

Keil, P. G. (2015). Human-sheepdog distributed cognitive systems: An analysis of interspecies cognitive scaffolding in a sheepdog trial. *Journal of Cognition and Culture*, *15*(5), 508–529. https://doi.org/10.1163/15685373-12342163

Kogan, L. R., Granger, B. P., Fitchett, J. A., Helmer, K. A., & Young, K. J. (1999, April). The human-animal team approach for children with emotional disorders: Two case studies. *In Child and Youth Care Forum*, *28*(2), 105–121. https://doi.org/10.1023/A:1021941205934

Lessick, M., Shinaver, R., Post, K. M., Rivera, J. E., & Lemon, B. (2004). Therapeutic horseback riding. *AWHONN Lifelines*, *8*(1), 46–53. https://doi.org/10.1177/1091592304263956

LLM Watch. (2023, November 21). *Augmented work: The AI teammates are coming*. LLM Watch. https://www.llmwatch.com/p/augmented-work-the-ai-teammates-are

Lou, B., Lu, T., Raghu, T. S., & Zhang, Y. (2025). *Unraveling human-AI teaming: A review and outlook*. https://doi.org/10.2139/ssrn.5211067

Lum, H. C., & Phillips, E. K. (2024). Understanding human–autonomy teams through a human–animal teaming model. *Topics in Cognitive Science*, *16*(3), 554–567. https://doi.org/10.1111/tops.12713

Martin, J., & Barber, K. S. (1996). Adaptive autonomy in multi-agent systems. *Proceedings of the AAAI spring symposium on adaptation, coevolution, and learning in multiagent systems* (pp. 1–8). AAAI Press. https://citeseerx.ist.psu.edu/document?repid=rep1&type=pdf&doi=02d4b63444942ad35f2b3141843dff807864be5a

McGrath, J. E. (1964). *Social psychology: A brief introduction*. Holt, Rinehart & Winston.

Melson, G. (2002). Psychology and the study of human-animal relationships. *Society & Animals*, *10*(4), 347–352. https://doi.org/10.1163/156853002320936791

Menna, L. F., Santaniello, A., Todisco, M., Amato, A., Borrelli, L., Scandurra, C., & Fioretti, A. (2019). The human–animal relationship as the focus of animal-assisted interventions: A one health approach. *International Journal of Environmental Research and Public Health*, *16*(19), 3660. https://doi.org/10.3390/ijerph16193660

Moyer, J. C. (2024, September). *Canine utilization in law enforcement* (LEMIT Report No. 2215, LEMIT Class 99). Law Enforcement Management Institute of Texas, Sam Houston State University. https://shsu-ir.tdl.org/items/24b9291c-d6b1-4c1f-bc4d-14425b3628ee

National Institute of Standards and Technology. (2025). *Trustworthy and responsible AI*. U.S. Department of Commerce. https://www.nist.gov/trustworthy-and-responsible-ai

O'Neill, T., McNeese, N., Barron, A., & Schelble, B. (2022). Human–autonomy teaming: A review and analysis of the empirical literature. *Human Factors*, *64*(5), 904–938. https://pmc.ncbi.nlm.nih.gov/articles/PMC9284085/

Phillips, E., Jenkins, M., & Jentsch, F. (2017). Human-animal teams as an analog for future human-robot teams. *Proceedings of the Human Factors and Ergonomics Society Annual Meeting*, *61*(1), 1355–1359. https://doi.org/10.5898/JHRI.5.1.Philli

Phillips, E., & Jentsch, F. (2016). Human-animal teaming as a model for human-AI-robot teaming: Advantages and challenges. *Proceedings of the international conference on human-computer interaction in aerospace* (pp. 1–8). ACM.

Phillips, E., Schaefer, K. E., Billings, D. R., Jentsch, F., & Hancock, P. A. (2016). Human-animal teams as an analog for future human-robot teams: Influencing design and fostering trust. *Journal of Human-Robot Interaction*, *5*(1), 100–125.

Poling, A., Weetjens, B., Cox, C., Beyene, N. W., Bach, H., & Sully, A. (2011). Using trained pouched rats to detect land mines: Another victory for operant conditioning. *Journal of Applied Behavior Analysis*, *44*(2), 351–355. https://doi.org/10.1901/jaba.2011.44-351

Poresky, R. H., & Hendrix, C. (1989). Companion animal bonding, children's home environments, and young children's social development [Paper presentation]. *Biennial meeting of the society for research in child development, Kansas City, MO*. Department of Human Development and Family Studies, Kansas State University. ERIC. https://files.eric.ed.gov/fulltext/ED312087.pdf

Prada, R., Homan, A. C., & van Kleef, G. A. (2024a). A framework for understanding human-agent team dynamics. *Proceedings of the 23rd international conference on autonomous agents and multiagent systems (AAMAS)*. https://dare.uva.nl/personal/pure/en/publications/towards-sustainable-humanagent-teams-a-framework-for-understanding-humanagent-team-dynamics(9b09cef2-5842-4c1b-9a59-b906a020ba75).html

Prada, R., Homan, A. C., & van Kleef, G. A. (2024b). Towards sustainable human-agent teams: A framework for understanding human-agent team dynamics. *Proceedings of the 23rd international conference on autonomous agents and multiagent systems (AAMAS 2024)* (pp. 2696–2700). International Foundation for Autonomous Agents and Multiagent Systems.

Premack, D., & Woodruff, G. (1978). Does the chimpanzee have a theory of mind? *Behavioral and Brain Sciences*, *1*(4), 515–526. https://doi.org/10.1017/S0140525X00076512

Rahwan, I., Cebrian, M., Obradovich, N., Bongard, J., Bonnefon, J.-F., Breazeal, C., Crandall, J. W., Christakis, N. A., Couzin, I. D., Jackson, M. O., Jennings, N. R., Kamar, E., Kloumann, I. M., Larochelle, H., Lazer, D., McElreath, R., Mislove, A., Parkes, D. C., Pentland, A. S., … Wellman, M. (2019). Machine behaviour. *Nature*, *568*(7753), 477–486. https://doi.org/10.1038/s41586-019-1138-y

Reichert, E. (1998). Individual counseling for sexually abused children: A role for animals and storytelling. *Child and Adolescent Social Work Journal*, *15*(3), 177–185. https://doi.org/10.1023/A:1022284418096

Ross, S., Weisz, J., & Singh, A. (2023). *Programming with AI teammates: A review of human-agent collaboration in software development*. arXiv. https://doi.org/10.48550/arXiv.2302.07080

Salas, E., Dickinson, T. L., Converse, S. A., & Tannenbaum, S. I. (1992). Toward an understanding of team performance and training. In R. W. Swezey & E. Salas (Eds.), *Teams: Their training and performance* (pp. 3–29). Ablex Publishing.

Salas, E., Sims, D. E., & Burke, C. S. (2005). Is there a "big five" in teamwork? *Small Group Research*, *36*(5), 555–599. https://doi.org/10.1177/1046496405277134

Scheutz, M., DeLoach, S., & Adams, J. A. (2017). A framework for developing and using shared mental models in human-agent teams. *Journal Title*, 1–29. https://doi.org/10.1177/1555343416682891

Serpell, J. A., McCune, S., Gee, N. R., & Griffin, J. A. (2017). Current challenges to research on animal-assisted interventions. *Applied Developmental Science*, *21*(3), 223–233. https://doi.org/10.1080/10888691.2016.1262770

Shapiro, K. (2020). Human-animal studies: Remembering the past, celebrating the present, troubling the future. *Society & Animals*, *28*(7), 797–833. https://doi.org/10.1163/15685306-BJA10029

Singh, V., Qin, J., & Flathmann, B. (2023). Enhancing creativity through human-agent collaboration: Empirical findings. *Proceedings of the international conference on computational creativity*.

Spataro, J. (2025, April 11). Human-agent teams will reshape your workforce. *LinkedIn*. https://www.linkedin.com/pulse/human-agent-teams-reshape-your-workforce-jared-spataro-get0c

Stiner, M. C. (2002). Carnivory, coevolution, and the geographic spread of the genus Homo. *Journal of Archaeological Research*, *10*, 1–63. https://doi.org/10.1023/A:1014588307174

Sultan, M., Al-Hunaishi, W., & Bistaraki, A. (2021). *Disaster collaborative exercises for healthcare teamwork*. Major Incident Medical Management and Support (MIMMS). https://pmc.ncbi.nlm.nih.gov/articles/PMC10088626/

Troisi, C. A., Mills, D. S., Wilkinson, A., & Zulch, H. E. (2019). Behavioral and cognitive factors that affect the success of scent detection dogs. *Comparative Cognition & Behavior Reviews*, *14*, 51–76. https://doi.org/10.3819/CCBR.2019.140007

Van Houtte, B. A., & Jarvis, P. A. (1995). The role of pets in preadolescent psychosocial development. *Journal of Applied Developmental Psychology*, *16*(3), 463–479. https://doi.org/10.1016/0193-3973(95)90030-6

Wang, G.-D., Zhai, W., Yang, H.-C., Wang, L., Zhong, L., Liu, Y.-H., Fan, R.-X., Yin, T.-T., Zhu, C.-L., Poyarkov, A. D., Irwin, D. M., Hytönen, M. K., Lohi, H., Wu, C.-I., Savolainen, P., & Zhang, Y.-P. (2016). Out of southern East Asia: The natural history of domestic dogs across the world. *Cell Research*, *26*(1), 21–33. https://doi.org/10.1038/cr.2015.147

Zhang, L., Ji, Z., & Chen, B. (2024). *CREW: Facilitating human-AI teaming research*. arXiv preprint arXiv:2408.00170. https://arxiv.org/abs/2408.00170

CHAPTER 13

THE FUTURE OF AI IN TEAMS*

Susannah B. F. Paletz[a] and Samantha R. Dubrow[b]

[a]*College of Information, University of Maryland College Park, USA*
[b]*The MITRE Corporation, USA*

ABSTRACT

For the conclusion of this book, we discuss the common themes that arose throughout the chapters, such as the potential benefits and weaknesses of artificial intelligence (AI), the importance of developing trust and trustworthy AI, potential uses of AI in teams, and the effects and requirements of deploying AI in the workplace (e.g., training for both the AI and teams). Then, we review what is not yet covered in the literature or in this book and tie that to recommendations for future research (e.g., team dynamics such as intragroup conflict, newly publicized harms of companion AI, and more). As AI technologies continue to change dramatically and people try to determine the appropriate regulations, the world of teams and research on them, will continue to develop.

Keywords: Artificial intelligence; teams; future of work; human–agent teams; human–AI teams; human–autonomy teams; mental health; conflict; norms; mental models; design; deskilling; augmentation

The dynamics of AI in the workplace have completely changed since we began soliciting chapters for this book. Even the industries that we once expected would be the last to be transformed by AI (e.g., law, intelligence) have integrated AI into daily practices, and some schools are not just allowing the use of generative

*Approved for public release. Distribution unlimited 25-01892-3.

AI in Teams: Research on Managing Groups and Teams, Volume 21, 235–249

ISSN: 1534-0856/doi:10.1108/S1534-085620260000021032

AI (gen AI), but teaching about how to best use those technologies (Augenstein, 2025). Thus, the contents of this book are even more relevant than we thought when we first set out to edit it. The purpose of this book was to apply historical teams research to ever-changing team dynamics, specifically, the entry of AI agents into human teams. This book draws on a variety of disciplines, with most chapters written by authors from multiple disciplines and domains. In our Introduction, we discuss the current debates about whether and how one or more AI could be teammates. We define human–agent teams (HATs) as at least one human (and Carter et al., in press, suggests at least two) and one autonomous agent that have a shared goal and are interdependent (as with O'Neill et al., 2022, 2023), interacting, have specific roles, and are inside a group perceived as a bounded team.

For the conclusion of this book, we discuss the common themes that arose throughout the chapters. Then, we will review the elements of HAT dynamics that were not covered in the book, including newly publicized harms, and make recommendations for future research related to HATs as the industries affected by HATs continue to dramatically change.

COMMON THEMES

There were some common themes across many of the chapters. For AI to be used appropriately, it needs to be trusted appropriately: Webb and Hunt (2026) and Wildman et al. (2026), specifically, take two different perspectives on AI and trust, both more nuanced than a simple over- versus under-trust perspective. Trust can and should change over time and reflect different perceptions of the different humans and AI. Another theme in this book is a general optimism about the promise that new AI technologies can offer to teams. Current AI tools, particularly large language models (LLMs), machine learning, and natural language processing (NLP), can offer a speed of processing and ability to process a large volume of data that humans cannot. In addition to a large volume of information, big data challenges include fast velocity (e.g., speed of receiving data), large variety (e.g., text, image, video, satellite, social media), and difficulty with assessing the veracity and value of data (Jin et al., 2015). AI can help humans deal with these big data challenges, whether in the context of teams or not. Roles that can assist teams, in particular, include help in automating the tasks of summarizing, searching, real-time transcription and translation, pattern matching, synthesis, and idea generation, among others (see, for instance, Kane et al. (2026)'s chapter).

Medeiros et al. (2026) and Allen et al. (2026) suggest different AI functions could help with different aspects of team creativity and team meetings, respectively. This book's authors argue that AI technologies can support additional, more complex team functions, such as prototyping and creating personas for design (Bonsignore et al., 2026; Clark & Graff, 2026), evaluation and optimization (Medeiros et al., 2026), and emotion detection, bias monitoring, and acting as a virtual assistant (Allen et al., 2026).

The kinds of roles the authors suggest are generally support roles. Most authors' suggestions imply or characterize the AI as tools, but some of this book's authors describe AI as a potential junior teammate. For instance, Allen et al. (2026)'s description of a virtual assistant would incorporate different AI functions to help with team meetings. Clark and Graff (2026) discuss the potential implications for the types of roles that different kinds of AI can play in the design process in a real company, some of which are teammates. In reflecting on the nature of AI in teams, Lum et al. (2026) compare and contrast human–AI teams with human–animal teams, making analogies between AI and animals, and describing potential human–animal–agent teams.

The chapters in this book cover many specific kinds of teams that could be helped by AI, such as virtual, hybrid teams (including asynchronous and/or geographically dispersed teams) and different kinds of knowledge worker teams (e.g., research teams, intelligence analysis teams; Fouse et al., 2026; Kane et al., 2026); action teams engaging in emergency medical care and hazard tasks (e.g., hazardous waste cleanup teams; Jamshad et al., 2026); professional designers (Clark & Graff, 2026); participatory design conducted by children and their families (Bonsignore et al., 2026); and tactical soldier teams (Canter, 2026). Each chapter examines ways in which the functions of AI could assist with those teams. These often touch on the team processes of team creativity, decision making, and collective intelligence (Woolley & Gupta, 2024).

The various chapters also point out some of the downsides and weaknesses of current AI technologies. One particular concern is that while gen AI specifically was created to offer predictive text based on training datasets, this process does not, nor should it, guarantee factually correct outputs (Narayanan & Kapoor, 2024). This limitation need not be a problem if the technology is used properly within its well understood limitations (Narayanan & Kapoor, 2024), something understood by the chapter authors in this book. In particular, most of the chapter authors express that having the appropriate levels of trust and reliance are important with these new technologies (e.g., Fouse et al., 2026; Webb & Hunt, 2026; Wildman et al., 2026). Some authors additionally point out that a substantial set of gen AI tools have been trained on text and images such that intellectual property rights were ignored and/or uncompensated; that using such tools can potentially violate data privacy and informed consent; that there were risks associated with emotion surveillance and/or manipulation; and that transparency in terms of how information is generated, and potential algorithmic bias are concerns (e.g., Allen et al., 2026). Fouse et al. (2026) also note challenges with obtaining back-end data access for an AI and ways of protecting data security.

Another theme is the ways in which adopting AI technologies could change organizational and work processes and impact humans as individuals and teams. Selection and training of both humans and AI are likely necessary to realize the benefits of, or even just appropriately work with, AI. Humans may need skills and training to work with AI and robots; humans could be selected for their existing skills and abilities to work with specific AI tools; and AI (and robots) could be selected, trained, and/or designed to work with humans (e.g., Canter, 2026; Clark & Graff, 2026; Jamshad et al., 2026; Kane et al., 2026; Medeiros et al., 2026). In chapters where AI is conceptualized as a teammate, the human training could be characterized as "getting to know their AI collaborators," but even without anthropomorphizing, understanding the strengths and limits of specific AI technologies, and its effects on teams, is important (e.g., Clark & Graff, 2026; Lum et al., 2026). Another obvious impact on organizational and team processes is the possibility of AI replacing humans in particular jobs (e.g., Clark & Graff, 2026). These effects are ongoing: As of 2025, layoffs due to AI have switched to limited rehiring. This switch occurred with an understanding (or at least a passionate debate) that in many cases, AI should be an enhancement rather than a replacement for humans in a variety of work roles (e.g., Ebert, 2025; Martinez, 2025, citing a study by Orgvue, 2025; Sadler, 2025; Zhou, 2025). In other words, adopting AI and laying off human workers can be accomplished, but need a strategy, plan, and research before being implemented (Martinez, 2025), as also pointed out in this book.

It is important to stress that the chapters in this book take both a hopeful and a deliberately human-centered approach to AI in teams. Prior scholars have argued strongly for human-centered and ethical approaches to designing AI (Shneiderman, 2022; Winter, 2024). At its best, AI technologies could be implemented *and* used in a way that augments and supports human creativity, productivity, satisfaction, and agency, whether in teams or individually. By examining team processes and team needs, we could use these rapidly advancing technologies to improve our lives.

WHAT IS MISSING FROM THIS BOOK AND FUTURE WORK

Given that AI represents multiple technologies with different limitations, strengths, and potential roles; the recent speed of the deployment of different AI technologies; and that no one book can cover every element of teams, let alone AI and teams, there were, of course, gaps in what this book could cover. Some of these gaps included additional types and functions of AI; different kinds of team processes; additional downsides of using AI that have unfolded over 2025 as both implementation and research grow; and considerations on the nature of teams and teamwork.

Additional Types and Functions of AI

In terms of content, this book did not go deeply into several other potential functions of AI, such as language translation for assisting multilingual teams (e.g., Zhang et al., 2022). In the future, one can imagine multilingual teams that are able to work together seamlessly without any language barrier, or at least with greater language support. However, there are still likely to be barriers around culture and time zone, such that workers might need different AI agents to assist their teams. Another consideration is that using AI as a translator may increase anxiety in some individuals (Zheng, 2025).

Similarly, while our chapters focused on team creativity, design, knowledge work, hybrid virtual teams, action teams, and more, additional versions of this book could also examine different domains and the different ways in which AI could assist with those domains, such as in transportation (e.g., trains, aviation), automation in manufacturing, construction, and sales. Computer programming and software development are seen as particularly vulnerable to replacement by AI (Zhou, 2025). Multiteam systems of people in extreme environments such as space missions have also welcomed research and theory on how to integrate AI (e.g., Lindhardt et al., 2025; Marquez et al., 2023). In addition, Amazon's remarkable advances in logistics and shipping are soon to be further enhanced by AI and robotics (Bensinger, 2025). While a single delivery driver would not be considered a team, the combination of warehouse robots, delivery drivers, and supportive AI identifying directions and obstacles for drivers could be considered a multiteam system. Early consumer testing with GPT-5 suggests its capabilities are far superior to that of GPT-4o, with more autonomy and utility, although transparency in how it creates solutions is still limited (Mollick, 2025). As AI advances touch these different domains, future versions of this book could include additional domains and AI functions.

Additional Team Processes

A significant gap is that there are many specific team processes not deeply examined in relation to AI in this book. As Steve Zaccaro (2025) stated, and as mentioned in the Introduction, whether an AI should be considered a teammate could depend on if it also contributes to transition (e.g., planning), action, or interpersonal (e.g., conflict resolution) team processes. This contention was above and beyond whether the AI in question is considered to have agency (Harris-Watson & Larson, 2025; Vanneste & Puranam, 2024). Relatedly, how could AI contribute to, or help mitigate, team conflict, negotiation, participation (equality and/or equity), social identity processes, and more? AI can influence perceptions of the team as a whole, including emergent states (Mathieu et al., 2019). For example, team entitativity is a concept about the perception of a group as a social unit (Blanchard et al., 2020). Recall that the definition of a team presumes it has an inside and an outside (e.g., Hackman, 2012). Future work could examine the degree to which an AI must be perceived as part of the team to be considered a teammate, or if humans can distinguish between AI teammates and AI as part of a social unit but not a teammate. Similarly, how does perceiving one or more AI as a teammate affect perceptions of team cohesion? Implicit coordination and humor have been proposed to help teams in high-stress situations to promote team well-being (Lindhardt et al., 2025). If an AI helps with those functions, does it contribute to team cohesion?

One team process that was covered less in this book than we anticipated was the concept of conflict in teams and how that changes with the introduction of AI. Some types of AI that were mentioned in this book, such as AI agents that can help with team meetings and creativity, may help to reduce overall team conflict. An important potential source of conflict worth further study is how the introduction of AI itself can cause conflict. Different individuals within the team may have different perceptions of how AI should be integrated into the team, which may be a source of conflict. This is particularly important when AI is more of a tool that some team members are using than others. Consider if different human teammates have different levels of trust, reliance, or norms regarding the same AI tool. For example, marketing teams that disagree about the use of AI may have conflict around how much AI can and should be used in the writing process. Some team members might think of using AI as cheating, while others might consider it an essential tool that the team would be unnecessarily handicapped without. Evolving and disparate industry and workplace norms can cause conflict over the use of AI (e.g., what is allowed in one domain vs. another, or changed from year to year). In this case, differences in trust, reliance, and mental models regarding team-shared AI tools could cause conflict just as much as differences in trust, reliance, and mental models regarding any other technology or process widely used by the team. Beyond conflicts caused by different norms and perceptions of AI, different kinds of AI technologies can cause conflict based on specific outputs. For instance, imagine that an LLM gives one answer to one human teammate and a different answer to another, generating a task conflict between them.

Resolving conflict around AI will need to go beyond using chatbots to help resolve conflict. Although not covered in this book, human–robot interaction and older (pre-chatGPT) AI research has examined the effects of interventions such as synchronization and verbal supports on conflict resolution (e.g., Jung & Hinds, 2018; Sebo et al., 2020a, 2020b). When AI is a source of team conflict, team leadership will be especially important. Teams will need to establish norms and expectations regarding the integration of AI, and these will need to be modified consistently as AI continues to develop. Without strong organizational and team leadership and transparency around how AI is being integrated, team members may choose to lie to and deceive one another about their use of AI. It is important for team members to be forthcoming about their use of AI so that others who are meant to engage in team backup behaviors (e.g., checking the work of their teammates) have a clear understanding as to how the work was developed. This process is similar to programmers within software development teams that want to share code rather than the final product with another team member. It is important to share both the back end of what was used to develop the product and the front end that the final user may see in order for teams to work together effectively and maintain their trust.

Specific work processes could also be benefited or hindered by the introduction of different kinds of AI. For example, group contracts, huddles, debriefs, and after-action reviews (for a review, see Tannenbaum & Salas, 2020; e.g., Tannenbaum & Cerasoli, 2013) could be benefitted by accurate transcribers and summarizers of team meetings (Allen et al., 2026) and of delivered products to help suggest whether and how well the team met its anticipated milestones in terms of both affective team processes and task success. However, inaccurate AI team monitors – such as one that claims poor team cohesion or negative affect when the team is relatively satisfied – would be enormously frustrating and detrimental to team processes. Even an accurate AI that violates privacy (e.g., reporting on an unhappy team to malevolent or petty management) could cause more problems than it would overcome.

A related issue is the implications of new AI technology on leadership more directly. How can an AI be used to fulfill some of the functions of a leader, support human leaders, influence emergent leadership, and/or complicate leaders' work (Larson & DeChurch, 2020)? Leaders, in turn, can establish norms around AI use or even choose whether and what technologies to have their teams use. Larson and DeChurch (2020) noted that leaders would need to "foster functional affective and cognitive states and behavioral processes among human and synthetic team members so that human-machine teams can perform effectively" (p. 24). Relatedly, when deploying new AI technology in a team, leaders need to manage the use of this technology, including, as noted previously, helping team members establish shared and accurate team models about it (Larson & DeChurch, 2020). As Canter (2026) notes in his historical analysis chapter about deploying AI, high-level leaders need to seriously consider not just the initial functions and features of an AI, but the actual physical deployment and training needs for their workforce. As he suggests, AI that is not on a network for security reasons can be a heavy additional physical burden in the field.

Additional Downsides and Research Regarding AI Use

As different kinds of AI are introduced in different products without being directly tested in teams (or society) first, additional downsides are becoming clearer. Primary of these is not just whether gen AI can be inaccurate because of its primary function of mimicking language (Hicks et al., 2024), but whether gen AI are likely to give outright bad or dangerous advice (Narayanan & Kapoor, 2024, e.g., CBS News, 2025; Center for Countering Digital Hate [CCDH], 2025; Moore et al., 2025). Scholars have argued and demonstrated that LLMs, as language models, are inherently biased because they are approximating human language, which is also biased (e.g., Resnik, 2025; Wilson & Caliskan, 2024). In high-stakes team domains and/or in extreme time pressure situations (e.g., military drone targeting; emergency medicine), the consequences of wrongly biased or dangerous advice could be horrific.

Beyond being based on the underlying biases that occur naturally, one question is whether the different kinds of AI technologies are being applied to appropriate tasks. Lum et al. (2026) in this book argue that AI lacks emotional intelligence such that humans are best at empathic tasks, while AI could be used for analytic and big data processing tasks. However, this is not the current situation with gen AI, which is advertised and used as a companion (CCDH, 2025). A recent court case demonstrates the danger of trying to mimic human empathy without proper design, testing, or an expert understanding of potential dangers. The programmed simulation of empathy and agreeability in GPT-4o, and lack of testing or listening to designers, are directly blamed in a court case where parents are suing OpenAI and CEO Sam Altman for their son's death by suicide (Godoy, 2026). The parents allege that the GPT-4o launch was rushed, with multi-turn conversations as a feature but only single prompts tested (Hendrix, 2025). As noted in the court documents, the teen easily avoided the minimal safety features and had lengthy conversations where the AI encouraged him to keep his suicidal ideation and attempts a secret and provided him with technical details on how to harm himself (Hendrix, 2025). The teen in the case had started using AI for schoolwork and perceived it as a friend with whom he could confide his mental health struggles (Hendrix, 2025).

This was also not an isolated case, and suicidal ideation is not the only troubling behavior or communication this kind of AI has encouraged young users to do. Research by the Center for Countering Digital Hate (CCDH, 2025) using a consistent set of prompts sent multiple times to ChatGPT's free version found that this situation was not unique, but that AI "fail at scale" (p. 6). CCDH researchers created three at-risk teen personas, covering young people with depression and suicidal ideation, eating disorders, and an interest in alcohol and drugs. This Center's research found that 53% of 1,200 responses to 60 harmful prompts resulted in harmful content; age verification and parental consent were easily avoided; and that by stating the query was "for a friend" or "for a presentation" allowed a user to easily avoid refusals to answer questions (CCDH, 2025, pp. 6–7). Even extreme harmful advice (e.g., detailed suicide plans) came within 65 minutes of conversing with ChatGPT.

As a result of this research, related cases, and advocacy by the American Psychological Association, the United States Federal Trade Commission (FTC), even as it states promoting innovation, "is issuing orders to seven companies that provide consumer-facing AI-powered chatbots seeking information on how these firms measure, test, and monitor potentially negative impacts of this technology on children and teens" (FTC, 2025). The inquiry requires these companies to report on their testing and evaluation, as there is growing evidence that some of these companies knew there were dangers but deployed AI to the public anyway. The AI technologies in question are gen AI, trained on massive datasets to simulate human communication, but beyond that designed to "communicate like a friend or confidant" (FTC, 2025) – a communication style that makes it also more likely to be anthropomorphized and thus perceived as a teammate or companion. By the time this book is published, more information will come to light from the FTC inquiry and the court case.

While not about teams, this research illustrates the potential problems (including underlying ethical ones, Perry, 2025) with one gen AI tool. These cases are focused on individual dangers, but the disruption to (and tragedy for) families and friends is also clear, suggesting potential impacts on team dynamics as well. It is possible that the underlying causes of these harms can also generate problems for individuals in workplaces and their teams. Research could be conducted on whether certain versions of gen AI, in being designed for engagement and agreeableness, can exacerbate faultlines or existing divisions within teams if workers trust and confide with gen AI rather than communicate directly with coworkers. Ideally, specific versions of gen AI will prompt arguing coworkers to listen to each other, repair relationships, and resolve their conflicts, but these findings suggest that more harmful advice could be given. In terms of teams of children, Bonsignore et al. (2026)'s chapter points to safe ways in which children and their families can engage in AI use and design, through deliberately valuing the agency, autonomy, privacy, and needs of all the humans involved. Clearly, human-centered design, extensive testing, and more thoughtful considerations of the variety of dangers that these types of gen AI could cause is necessary for these technologies to eventually be primarily beneficial (Cummings, 2025).

In general, the chapters in this book focus on the potential cases and uses of AI in teams, and they are not written from a sociological perspective. So, most do not discuss the potential for exploitation in the creation or use of AI tools (e.g., intellectual property, underpaid annotators, or job loss, with few exceptions such as Allen et al., 2026; Lum et al., 2026). However, these issues are also currently being raised in court cases and the media (e.g., Crawford, 2021), as are concerns about the sizable water and power requirements to run gen AI. Relatedly, the adoption of AI is often an organizational rather than an individual decision: companies as varied as Meta, Apple, Microsoft, and Alphabet (Google) include different kinds of AI products, and universities are instituting widespread AI adoption, whether or not individuals are eager to use these technologies (Guest et al., 2025). These sociological considerations can still influence teams, such as whether student project teams are expected to use, or learn to use, AI, and can be the cause of friction between different units or subgroups within organizations.

An additional growing concern is that relying on AI can potentially cause a loss of skills – and one with more significant consequences than, for instance, using a calculator (Budzyń et al., 2025; Kosmyna et al., 2025). More research is important to understand which skills degrade with using which specific kinds of AI and how quickly, which skills are maintained (and how), and how best to leverage these AI technologies to fulfill their promise for productivity gains without losing important skills. Our book currently also rarely discusses in a systemic way how different kinds of AI (e.g., LLMs vs. NLP that does topic modeling) and different versions of the same type of AI (e.g., Claude vs. GPT-4o vs. GPT-5) have different pros and cons. As more researchers tackle the distal effects on individuals and teams of using AI, we hope that these benefits and disadvantages will become more clear, including the degree to which deskilling is a concern, is overblown, and/or is specific to particular types and cases of AI use.

As AI technologies are developed and deployed at a furious rate, countries, regions, and organizations are trying to keep up with guidelines, regulations, and policies (e.g., European Commission, 2025). Many of these restrictions are reactive, as with the FTC's (2025) inquiry and court cases (e.g., Hendrix, 2025). We look forward to seeing whether this pace and pattern of AI deployment continue in 2026, or whether a more measured approach to AI introductions occur, which would also enable more careful exploration and testing of the effects of AI on individuals, team dynamics, and team processes and cognition. Researchers continue to call for ethical and human-centered design (Shneiderman, 2022; Winter, 2024) and note the importance of fully testing new AI tools in realistic situations (e.g., Kane et al., 2025; Paletz et al., 2025). A promising technique is participatory design, as used by Bonsignore et al. (2026) in their work with children and families. A group of scholars recently recommended participatory design to center humans, human needs, and human choice in developing AI technologies (Elmqvist et al., 2025). This technique was developed in Scandinavia to deliberately and democratically develop technologies that serve humans in the workplace (Bonsignore et al., 2026; Elmqvist et al., 2025). AI could similarly be developed with the participatory design principles of: mutual learning between designers and users; exploration and debate of potential future alternatives to the technology; understanding that technologies operate within existing sociotechnical systems; empowerment of communities and individuals with technology that mediates human activities; and supporting multiple communities, groups, and interests by democratic decision making that takes into account existing power structures and imbalances (Elmqvist et al., 2025, see pp. 5–6). Beyond specific regulations, we contend that this and related approaches could better take into account teamwork and the needs of teams.

Considerations for the Nature of Teams and Teamwork

As the distinction between tool and teammate starts to blur with gen AI, an area rich for future research is what these new technologies mean for the nature of teams. A related question is how the number of AI agents being used in a team affects team dynamics. When the research literature discusses human teams, groups of 30 or more, for example, are considered too big to be considered true teams because they cannot have interpersonal dynamics between all team members. Generally, many researchers characterize these larger group sizes as organizations or multiteam systems. However, a potentially unlimited number of AI agents could engage in teamwork with each other, although human teammates may still have limitations on the number of agents that they can work with at any given time. Humans are limited in the amount of information that they can monitor. This imbalance suggests we should consider, and research, whether being aware of what teammates are doing, including AI agents, is truly important for teaming, or if the future of teamwork may include not being fully cognizant of all the teammates' work. For instance, what would be the implications of not knowing everything one's teammates are doing on team outputs. While human teams are often not aware of everything everyone is doing at any one moment, whole areas of research (e.g., on transactive memory systems) suggest that having knowledge of each other's expertise and ongoing task progress are important to team functioning and performance (Tannenbaum & Salas, 2020).

The chapters in this book also do not cover the concept of measuring performance in HATs. Because most teams engage in some degree of reciprocal or intensive, rather than additive, tasks, team performance is not usually measured by adding up the performance of individual teammates. Rather, team outcomes are graded on their performance as a whole. In the workplace, awards are often given at the team level. Future research is needed to consider the implications of measurement and the perceived fairness of measurement performance in HATs. Unlike humans, AI can produce huge amounts of content in just a few seconds. Also unlike humans, AI does not need vacation days, time to spend with family, or to sleep. Therefore, conflict and competition between humans and AI teammates may come up as important issues in measuring team performance in the years to come.

Despite all the unique considerations for AI in teams that *are* addressed throughout the chapters in this book, we are left with many lingering questions regarding the nature and impact of AI in teams. We let the chapter authors choose how they wanted to characterize AI: as a teammate, a tool, a support, some mix, or unspecified. An additional question regarding the nature of HATs revolves around the anthropomorphism of AI and how this influences perceptions, psychological processes, and team dynamics. There are continuing calls to ensure that anthropomorphism of AI, including as a teammate, does not absolve companies and humans (e.g., designers; teams of designers) of their accountability for potential harms (Bender & Hanna, 2025; Shneiderman, 2022). A related, more philosophical question, is, what does it mean to anthropomorphize an AI that is not autonomous? In the past, did people consider typewriters or word processors to be teammates, even though they were not autonomous, if they did replace, enhance, or create different jobs? As AI technologies are deployed and new versions are developed, the answers to these questions may also change. Recent research suggests, for instance, that AI-led job interviews for customer service positions increases job offers and 30-day retention among applicants and elicits more relevant information than human interviewers (Jabarian & Henkel, 2025). Human recruiters still reviewed the transcripts and made the hiring decisions. This kind of research points to the potential for AI to counter biases and improve efficiency, augmenting human capabilities rather than replacing them. Further research could examine the degree to which AI interviewers are perceived as agentic and teammates or not. In general, we would recommend that specific AI technologies be developed for particular uses and that their limitations and strengths be fully known so that teams can use them appropriately. Research could then be conducted to evaluate the effects of these AI, distinguishing between different technologies in terms of their effects on team dynamics, and the effects of teams on the development, acceptance, and use of these AI.

CONCLUSION

At the time of writing this conclusion, AI in the workplace is still most typically seen as a tool to assist and augment human team members (e.g., summarizing meetings, assisting with brainstorming). Countries and other groups are still developing regulations and policy, with both hype and doomerism surrounding AI dominating the discourse (Bender & Hanna, 2025). Thoughtful, technology- and use-specific designs, policies, and safeguards for individuals, teams, organizations, and societies are still needed. Whether perceived (or regulated) as a product, a tool, or a teammate, AI can and will be implemented in, support, and impact teams and teamwork. While AI has started to change the dynamics of the workplace in terms of jobs that are available, reducing the need for some jobs and increasing the need for others, AI has yet to fully become part of the organizational chart (Nolan, 2025). We predict that future iterations of the chapters in this book will need to look beyond the team construct and begin to investigate how AI is transforming multiteam systems as well as complete organizational structures. In multiteam systems, between-team distance and conflict may increase when AI is integrated into component teams differently, and teams have to actively work to reconcile their differences around how to integrate AI into the multiteam system (Zaccaro, 2025). Different kinds of AI technologies still hold great promise for supporting teams and the individuals in them. Within organizations, AI will change team dynamics as it becomes less of a tool and takes over distinct roles in the organization more clearly. Research should continue to examine the role of AI in teams, and how AI changes human team dynamics.

REFERENCES

Allen, J., Grabowski, M., Thiese, M. S., & Eden, M. (2026). Artificial intelligence (AI) in the team meeting landscape. In S. B. F. Paletz & S. Dubrow (Eds.), *AI in teams* (pp. 59–77). Emerald Publishing.

Augenstein, N. (2025, August 18). 'Letting us learn how to use it instead of hiding it away': Prince William Co. schools readies students to use AI. *WTOP News*. https://wtop.com/prince-william-county/2025/08/letting-us-learn-how-to-use-it-instead-of-hiding-it-away-prince-william-co-schools-readies-students-to-use-ai/

Bender, E. M., & Hanna, A. (2025). *The AI con: How to fight big tech's hype and create the future we want*. HarperCollins.

Bensinger, G. (2025, June 4). Amazon's delivery, logistics get an AI boost. *Reuters*. https://www.reuters.com/business/retail-consumer/amazons-delivery-logistics-will-get-an-ai-boost-2025-06-04/

Blanchard, A., Caudill, L. E., & Walker, L. S. (2020). Developing an entitativity measure and distinguishing it from antecedents and outcomes within online and face-to-face groups. *Group Processes & Intergroup Relations*, *23*(1), 91–108. https://doi.org/10.1177/1368430217743577

Bonsignore, E., Nanduri, D. K., Blinder, E., Lin, Y.-H., Dwivedi, U., Guha, M. L., Tare, M., & Kacorri, H. (2026). Participatory AI: Children and families co-designing and collaborating with AI systems. In S. B. F. Paletz & S. Dubrow (Eds.), *AI in teams* (pp. 173–197). Emerald Publishing.

Budzyń, K., Romańczyk, M., Kitala, D., Kołodziej, P., Bugajski, M., Adami, H. O., Blom, J., Buskiewicz, M., Halvorsen, N., Hassan, C., Romańczyk, T., Holme, O., Jarus, K., Fielding, S., Kunar, M., Pellise, M., Pilonis, N., Kamiński, M. F., Kalager, M., Bretthaver, M., & Mori, Y. (2025). Endoscopist deskilling risk after exposure to artificial intelligence in colonoscopy: A multicentre, observational study. *Lancet Gastroenterology and Hepatology*. https://doi.org/10.1016/S2468-1253(25)00133-5

Canter, S. (2026). "It's your turn to carry the AI, soldier!" Artificial intelligence and the challenges of introducing new technologies to tactical military teams. In S. B. F. Paletz & S. Dubrow (Eds.), *AI in teams* (pp. 199–214). Emerald Publishing.

Carter, B. M., Paletz, S. B. F., Campbell, S. G., O'Rourke, P., Carraway, M. J., Vahlkamp, S. H., & Schwartz, J. (in press). There is no "AI" in teams: A multi-disciplinary framework for AIs to work in human teams. In B. Bonner & M. Baumann (Eds.), *Research handbook on group decision making. Research handbooks on social psychology series. Cheltenham, United Kingdom*. Edward Elgar Publishing.

CBS. (2025, August 7). ChatGPT gave alarming advice on drugs, eating disorders to researchers posing as teens. *CBS News*. https://www.cbsnews.com/amp/news/chatgpt-alarming-advice-drugs-eating-disorders-researchers-teens/

Center for Countering Digital Hate (CCDH). (2025, August 6). *Fake friend: How ChatGPT betrays vulnerable teens by encouraging dangerous behavior*. Center for Countering Digital Hate. https://counterhate.com/wp-content/uploads/2025/08/Fake-Friend_CCDH_FINAL-12Sep.pdf

Clark, M. A., & Graff, D. (2026). AI and design collaboration: Not a full member (yet). In S. B. F. Paletz & S. Dubrow (Eds.), *AI in teams* (pp. 153–171). Emerald Publishing.

Crawford, K. (2021). *Atlas of AI: Power, politics, and the planetary costs of artificial intelligence*. Yale University Press.

Cummings, M. (2025, October 17). The future of human factors and AI innovation. *Creating AI that works for people: Human-centered innovation* [Symposium]. *Advancing systems and practice through innovation, research and education (ASPIRE): Human factors and ergonomics society (HFES) 69th international annual meeting*, Chicago, IL.

Ebert, A. (2025, July 16). The companies laying off staff for AI today will regret it in five years. *Fortune*. https://fortune.com/2025/07/16/ai-layoffs-regrets/

Elmqvist, N., Hoggan, E., Schulz, H.-J., Petersen, M. G., Dalsgaard, P., Assent, I., Bertelsen, O. W., Arora, A., Grønbæk, K., Bødker, S., Klokmose, C. N., Smith, R. C., Hubenschmid, S., Johns, C. A., León, G. M., Wolter, A., Ellemose, J., Dhanoa, V., Enni, S. A., … & Iversen, O. S. (2025, September 16). *Participatory AI: A Scandinavian approach to human-centered AI*. https://doi.org/10.48550/arXiv.2509.12752

European Commission. (2025, February 4). *Commission publishes the Guidelines on prohibited artificial intelligence (AI) practices, as defined by the AI act*. European Union. https://digital-strategy.ec.europa.eu/en/library/commission-publishes-guidelines-prohibited-artificial-intelligence-ai-practices-defined-ai-act

Federal Trade Commission. (2025, September 11). *FTC launches inquiry into AI chatbots acting as companions*. Federal Trade Commission. https://www.ftc.gov/news-events/news/press-releases/2025/09/ftc-launches-inquiry-ai-chatbots-acting-companions

Fouse, A., Ganberg, G., Bruni, S., Volkova, S., Orbis, K. L., & Klinefelter, Z. (2026). AI-powered dynamic hybrid teaming. In S. B. F. Paletz & S. Dubrow (Eds.), *AI in teams* (pp. 99–116). Emerald Publishing.

Godoy, J. (2026, August 26). OpenAI, Altman sued over ChatGPT's role in California teen's suicide. *Reuters*. https://www.reuters.com/sustainability/boards-policy-regulation/openai-altman-sued-over-chatgpts-role-california-teens-suicide-2025-08-26/

Guest, O., Suarez, M., Müller, B., van Meerkerk, E., Oude Groote Beverborg, A., de Haan, R., Reyes Elizondo, A., Bickpoel, M., Scharfenberg, N., Kleinherenbrink, A., Camerino, I., Woensdregt, M., Monett, D., Brown, J., Avraamidou, L., Alenda-Demoutiez, J., Hermans, F., & van Rooij, I. (2025, September 5). Against the uncritical adoption of 'AI' technologies in academia. *Zenodo*. https://doi.org/10.5281/zenodo.17065098

Hackman, J. R. (2012). From causes to conditions in group research. *Journal of Organizational Behavior*, *33*, 428–444.

Harris-Watson, A. M., & Larson, L. E. (2025, July 19). What's in a name? Framing AI roles for successful human-AI teaming. *Exploring human-AI team dynamics: Core constructs and assessment strategies* [Symposium]. *The 20th annual interdisciplinary network for group research (INGRoup) conference*, Rotterdam, Netherlands.

Hendrix, J. (2025, August 26). *Breaking down the lawsuit against OpenAI over teen's suicide*. Tech Policy Press. https://www.techpolicy.press/breaking-down-the-lawsuit-against-openai-over-teens-suicide/

Hicks, M. T., Humphries, J., & Slater, J. (2024). ChatGPT is bullshit. *Ethics and Information Technology*, *26*, 38. https://doi.org/10.1007/s10676-024-09775-5

Jabarian, B., & Henkel, L. (2025, August 18). Voice AI in firms: A natural field experiment on automated job interviews. *SSRN*. http://dx.doi.org/10.2139/ssrn.5395709

Jamshad, R., Simkins, S., & Riek, L. D. (2026). Proactive robots in human-robot action teams. In S. B. F. Paletz & S. Dubrow (Eds.), *AI in teams* (pp. 137–151). Emerald Publishing.

Jin, X., Wah, B. W., Cheng, X., & Wang, Y. (2015). Significance and challenges of big data research. *Big Data Research*, *2*(2), 59–64. https://doi.org/10.1016/j.bdr.2015.01.006

Jung, M., & Hinds, P. (2018). Robots in the wild: A time for more robust theories of human-robot interaction. *ACM Transactions on Human-Robot Interaction*, *7*(10), Article 2. https://doi.org/10.1145/3208975

Kane, A. A., Diep, M. M., Porter, A. A., & Paletz, S. B. F. (2026). Operationalizing and optimizing human-agent teaming for knowledge work. In S. B. F. Paletz & S. Dubrow (Eds.), *AI in teams* (pp. 117–133). Emerald Publishing.

Kane, A. A., Paletz, S. B. F., Diep, M., Hajkowski, A., & Porter, A. A. (2025). *Virtual collaborative analysis: Effects of an entity-based versus a simple AI summarizer*. Small Group Research, *56*(5), 821–863. https://doi.org/10.1177/10464964251361563

Kosmyna, N., Hauptmann, E., Yuan, Y. T., Situ, J., Liao, X.-H., Beresnitzky, A. V., Braunstein, I., & Maes, P. (2025). *Your brain on ChatGPT: Accumulation of cognitive debt when using an AI assistant for essay writing task*. https://arxiv.org/pdf/2506.08872

Larson, L., & DeChurch, L. A. (2020). Leading teams in the digital age: Four perspectives on technology and what they mean for leading teams. *The Leadership Quarterly, 31*(1), 1–18. https://doi.org/10.1016/j.leaqua.2019.101377

Lindhardt, R. M., Berger, L., & Salas, E. (2025). No laughing matter: How autonomous agents can improve well-being and teamwork. *Acta Astronautica, 226*, 385–397.

Lum, H. C., Evans, S., Jayakumar, R., Inderberg, L. H., & Suresh, S. (2026). Human-animal team modeling for more effective human-agent teaming design. In S. B. F. Paletz & S. Dubrow (Eds.), *AI in teams* (pp. 217–236). Emerald Publishing.

Marquez, J. J., Landon. L. B., & Salas, E. (2023). The next giant leap for space human factors: The opportunities. *Human Factors, 65*(6), 1279–1288. https://doi.org/10.1177/00187208231174955

Martinez, A. (2025, May 1). 55% of companies regret AI layoffs, HR leaders need to take note. *The HR Digest*. https://www.thehrdigest.com/55-of-companies-regret-ai-layoffs-hr-leaders-need-to-take-note/

Mathieu, J. E., Gallagher, P. T., Domingo, M. A., & Klock, E. A. (2019). Embracing complexity: Reviewing the past decade of team effectiveness research. *Annual Review of Organizational Psychology and Organizational Behavior, 6*, 17–46.

Medeiros, K., Marrone, R., & Reiter-Palmon, R. (2026). A time-saving dishwasher: AI's role in team creative processes. In S. B. F. Paletz & S. Dubrow (Eds.), *AI in teams* (pp. 79–96). Emerald Publishing.

Mollick, E. (2025, August 7). GPT-5: It just does stuff. *One Useful Thing*. https://www.oneusefulthing.org/p/gpt-5-it-just-does-stuff

Moore, J., Grabb, D., Agnew, W., Klyman, K., Chancellor, S., Ong, D. C., & Haber, N. (2025). Expressing stigma and inappropriate responses prevents LLMs from safely replacing mental health providers. *FAccT '25*, Athens, Greece. https://doi.org/10.1145/3715275.3732039

Narayanan, A., & Kapoor, S. (2024). *AI snake oil: What artificial intelligence can do, what it can't, and how to tell the difference*. Princeton University Press.

Nolan, B. (2025). AI is already upending the corporate org chart as it flattens the distance between the C-suite and everyone else. *Fortune*. https://fortune.com/2025/08/07/ai-corporate-org-chart-workplace-agents-flattening/

O'Neill, T. A., Flathmann, C., McNeese, N. J., & Salas, E. (2023). Human-autonomy teaming: Need for a guiding team-based framework? *Computers in Human Behavior, 146*, 107762. https://doi.org/10.1016/j.chb.2023.107874

O'Neill, T. A., McNeese, N. J., Barron, A., & Schelbe, B. (2022). Human-autonomy teaming: A review and analysis of the empirical literature. *Human Factors, 64*(5), 904–938. https://doi.org/10.1177/0018720820960865

Orgvue. (2025, April 29). *55% of businesses admit wrong decisions in making employees redundant when bringing AI into the workforce*. Orgvue.com. https://www.orgvue.com/news/55-of-businesses-admit-wrong-decisions-in-making-employees-redundant-when-bringing-ai-into-the-workforce/

Paletz, S. B. F., Kane, A. A., Diep, M., Nelson, T. M., Porter, A., & Vahlkamp, S. H. (2025, November). Human-agent teaming on intelligence tasks (HATIT): A testbed for evaluating AI in intelligence analysis. *88th Annual meeting of the association for information science and technology (ASIS&T)* (pp. 474–485). Wiley.

Perry, D. (2025, October 25). How can AI be used ethically when it's been linked to suicide? *The Minnesota Star Tribune*. https://www.startribune.com/adam-raine-chatgpt-lawsuit-teen-mental-health-education/601498318

Resnik, P. (2025). Large language models are biased because they are large language models. *Computational Linguistics, 51*(3), 885–906. https://doi.org/10.1162/coli_a_00558

Sadler, D. (2025, May 26). Companies backtrack after going all in on AI. *ACS Information Age*. https://ia.acs.org.au/article/2025/companies-backtrack-after-going-all-in-on-ai.html

Sebo, S., Dong, L. L., Chang, N., Lewkowicz, M., Schutzman, M., & Scassellati, B. (2020a). The influence of robot verbal support on human team members: Encouraging outgroup contributions and suppressing ingroup supportive behavior. *Frontiers in Psychology, 11*, 590181. https://doi.org/10.3389/fpsyg.2020.590181

Sebo, S., Stoll, B., Scassellati, B., & Jung, M. F. (2020b). Robots in groups and teams: A literature review. *Proceedings of the ACM on Human-Computer Interaction, 4*(CSCW2), 1–36. Article 176. https://doi.org/10.1145/3415247

Shneiderman, B. (2022). *Human-centered AI*. Oxford University Press.

Tannenbaum, S. I., & Cerasoli, C. P. (2013). Do team and individual debriefs enhance performance? A meta-analysis. *Human Factors, 55*(1), 231–245. https://doi.org/10.1177/0018720812448394

Tannenbaum, S. I., & Salas, E. (2020). *Teams that work: The seven drivers of team effectiveness*. Oxford.

Vanneste, B. S., & Puranam, P. (2024). Artificial intelligence, trust, and perceptions of agency. *Academy of Management Review*. https://doi.org/10.5465/amr.2022.0041

Webb, N., & Hunt, E. R. (2026). Active trust management for successful human-robot teaming: Moving from a trust repair to a trust satisficing perspective. In S. B. F. Paletz & S. Dubrow (Eds.), *AI in teams* (pp. 17–37). Emerald Publishing.

Wildman, J. L., Carroll, M., Thayer, A. L., Carmody, K., Nguyen, D., Akib, M., Addis, A., Fickle, C., & Robbins-Roth, V. (2026). Trust in human-agent teams: Temporal, multilevel, and multimodal perspectives. In S. B. F. Paletz & S. Dubrow (Eds.), *AI in teams* (pp. 39–56). Emerald Publishing.

Wilson, K., & Caliskan, A. (2024). Gender, race, and intersectional bias in resume screening via language model retrieval. *Proceedings of the Seventh AAAI/ACM Conference on AI, Ethics, and Society (AIES 2024), 7*(1), 1578–1590. https://doi.org/10.1609/aies.v7i1.31748

Winter, S. J. (2024). The road less taken: Pathways to ethical and responsible technologies. In H. Werthner, C. Ghezzi, J. Kramer, J. Nida-Rümelin, B. Nuseibeh, E. Prem, & A. Stanger (Eds.), *Introduction to digital humanism* (pp. 267–281). Springer. https://doi.org/10.1007/978-3-031-45304-5_18

Woolley, A. W., & Gupta, P. (2024). Understanding collective intelligence: Investigating the role of collective memory, attention, and reasoning processes. *Perspectives on Psychological Science, 19*(2), 344–354. https://doi.org/10.1177/17456916231191534

Zaccaro, S. (2025, July 19). What is a teammate? An interactive discussion [Interactive panel]. *20th Annual interdisciplinary network for group research (INGRoup) conference*. Rotterdam, Netherlands.

Zhang, Y., Owusu, D. A., Carpuat, M., & Gao, G. (2022). Facilitating global team meetings between language-based subgroups: When and how can machine translation help? *PACM on Human-Computer Interaction, 6*(CSCW1), Article 90. 1–26. https://doi.org/10.1145/3512937

Zheng, K. (2025). You don't need to prove yourself: A raciolinguistic perspective on Chinese international students' academic language anxiety and ChatGPT use. *Linguistics and Education, 86*, 101406. https://doi.org/10.1016/j.linged.2025.101406

Zhou, Y. (2025, July 28). How AI is impacting 700 professions – And might impact yours. *The Washington Post*. https://www.washingtonpost.com/opinions/interactive/2025/ai-jobs-layoffs-tech/

INDEX

Printed and bound by CPI Group (UK) Ltd, Croydon, CR0 4YY

15/09/2026

14962483-0007